Washington DC

THE ROUGH GUIDE

There are one hundred Rough Guide titles
covering destinations from Amsterdam to Zimbabwe

Forthcoming titles include
Jamaica • New Zealand •
South Africa • Southwest USA

Rough Guide Reference Series
Classical Music • The Internet • Jazz • Opera• Rock Music • World Music

Rough Guide Phrasebooks
Czech • French • German • Greek • Hindi & Urdu • Indonesian • Italian •
Mandarin Chinese • Mexican Spanish • Polish • Portuguese • Russian •
Spanish • Thai • Turkish • Vietnamese

Rough Guides on the Internet
http://www.roughguides.com/
http://www.hotwired.com/rough

Rough Guide Credits

Editor:	Samantha Cook
Series Editor:	Mark Ellingham
Editorial:	Martin Dunford, Jonathan Buckley, Jo Mead, Amanda Tomlin, Ann-Marie Shaw, Paul Gray, Vivienne Heller, Sarah Dallas, Chris Schüler, Helena Smith (UK); Andrew Rosenberg (US)
Online Editors:	Alan Spicer (UK); Andrew Rosenberg (US)
Production:	Susanne Hillen, Andy Hilliard, Judy Pang, Link Hall, Nicola Williamson, Helen Ostick
Cartography:	Melissa Flack, David Callier
Finance:	John Fisher, Celia Crowley, Catherine Gillespie
Marketing & Publicity:	Richard Trillo, Simon Carloss, Niki Smith (UK); Jean-Marie Kelly, Jeff Kaye (US)
Administration:	Tania Hummel, Mark Rogers

Acknowledgements

Suitably monumental thanks must go to Sam Cook, who guided without erring and without whom this book would be four times longer – editing was never less obtrusive and more welcome. I'd also like to thank the original authors of the *Rough Guide to the USA*, especially Greg Ward, and the incomparable Katie who stuck by me through thick and thin (mainly thick) despite severe writer's grumpiness on occasion. And praise the gods for the safe return of Capt. I Little, presumed lost at sea, but washed up in his coracle on Chesapeake Bay.

In Washington, I'm grateful for the help of Lisa Holland of the Washington DC Convention and Visitors Association, and of Peter Green, Jutta Whitfield, Lorna Hobell, Joe Fab, Jennifer Schroeder, Diana Kaiser, Tricia Messerschmitt, Robin Reath and Rick Fenstermaker. Thanks, too, to Darren Colby, to Robert Anderson for his political updates, and Jean-Marie Kelly for encouragement. Finally, thanks to Helen Ostick for typesetting; MicroMap, Romsey, Hants, and Melissa Flack and David Callier for the wonderful maps; Andrew Tibber for proofreading; and Nick Thomson and Narrell Leffman for their work on *Basics*.

This edition published March 1997 by Rough Guides Ltd, 1 Mercer Street, London WC2H 9QJ. Distributed by the Penguin Group:

Penguin Books Ltd, 27 Wrights Lane, London W8 5TZ.

Penguin Books USA Inc, 375 Hudson Street, New York 10014, USA.

Penguin Books Australia Ltd, 487 Maroondah Highway, PO Box 257, Ringwood, Victoria 3134, Australia.

Penguin Books Canada Ltd, 10 Alcorn Avenue, Toronto, Ontario, Canada M4V 1E4.

Penguin Books (NZ) Ltd, 182–190 Wairau Road, Auckland 10, New Zealand.

Printed in the United Kingdom by The Bath Press.

Typography and **original design** by Jonathan Dear and The Crowd Roars.

Illustrations throughout by Edward Briant.

A catalogue record for this book is available from the British Library.

ISBN 1-85828-246-2

Washington DC

THE ROUGH GUIDE

Written and researched by
Jules Brown

THE ROUGH GUIDES

Help us update

We've gone to a lot of trouble to ensure that this first edition of the *Rough Guide to Washington DC* is accurate and up-to-date. However, things inevitably change, and if you feel we've got it wrong or left something out, we'd like to know: any suggestions, comments or corrections would be much appreciated. We'll credit all contributions and send a copy of the next edition – or any other *Rough Guide* if you prefer – for the best correspondence.

Please mark letters "Rough Guide to Washington DC" and send to:
Rough Guides, 1 Mercer St, London WC2H 9QJ or
Rough Guides, 375 Hudson St, 9th floor, New York, NY 10014.

E-mail should be sent to:
washingtondc@roughtravl.co.uk

Online updates about Rough Guide titles can be found on our website at http://www.roughguides.com/

Rough Guides

Travel Guides • Phrasebooks • Music and Reference Guides

We set out to do something different when the first Rough Guide was published in 1982. Mark Ellingham, just out of University, was travelling in Greece. He brought along the popular guides of the day, but found they were all lacking in some way. They were either strong on ruins and museums but went on for pages without mentioning a beach or taverna. Or they were so conscious of the need to save money that they lost sight of Greece's cultural and historical significance. Also, none of the books told him anything about Greece's contemporary life – its politics, its culture, its people, and how they lived.

So with no job in prospect, Mark decided to write his own guidebook, one which aimed to provide practical information that was second to none, detailing the best beaches and the hottest clubs and restaurants, while also giving hard hitting accounts of every sight, both famous and obscure, and providing up-to-the-minute information on contemporary culture. It was a guide that encouraged independent travellers to find the best of Greece, and was a great success, getting shortlisted for the Thomas Cook travel guide award, and encouraging Mark, along with three friends, to expand the series.

The Rough Guide list grew rapidly and the letters flooded in, indicating a much broader readership than had been anticipated, but one which uniformly appreciated the Rough Guides' mix of practical detail and humour, irreverence and enthusiasm. Things haven't changed. The same four friends who began the series are still the caretakers of the Rough Guide mission today: to provide the most reliable, up-to-date and entertaining information to independent-minded travellers of all ages, on all budgets.

We now publish 100 titles and have offices in London and New York. The travel guides are written and researched by a dedicated team of more than 100 authors, based in Britain, Europe, the USA and Australia. We have also created a unique series of phrasebooks to accompany the travel series, along with the acclaimed series of music guides, and a best-selling pocket guide to the Internet and World Wide Web. We also publish comprehensive travel information on our two websites: http://www.hotwired.com/rough and http://www.roughguides.com/

The Author

Jules Brown has travelled extensively in North America. Apart from this book, he has written and researched four more *Rough Guides*, as well as various titles for other travel publishers and numerous newspaper and magazine articles.

Contents

List of Maps

MAP SYMBOLS

Interstate		Tourist office	
US Highway		Memorial	
Tunnel		Statue	
Minor road		Hospital	
Railway		Building	
Waterway		Church	
Chapter division boundary		Cemetery	
Airport		Park	
Metro station			

*This book is dedicated to my parents, who, happily, show
no signs of slowing down.*

Introduction

As a nation's capital, **Washington DC** – showtown USA – takes some beating. Along its triumphant avenues stand historic buildings that define a world-view, while on either side of the central Mall sit the various museum buildings of the planet's greatest cultural collection, the Smithsonian Institution. For an introduction to America or a crash course in politics, portraiture or paleontology look no further than the spacious, well-ordered, Neoclassical sweep that is downtown DC.

Just don't expect Washington to fulfill any reasonable expectations of a living, breathing, warts-and-all American city. Born of compromise, it was built as an experiment, and in many ways continues as one – careering along in political turmoil, without representation, bankrupt, neglected, socially psychotic: a federal basket case. These attributes don't necessarily preclude a city from greatness – look at New York – but in Washington's case, history and politics have combined to produce a city full of fine buildings, soaring monuments and improving experiences but short on soul and long on contradictions.

Its very foundation – the result of political wrangle – proved a harbinger of what was to come. In the late eighteenth century, Congress

---

One of these days this will be a very great city if nothing happens to it.
Henry Adams, 1877

I went to Washington as everybody goes there, prepared to see everything done with some furtive intention, but I was disappointed – pleasantly disappointed.
Walt Whitman, 1888

Past a certain hour of the night, when all the good people have gone – or been chased – indoors, the nation's capital turns into a life style septic tank.
P J O'Rourke, *Parliament of Whores*, 1991

My home city of Washington has become a vast memorial to those dead in wars that have glorified the odd president [and] enriched the military industrial complex.
Gore Vidal, 1996

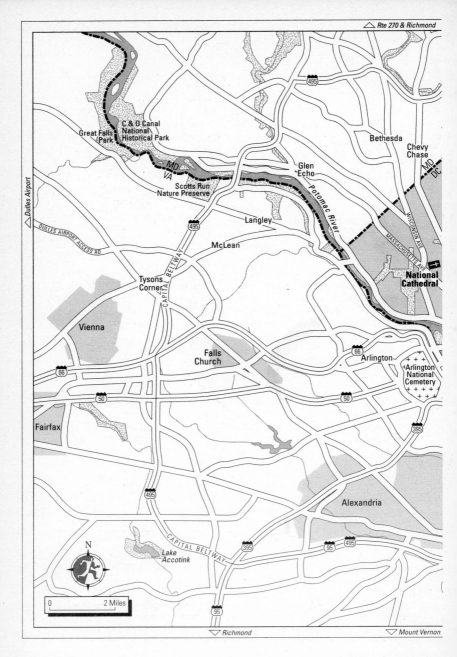

WASHINGTON DC

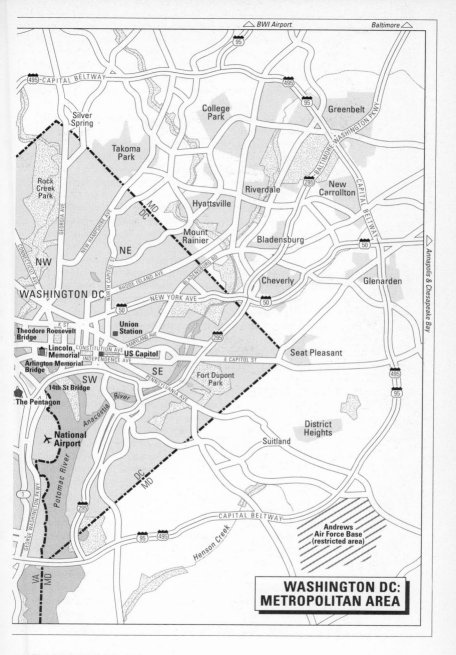

WASHINGTON DC: METROPOLITAN AREA

acceded to the demands of the Northern states to assume their Revolutionary War debts, but squeezed a key concession for the South – rather than being sited in one of the big Northern cities the new federal capital would be built from scratch on the banks of the Potomac River, midway along the eastern seaboard. And while not actually *in* the Deep South, Washington – named for the republic's first president – in the Territory (later District) of Columbia, was very definitely *of* the South. French architect Pierre L'Enfant planned the city on a diamond-shaped piece of land donated by the tobacco-rich states of Virginia and Maryland; slave-labour drained the floodlands and erected the public buildings, and Virginian high society frequented the townhouses and salons which flourished after the government moved in during 1800. Capital of all America it may have been, but in its early years Washington rejoiced in its southern proclivities – bolstered by the fact that during the first fifty years of its existence, eight out of eleven presidents (and their entourage), between the administrations of John Adams and Zachary Taylor, were from the South.

But to paint DC as a Southern city is to miss the point. John F Kennedy, a resident before he was president, famously pointed out its contradictions in his waspish comment that Washington was "a city of southern efficiency and northern charm". Even more important than its geographical character or location was its unique experimental nature – a modern, planned capital built for a disparate collection of states seeking security in unity. As a symbol of union, its finest hour came within a generation of its foundation when the city that was built largely by slaves became the frontline headquarters of the fight against slavery, as Abraham Lincoln directed the Union troops from the capital's halls and offices. With Virginia and the Confederate states only a river crossing away, DC was secure only when peace was at hand: relief was palpable in the unconfined joy of the victorious Union Army parade down Pennsylvania Avenue in May 1865. After the Civil War, thousands of southern blacks arrived in search of a sanctuary from racist oppression: to some extent they found one. Racial segregation was banned in public places and Howard University, the only US institution of higher learning that enrolled black people, was set up in 1867. By the 1870s African-Americans made up over a third of the population, but economic resources were soon stretched to breaking point. As poverty and squalor worsened, official segregation was re-introduced in 1920, banning blacks from government buildings and the jobs they had come to find.

For much of this century, DC has been both a predominantly black city and a federal fortress. Shunned by the white political aristocracy, the city is run as a virtual colony of Congress, where residents have only non-voting representation and couldn't even participate in presidential elections until the 1970s. Suffering an endless cycle of boom and bust, the city has one of the country's highest crime rates, and appalling levels of unemployment, illiteracy and drug abuse – much bandied-about statistics usually dub it the nation's "murder and crack cocaine capital". Federal government money props up the city, pays its administrators and affects virtually every aspect of local commerce and industry – galling in the extreme to the majority of American citizens to whom Washington is a dirty word, inhabited only by self-seeking politicians isolated within the fabled Beltway, the ring road which circles the city and is used as a metaphor for all that's different about DC.

Meanwhile, twenty million visitors come to Washington each year for fun, making it one of the most visited destinations in the country. Kept away from the city's peripheral dead zones, they tour a scrubbed, policed and largely safe downtown swathe where famous landmark follows world-class museum with unending and uplifting regularity. Politics and power are the daily spectacle in the **White House, US Capitol** and **Supreme Court**, as well as the **FBI** and Arlington's military **Pentagon** building – all open to the general public. Overpowering **memorials and monuments** to George Washington, Abraham Lincoln, Thomas Jefferson and the Vietnam and Korean War Veterans punctuate the magnificent showpiece Mall; the **National Gallery of Art** or any of the thirteen **Smithsonian** museums (and its zoo) hold collections unrivalled in their field; while just outside the city, **Arlington National Cemetery** – most famously, burial place of the Civil War dead and the Kennedys – and **Mount Vernon**, George Washington's birthplace, elevate DC to pilgrimage centre. Even better, most of what you see in Washington is free and getting around (on a subsidized transport system that has few equals in the United States) is easy.

True, a sense of community, or even neighbourhood, is rare – especially downtown, where like in so many American cities the entire place falls strangely silent after 6pm and at weekends. But pockets of vitality do stand out, in historic Georgetown, arty Dupont Circle or trendy Adams-Morgan, where what nightlife there is shakes its fist at the otherwise conservative surroundings. You wouldn't necessarily choose to come shopping or clubbing in DC, but you'll eat well, from a bounty of different cuisines, and nowhere will you be better informed about what's happening in America. Pick up the paper, switch on the TV or radio, and tune in to the thousands of broadcasters, lobbyists, journalists and politicians who shape the views of the world from a medium-sized east coast city of glorious compromise and dubious future.

Climate

Before air conditioning Washington was deserted from mid-June to September . . . But [now] Congress sits and sits while the presidents – or at least their staffs – never stop making mischief.

Gore Vidal, *Armageddon? Essays*, 1987

The local climate isn't great, it has to be said – often unbearably hot and humid in summer and bitterly cold in winter. It's claimed, with some measure of truth, that such an inauspicious spot was picked precisely to discourage early elected leaders from making government a full-time job. The advent of widespread air-conditioning during the 1950s alleviated matters, though, and as long as you're suitably kitted out for venturing outdoors you'll encounter few periods when sightseeing becomes unpleasant. **Best times to visit** are spring, early summer and fall, when the weather is at its most benign; there's usually snow (occasionally severe) in January and February, while late summer (July and August) is too hot and humid. Whenever you come, bring suitable, comfortable shoes – there's a lot of walking to be done.

Washington DC Climate

	Jan	Feb	Mar	Apr	May	Jun	July	Aug	Sept	Oct	Nov	Dec
Average daily max temp (°F)	42	44	53	64	75	83	87	84	78	67	55	45
Average daily min temp (°F)	27	28	35	44	54	63	68	66	59	48	38	29
Average rainfall (in)	3.4	3	3.6	3.3	3.7	3.9	4.4	4.3	3.7	2.9	2.6	3.1

Basics

Getting There from North America

The easiest way to get to DC from within the US is to fly. Three airports serve the DC area: Washington National, Dulles, and Baltimore (BWI). See p.35 for more on points of arrival.

Competition is such between the major airlines that you'll find little variation between them on their basic fares at any one time. However, airfares do vary wildly throughout the year, depending on the time, seat availability, and whether there's a price war going on. Though there are no official **seasonal variations** for domestic flights, travelling during the week tends to be cheaper than at the weekend, and you should book well in advance during the major holidays (Fourth of July, Christmas,

See p.35 for more on points of arrival.

Airlines	
Air Canada	☎ 1-800/776-3000
American Airlines	☎ 1-800/433-7300
Continental	☎ 1-800/525-0280
Delta	☎ 1-800/221-1212
Southwest	☎ 1-800/435-9792
TWA	☎ 1-800/221-2000
United	☎ 1-800/241-6522
USAir	☎ 1-800/428-4322
Valujet	☎ 1-800/825-8538

Discount Agents	
Council Travel	☎ 1-800/226-8624
STA Travel	☎ 1-800/777-0112
Travel Avenue	☎ 1-800/333-3335
UniTravel	☎ 1-800/325-2222 or 314/569-2501

Thanksgiving, even college spring break). The cheapest option when dealing with the airlines direct is usually to buy an **Apex fare**, though these can come with a myriad of restrictions (travelling at a certain time of day, on certain days of the week, staying for a fixed length of time, having to include a Saturday night and so forth). They operate on a sliding scale depending on how early you're able to book (7 days, 14 days, or, for the cheapest fares, 21 days). If you're under 26 and have flexible travel plans, you might find that airlines can quote you an even cheaper standby rate.

As an example of Apex **round-trip fares** for direct flights to DC, bookable 14 days in advance, travelling mid-week and entailing a Saturday night stay, you're looking at around $150 from New York (1hr 30min); $230 from Chicago (2hr 40min), and $250 from Miami (2hr 15min). Only *United* fly direct from San Francisco, for $390 (4hr 30min). If you don't mind flying into Baltimore, check out *Southwest*'s excellent deals: from Chicago $110, from San Francisco $286, and from Fort Lauderdale $112. Although these fares are non-refundable, most airlines will allow you to change your plans for a fee of about $50.

If money concerns are less important than flexibility, *Delta* and *US Air* both offer a walk-up weekend fare from New York of $79 one-way, valid all day Saturday and on Sunday until 2.30pm (*Delta*)/3pm (*US Air*), and a three-day advance purchase fare of $51 one-way, valid all day Saturday, Sunday until 11.30am (*Delta*)/noon (*US Air*). Both airlines also run **shuttles** from La Guardia to Washington National.

These run hourly from about 7am to 9pm and the flight takes around an hour. In theory, they'll send you off in your own otherwise empty plane if the preceding one is full, so the advertised weekday one-way fare of $173 is accordingly steep. However, both airlines offer discount "flight packs", valid for a year, which cost $230 for four one-way tickets and $420 for eight one-way tickets.

Look out for other special deals offered by the major airlines: these tend to be advertised in newspapers, often last only a few days, and may require booking months in advance. See p.6 for details of **air passes** available to overseas visitors.

You'll save yourself a lot of time and stress, and maybe big bucks, by checking out the **discount agents** first. Some, like STA and *Council Travel,* specialize in youth/student fares, and even if you don't fit into that category, they'll do their best to find you the cheapest available flight – though these, of course, may not be by the most direct route. STA currently offers a special youth/student fare, 3-day advance purchase, 60-day maximum stay, San Francisco–DC round-trip flight on US Air for $355, and even non-student/youth fares can offer savings of up to as much as $100. Note that there's a $3 **airport tax** on all domestic flights.

For details of flights **from Canada**, see p.7.

Tours

A number of operators, including most of the major airlines, offer **city breaks** to DC. One of the most reliable outfits, *Collette Tours,* offers a 4 night/3 day DC vacation, including flight, 4-star hotel, meals, and guided tours; the price from San Francisco is $830, going up to about $850 during April and May. From Chicago it costs $680–700. They don't arrange air travel from East Coast cities. If you're after a little more flexibility, *Adventure Vacations* allows you to choose tailor-made tours, for any number of days, with various extras such as car rental and the like, at competitive prices. For example, booking a flight from San Francisco, with four nights accommodation at a 3-star hotel, two evening meals and a trolley tour, costs around $1000. Operating under the banner of *Smithsonian Odyssey Tours, Saga,* an organization that caters mostly (though not exclusively) for the over-50s, has a five-night tour called

Washington DC – An Insider's Look. Though expensive, the price tag includes air-fare, 4-star accommodation, guided tours of the Smithsonian's many museums and the White House, a performance at the Kennedy Center, and other entertainments. Prices range from $900 from New York to $1050 from Chicago and $1350 from the West Coast.

Of the packages offered in conjunction with the airlines, *Continental Vacations/Grand Destinations* offer good deals, including air fare, accommodation, and at least one guided city tour. Prices per person, double occupancy, leaving from Sunday to Wednesday (travelling Thurs–Sat costs a few dollars extra), are: $350 (2 nights)/$595 (7 nights) from Chicago; $400/$650 from Miami, or $520/$770 from San Francisco. From New York (flight not included) packages cost from $130/$370. *Delta Dream Vacations/Certified Vacations* have a more expensive 3 night/4 day DC package that includes flight and 5-star hotel only; prices for two (no packages for singles) start at $580 from New York; $860 from Chicago; $900 from Miami, and $1320 from San Francisco. *Amtrak's Great American Vacations* will mix and match accommodation at a choice of 3- to 5-star hotels in DC, a trolley tour, and round-trip travel by train or a combination of train and plane. Prices start at $287 (per person, double occupancy), travelling from New York and including two nights in a 4-star hotel. Travelling from the West Coast, naturally, works out far more expensive.

A few tour operators include Washington DC on **longer East Coast and southern itineraries**. *Globus* has a seven-day bus tour that covers New York, Niagara Falls, Pennsylvania Dutch Country and includes two nights in DC. Prices start at $750 and include food, first-class hotel, transportation and tour guide. *American Adventures* offers a variety of camping/youth hostel tours that include DC; of particular interest is their *Eastern Highlights* tour, which hits Washington, upstate New York, New York City, Boston and Cape Cod. The tour runs from May to July, with prices ranging from $399 (7 days, 1 night in DC)/$499 (10 days, 2 nights in DC) in May to $499/$599 in July. You'll need to budget an extra $50 per person per week for the food kitty and an estimated $20 per person (4 per room) for 2-star hotel accommodation in DC.

BASICS

Specialist Operators

Adventure Vacations	☎ 1/800-638-9040	Continental Vacations/Grand Destinations	
American Adventures	☎ 1-800/864-0335		☎ 1-800 /634-5555
Amtrak Great American Vacations		Delta Dream Vacations	☎ 1-800/872-7786
	☎ 1-800/321-8684	Globus	☎ 1-800/221-0090
Certified Vacations	☎ 1-800/233 7260	Saga Holidays	☎ 1-800/343-0273
Collette Tours	☎ 1-800/832-4656	Trek America	☎ 1-800/221-0596

Between May and October, *Trek America's* popular 14-day *Atlantic Dream* ($687–803) takes you from New York to Miami and allows a generous two to three days in Washington. At the other end of the price range, *Saga Holidays* (see above) offers a Colonial Virginia and Blue Ridge Mountains tour beginning in Charleston, South Carolina and ending in Washington DC, staying in 2/3-star hotels. It costs $2099–2199 (as usual, depending on the time of year).

By train

Travelling by **Amtrak** (☎ 1-800/USA-RAIL), isn't particularly cheap, and if you want extras (like a sleeping compartment) you'll have to pay a whole lot more than the prices quoted in the box below. If you want a relatively comfortable journey from San Francisco, for example, then you can expect to add either $211 (depending on availability) or $344 per night for *Amtrak's* so-called "economy sleeper" on top of the total fare. But for long journeys, the comfort – especially compared to the bus – and the stunning scenic views on many routes make the extra cost well worthwhile. In particular, the *Silver Star,* which travels from Miami through Georgia, the Carolinas and Virginia to DC, makes for a pleasant 22 hours travel time.

Amtrak's **All Aboard pass**, for US travellers only, is valid for 45 days and permits three stopovers within certain geographical zones. DC is included in the eastern zone, which stretches as far west as Chicago, up to Montréal (but excludes Toronto) and down to Miami. The price is $198 (off peak) or $228 (summer and Christmas). For details of rail passes available to overseas visitors, see p.6.

Amtrak also organizes packages to DC; for details see above. And for rail arrivals in the city, see p38.

By bus

Buses are cheaper than the train, and run far more regularly. But they do take forever. And you might need to use one of those toilets . . . The chief operator to DC is *Greyhound* (☎ 1-800/231-2222), who run especially frequent routes from New York. They also offer a *Greyhound* **Ameripass**, which gives unlimited travel on the network for $179 (7 days), $289 (15 days), $399 (30 days) and $599 (60 days). All passes are unrefundable, and are only really worthwhile for domestic travellers who are including DC as part

---

Sample Rail Fares to DC

Note that round-trip fares on some routes vary according to seat availabilty.

From Chicago (17hr 20min): $139 (one-way), $141–278 (round-trip)

From Miami (22hr): $204 (one-way), $182–408 (round-trip)

From New York (3hr–3hr 30min): $60 (one-way), $120 (round-trip)

From San Francisco via Chicago (3 days): $259 (one-way), $266–518 (round-trip)

Sample Greyhound Fares to DC

The following are standard weekend fares: you'll pay a few bucks less if you travel between Monday and Thursday. Regular tickets allow three stop overs, and some have a 15 percent cancellation fee.

From Chicago (18hr): $83 (one-way), $168 (round-trip)

From Miami (22–29hr): $89 (one-way), $139 (round-trip)

From New York (4hr 30min–5hr): $28 (one-way), $52 (round-trip)

From San Francisco (3 days): $125 (one-way), $209 (round-trip)

TRAVEL PASSES FOR OVERSEAS TRAVELLERS

Overseas visitors travelling around the US have a choice of train, bus and air passes, which must usually be bought in advance of their trip. They're of little use if you plan simply to visit Washington DC, but if the city forms part of a wider East Coast or cross-country trip you may find them worthwhile.

Amtrak Rail Passes

The most relevant *Amtrak* rail passes for Washington are the *Eastern Pass* (June 19–Aug 22 $200 for 15 days, $255 for 30; rest of year $179 /$229), which covers the country east of the Mississippi; and the *North Eastern Rail Pass*, which covers the east coast from Montréal via Niagara Falls (excluding Toronto) down to DC (June 19–Aug 22 $175 for 15 days, $205 for 30; rest of year $155/$195). On production of a passport issued outside the US or Canada, the passes can be bought at *Amtrak* stations in the US. In the UK, you can buy them from specialist holiday operators (see p.10) or *Destination Marketing* (☎0171/978 5212); in Ireland, contact *USIT* (see p.11); in Australasia, *Walshes World* (Sydney ☎02/9232 7499 or 1800/227 122; Auckland ☎09/379 3708) or *Thomas Cook World Rail* (Sydney ☎1800/42747).

Greyhound Ameripasses

The *Greyhound* Ameripass offers unlimited bus travel within a set time limit (4–60 days; £70–330). It is only available before leaving home: most travel agents can oblige. In the UK, *Greyhound*'s office is at Sussex House, London Rd, East Grinstead, West Sussex RH19 1LD (☎01342/317317). The first time you use your pass, it will be dated by the ticket clerk; this becomes the starting date of the ticket.

Air Passes

All the main American airlines offer air passes for travel within the US: these have to be bought in advance, and are usually sold with the proviso that you reach the US with the relevant airline. All the deals are broadly similar, involving the purchase of at least three coupons (for around US$300–350 for the first three coupons and US$50–75 for each additional one), each valid for a flight of any duration in the US.

of a longer itinerary, or for those coming from the West Coast. For details of bus pass deals available to overseas travellers, see the box above.

For details of bus arrivals in DC, see p.38.

By car

Renting a car to get to DC gives you the greatest freedom and flexibility, but will be of little use in the city itself (see p.44). Though rates and bargain offers vary wildly, in general you'll get a better deal at the weekend (usually Thurs–Mon, inclusive) than during the week. The lowest rates are usually available at airports, where $150 a week for a subcompact is fairly standard. The best bet, however, is to wait until you know exactly when you'll be needing a car, check any discounts from airlines, credit cards and the like that you might qualify for, then shop around. Be sure to get free unlimited mileage, and be aware that drop-off charges can be as much as $200 or more. Always read the small print carefully for details on Collision Damage Waiver (CDW), sometimes called Liability Damage Waiver (LDW), a form of insurance which often isn't included in the initial rental charge but is well worth considering. This specifically covers the car that you are driving yourself – you are in any case insured for damage to other vehicles. At $9–13 a day, it can add substantially to the total cost, but without it you're liable for every scratch to the car – even those that aren't your fault.

One option worth considering is a **driveaway**, whereby you drive a car from one place to another on behalf of the owner, paying only for the petrol you use. Current offers can be found in the *Yellow Pages* under "Automobile Transporters" and "Drive-Away Companies". You

Driving to DC

From Chicago: 16hr (710 miles)
From Miami: 24hr (1057 miles)
From Montréal: 14hr (610 miles)
From New York: 5hr 30min (240 miles)
From San Francisco: 72hr (2845 miles)
From Toronto: 12hr (570 miles)

Car Rental Companies

Alamo	☎ 1-800/354-2322	Holiday Autos	☎ 1-800/422-7737
Avis	☎ 1-800/331-1212	National	☎ 1-800/CAR-RENT
Budget	☎ 1-800/527-0700	Rent-A-Wreck	☎ 1-800/535-1391
Dollar	☎ 1-800/421-6868	Thrifty	☎ 1-800/367-2277
Hertz	☎ 1-800/654-3131		

Most agencies in DC have offices at National and Dulles airports and Union Station. For associated car rental companies in foreign countries, see p.10 (Britain), p.11 (Ireland), & p.14 (Australia and New Zealand).

must be 21 or older with a valid driver's licence and, possibly, prove you have a "good" driving record. The deposit, refundable on delivery, can vary from $200 to $500 and may depend on the age of the driver. Some companies will only accept cash or travellers' cheques. Note that you might be expected to average 400 miles a day.

From Canada

Of the major airlines, only *US Air* and *Air Canada* have **direct flights to DC** from Toronto and Montréal. Although *US Air* has the edge on special deals, *Air Canada* offers better overall standard fares. They run four daily direct flights from Toronto (1hr 20min; Can$420) and Montréal (1hr 20min; Can$360). Their cheapest fare from Vancouver is via Toronto (7hr; Can$1071). Fares quoted are 14 day advance round-trip (requiring 1 Saturday night stay).

You can also get to DC from Canada by **bus**: *Greyhound's* Montréal–DC fare is $82 one way/ $109 round-trip. The travel time varies between thirteen and sixteen hours. From Toronto it's $59/$109, and takes fifteen to nineteen hours. If you want a more leisurely trip you can even travel by **Amtrak**, which from Toronto weaves its way down via Niagara Falls, upstate New York and New York City, and from Montréal takes you via New England. For more details on *Amtrak* see p.5.

Insurance

You may already be covered by your existing **insurance** – some homeowners' policies are valid on vacation, and credit cards such as *American Express* often include some medical or other insurance, while most Canadians are covered for medical mishaps overseas by their provincial health plans. If you only need trip cancellation/interruption coverage (to supplement your homeowners/credit card/student health plan), this is generally available at around $6 per $100. If you aren't already covered, however, you should consider taking out specialist **travel insurance**. Reasonably priced deals include those offered by *Access America* (☎ 1-800/284-8300), whose policy, valid up to 31 days, covers trip cancellation, life, emergency medical and dental, medical evacuation, lost or stolen baggage, baggage and travel delay and default protection (in case your airline or travel agent goes broke). It costs $45, with extensions available at $3 a day. *Travel Guard's* (☎ 1-800/826-1300) full package for a trip costing up to $500 is $40. Cover for trips costing up to $1000 is $65, and it's $82 for trips up to $1500. Children under sixteen travelling with an insured adult are covered at no extra charge.

Getting There from Britain and Ireland

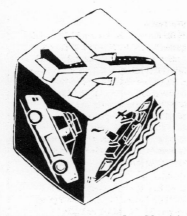

It's not quite as cheap yet to fly to DC as it is to New York, so whatever kind of travel deal you're looking for – flight-only, fly-drive or package – it pays to shop around for the best offers. Calling a specialist flight agent or tour operator can give you an overview of the available options, while competition is such that it's always worth phoning the airlines direct to check on current deals. Other useful resources include the travel ads in the weekend papers, and, in London, *Time Out* and the *Evening Standard*.

Flights from London

There are **non-stop direct flights to Washington DC** from London Heathrow with *United Airlines*, *British Airways* and *Virgin Atlantic*, which take around seven hours. Following winds ensure that return flights are always an hour or so shorter than outward journeys. Flights usually leave Britain in mid-morning, while flights back from the US tend to arrive in Britain early in the morning. All other airlines serving DC fly via their respective American or European hubs, so you can expect these flights to take an extra two to three hours each way.

Fares vary widely according to season, availability and the current level of inter-airline competition – which, since the advent of direct *Virgin* flights, is considerable. In general you're best buying an **Apex** ticket. The conditions on these are pretty standard whoever you fly with – seats must be purchased at least 7, 14 or 21 days in advance, and you must stay at least one Saturday night; tickets are normally valid for between one and six months and are usually not refundable or changeable. The most expensive time to fly is **high season**, roughly between June and August and around Easter and Christmas; May and September/October are slightly less pricey (shoulder season), and the rest of the year is considered low season and cheaper still. **Weekend rates** for all return flights tend to be around £30 more expensive than those in the week. And remember to add £25–35 **airport tax**, whenever you travel.

The **cheapest return fares** to Washington DC (booking at least 21 days in advance, staying minimum one week, maximum one month) currently cost around £400 (high season), dropping to £320 (shoulder) and as little as £205 in low season; tickets with more flexibility and less advance-booking time cost around £100 more whenever you buy. If you're under 26 or a student, an **agent** specializing in low-cost flights (like *Campus Travel* or *STA*; see below) may be able to undercut the regular fares, bringing low-season prices to DC down to around £180 return.

International flights to DC use Dulles airport, though it's also worth checking fares to **Baltimore** (BWI), which is just an hour from downtown DC. With an **open-jaw** ticket you can fly into one city (DC) and out of another (say New York); fares are calculated by halving the return fares to each destination and adding the two figures together. This is a convenient option for those who want a fly-drive holiday (see "Package holidays and travel passes" opposite).

For details on how to reach downtown DC from the various airports, see *Introducing the City*, p.35.

AIRLINES

Air France	☎0181/742 6600	Lufthansa	☎0181/740 2626
American Airlines	☎0181/572 5555	Northwest	☎01293/561000
British Airways	☎0345/222111	TWA	☎0171/439 0707
Continental	☎0800/776464	United	☎0181/990 9900
Delta	☎0800/414767	Virgin Atlantic	☎01293/747747
KLM	☎0181/750 9000		

DISCOUNT FLIGHT AGENTS

Alpha Flights
173 Uxbridge Rd,
London W11 ☎0171/579 8444

APA Travel
138 Eversholt St,
London NW1 ☎0171/387 5337

Campus Travel
52 Grosvenor Gardens, London SW1W 0AG
☎0171/730 2101; 541 Bristol Rd, Selly Oak,
Birmingham B29 6AU ☎0121/414 1848; 61
Ditchling Rd, Brighton BN1 4SD
☎01273/570226; 39 Queen's Rd, Clifton,
Bristol BS8 1QE ☎0117/929 2494; 5 Emmanuel
St, Cambridge CB1 1NE ☎01223/324283; 53
Forest Rd, Edinburgh EH1 2QP ☎0131/668
3303; 166 Deansgate, Manchester M3 3FE
☎0161/833 2046; 105–106 St Aldates, Oxford
OX1 1DD ☎01865/242067

Council Travel
28a Poland St,
London W1V 3DB ☎0171/437 7767

Destination Group
41–45 Goswell Rd,
London EC1 ☎0171/253 9000

Nouvelles Frontières
11 Blenheim St,
London W1Y 9LE ☎0171/629 7772

STA Travel
86 Old Brompton Rd, London SW7 3LH, 117
Euston Rd, London NW1 2SX, 38 Store St
London WC1 ☎0171/ 361 6262; 25 Queen's Rd,
Bristol BS8 1QE ☎0117/929 4399; 38 Sidney
St, Cambridge CB2 3HX ☎01223/366966; 75
Deansgate, Manchester M3 2BW ☎0161/834
0668; 88 Vicar Lane, Leeds LS1 7JH
☎0113/244 9212; 36 George St, Oxford OX1
2OJ ☎01865/792800; and branches in
Birmingham, Canterbury, Cardiff, Coventry,
Durham, Glasgow, Loughborough, Nottingham,
Warwick and Sheffield

Trailfinders
42–50 Earls Court Rd, London W8 6FT
☎0171/938 3366; 194 Kensington High St,
London, W8 7RG ☎0171/938 3939; 58
Deansgate, Manchester M3 2FF ☎0161/839
6969; 254–284 Sauchiehall St, Glasgow G2 3EH
☎0141/353 2224; 22–24 The Priory,
Queensway, Birmingham B4 6BS ☎0121/236
123; 48 Corn St, Bristol BS1 1HQ ☎0117/929
9000

Travel Bug
597 Cheetham Hill Rd,
Manchester M8 5EJ ☎0161/721 4000

Union Travel
93 Piccadilly,
London W1 ☎0171/493 4343

Package holidays and travel passes

Typically, a summer **city break** – return flight plus
3-star (room-only) accommodation for three
nights in Washington DC – costs from around
£399–489 per person, perhaps £100 more in a
5-star hotel; prices drop a little in low season.
Some of the specialist operators over the page
can arrange tailor-made holidays of a week or
more, using DC as a base to visit nearby Civil and
Revolutionary War sites; others include two or

three days in DC as part of a longer American
tour, camping holiday or adventure trip.
Obviously, these are considerably more expensive (and prices vary wildly according to what's
being offered) but the DC element of the trip
makes a suitably monumental start or finish to
an American holiday.

Many American hotel chains also offer **pre-
paid discount accommodation vouchers**. British
travellers must buy the vouchers in the UK, at a
cost of between £30 and £60 per night for a

Specialist Holiday Operators in the UK

AmeriCan Adventures
45 High St, Tunbridge Wells,
Kent TN1 1XL   ☎ 01892/511894

Bon Voyage
18 Bellevue Rd, Southampton,
Hants SO15 2AY   ☎ 01703/330332

British Airways Holidays
Astral Towers, Bettsway,
London Rd, Crawley
W Sussex RH10 2XA   ☎ 01293/722727

Destination USA
41–45 Goswell Rd,
London EC1   ☎ 0171/253 2000

First Choice
First Choice House,
London Rd, Crawley,
W Sussex RH10 2HB   ☎ 01293/560777

Key to America
1–3 Station Rd, Ashford,
Middlesex TW15 2UW   ☎ 01784/248777

North America Travel Service
7 Albion St,
Leeds LS1 5ER   ☎ 0113/246 1466

Northwest Flydrive
PO Box 45, Bexhill-on-Sea,
E Sussex TN40 1PY   ☎ 01424/224400

Premier Holidays
Westbrook, Milton Rd,
Cambridge CB4 1YQ   ☎ 01223/516516

Trans Atlantic Vacations
3A Gatwick Metro Centre, Balcombe Rd,
Horley, Surrey RH6 9GA   ☎ 01293/774441

TrekAmerica
4 Waterperry Court, Middleton Rd,
Banbury, Oxon OX16 8Q6   ☎ 01869/338777

Unijet
"Sandrocks", Rocky Lane, Haywards Heath,
W Sussex RH16 4RH   ☎ 01444/459191

Virgin Holidays
The Galleria, Station Rd, Crawley,
W Sussex RH10 1WW   ☎ 01293/617181

minimum of two people sharing (the higher amount is more likely in DC). However, good-value accommodation is not exactly difficult to find in the US (see "Accommodation", p.259) – and, once you've arrived, if you intend to travel outside DC you may well regret the inflexibility imposed upon your travels. Most UK travel agents carry details of the various voucher schemes; the cheapest is the "Go As You Please" deal offered by *Days Inn* (☎ 01483/440 0470 in Britain).

British visitors can also buy **train, bus and air passes** for travel throughout the United States. They usually have to be bought in advance of your trip; for more details, see p.6.

Fly-drive holidays

You won't need a car in Washington DC, but if you plan to see more of the country, **fly-drive** deals – which give cut-rate (sometimes free) car rental when buying a transatlantic ticket from an airline or tour operator – are always cheaper than renting on the spot. Several of the companies listed in the "Specialist Holiday Operators" box above offer fly-drive packages, though watch out

for hidden extras, such as local taxes, "drop-off" charges and extra insurance, and note that you'll probably have to pay more for the flight than if you booked it through a discount agent. It's not necessary to rent a car by the week (although it's cheaper to do so): most operators can arrange a daily tariff if all you want is a couple of days' local sightseeing around DC.

You can also save up to 60 percent by booking **car rental** in advance with a major firm which has representation in Washington DC (see the list of rental companies below). If you choose not to pay until you arrive, take a written confirmation of the price with you. If you need to arrange car

Car Rental Companies in the UK

Alamo	☎ 0800/272200
Avis	☎ 0181/848 8733
Budget	☎ 0800/181181
Dollar (Eurodollar)	☎ 01895/233300
Hertz	☎ 0990/996699
Holiday Autos	☎ 0990/300400
National (EuropCar/InterRent)	
	☎ 01345/222525

rental once you're **in Washington**, see p.7; while for the hideous intricacies of driving in DC itself, see p.44.

Flights from Ireland

There are no direct flights from Ireland to Washington DC, though *Delta* and *Aer Lingus* offer services from **Dublin via New York**, which take between nine and eleven hours. Other airlines (like *BA*, *Virgin Atlantic* and *United*) will route you through London on a connecting flight with another carrier; with more time, you could always arrange your own discount Dublin/Belfast –London flight and pick up an onward service from there; see "Flights from London" p.8. Low-season fares from Dublin to DC run from around IR£320 to IR£420 depending on the route; in high season you'll pay IR£510–590; tax of around IR£25 is added to all flights. You can call the airlines direct, but it's best to deal with a **discount agent** specializing in low-cost flights, some of which are listed below. If you're under 26 or a student, contact *USIT* or *Student & Group Travel* for the most competitive fares.

USEFUL ADDRESSES AND CONTACTS IN IRELAND

Airlines

Aer Lingus Belfast ☎0645/737747; Dublin ☎01/844 4777; Cork ☎021/327155; Limerick ☎061/474239

British Airways Belfast ☎0345/222111; Dublin ☎1800/626747

Delta Belfast ☎01232/480526; Dublin ☎01/676 8080; or 1800/768080

Virgin Atlantic Dublin ☎01/873 3388

Car Rental Agencies

Avis	☎01232/240404
Budget	☎01232/230700
Hertz	☎01/660 2255

Holiday Autos ☎01/454 9090

National (EuropCar/InterRent) ☎01232/450904 or 423444

Discount Flight Agents and Tour Operators

American Holidays
Lombard House, Lombard St,
Belfast 1 ☎01232/238762;
38 Pearse St,
Dublin 2 ☎01/679 8800

Apex Travel
59 Dame St,
Dublin 2 ☎01/671 5933

Discount Travel
4 South Great Georges St,
Dublin 2 ☎01-679 5888

Flight Finders International
13 Baggot St Lower,
Dublin 2 ☎01/676 8326

Inflight Travel
92–94 York Rd,
Belfast 15 ☎01232/740187 or 743341

Joe Walsh Tours
8–11 Baggot St,
Dublin ☎01/676 3053

Student & Group Travel
71 Dame St,
Dublin 2 ☎01/677 7834

Thomas Cook
11 Donegall Place,
Belfast ☎01232/240833
118 Grafton St,
Dublin ☎01/677 1721

Travel Shop
35 Belmont Rd,
Belfast 4 ☎01232/471717

USIT
Fountain Centre, Belfast BT1 6ET
☎01232/324073; 10–11 Market Parade, Patrick St, Cork ☎021/270900; 33 Ferryquay St, Derry ☎01504/371888; Aston Quay, Dublin 2 ☎01/679 8833; Victoria Place, Eyre Square, Galway ☎091/565177; Central Buildings, O'Connell St, Limerick ☎061/415064; 36–37 Georges St, Waterford ☎051/72601

For information about **package holidays** and city breaks, call any of the high-street travel agents. These (as well as the discount agents listed on the previous page) can also advise about **fly-drive** deals; to compare prices, call one of the car rental agencies in Ireland with representation in DC. There's more on driving in the US given above under "Fly-drive holidays" and on p.6.

Insurance

Though not compulsory, **travel insurance** including medical cover is *essential* in view of the high costs of health care in the US. Credit cards (particularly *American Express*) often have certain levels of medical or other insurance included, especially if you use them to pay for your trip; in addition, if you have a good "all risks" home insurance policy it may well cover your possessions against loss or theft even when overseas,

and many private medical schemes also cover you while abroad. Note that if visiting Washington DC is part of a wider American trip and you later plan to participate in watersports, or do some hiking or skiing, you'll almost certainly have to pay an extra premium; check carefully that your policy will cover you in case of an accident. Most travel agents and tour operators will offer you travel insurance – those policies offered by *Campus Travel* or *STA* in the UK and *USIT* in Ireland are usually reasonable value. If you feel the cover is inadequate, or you want to compare prices, any insurance broker, bank or specialist travel insurance company should be able to help: call *Columbus Travel Insurance* (☎0171/375 0011), *Endsleigh Insurance* (☎0171/436 4451), or *Frizzell Insurance* (☎01202/292333). Two weeks' cover for a trip to DC should cost around £40, a month around £47.

Getting There from Australia and New Zealand

There are no direct scheduled flights to Washington DC from Australia or New Zealand and most people reach the capital flying via

Honolulu or Los Angeles, with a stopover or transfer in an Asian or Pacific hub. Specialist agents can help sort out all the routes and several of the best are listed opposite; *Flight Centres* and *STA Travel* generally have the best discounts.

Flights

The **high season** for airfares to the USA runs from the beginning of December to mid-January; **low season** is February/March and mid-October/November; shoulder season is mid/end January, April, May and July to mid-October.

Fares to DC on major airlines like *United* and *Qantas* run from A$2300–3000/NZ$2500–3100, roughly the same as a "Round-the-World" fare (see p.14). *Korean Airlines* can get you there slightly cheaper, flying to DC with an overnight stopover in Seoul for around A$1900–2200/NZ$2250–2500. *United* and *Qantas* have daily flights to DC via LA from major

Airlines

Air New Zealand Sydney ☎ 02/9223 4666 or Auckland ☎ 09/366 2803

Air Pacific Sydney ☎ 02/9957 0150 or 1800/230150

American Airlines Sydney ☎ 02/9299 3600 or 1800/227101

Cathay Pacific Sydney ☎ 02/9931 5500, local-call rate 131747; Auckland ☎ 09/379 0861

Delta Sydney ☎ 02/9262 1777; Auckland ☎ 09/379 3370

Garuda Sydney ☎ 02/9334 9944; Auckland ☎ 09/366 1855

Korean Airlines Sydney ☎ 02/9262 6000; Auckland ☎ 09/307 3687

Malaysian Airlines Sydney local-call rate ☎ 13/2627; Auckland ☎ 09/373 2741

Philippine Airlines Sydney ☎ 02/9262 3333

Qantas Sydney ☎ 02/9957 0111; Auckland ☎ 09/357 8900

Thai Airways Sydney ☎ 02/9844 0999 or 1800/422020; Auckland ☎ 09/377 3886

United Airlines Sydney ☎ 02/237 8888; Auckland ☎ 09/307 9500

Discount Travel Agents

Anywhere Travel
345 Anzac Parade, Kingsford,
Sydney ☎ 02/9663 0411

Brisbane Discount Travel
260 Queen St,
Brisbane ☎ 07/3229 9211

Budget Travel
6 Fort St,
Auckland; other branches around the city
☎ 09/366 0061; 0800/808040

Destinations Unlimited
3 Milford Rd, Milford,
Auckland ☎ 09/373 4033

Flight Centres
Australia: Level 11, 33 Berry St, North Sydney
☎ 02/9241 2422; Bourke St, Melbourne
☎ 03/9650 2899; plus other branches nationwide
New Zealand: National Bank Towers, 205–225
Queen St, Auckland ☎ 09/209 6171; Shop 1M,
National Mutual Arcade, 152 Hereford St,
Christchurch ☎ 03/379 7145; 50–52 Willis St,
Wellington ☎ 04/472 8101; other branches
countrywide

Northern Gateway
22 Cavenagh St,
Darwin ☎ 08/8941 1394

Passport Travel
320b Glenferrie Rd,
Malvern ☎ 03/9824 7183

STA Travel
Australia: 702–730 Harris St, Ultimo, Sydney
☎ 02/9212 1255; 1800/637444; 256 Flinders St,
Melbourne ☎ 03/9654 7266; other offices in
state capitals and major universities
New Zealand: Travellers' Centre, 10 High St,
Auckland ☎ 09/309 0458; 233 Cuba St,
Wellington ☎ 04/385 0561; 90 Cashel St,
Christchurch ☎ 03/379 9098; other offices in
Dunedin, Palmerston North, Hamilton and
major universities

Thomas Cook
Australia: 321 Kent St, Sydney ☎ 02/9248
6100; 257 Collins St, Melbourne ☎ 03/9650
2442; branches in other state capitals
New Zealand: Shop 250a St Luke's Square,
Auckland ☎ 09/849 2071

Topdeck Travel
65 Glenfell St,
Adelaide ☎ 08/8232 7222

Tymtro Travel
428 George St,
Sydney ☎ 02/9223 2211

Australian and New Zealand cities; *Korean Airlines* flies several times a week to Washington from Brisbane, Sydney and Auckland.

Alternatively, you can pick up a cheaper flight **to the West Coast** (usually LA) and then either buy an add-on fare to Washington DC (around A$420/NZ$490), travel overland, or take advantage of coupons available with your international ticket for discounted flights within the US (see p.6). The cheapest fares to the West Coast (A$1550–2200/NZ$1800–2400) are with *Air New Zealand, Philippine Airlines* and *Garuda*;

Package Tour Operators

Adventure World

73 Walker St, North Sydney ☎02/9956 7766
or 1800/221931; level 3, 33 Adelaide St,
Brisbane ☎07/3229 0599; 8 Victoria Ave,
Perth ☎08/9221 2300; 101 Great South Rd,
Remuera, Auckland ☎09/524 5118

Creative Tours
Grafton St, Woollahra,
Sydney ☎02/386 2111

Drive-A-Rama
41 Dora St,
Hurstville NSW ☎02/580 6555 or 1800/251354

Wiltrans/Maupintour
Level 10, 189 Kent St,
Sydney ☎02/9255 0899

Car Rental Agencies

AUSTRALIA	
Avis	☎1800/225 533
Budget	☎13/2848
Hertz	☎13/3039
NEW ZEALAND	
Avis	☎09/579 5231
Budget	☎09/375 2220
Hertz	☎09/309 0989

Malaysian Airlines, United Airlines, Cathay Pacific, Thai Airways and *Air Pacific* are slightly more expensive. Departures vary, but are at least several times weekly for all carriers.

As far as **Round-the-World** fares go, you should be able to get six stopovers worldwide (including DC) for A$2400–2900/NZ$2700–3300. More US-oriented, but only available in Australia, is *Cathay Pacific-TWA*'s RTW fare (A$3240), allowing unlimited stopovers worldwide (with a maximum of 8 within the US) and limited backtracking within the US. Call any of the agents or airlines on p.13 for more information.

Packages, passes and car rental

Several agencies organize **package holiday** tours that include DC, from city breaks and tours of historical and Civil War sites to longer overland camping trips; some of the best operators are picked out in the box on this page. If you're planning a wider trip in the US, you may also want to check prices for **rail and bus passes** (see p.6), which are available in Australia and New Zealand before you leave. **Car rental**, too, can be arranged in advance, either by calling one of the major rental companies with representatives in DC (listed above) or by buying a fly-drive holiday from one of the specialist operators listed above. For more on **driving in the US and DC**, see p.6, p.39, and p.44.

Insurance

Travel insurance is put together by the airlines and travel agent groups such as *United Travel Agents Group* (UTAG; ☎1800/809462), *Australian Federation of Travel Agents* (AFTA; ☎02/956 4800), *Cover-More* (☎02/9202 8000 or 1800/251881) and *Ready Plan* (☎1800/337 462) in conjunction with insurance companies. They are all similar in premium and coverage, though *Ready Plan* usually gives the best value for money. A typical policy for the US costs A$190/NZ$220 for one month, rising to A$330/NZ$400 for three months. Contact *STA* or any of the *Flight Centres* (see p.13) for details.

Entry Requirements for Foreign Visitors

Visas

Under the **Visa Waiver Scheme**, if you're a citizen of the UK, Ireland, New Zealand or most western European countries (check with your nearest US embassy or consulate to be sure) and visiting the United States for a period of less than ninety days, you only need a full passport and a visa waiver form. The latter (an I-94W) will be provided either by your travel agency, or by the airline during check-in or on the plane, and must be presented to immigration on arrival. The same

form covers entry across the land borders with Canada and Mexico.

Prospective visitors **from Australia** and most other parts of the world not mentioned above require a valid passport and a **non-immigrant visitor's visa**. For a brief excursion into the US, **Canadian citizens** do not necessarily need even a passport, just some form of ID, though for a longer trip you should carry a passport, and if you plan to stay for more than ninety days you need a visa, too. If you cross into the States by car, your vehicle is subject to spot searches by US Customs personnel, though this sort of surveillance is likely to decrease as remaining tariff barriers fall over the next few years. Remember, too, that Canadians are legally barred from seeking gainful employment in the US.

How you **obtain a visa** depends on what country you're in and your status on application, so telephone your nearest US embassy or consulate, listed in the box below.

Extensions

The date stamped on your passport is the latest you're legally allowed to stay. Leaving a few days later may not matter, especially if you're heading home, but more than a week or so can result in

---

US Embassy and Consulates

Australia
Moonah Place,
Canberra, ACT 2600 ☎ 06/270 5000

Canada
100 Wellington St,
Ottawa, ON K1P 5T1 ☎ 613/238 5335

Ireland
42 Elgin Rd,
Ballsbridge, Dublin ☎ 01/668 7122

New Zealand
29 Fitzherbert Terrace,
Thorndon, Wellington ☎ 4/472 2068

UK
5 Upper Grosvenor St,
London W1A 1AE ☎ 0171/499 9000
visa hotline ☎ 0891/200290

3 Regent Terrace,
Edinburgh EH7 5BW ☎ 0131/556 8315

Queens House, 14 Queen St,
Belfast BT1 6EQ ☎ 01232/328239

For details of foreign embassies and consulates in Washington DC, see p.308.

---

a protracted, rather unpleasant, interrogation from officials, which may cause you to miss your flight. Overstaying may also cause you to be turned away next time you try to enter the US.

To get an extension before your time is up, apply at the nearest **US Immigration and Naturalization Service** (INS) office, whose address will be under the Federal Government Offices listings at the front of the phone book. In DC they're at 425 I St NW (☎514-4316). They will assume that you're working illegally and it's up to you to convince them otherwise, by providing evidence of ample finances. If you can, bring along an upstanding American citizen to vouch for you. You'll also have to explain why you didn't plan for the extra time initially.

Work and study

Anyone planning an extended legal stay in the United States – even those eligible for the Visa Waiver Scheme (see p.15) – should apply for a special **working visa** at any American embassy before setting off. Different types of visas are issued, depending on your skills and length of stay, but unless you've got relatives (parents or children over 21) or a prospective employer to sponsor you, your chances are at best slim.

Illegal work is nothing like as easy to find as it used to be, and the government has intro- duced fines as high as $10,000 for companies caught employing anyone without the legal right to work in the US. Even in the traditionally more casual establishments, like restaurants and bars, things have really tightened up, and if you do find work it's likely to be of the less visible, poorly paid kind – washer-up instead of waiter.

Foreign students have the best chance of prolonging their stay in the US. If you want to **study** at an American university, apply to that institution directly; if they accept you, you're more or less entitled to unlimited visas so long as you remain enrolled in full-time education.

Another option for work, peculiar to DC, is to acquire a place as an **intern**, basically a general administrative dogsbody serving someone con- nected, however tenuously, to the nation's polit- ical system. Senators, representatives, White House staff, federal agencies and lobbyists all hire interns over the summer and applications should be made early in the New Year to anyone you can think of that might be interested in your skills and experience; large city bookshops carry guides to applying for internships. Most posts are unpaid and filled by college students keen to get on in American politics, though foreign visitors with a special interest can try writing in the first instance to their local parliament members, who often have contacts or reciprocal arrangements with American members of Congress.

Information and Maps

There's a wealth of information available about Washington DC, but you'll have to be specific about your enquiries to get anything more than a map and a list of museums. When contacting the relevant offices, write well in advance of your visit, and be as focused as possible about your interests.

Information

The main city information source for tourists is the **Washington DC Convention and Visitors Association**, which has various foreign branches as well as a useful office in the city itself – see the box on the facing page for details. You can also contact other organizations **in Washington**

Tourist Information Offices

Washington DC

DC Chamber of Commerce, 1301 Pennsylvania Ave NW, Suite 309, Washington DC 20004 ☎ 202/347-7201, fax 347-3538

DC Committee to Promote Washington, 1212 New York Ave NW, Suite 200, Washington DC 20005 ☎ 202/347-2873, fax 724-2445, free brochures on ☎ 1-800/422-8644

National Park Service, National Capital Region, 1100 Ohio Drive SW, Washington DC 20242 ☎ 202/619-7222, fax 619-7302

Washington DC Convention and Visitors Association, 1212 New York Ave NW, Suite 600, Washington DC 20005 ☎ 202/789-7000, fax 789-7037; http://www.washington.org

Maryland

Maryland Office of Tourism, 217 E Redwood St, Baltimore MD 21202 ☎ 410/333-6611 or 1-800/543-1036

Virginia

Virginia Division of Tourism, 901 E Byrd St, Richmond VA 23219 ☎ 804/786-2051 or 1-800/847-4882

West Virginia

West Virginia Division of Tourism and Parks, State Capitol Complex, 2101 Washington St, E Charleston WV 25305 ☎ 304/348-2286 or 1-800/CALL-WVA

UK

Washington DC Convention and Visitors Association (UK), 375 Upper Richmond Rd West, London SW14 7NX ☎ 0181/392 9187

DC in advance of your trip for special brochures, information leaflets, visitor guides, events calendars and maps – although you can call these while in the city for specific help, they are not set up for walk-in visits. However, some **information offices** in DC can be visited in person, particularly those staffed by rangers of the National Park Service, which oversees most of the city's monuments and memorials. For more on city offices and information line numbers, see p.40, and for details of city newspapers and listings magazines see p.309.

Also note the addresses and numbers of tourist offices and visitor bureaux in **the surrounding states** (see box above), useful if you're planning to travel on from Washington.

Maps

The maps in this guide, together with the untold number of free city plans you'll pick up from tourist offices, hotels and museums, should be sufficient to help you find your way around. For something more durable, best is the small, shiny, fold-out *Streetwise Washington DC* map ($4.95), available from book, travel and map stores (see p.301 for store locations in DC). Once you've got your map, turn to p.39 for how to **orientate** yourself in the city.

Moving on from DC, the **free road maps** issued by each state are usually fine for general driving and route planning. To get hold of one, either write to the state tourist office directly or stop by any state Welcome Center or visitor centre. *Rand McNally* (Americans can call ☎ 1-800/333-0136 for the location of their nearest store) produces good commercial state maps, while for something more detailed, say for **hiking**, camping shops generally have a good selection, and ranger stations in national parks, state parks and wilderness areas sell good-quality local hiking maps for $1 to $3.

The *American Automobile Association* (*AAA*; ☎ 1-800/222-4357) provides free maps and assistance to its members, and to British members of the *AA* and *RAC*.

Costs, Money and Banks

DC may be the nation's capital, but it's a lot more affordable to vacation here than in most American cities: nearly all the major museums, monuments and sights are free, public transit is cheap and efficient, and the presence of so many students, interns and public service officials means great deals on drinks and food in many establishments. That's not to say that you can't spend money in Washington – the city has some of the nation's finest and most expensive hotels and restaurants. But if you're sticking to any kind of budget, you're unlikely to have too hard a time.

Average costs

Accommodation will be your biggest single expense, with the cheapest, reasonable double hotel rooms going for $70–110 a night, though a few spartan hostels, dingy budget hotels and rather nicer B&Bs undercut this. However, within that price range you'll be able to cut some good deals at weekends and in the less popular summer months – all the details are on p.259. After you've paid for your room, count on a **minimum** of $30 a day, which will buy you breakfast, fast-food lunch, a budget dinner and a beer, but not much else. Eating fancier meals, taxi-taking and drinking and socializing (especially drinking and socializing) will mean allowing for more like $50–60 a day; if you want to go regularly to the theatre or major concerts, rent a car or take a tour, then double that figure.

What's good about DC is how much is **free**. Visiting the major national museum and art collections (and taking specialist guided tours around them); tours of the White House, US Capitol, FBI, and Pentagon; spring and summer concerts, festivals, parades, gatherings, children's events – none costs a cent. The Metro and bus system gets you everywhere you want to go for a dollar or two at a time (or five bucks a day with a special ticket); taxis are inexpensive, and bars and restaurants routinely offer happy hour (ie half-price) drinks and food.

However, note that **sales tax** in Washington DC is 10 percent (and isn't part of the marked price on goods); **hotel tax** is 13 percent on top of the room rate, and there's an extra $1.50 occupancy tax per night wherever you stay.

Currency Exchange in DC

Banks

American Security Bank ☎371-4023

Crestar Bank ☎879-6000

First American Bank ☎637-6210

Riggs National Bank ☎835-6000

American Express

1150 Connecticut Ave NW ☎457-1300

1776 Pennsylvania Ave NW ☎289-8800

Thomas Cook

1800 K St NW ☎872-1233

Union Station ☎371-9219

Opening hours of most banks in Washington DC are Monday to Friday 9am–3pm; some stay open until 5pm or 6pm on Friday, a few open Saturday 9am to noon. For currency exchange outside normal business hours and at weekends try Thomas Cook at Georgetown Park Shopping Mall, 3222 M St NW, or National (7am–9pm) or Dulles (7am–11pm) airports.

Taking, changing and accessing money

US dollar travellers' cheques are the safest way to carry money, for both American and foreign visitors. Be sure to have plenty of $10 and $20 denominations for everyday transactions. Many banks will **change foreign travellers' cheques and currency**; exchange bureaux, always found at airports, tend to charge less commission.

For many services, however, it's simply taken for granted that you'll be paying with plastic. When renting a car or checking into a hotel, you may well be asked to show a **credit card** – even if you intend to settle the bill in cash. Most major credit cards issued by foreign banks are honoured in the US. *Visa, Mastercard, Diners Club, American Express* and *Discover* are the most widely used. With *Mastercard* or *Visa* it is also possible to **withdraw cash** at any bank displaying relevant stickers, or from appropriate automatic 24-hour teller machines (**ATMs**). *Diners Club* cards can be used to cash personal cheques at *Citibank* branches. *American Express* cards can only get cash, or buy travellers' cheques, at *American Express* offices or from the travellers' cheque dispensers at most major airports. American holders of ATM cards from out of state are likely to discover that their cards work in the machines of certain banks in DC (check with your bank before you leave home). Foreign cash-dispensing cards linked to international networks such as *Cirrus* and *Plus* are also accepted in the US – check with your home bank before you set off, as otherwise the machine may simply gobble up your plastic friend.

To find the location of your nearest **ATM**, call:

Amex	☎ 1-800/CASH-NOW
Plus	☎ 1-800/843-7587
Cirrus	☎ 1-800/424-7787

Emergencies

Emergency phone numbers to call if your cheques and/or credit cards are stolen are on p.24. Assuming you know someone who is prepared to send you money in a crisis, the quickest way is to have them take the cash to the nearest **American Express Moneygram** (☎ 1-800/543-4080) office and have it instantaneously **wired** to the office nearest you, subject to the deduction of 10 percent commission. In the US this process should take no longer than ten minutes. They charge according to the amount sent (ranging from $13 to wire $100, to $49 for $1000). See the box on the previous page for addresses of the main AmEx offices in DC. **Western Union** offer a similar service, at slightly higher rates (☎ 1-800/325-6000 in the US, or ☎ 0800/833833 in the UK); if credit cards are involved they charge an extra $10.

If you have a few days' leeway, sending a postal money order, which is exchangeable at any post office, through the mail is cheaper. The equivalent for foreign travellers is the **international money order**, for which you need to allow up to seven days in the mail before arrival. An ordinary cheque sent from overseas takes two to three weeks to clear.

As a last resort, foreign visitors can have money wired directly from a bank in their home

---

Money: a Note for Foreign Travellers

Generally speaking, one **pound sterling** will buy between $1.50 and $1.70; one **Canadian dollar** is worth between 70¢ and 90¢; one **Australian dollar** is worth between 70¢ and 90¢; and one **New Zealand dollar** is worth between 60¢ and 75¢.

  US currency comes in **bills** of $1, $5, $10, $20, $50 and $100, plus various larger (and rarer) denominations. All are the same size and same green colour, making it necessary to check each bill carefully. The dollar is made up of 100 cents in **coins** of 1 cent (known as a **penny**), 5 cents (a **nickel**), 10 cents (a **dime**) and 25 cents

(a **quarter**). Change (quarters are the most useful) is needed for buses, vending machines and telephones, so always carry plenty.

  When working out your daily budget allow for **tipping**, which is universally expected. You really shouldn't depart a bar or restaurant without leaving a tip of *at least* 15 percent (unless the service is utterly disgusting), 20 percent in more upmarket places. About the same amount should be added to taxi fares – and round them up to the nearest 50¢ or dollar. A hotel porter should get $1 a bag, $3–5 for lots of baggage; chambermaids $1–2 a day, valet parking attendants $1.

country to a bank in the US: the person wiring the funds to you will need to know the telex number of the bank the funds are being wired to. Foreign travellers in real difficulties also have the final option of throwing themselves on the mercy of their nearest national **consulate** (see p.308), who will – in worst cases only – repatriate you, but will *never*, under any circumstances, lend money.

Telephones and Mail

Telephones

All telephone numbers in this guide have a ☎ **202** telephone **area code** (for Washington DC), unless otherwise stated. You do not need to dial the area code within the District. Outside DC, dial 1 before the area code and number; calls within the greater DC metropolitan area are counted as local even if they require a different code (☎ 703 for northern Virginia, for example). Making **long-distance calls** to a different area code you'll need plenty of change – when necessary, a voice comes on the line telling you to pay more. Such calls are much less expensive if made between 6pm and 8am – the **cheapest rates** are from 11pm to 8am. In general telephoning from your **hotel room** is more expensive than using a pay-phone, costing up to 75¢–$1 for a local call; that said, some budget hotels offer free local calls. An increasing number of public phones accept **credit cards**, while all the major US phone companies issue their own charge cards. Detailed information about calls, codes and rates is listed at the front of the **telephone directory** in the *White Pages*.

International telephone calls

International calls can be dialled direct from public phones. You can get assistance from the

---

Area Codes

Washington DC ☎ 202

Maryland
Baltimore ☎ 410
rest of the state ☎ 301

Virginia
Richmond, the Tidewater and Atlantic Coast
☎ 804
Northern Virginia ☎ 703
Lexington and western Virginia ☎ 540

West Virginia ☎ 304

Service Numbers

Emergencies ☎ 911 for fire, police or ambulance

Local directory information ☎ 411

Long-distance directory information
☎ 1 (Area Code)/555-1212

Operator ☎ 0

Toll-free directory information
☎ 1-800/555-1212

For other information line and emergency numbers in DC, see City Directory *(p.308) and* Introducing the City *(p.40).*

---

international operator (☎00). The **lowest rates** for international calls to Europe are between 6pm and 7am, when a direct-dialled three-minute call will cost roughly $5.

In **Britain**, it's possible to obtain a free **BT Chargecard** (☎0800/800 838). To use these cards in the US, or to make a **collect call**/reverse the charges, contact the carrier: *AT&T* ☎1-800/445-5667; *MCI* ☎1-800/444-2162; or *Sprint* ☎1-800/800-0008. In the same way, Australia's **Telstra Telecard** (application forms available from Telstra offices) and **New Zealand Telecom**'s **Calling Card** (☎04/382-5818) can be used to make calls charged to a domestic account or credit card.

To make an international call **to Washington DC**, dial your country's international access code, then 1 for the US, followed by 202 for DC. To call **from DC to the rest of the world**, dial 011, then the country code (Britain is 44, Ireland 353, Canada 1, Australia 61 and New Zealand 64), and finally the number (minus the initial 0 of the area code.

For details of **time differences** between the US and the rest of the world, see "Time", p.27.

US mail

Air mail between the US and Europe generally takes about a week. Letters that don't carry the **zip code** are liable to get lost or at least delayed; phone books carry a list for their service area, and post offices – even abroad – have directories. In this guide the zip code for addresses is given where it may be necessary to write in advance.

Letters sent to you c/o **General Delivery** (known elsewhere as **poste restante**), *must* include the post office zip code and will only be held for thirty days before being returned to sender – so make sure there's a return address on the envelope. In DC, the post office which handles General Delivery mail is miles out of the centre at 900 Brentwood Rd NE (Mon–Fri 8am–8pm, Sat 10am–6pm, Sun noon–6pm; ☎635-5300; zip code 20090) – try and have mail held at a hotel, *American Express* office or some other address.

DC's main **downtown post office** is across from Union Station at Massachusetts Ave and N Capitol St NE (Mon–Fri 7am–midnight, Sat & Sun 7am–8pm; ☎523-2628; zip code 20002); there's also a useful counter in the Old Post Office building on Pennsylvania Ave NW (see p.175) and in the US Capitol (see p.109). Downtown **mail boxes** are on Constitution Ave NW at 11th, 14th and 21st; on Independence at 14th; and on 15th outside the Bureau of Engraving and Printing.

Telegrams and faxes

To send a **telegram**, go to a *Western Union* office (listed in the *Yellow Pages*; and see p.19). Credit card holders can dictate messages over the phone. **International telegrams** sent in the morning from the US should arrive at their overseas destination the following day. For domestic telegrams ask for a **mailgram**, which will be delivered to any address in the country the next morning.

Public **fax** machines, which may require your credit card to be "swiped" through an attached device, are found at city photocopy centres and, occasionally, bookstores.

Opening Hours, Public Holidays and Festivals

Opening hours

Museums generally open daily 10am–5.30pm, though some have extended summer opening hours; a few art galleries stay open until 9pm or so one night a week. Smaller, private museums close for one day a week, usually Monday or Tuesday. **Federal office buildings** (some of which incorporate museums) open Monday–Friday 9am–5.30pm and are closed at weekends. Most of the national **monuments** in the city are open daily 24 hours, though they tend to be staffed only between 8am and midnight. Finally, **stores** are usually open Monday–Saturday 10am–7pm, while some have extended Thursday night hours. In neighbourhoods like Georgetown, Adams-Morgan and Dupont Circle many stores open on Sunday, too (usually noon–5pm); **malls** tend to be open Monday–Saturday 10am–9pm or later, and Sunday noon–6pm.

For the opening hours for specific attractions, see the relevant accounts in the *Guide*. Telephone numbers are provided throughout so that you can check current information with the places themselves.

National public holidays

On the national **public holidays** listed below, shops, banks and public and federal offices are liable to be closed all day. The Smithsonian museums and galleries, on the other hand, close only on Christmas Day. The traditional **summer season** for tourism, when many attractions have extended opening hours, runs from **Memorial Day to Labor Day**.

Festivals

Washington has a huge variety of **annual festivals and events**, many of them national in scope: America's Christmas Tree is lit each year

---

National Public Holidays

January
1: New Year's Day
3rd Monday: Dr Martin Luther King Jr's Birthday

February
3rd Monday: President's Day

March/April
Easter Monday

May
Last Monday: Memorial Day

July
4: Independence Day

September
1st Monday: Labor Day

October
2nd Monday: Columbus Day

November
11: Veterans' Day
Last Thursday: Thanksgiving Day

December
25: Christmas Day

on the Ellipse in front of the White House; the grandest Fourth of July Parade in the country takes place along and around the Mall; while every four years the new President makes a triumphal Inaugural Parade up Pennsylvania Avenue. Many of the national holidays listed above also feature special events and celebrations in the city. Such is the range of festivals throughout the year, it's hard to turn up without coinciding with at least one; DC's full **festival calendar** is detailed in Chapter 18. Note, however, that at all major festival periods – Cherry Blossom Festival and Easter, Memorial Day and Fourth of July particularly – it can be very difficult to find available accommodation in the city: book well in advance.

Crime and Personal Safety

Emergency Numbers

See *City Directory* for **emergency numbers** for the police, Travelers Aid and the hospital.

For many years Washington has had a poor reputation in terms of crime and personal safety. You'll be confidently told that it's the "Murder Capital" of the United States (even though, statistically, that's no longer true), and stories of drug dealers in business just blocks from the White House are in routine circulation amongst visitors and locals alike.

It's true, DC ain't Kansas: scan any copy of the *Washington Post* for a rundown of the latest daily drive-by shootings and crack-war escapades. However, to get things in perspective, almost all the crime that makes the newspaper headlines takes place in **neighbourhoods** (most of NE, SE and distinct parts of upper NW) that tourists have no business venturing into – there's nothing there to see and certainly no "real" Washington that you'd want to experience. Where neighbourhoods are borderline in terms of personal security, this guide makes it clear where you should

and shouldn't go; if there's a sight or museum you really want to see, get a cab there and back. However, in the places you will be spending most of your time – downtown, along the Mall, in Georgetown – all the major tourist sights, the Metro system and the main nightlife zones are invariably well lit and well policed. Indeed, the Mall between the US Capitol, White House and Lincoln Memorial is probably the most heavily policed district in America, brimming with regular police officers, secret service operatives and park rangers.

Mugging and theft

Most people will have few problems and if things do go wrong, foreign visitors tend to report that the **police** are helpful and obliging, although they'll be less sympathetic if they think you brought the trouble on yourself through carelessness.

You shouldn't be complacent. The fact that DC attracts so many tourists means that it has more than its share of **petty crime**, simply because there are more unsuspecting holidaymakers to prey on. Keep your wits about you in crowds; know where your wallet or purse is, and, of course, avoid parks, parking lots and dark streets at night. After the Metro has closed down, take taxis back from bars, restaurants and clubs. And if you have to ask directions, choose your target carefully (try a shopkeeper if possible).

Should the worst happen, hand over your money, and afterwards, despite your shock, try to find a phone and dial ☎911, or hail a cab and ask the driver to take you to the nearest police station. Here, report the theft and get a reference number on the report to claim insurance and travellers' cheque refunds. Ring the local *Travelers Aid* (see *City Directory*, p.309) for sympathy and practical advice.

Another potential source of trouble is having your **hotel room burgled**. Always store valuables in the hotel safe when you go out; when inside, keep your door locked and don't open it to anyone you are suspicious of; if they claim to be hotel staff and you don't believe them, call reception to check. In hostels and budget hotels, you may want to keep your valuables on your person, unless you know the security measures to be reliable.

Needless to say, having bags that contain travel documents snatched can be a big headache, none bigger for foreign travellers than **losing your passport**. Make photocopies of everything important before you go (including the business page of your passport) and keep them separate from the originals. If the worst happens, go to the nearest consulate and get them to issue you a **temporary passport**, basically a sheet of paper saying you've reported the loss, which will get you back home.

Finally, it goes without saying that you should *never* **hitch** anywhere in DC, or indeed the entire United States.

Car crime

Crimes committed against tourists driving **rented cars** have garnered headlines around the world in recent years, but there are certain precautions you can take to keep yourself safe. Not driving in DC itself would be a good first step: it's not necessary, since public transportation and cheap taxis can get you most places you'd want to go; on longer trips, pick up your rental car on the day you leave the city. Any car you do rent should have nothing on it – such as a particular licence plate – that makes it easy to identify as a rental car. When driving, under no circumstances stop in any unlit or seemingly deserted urban area – and especially not if someone is waving you down and suggesting that there is something wrong with your car. Similarly, if you are "accidentally" rammed by the driver behind, do not stop but drive on to the nearest well-lit, busy area and **phone** ☎911. Keep your doors locked and windows never more than slightly open. Do not open your door or window if someone approaches your car on the pretext of asking directions. Hide any valuables out of sight, preferably locked in the boot or in the glove compartment (any valuables you don't need for your journey should be left in your hotel safe).

Outside the city, if your **vehicle breaks down** on an interstate or heavily travelled road, wait in the car for a patrol car to arrive. One option is to rent a portable telephone with your car, for a small additional charge – a potential lifesaver.

Stolen Travellers' Cheques and Credit Cards

Keep a record of the numbers of your **travellers' cheques** separately from the actual cheques; if you lose them, ring the issuing company on the toll-free number below. They'll ask you for the cheque numbers, the place you bought them, when and how you lost them and whether it's been reported to the police. All being well, you should get the missing cheques reissued within a couple of days – and perhaps an emergency advance to tide you over.

Emergency Numbers

American Express Cards	☎1-800/528-4800	**Mastercard/Access**	☎1-800/826-2181
American Express Cheques	☎1-800/221-7282	**Thomas Cook/Mastercard**	☎1-800/223-9920
Citicorp	☎1-800/645-6556	**Visa Cheques**	☎1-800/227-6811
Diners Club	☎1-800/234-6377	**Visa Cards**	☎1-800/336-8472

Travellers with Disabilities

Washington DC is one of the most accessible cities in the world for travellers with special needs. All public buildings, including hotels and restaurants, have to be wheelchair accessible and provide suitable toilet facilities. Almost all street corners have dropped kerbs, and the public transport system has such facilities as subways with elevators, and buses that "kneel" to let people board.

Planning your trip

It's always a good idea for people with special needs to alert their travel agents when booking: things are far simpler when the various travel operators or carriers are expecting you. A **medical certificate** of your fitness to travel, provided by your doctor, is also useful; some airlines or insurance companies may insist on it. Most **airlines** do whatever they can to ease your journey, and will usually let attendants of more seriously

---

Contacts for Travellers with Disabilities

Australia
ACROD (Australian Council for Rehabilitation of the Disabled), PO Box 60, Curtin ACT 2605 ☎ 06/682 4333; 55 Charles St, Ryde ☎ 02/9809 4488

Ireland
Disability Action Group, 2 Annadale Ave, Belfast BT7 3JH ☎ 01232/91011
A good source of general advice.

Irish Wheelchair Association, Blackheath Drive, Clontarf, Dublin 3 ☎ 01/833 8241
National voluntary organization with services for holidaymakers.

New Zealand
Disabled Persons Assembly, PO Box 10–138, The Terrace, Wellington ☎ 04/472 2626

North America
Directions Unlimited, 720 N Bedford Rd, Bedford Hills, NY 10507 ☎ 914/241-1700
Tour operator specializing in custom tours for people with disabilities.

Mobility International USA, PO Box 10767, Eugene, OR 97440 Voice and TDD: ☎ 541/343-1284
Information and referral services, access guides, tours and exchange programmes. Annual membership $25 (includes quarterly newsletter).

National Tour Association, 546 East Main St, PO Box 3071, Lexington KY 40596 ☎ 606/226-4444
Can recommend organizations facilitating travel for the disabled.

Society for the Advancement of Travel for the Handicapped (SATH), 347 5th Ave, Suite 610, New York, NY 10016 ☎ 212/447-7284
Non-profit travel industry grouping which includes travel agents, tour operators, hotel and airline management, and people with disabilities. It will pass on any enquiry to the appropriate number; allow plenty of time for a response.

Travel Information Service ☎ 215/456-9600; deaf/hearing impaired ☎ 215/456-9602
Telephone information and referral service.

Twin Peaks Press, Box 129, Vancouver, WA 98666 ☎ 360/694-2462 or 1-800/637-2256
Publishes Directory of Travel Agencies for the Disabled *($19.95) and* Travel for the Disabled *($14.95).*

UK
Holiday Care Service, 2nd floor, Imperial Building, Victoria Rd, Horley, Surrey RH6 9HW ☎ 01293/774535
Information on all aspects of travel.

RADAR, 12 City Forum, 250 City Rd, London EC1V 8AS ☎ 0171/250 3222; Minicom ☎ 0171/250 4119
A good source of advice on holidays and travel abroad.

---

disabled people accompany them at no extra charge. The Americans with Disabilities Act 1990 obliged all air carriers to make the majority of their services accessible to travellers with disabilities within five to nine years. Almost every **Amtrak train** includes one or more coaches with accommodation for passengers with disabilities. Guide dogs travel free and may accompany blind, deaf or disabled passengers in the carriage. Be sure to give 24 hours' notice. Hearing-impaired passengers can get information on ☎1-800/523-6590. *Greyhound* buses are not equipped with lifts for wheelchairs, though staff will assist with boarding, and the "Helping Hand" scheme offers two-for-the-price-of-one tickets to passengers unable to travel alone (make sure to carry a doctor's certificate).

The American Automobile Association produces the *Handicapped Driver's Mobility Guide* for **disabled drivers** (available from *Quantum-Precision Inc*, 225 Broadway, Suite 3404, New York, NY 10007). The larger car rental companies provide cars with hand-controls at no extra charge, though only on their full-size (ie most expensive) models; reserve well in advance.

Disabled access in the city

The **Washington DC CVA** (see p.17) produces a free handout on accessibility in the city: call ☎202/789-7000. You can also contact *Washington Ear, Inc* (☎301/681-6636) for large-print and tactile atlases of the DC area; *Columbia Lighthouse for the Blind* (☎202/462-2900) has free tactile maps of the Metro system and pamphlets on how best to get around the city. Other helpful information is available from the *Center for Independent Living* (☎202/388-0033) and from

the *Information, Protection and Advocacy Center for People with Disabilities* (☎202/966-8081).

The *American Public Transit Association*, 1201 New York Ave, Suite 400, Washington DC 20005 (☎202/898-4000), provides information about the accessibility of **public transport** in American cities, including, of course, DC. Each station on the **Metro** (subway) system has an elevator (with braille controls) to the platforms; the wide train aisles can accommodate wheelchairs; there are reduced fares and priority seating available, and some Metro buses have wheelchair lifts. For a free guide offering complete information on Metro access for the disabled, call ☎202/635-6434.

Most of the **monuments and memorials** in DC have elevators to viewing platforms and special parking facilities, and at some sites large-print brochures and sign-language interpreters are available. The White House has a special entrance reserved for visitors in wheelchairs, who don't need to queue for a ticket. For more information on any site operated by the National Park Service call ☎202/619-7222. All **Smithsonian museum** buildings are wheelchair accessible and with notice staff can serve as sign-language interpreters or produce large-print, braille or cassette material. The free *Smithsonian Access* is available in large print, braille or audio cassette, or by calling ☎202/357-2700.

In addition, most new downtown **shopping malls** have wheelchair ramps and elevators. **Union Station** (shops, trains and cinema) is fully accessible, as are the **Kennedy Center** (p.297) and **National Theater** (p.297), both of which also have good facilities for visually and aurally impaired visitors.

Directory

AREA CODE The telephone area code for Washington DC is ☎202; see p.20 for more details.

CLIMATE For details of DC's climate, see the *Introduction*, p.xiii.

DATES Dates are written the other way around to Europe: 4-1-98 is not the fourth of January but the first of April.

ELECTRICITY The US electricity supply is 110 volts AC. Plugs are standard two-pins – foreign visitors will need an adaptor and voltage converter for their own electrical appliances.

FLOORS The first floor in the US is what would be the ground floor in Britain; the second floor would be the first floor and so on.

HEALTH MATTERS Most travellers do not require inoculations to enter the US, though you may need certificates of vaccination if you're en route from cholera- or typhoid-infected areas in Asia or Africa – check with your doctor before you leave. For an ambulance, dial ☎911 (or whatever variant may be on the information plate of the pay phone). To find a doctor or pharmacy in DC, see *City Directory*, p.308.

ID Should be carried at all times. Two pieces should suffice, one of which should have a photo: a passport or driving licence and credit card(s) are best. Not having your licence with you while driving is an arrestable offence.

MEASUREMENTS AND SIZES US measurements are Imperial, though American pints and gallons are about four-fifths of Imperial ones. Clothing sizes are two figures less than in the UK – a British women's size 12 is a US size 10 – while British shoe sizes are half below American ones for women, and one size below for men.

SENIOR TRAVELLERS Anyone over the age of 62, who can produce suitable ID, can enjoy certain discounts. *Amtrak* and *Greyhound*, for example, offer (smallish) percentage reductions on fares to older passengers. US residents aged over fifty can join the *American Association of Retired Persons*, 601 E St NW, Washington DC 20049 (☎202/434-2277), which organizes group travel for senior citizens and can provide discounts on accommodation and vehicle rental.

TAXES For a rundown of local taxes, see p.18.

TEMPERATURES Always given in Fahrenheit.

TIME Washington DC is in the Eastern zone, which covers the area inland to the Great Lakes and the Appalachian Mountains; this is five hours behind Greenwich Mean Time (-5 GMT), so 10am London time is 5am in Washington DC. Daylight saving time operates between April and October (check newspapers for specific dates), when the clocks go back an hour.

VIDEOS The standard format used for video cassettes in the US is different from that used in Britain. You cannot buy videos in the US compatible with a British video camera.

The City

Chapter 1

Introducing the City

Washington isn't a city, it's an abstraction.

Dylan Thomas, 1956

I t comes as some surprise to find that **Washington DC**, capital of a thriving nation of 250 million people and self-professed political arbiter of the Free World, is a small-fry in city terms. With a population of just 600,000 it comes way down the list of American cities and is outnumbered by just about every foreign capital you could think of. Sparsely populated it may be, but it's certainly not small in scale. Everywhere, Washington boasts the sweeping expanses, generous sightlines and monumental architecture of a carefully planned city which, originally, at least, was destined to fill a hundred square-mile diamond of land between Virginia and Maryland – Virginia later demanded its chunk of land back, which is why there's a bite out of the diamond shape across the Potomac River. So while locals (and boozy Welsh poets) talk about DC as being more a collection of disparate neighbourhoods than a coherent whole, and critics sneer that it can't hold a candle to a "real" city like New York, visitors get on with familiarizing themselves with the bus and Metro systems – essential if they're to get around every nook and cranny of America's capital.

See the colour map of central DC at the centre of this book.

This isn't to say that DC is not a city for walking around. There's no better way to get to grips with the "magnificent distances" trumpeted by nineteenth-century boosters than a two-mile stroll along the grassy reach of the **Mall** (Chapter 2) – the city's principal thoroughfare – where the views unfold from the US Capitol through the Washington Monument to Lincoln Memorial. The majority of the peerless Smithsonian museums and galleries reside here, as does the overwhelming art collection in the National Gallery of Art and the major memorials to Thomas Jefferson, the Vietnam and Korean Vets and, soon, to FDR.

The US Capitol, at the Mall's eastern end, marks the geographical centre of the city, all neighbourhoods and quadrants radiating out from its familiar white dome. **Capitol Hill** (Chapter 3), is one of DC's oldest neighbourhoods, rich in nineteenth-century row houses,

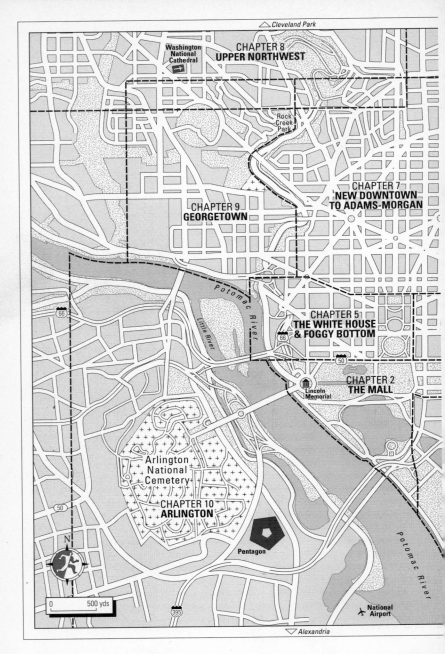

△ Cleveland Park

Washington
National
Cathedral

CHAPTER 8
UPPER NORTHWEST

Rock
Creek
Park

CHAPTER 7
NEW DOWNTOWN
TO ADAMS-MORGAN

CHAPTER 9
GEORGETOWN

Potomac River

Little River

66

CHAPTER 5
THE WHITE HOUSE
& FOGGY BOTTOM

66

50

Lincoln
Memorial

CHAPTER 2
THE MALL

Arlington
National
Cemetery

CHAPTER 10
ARLINGTON

50

N

Pentagon

Potomac River

0   500 yds

395

National
Airport

▽ Alexandria

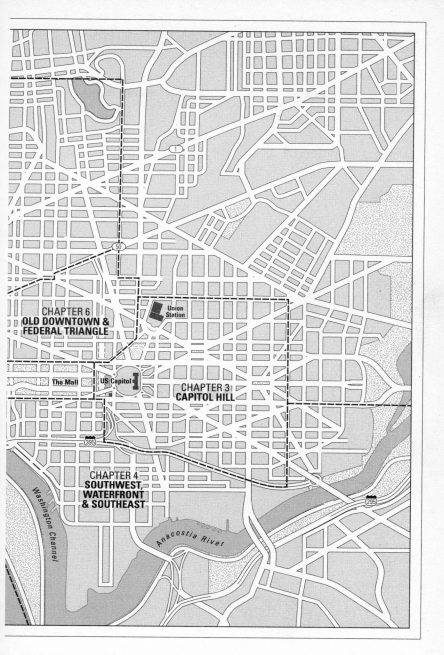

CHAPTER 6
OLD DOWNTOWN &
FEDERAL TRIANGLE

Union Station

The Mall

US Capitol

CHAPTER 3
CAPITOL HILL

CHAPTER 4
SOUTHWEST,
WATERFRONT
& SOUTHEAST

Washington Channel

Anacostia River

and ripe for a stroll from the Capitol itself to other defining buildings such as the Supreme Court and Library of Congress. Immediately south of the Mall, two of the most popular attractions in DC – the Federal Bureau of Printing and Engraving and the Holocaust Memorial Museum – are the undisputed highlights of the Southwest/Waterfront (Chapter 4). Monolithic federal office buildings occupy the rest of the no-man's-land between the Mall and the Washington Channel, though a thriving fish market and popular waterfront seafood restaurants pull visitors away from the museums. To the Southeast (also Chapter 4), hard against the Anacostia River, the neighbourhood toughens: there are sporadic attractions at the Navy Yard and, across the river, in Anacostia itself, but these areas do not lend themselves to casual exploration – certainly not by tourists on foot. There are no such caveats about the heavily visited area around the White House and Foggy Bottom (Chapter 5), a neighbourhood which stretches along the northwest side of the Mall. Quite apart from the President's house, this compact block of streets holds heavyweight attractions like the Corcoran Gallery of Art, the renowned Kennedy Center and the infamous Watergate building.

See everything along and around the Mall and you've seen the greater part of monumental Washington, but you still won't have much impression of a living, working city. What's known as Old Downtown (Chapter 6) – north of the Mall between the White House and Union Station – was where nineteenth-century Washington first set out its shops and services, along the spine of Pennsylvania Avenue, the country's most prominent parade route. After years of neglect, it's today facing spirited restoration and numbers revitalized plazas, galleries and restaurants alongside its traditional attractions: the FBI Building, Old Post Office, Chinatown and the buildings associated with President Lincoln's assassination. Wedged against the Mall, Federal Triangle (also Chapter 6) siphons off downtown sightseers to the National Archives; fewer make the effort to tour the district's other splendid Neoclassical buildings.

Hardcore business and commerce takes place these days in New Downtown, along and around K Street, which is where Washington most resembles any other modern American city. From here, long diagonal avenues march off through a number of neighbourhoods that mark the end of the line for most tourists. The historic townhouses and mansions of chic Dupont Circle hide a gaggle of low-key museums and an expanding enclave of art galleries; the bar and restaurant zone of Adams-Morgan to the north gets trendier by the day at the same time as it squeezes out its Latino heritage; while, to the east, the historic black neighbourhood of Shaw – off-limits in places – boasts the thriving nightlife corridor of U Street. All these neighbourhoods, from New Downtown to Adams-Morgan, are covered in Chapter 7.

The first *bona fide* city suburbs were in the **Upper Northwest** (Chapter 8), where the nineteenth-century wealthy created picket-fence paradise in areas like Woodley Park and Cleveland Park. The Metro brings visitors out here today for the hugely enjoyable National Zoological Park and the landmark National Cathedral; with more time and your own transport, you can get to the glades, dales and riverbanks of Rock Creek Park. West of downtown, across Rock Creek, **Georgetown** (Chapter 9) is the other major draw. Once a thriving town in its own right (pre-dating DC), this historic neighbourhood is now the quintessential hangout of the chattering classes and the students of Georgetown University, who make the shops, galleries, bars and restaurants very much their own.

As a cursory glance at the map will tell you, that still leaves a lot of Washington to cover. Seventy percent of the city's population, predominantly black, lives outside the environs of the Mall and the affluent Northwest – what PJ O'Rourke calls the "white pipeline" of the city. But there's little that tourists are encouraged to see in the disparate neighbourhoods of Northeast and Southeast Washington – with just a few exceptions, some of the poorest, most run-down areas in the city. Instead visitors are steered south and west across the Potomac into Virginia, to **Arlington** (Chapter 10), easily accessible by Metro and holding the city's major military sights – Arlington National Cemetery, the Marine Corps (Iwo Jima) Memorial and the Pentagon. Further **out from the city** (Chapter 11), most people make day-trips to the historic town of Alexandria (fifty years older than Washington DC) and to Mount Vernon, the beloved family estate and burial place of George Washington.

For more on the slow progress of the building of the city, see the accounts of the Mall (p.49), US Capitol (p.109), White House (p.144) and Old Downtown (p.172 and p.177).

Arriving in DC

The most central points of arrival are for those reaching the city by **train** (at Union Station), or **bus** (downtown *Greyhound* terminal). From the **airports**, you can't count on being downtown much within the hour, though the various bus, train and Metro transfers are smooth enough; at National and BWI, free shuttle buses run from the airports to the relevant stations. Taking **taxis** from any airport won't save much time, especially if you arrive during rush hour, though filling a cab with three or four people may save a few dollars.

Telephone area codes for organizations and services listed in this chapter are ☎202, for Washington DC, unless otherwise stated.

By air

Domestic arrivals land at **National Airport** (☎703/419-8000 or 685-8000), four miles south of downtown. Driving or by bus it takes

The Planning of a Capital City

It is sometimes called the City of Magnificent Distances, but it might with greater propriety be termed the City of Magnificent Intentions; for it is only on taking a bird's-eye view of it from the top of the Capitol that one can at all comprehend the vast designs of its projector, an aspiring Frenchman.

Charles Dickens, American Notes, 1842

In 1790, the year after George Washington was inaugurated as first President of the United States, it fell to Congress to decide upon a permanent site for the country's capital. Since Independence, Congress had met in half a dozen different cities – the President was inaugurated in New York – and a dozen others, in North and South, had competing claims and loud promoters. Ultimately the decision came down to political wrangling: in return for Congress assuming the states' debts from the Revolutionary War (a key Northern demand), the new federal capital would be sited in the South, somewhere on the sparsely populated banks of the Potomac River.

With the help of Major Andrew Ellicott, a surveyor from Maryland, and the black mathematician and scientist Benjamin Banneker, Washington – no mean surveyor himself – suggested a diamond-shaped, hundred-square-mile site at the confluence of the Potomac and Anacostia rivers. It seemed a canny choice – centring on the confluence, and thus ripe for trade, the site incorporated the ports of Alexandria in Virginia and Georgetown in Maryland; it would have its own port in Anacostia, and, no small matter for Washington, it was only eighteen miles upriver from his home at Mount Vernon. Maryland ceded roughly seventy square miles of land, Virginia thirty; all Washington had to do was find someone to plan his city, which Congress – in honour of the President – decreed would be named **Washington**, in the Territory (later District) of Columbia (a reference to Christopher Columbus).

Washington found his "aspiring Frenchman", **Major Pierre Charles L'Enfant**, who had been a member of Washington's Continental Army staff. His reputation as an engineer stemmed from his successful redesign of New York's Federal Hall for the presidential inauguration; now the President gave him the chance to create an entire city. Within a year L'Enfant had come up with an ambitious plan to transform a wilderness into gridded streets and

twenty to thirty minutes to reach the centre, depending on traffic; the National Airport Metro station (across from North Concourse), is linked directly to Metro Center, L'Enfant Plaza and Gallery Place-Chinatown (for more on the Metro, see p.41). A taxi downtown costs around $12–15, or catch the *Washington Flyer Express* bus (every 30–60min, daily 6.25am–9.25pm; one-way $8, round-trip $14), which runs from the airport to its city terminal at 1517 K St NW (see "Leaving DC" on p.38).

Washington's major airport, **Dulles International** (☎703/661-2700), 26 miles west in northern Virginia, handles most international and some domestic services. The drive in or out can take between forty minutes and an hour; taxis downtown run to around $45–50. It's cheaper to take the *Washington Flyer Express* bus (every 20–30min,

diagonal avenues, radiating from ceremonial squares and elegant circles. A "Grand Avenue" (later known as the Mall) formed the centrepiece; government buildings were assigned their own plots; a central canal linked the city's ports; sculptures, fountains and parks punctuated the design. Its initial inspiration was the city of Paris and the seventeenth-century palace of Versailles, though L'Enfant did adopt suggestions made by others – not least Secretary of State Thomas Jefferson, who proposed the sites of the US Capitol and the President's Mansion (later called the White House). The plan named avenues after the fifteen states that existed in 1791, placing northern states and avenues north of the Capitol, southern ones to the south – the most populous states, Virginia, Pennsylvania and Massachusetts, were represented by the longest avenues.

Washington was delighted with the scheme, though the existing landowners were less than pleased with the injunction to donate any land to be used for public thoroughfares. L'Enfant was planning avenues 100ft wide – whether he knew it or not, clearly following the Parisian model of making streets too broad for the public to barricade and big enough for troops to manoeuvre in during times of unrest. Disagreements with the landowners aside, L'Enfant found himself in constant dispute with the District Commissioners who had been appointed by Washington to oversee the construction. His obstinacy cost him his job in 1792, and the design of the Capitol and White House were both later thrown open to public competition. L'Enfant turned down the $2500 he was offered as payment for his services, sued Congress (unsuccessfully) for $100,000, harried the legislature with his grievances for the rest of his life and died in penury in 1825.

For decades L'Enfant's plan seemed full of empty pretensions as Washington DC struggled to make its mark. Any number of nineteenth-century observers commented upon the hilarious contrast between such "vast designs" and the less-than-impressive reality. But for all that, this unique attempt to create a capital city that could define a nation was a remarkable enterprise. Perhaps the last word should be with nineteenth-century abolitionist and orator Frederick Douglass, who said:

It is our national center. It belongs to us, and whether it is mean or majestic, whether arranged in glory or covered with shame, we cannot but share its character and its destiny.

Mon–Fri 6am–10.30pm, Sat & Sun 7.30am–10.30pm; one-way $8, round-trip $14) to the **West Falls Church Metro** station, a twenty-minute ride; from here, trains run into Metro Center (20min) and on to downtown. There's also a bus from Dulles to the *Washington Flyer* downtown terminal at 1517 K St NW (every 30–60min, daily 5.20am–10.20pm; one-way $16, round-trip $26), where you can link up with courtesy shuttles to various hotels (see "Accommodation", p.264).

Other international and domestic arrivals land at **Baltimore-Washington International (BWI) Airport** (☎301/261-1000), 25 miles northeast of DC (and 10 miles south of Baltimore). This, too, is up to an hour's drive from downtown DC, with taxis costing $50–55 – agree the price before setting off. *BWI Super Shuttle* buses into Washington (hourly, daily 6am–11pm; one-way $19,

There's also a Flyer bus service between National and Dulles airports (every 1–2hr, 5am–11pm; one-way $16, round-trip $26).

Arriving in DC

Leaving DC: Getting to the Airports

Give yourself plenty of time to get to the airport, especially if you're driving: in rush hour, it can take up to thirty minutes to reach National, more like an hour to Dulles or BWI. For a list of taxi companies, see "Taxis", p.44.

Two companies run buses to the airports from the same downtown **bus terminal** at 1517 K St NW, three blocks north of the White House; nearest Metro is Farragut North. Note that the terminal has a check-in service for all *United* flights (Mon–Fri 10am–5pm).

Washington Flyer Express
☎703/685-1400

To National from the terminal: every 30–60min, 6.05am–9.05pm. $8, round-trip $14.

To Dulles from the terminal: every 30–60min, 6.15am–9.15pm. $16, round-trip $26.

To Dulles from West Falls Church Metro: every 20–30min, Mon–Fri

6.30am–11pm, Sat & Sun 8am–11pm. $8, round-trip $14.

Between National and Dulles: every 1–2hr, 5am–11pm. $16, round-trip $26.

BWI Supershuttle ☎301/369 0009 or 1-800/809-7080

To BWI from the terminal: hourly, 6.10am–10.10pm. $19, round-trip $29.

There are information counters and car rental desks at each airport.

round-trip $29) drop off at the 1517 K St NW terminal an hour later. It's cheaper, however, to take the train from BWI Airport station (train information on ☎410/672-6167): either the frequent peak-hour departures of the *MARC* commuter line (Mon–Fri only, 5.30–8am & 3.45–6.45pm; one way $5, round-trip $8.75) or the regular *Amtrak* trains (one-way $12, round-trip $24), which run daily – both services take around 45 minutes and terminate at Washington's Union Station (see "By train and bus" below).

By train and bus

See p.123 for an account of Union Station. Train and bus enquiries and departures are detailed on p.309 and p.308 respectively.

The gleaming malls of **Union Station**, 50 Massachusetts Ave NE, three blocks north of the Capitol, see arrivals from all over the country, including local **trains** from Baltimore, Richmond, Williamsburg and Virginia Beach, and major East Coast connections from Philadelphia, New York and Boston. Trains are operated either by *Amtrak* (☎1-800/872-7245 or 484-7540) – which has regular and Metroliner (quicker, more expensive) services to most destinations – or the *Maryland Rail Commuter Service* (*MARC*; ☎1-800/325-7245), which connects DC to Baltimore, BWI and suburban Maryland. Union Station has a connecting Metro station, and taxis line up outside. There are car rental desks here, too.

Greyhound (☎1-800/231-2222) and *Peter Pan Trailways* (☎371-2111) **buses** – from Baltimore, Philadelphia, New York, Boston, Richmond and other cities – stop at the modern station at 1005 1st St NE at L St, in a fairly unsavoury part of town, five long blocks north of Union Station; take a cab, especially at night, at least as far as Union Station Metro (around $5).

By car

Driving into DC is a sure way to experience some of the worst traffic on the East Coast. The six- to eight-lane freeway, known as the **Capital Beltway,** circles the city at a ten-mile radius from the centre and is busy eighteen hours a day. It's made up of two separate highways: I-495 on the western half and I-95/I-495 in the east. If it's the Beltway you want, follow signs for either.

Approaching the city **from the northeast** (New York/Philadelphia) you need I-95 (south), before turning west on Rte 50, which will take you to New York Avenue; **from Baltimore** there's the direct Baltimore–Washington Parkway, which also joins Rte 50. Route 50 itself is the main way in **from the east** (Annapolis, MD, and Chesapeake Bay). **From the south**, take I-95 to I-395, which crosses the river via the 14th Street (George Mason Memorial) Bridge to reach 14th Street. **From the northwest** (Frederick, MD, and beyond), come in on I-270 until you hit the Beltway, then follow I-495 (east) for Connecticut Avenue south. **From the west** (Virginia) use I-66, which runs across the Theodore Roosevelt Bridge for Constitution Avenue. At peak periods inside the Beltway, high occupancy vehicle restrictions apply on I-66 eastbound (6.30–9am) and westbound (4–6.30pm); at these times cars with less than three people face a surcharge at the toll booths.

Arriving in DC

For DC road and traffic information call ☎727 6161

For road routes into Washington DC, see the map in Prelims.

Orientation

Washington is divided into four **quadrants** – northeast (NE), northwest (NW), southeast (SE), southwest (SW) – whose axes centre on the US Capitol. Separating the quadrants, a central cross is formed by North Capitol Street (stretching north of the Capitol), East Capitol Street, South Capitol Street and – in the first of many exceptions – the grassy expanse of the Mall (West Capitol Street doesn't exist). The few sights in the NE, SE and SW quadrants cluster around the Capitol and south of the Mall; almost all other sights and neighbourhoods of note (including Georgetown) are in the NW quadrant.

Within the city, there's a simple right-angled grid plan in which, progressing away from the Capitol, **north–south streets are numbered** (in numerical order, from 1), **east–west ones are lettered** (in alphabetical order, from A). After W (there are no X, Y or Z streets), two-syllable names, still in alphabetical order, are used for east–west streets (Adams, Bryant, College), changing to three-syllable names even further out. In addition, broad **avenues**, all named for states, run diagonally across the grid of streets, meeting up at monumental **traffic circles** like Dupont Circle and Washington Circle. The system only breaks down in **Georgetown**, which predates the city – here quite a few streets retain their older names. Other **oddities** to note are that the Mall has swallowed up A and B streets NW and SW (what would be B St NW is now Constitution Ave NW, and so forth); I Street is often written Eye

Street; and there's no J Street in any quadrant (probably because the eighteenth-century city plan used the Latin alphabet, which has no J).

It's crucial to note the relevant two-letter **quadrant code** (NW, NE, SW, SE) in any address or direction. Each grid address (say 1200 G St) could be in one of four quadrants and impossible to find without the code; 1200 G St NW is a long way from 1200 G St SE. As in other grid plans, **addresses** of avenues and lettered streets relate to the numbered cross-streets – thus, the White House, 1600 Pennsylvania Ave NW, is at 16th St, while 1220 E St NW is between 12th and 13th. On numbered streets, the address is keyed to the numerical letter of the street at the intersection, so 800 9th St NW is at H St (H being the eighth letter of the alphabet); remember that there's no J St, so 1000 9th St is at K St, and so on.

Information

To acquire information on DC before you arrive, see "Information and Maps" (*Basics*, p.16). Most useful is the free *Washington DC Visitors Guide*, with endless listings, reviews and contact numbers. You'll also be able to pick up maps and information at desks in the airports, Union Station and in most hotels. For **accommodation services**, contact one of the agencies listed on p.259.

Once in the city either call one of the numbers listed in the box below or drop by the **White House Visitor Information Center**, 1450 Pennsylvania Ave NW (see p.150), which has details on sights all over DC; the **Smithsonian Castle** (see p.105) on the Mall is the best stop for Smithsonian museum information. Out and about in Washington, you'll come across National Park Service **rangers** – in kiosks on the Mall, at the major memorials, etc – who should also be able to answer general queries. One of the most useful sites is the **Ellipse Visitor Pavilion** (daily 8am–4pm), on the east side of the Ellipse near the bleachers. The **National Park Service information office** (Mon–Fri 9am–5pm), inside the Department of the Interior,

---

Useful Information Numbers

DC Committee to Promote Washington ☎347-2873
Information on festivals, current events, transportation and accommodation services.

Dial-A-Museum ☎357-2020
Smithsonian Institution exhibits and special events.

Dial-A-Park ☎619-7275
Events at National Park Service attractions.

Post-Haste ☎334-9000
Washington Post information line for news, weather, sports, restaurants, events and festivals.

Washington DC Convention and Visitors Association ☎789-7000
Main city information source.

White House Visitor Information Center ☎208-1631
Maps, brochures and information about most city sights.

on C St NW, between 18th and 19th, has information about all the city's national monuments and memorials.

For details of the various local newspapers and listings magazines see chapters 13, 14 and 15. Basically, though, armed with a free copy of the weekly *CityPaper* (available in stores, bars and restaurants) and Friday's *Washington Post* you can't go far wrong. Many neighbourhoods (Georgetown in particular) and all the universities also issue free weekly or monthly papers, full of news, reviews and listings peculiar to their area.

City transit

Most places downtown, including the Mall museums, the major monuments and the White House are within walking distance of each other; an excellent public transportation system connects downtown to outlying sites and neighbourhoods. The **Washington Metropolitan Area Transit Authority** (*WMATA*) operates a subway system (Metrorail) and a bus network (Metrobus), while other options include using taxis or even renting a bike; car rental (at least within the city) is less appealing. For details of city tours, see p.45.

The Metro

Washington's subway – **Metrorail**, or simply the **Metro** – is quick, cheap, easy and safe. It currently runs on five lines covering most of the downtown areas and suburbs (with the notable exception of Georgetown), though the system is in a state of constant expansion, and a number of new stations are due to open over the next decade.

See the colour map of the Metro system at the centre of this book.

Each line is **colour-coded** and studded with various **interchange stations**: Metro Center, L'Enfant Plaza and Gallery Place-Chinatown are the most important downtown. Stations are identifiable outside only by the letter "M" on top of a brown pylon; inside, the well-lit, uncluttered, vaulted halls make the Washington Metro one of the safest in the world. That said, you should, of course, **take the usual precautions** – the system itself may be substantially safe but a few of its stations are in fearsome neighbourhoods.

Operating hours are Mon–Fri 5.30am–midnight, Sat, Sun and most public holidays 8am–midnight. During rush hour, services run every 5min on most lines, and every 10–12min at other times.

Fares and passes
Each passenger needs a **farecard**, bought from machines before passing through the turnstiles. Fares are based on when and how far you travel; maps and ticket prices are posted by the machines. **One-way fares** range from $1.10 (base rate, off-peak) to $3.50; the higher, **peak-rate** fares are charged Mon–Fri 5.30–9.30am and 3–8pm. If you're going to use the Metro several times, it's worth putting in more

*The transit
system and
sights in DC
are surpris-
ingly access-
ible for trav-
ellers with dis-
abilities; see
p.25 for
details.*

money – cards with a value of over $20 get you ten percent extra free.
Then feed the card through the turnstile and retrieve it; when you do
the same thing at the end of your journey, the machine prints out on
the card how much fare remains. If you've paid the exact amount, the
turnstile keeps the card; if you don't have enough money remaining
on the card for the journey, insert it into one of the special exit-fare
machines, deposit more money and try the turnstile again. Finally, if
you're catching a bus after your Metrorail ride, get a **rail-to-bus
transfer** pass from the machine on the platform.

The useful **Metrorail One Day Pass** ($5) gives unlimited travel
after 9.30am on weekdays or all day at the weekend. There's also a
Fast Pass ($50), for 14 consecutive days' unlimited travel, and the
28-Day Pass ($100) for 28 consecutive days. If you're using buses,
too (see below), you might consider the **Bus/Rail Super Pass** ($65),
valid for 14 days' unlimited bus and Metro travel. All passes are available at Metro Center station, at Metro Headquarters (see below), at
most *Safeway*, *Giant* and *SuperFresh* stores; or through
TicketMaster (☎432-7328).

Buses

WMATA is also responsible for most of DC's **buses**, which operate
for largely the same hours as the Metro (though some go on until
2am). We've listed the most useful services below; the entire system
is shown on two **Metro System Route Maps** (one for DC/Virginia,
one for DC/Maryland; $1.50 each), which also mark the Metrorail
interchanges. They're available from Metro sales offices (see above).

Fares and passes

The **base fare** for most bus journeys is $1.10, payable to the driver,
though surcharges and zone crossings can increase this; the same
peak-hour rates apply as on the Metro. If you're transferring from the
Metro, give your pass to the driver, who'll give you a small discount

Useful Bus Routes

• **Foggy Bottom to Woodley Park: #L1**
via Virginia Ave, C St, 23rd St, Washington Circle, New Hampshire Ave, Dupont Circle, Connecticut Ave (National Zoological Park).

• **L'Enfant Plaza to McPherson Square: #52**
via 6th St, Independence Ave, 14th St.

• **McPherson Square to Woodley Park: #L2**
via K St, 20th St, Dupont Circle, 18th St (Adams-Morgan), Calvert St, Connecticut Ave (National Zoological Park).

• **Metro Center to Adams-Morgan: #42**
via Metro Center (10th and F), H St, Connecticut Ave, Dupont Circle, Columbia Rd (Adams-Morgan).

• **Pennsylvania Ave to Georgetown: #30, 32, 34, 35, 36**
via Eastern Market, US Capitol, Independence Ave, 7th St, Pennsylvania Ave, 15th St, Pennsylvania Ave, Wisconsin Ave (Georgetown).

• **Pentagon–Mall Loop: #13A, 13B**
via 14th St Bridge (Jefferson Memorial), Bureau of Engraving & Printing/Holocaust Museum, Independence Ave, 7th St, Constitution Ave, Lincoln Memorial, Arlington.

• **Union Station to Georgetown: #D2, D4**
via E St, 13th St, K St, Dupont Circle, Q St (Georgetown).

• **Union Station to Kennedy Center: #80, 81**
via North Capitol St, Massachusetts Ave, H St, New York Ave, Pennsylvania Ave, Foggy Bottom, Watergate Complex.

on the fare. Tourists are unlikely to get full value out of a bus pass – the two most relevant are the Bus/Rail Super Pass and the **DC Base Flash Pass** ($20) which gives 14 days' unlimited base-fare trips in DC only. **Outside DC, Maryland and Virginia have their own local bus systems.** The only time you're likely to need these is in Alexandria (whose system is called *DASH*) and en route to Mount Vernon, which you can reach on a *Fairfax Connector* bus. Both systems link with the Metro: for timetable information call *DASH* on ☎ 703/370-3274, or *Fairfax Connector* on ☎ 703/339-7200.

Taxis

Taxis are a useful adjunct to the public transportation system, especially in outposts like Georgetown and Adams-Morgan, which aren't on the Metro; if you know you're going to be out late in these neighbourhoods, it's a good idea to book a taxi in advance.

There are plans to install meters in all taxis by 1998, but for now **fares** are charged on a concentric zoned basis. Standard rates are posted in each cab; a ride at the basic rate within one zone costs $3.70. Most crosstown fares run from $3.70 to $10.70 (the maximum for any ride in the city limits) – Georgetown to Dupont Circle,

For more information on DC cabs, zones and fares, call the Taxicab Commission *on* ☎ 767-8319.

say, costs around $5. During evening rush hours (Mon–Fri 3.30–6.30pm) there's a $1 surcharge, and if travelling in a group you may be asked to pay $1.25 for each extra person. Don't be surprised if the driver pulls over to pick up another passenger: this is perfectly legal, provided they don't have to go more than five blocks out of the way to reach your destination – everybody pays the set amount for their journey. Once you get out of DC, into Maryland or Virginia, you'll be charged as normal on the meter; this can prove expensive.

Either flag cabs down on the street or use the ranks at hotels and transport terminals. To **call a taxi in advance** ($1.50 surcharge), try *Yellow Cab* (☎ 544-1212), *Capitol Cab* (☎ 546-2400) or *Diamond Cabs* (☎ 387-6200). *Washington Flyer Taxi* (☎ 703/661-8230) offers 24-hour service to Dulles airport.

Driving

It's not worth driving in the capital unless you have to. If you're heading out of the city by car, either pick up your vehicle at the end of your stay (there are rental desks at Union Station; you don't have to go back to the airports) or leave your own car at your hotel for the duration. For a list of car rental agencies, see *Basics*, p.7.

One-way streets can play havoc with the best-formulated driving routes, while the city's **rush hour** (Mon–Fri 6.30–9.30am & 4–7pm, plus lunchtime) traffic control system means that many lanes, or even whole streets, **change direction** at particular times of the day, and left turns are often periodically forbidden; read the signs carefully. To top it all, the roads are diabolical – even on major thoroughfares you'll want to keep a wary eye out for potholes and ridges.

Most mid- and upper-range hotels have secure parking (from around $10 per night); **parking lots and garages** cost from $4 per hour to $15 a day. Looking for free **on-street parking** is not likely to pay for itself in terms of time and energy expended: there are free, limited-wait (2–3hr) parking spots around the Mall (Jefferson and Madison Drives, Independence Ave SW) and in West Potomac Park, but they're heavily subscribed. **Parking meters** tend to operate between 9.30am and 6.30pm, usually giving a maximum stay of two hours; stay longer and you'll get a $15 ticket. At other times, just when you think you've found the perfect spot, it will almost certainly be reserved for local workers, or on a street that becomes one-way during rush hour, or temporarily illegal to park because it *is* rush hour, or in a clearway reserved for snow ploughs, or rendered useless for a million and one other reasons. Naturally, the places you might want to drive to for an evening out, like Georgetown, Dupont Circle or Adams-Morgan, are, again, heavily cruised for parking space.

*If your car gets **towed** away, call* ☎ 939-8000 *and expect to pay up to $100 to get it back.*

Bikes and boats

Given the traffic, few visitors will want to brave the streets on a **bicycle**, though several outfits can fix you up and provide maps and advice on local trails: *Big Wheel Bikes* (Georgetown, ☎337-0254 or Eastern Market, ☎543-1600), *City Bikes* (Adams-Morgan, ☎265-1564) and *Better Bikes* (☎293-2080 – will deliver anywhere in DC) all rent bikes for around $25 a day, $100 a week (slightly more for mountain bikes); you'll need to leave a deposit and/or a credit card or passport. A number of operators offer **cycling tours** – see p.46.

The nicest option is to rent a bike for short **rides along the Potomac River** or the **C&O Canal** towpath, something you can do at *Thompson's Boat Center*, 2900 Virginia Ave NW at Rock Creek Parkway (March–Oct only; ☎333-4861), near the Watergate complex, and *Fletcher's Boat House*, 4940 Canal Rd NW (☎244-0461), two miles further up the canal towpath. This costs just $20 a day and is infinitely safer than careering around the city. Long-distance **cycle paths** include the one in Rock Creek Park (see p.229), the 18.5-mile Mount Vernon Trail (see p.249), and the 184-mile length of the C&O towpath (see p.235).

Thompson's and *Fletcher's* also rent out **rowboats and canoes**, as do *Jack's Boats*, 3500 K St NW, Georgetown (☎337-9642), and *Swain's Lock Boat House* (☎301/299-9006), twenty miles up the canal: reckon on $6–8 per hour, $20–25 per day for either.

City tours

There are any number of operators prepared to show you the sights, though even with just a couple of days it's easy to see most things on your own. Some of the more popular services, however, are useful – like the *Tourmobile* – since they allow you to get on and off the bus at will and shuttle you out to the more far-flung sights. **River cruises**, too, can be worth considering, especially in high summer when the offshore breeze comes as a welcome relief. **Specialist tours** show you a side of Washington you may not otherwise see; some of the best are picked out below.

All telephone numbers are area code ☎202 unless otherwise stated.

Walking tours

Anthony S Pitch ☎301/294-9514. Highly recommended historical walking tours, led by the amiable Mr Pitch, of Adams-Morgan (Sun 11am), Lafayette Square (Sat, usually 10am & 11.30am) and Georgetown (call for times). They last 1–2hr and cost $5–6.

DC Foot Tour ☎703/461-7364. Customized walking tours around the major sights and off-the-beaten-track neighbourhoods.

Bus and trolley tours

Gray Line ☎289-1995. City bus tours ($20–40), trolley tour ($16) and black heritage tour ($20), from the *Gray Line* terminal in Union Station.

Old Town Trolley Tours ☎301/985-3021. Motorized, board-at-will trolleys covering downtown, Georgetown and National Cathedral.

City Tours

Tickets cost $16 a day, available at trolley stops and downtown hotels.

Tourmobile ☎554-5100. Narrated, open-sided *Tourmobile* buses allow unlimited stops at 18 locations. A $12 day ticket covers downtown and Arlington Cemetery; an extra $20 gets you to Mount Vernon and back, and $6 to the Frederick Douglass Home; two-day tickets for unlimited travel on both routes cost $32 (DC and Mount Vernon) or $24 (DC and Frederick Douglass). Bought after 2pm (after 4pm, mid-June to Labor Day), the $12 ticket is also valid for all the next day. Tickets from the office on the Ellipse, kiosks on the Mall (there's one at the Washington Monument) or on the bus itself.

Bicycle tours

DC Bike Tours ☎466-4486. Guided group rides (up to 10 people) throughout DC; there are frequent stops along the three-hour (8-mile) route. $24 per person including bike, helmet and guide.

Potomac Pedicabs ☎332-1732. Short, customized, three-wheeler pedicab tours of the city from around $10 per couple, with longer tours charged at around 50¢ a minute.

Cruises

DC Ducks ☎966-DUCK. Converted amphibious carriers which cruise the Mall and then splash into the Potomac on a cruise (90min). Tickets from 1323 Pennsylvania Ave NW, next to the National Theater (March–Nov Mon–Fri 10am, noon, 2pm & 4pm, Sat & Sun hourly 10am–4pm; $16).

Spirit Cruises ☎554-8000. Swish two-hour river cruises with bar and showbands, $25–30 plus lunch; three-hour dinner cruises for $55; narrated cruises to Mount Vernon $25. Tickets and departures (not Mon) from Pier 4, 6th and Water St SW (Waterfront Metro).

Building Tours

For special, extended tours of the following buildings you must make reservations; see the relevant accounts for details. American citizens should contact their Congressional representatives well in advance for special tours of government buildings. Tours arranged like this will be on a specific day, usually outside opening hours; most last longer than the normal walk-in tours and show you areas or rooms not usually open to the public.

Bureau of Engraving and Printing; see p.135.

Department of State; see p.162.

Federal Bureau of Investigation; see p.174.

Federal Reserve Building; see p.161.

National Archives; see p.179.

Old Executive Office Building; see p.153.

Treasury Building; see p.153.

US Capitol; see p.189.

Washington Post; see p.207.

White House; see p.142.

Specialist tours and activities

Capitol Entertainment Services Inc ☎636-9203. Black heritage
tours (3hr; $22) run by an African-American company.

Goodwill Embassy Tour ☎636-4225. Every May, some of DC's
finest embassy buildings throw open their doors; call well in advance
to book ($25). Many embassies also offer free guided tours provided
you reserve in advance; for numbers, see *City Directory*, p.308.

Smithsonian Associates, 1100 Jefferson Drive SW ☎357-3030.
Full programme of after-hours tours, performances, lectures and
films in the museums and galleries. *The Associates* magazine (from
Smithsonian museum shops), carries a monthly list of activities.

Museums, galleries, monuments and memorials

Full details are given for each **museum, gallery, monument, memorial and public building** reviewed in this guide – address, telephone
number (all area code ☎202 unless otherwise stated), public transport links, opening hours and adult admission price (where applic-
able). The majority of DC's museums and sights are **free**; where
there is an admission charge, **children** and, usually, **senior citizens**,
get in for half-price. For details of specific exhibits and events call in
advance. Note that all the Smithsonian museums and galleries have
the same information line. Most museums and attractions are **closed**
on December 25 and over New Year; many are closed on public holidays, too (for a list of which, see p.22).

Chapter 2

The Mall

Scrubbed, manicured and heavily policed, the showpiece greensward of **THE MALL** is quite unlike the centre of any other American city, though European visitors, used to triumphal structures, royal parks and boulevards, will feel right at home. Laid out along two carefully tended miles between the US Capitol and the Potomac River are nine Smithsonian **museums**, unrivalled in their field; the two buildings of the National Gallery of Art, and the city's three most famous **monuments and memorials** – to George Washington, Abraham Lincoln and the Vietnam Veterans. A fourth, to Thomas Jefferson, as well as the White House itself, stand perfectly aligned on either side.

The Mall is also where Washington comes to relax – on his visit in 1946, Albert Camus talked fondly of "placid evenings on the vast lawns" – and to party, not least at the annual Festival of American Folklife and on the Fourth of July. Yet its central role in a planned capital city also places it at the very heart of the country's **political and social** life. When there's a protest to be made, the National Mall – to give it its full title – is the place to make it. The 1963 March on Washington brought the Rev Dr Martin Luther King Jr to the steps of the Lincoln Memorial to deliver his "I have a dream" speech; in 1967, at the height of the anti-war protests, the notorious March on the Pentagon started from the same place; three decades later, in 1995, the controversial minister, Louis Farrakhan of the Nation of Islam, brought hundreds of thousands of black men here on the Million Men March. The sheer expanse of the Mall inspires grand gestures: on several occasions the AIDS Memorial Quilt – a patchwork of 40,000 individual quilts remembering America's AIDS victims – has been laid in commemoration the full mile from the Capitol to the Washington Monument.

As a visitor, you'd have to concoct a fairly perverse **itinerary** to avoid setting foot on the Mall. Given a normal appetite for museums, galleries and monuments, and a fair constitution, you could get around most things in three days or so. But it's better to return at various times during your stay, if only to avoid complete cultural overload. Many of the attractions lend themselves to being seen with a combination of other city sights: the western monuments with the White House (Chapter 5); the Jefferson Memorial with the Holocaust Museum or Bureau of Engraving and Printing (Chapter 4); the museums on the Mall's north side interspersed with a stroll around Old Downtown (Chapter 6).

History

When French military engineer **Pierre Charles L'Enfant** produced his plan for the new capital city in 1791, at its heart was a 400-foot-wide Grand Avenue, leading west from the site of the Capitol. Along it he envisaged gardens and mansions for the political elite and, where a line drawn west from the Capitol met one drawn south from the President's Mansion (today's White House), a commemorative monument to George Washington – ambitious schemes indeed for a piece of land that was, at the time, little more than a muddy, bug-infested swamp. Due to lack of funds, work didn't start on the Washington Monument until 1848, by which time any prospect of what had become known as "The Mall" transforming itself into a splendid avenue was laughable: cows, pigs and goats grazed on the open land, while along the north side ran the malodorous city canal (linking the C&O in Georgetown with the Anacostia River) stinking with rotting refuse, spoiling fish, entrails and dead animals from Washington's 7th Street Center Market.

For more on L'Enfant's plan, see p.36–37.

Following the building of the **Smithsonian Institution** "Castle" between 1849 and 1855, eminent landscape gardener **Andrew Jackson Downing** was employed to design an elegant green space in keeping with L'Enfant's original plan, but the money only stretched to one tree-planted park by the Smithsonian. Even here, people dared not venture at night since it soon became the haunt of footpads and ne'er-do-wells. What's more, by 1855 work had been halted on the nearby Washington Monument, which stood incomplete for the next twenty years. The Mall continued to deteriorate and, as the city grew, its south side became home to meat-markets and warehouses, while the avenue itself was criss-crossed by the ungainly tracks of the Baltimore and Potomac Railroad.

During the **Civil War**, President Lincoln had been determined to continue building as "a sign we intend the Union shall go on" and post-war Reconstruction saved the Mall from further decline. The city canal was filled in (it's now Constitution Ave) and Center Market was closed; a Board of Public Works was established to build sewers, sidewalks and streets; mature trees were planted; and in 1884 the Washington Monument was finally completed. Several of Downing's other schemes were resurrected, extending beyond the Mall to incorporate the Ellipse and the gardens on either side of the White House – finally placing the Mall at the ornamental heart of the city.

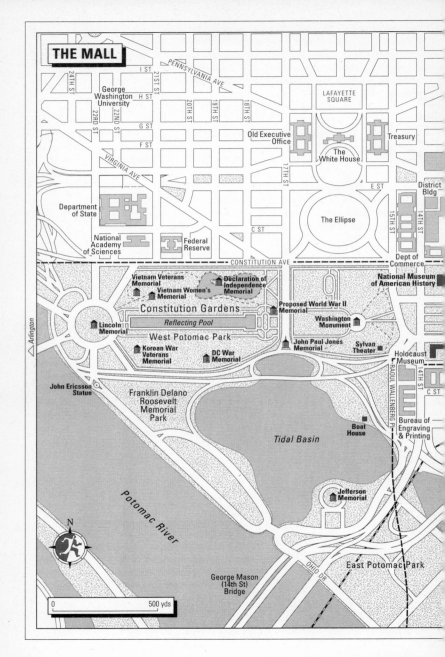

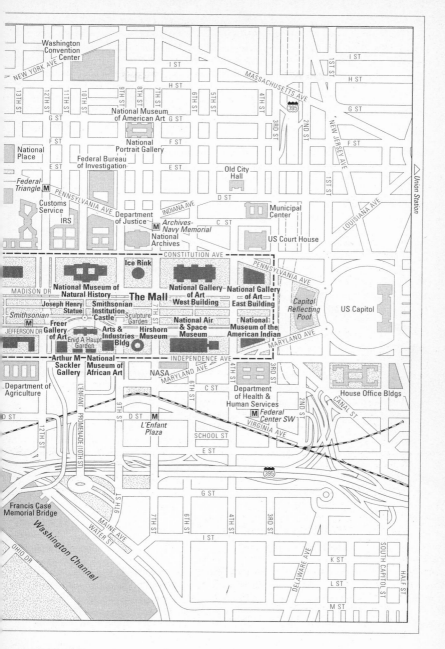

THE MALL

With the addition of the **Arts and Industries Building** in 1881 – America's first national museum – the Mall became seen as the natural site for grand public institutions (following L'Enfant's hope that it would be "attractive to the learned and afford diversion to the idle"). The Botanic Gardens followed in 1902, the Museum of Natural History in 1911, and, eventually, the Smithsonian's first art gallery, the Freer, in 1923. Meanwhile, members of the **McMillan Commission** of 1901, under Senator James McMillan, charged with improving the Mall and the city's park system, returned from Europe fired up with plans to link the Mall with a series of gardens and memorials and to demolish the unsightly railroad station (later replaced by Union Station). Not everyone concurred: House Speaker Joseph Cannon railed that he "would rather see the Mall sown in oats than treated as an artistic composition". However, McMillan's proposals prevailed and following the completion of the Lincoln Memorial in 1922, the Mall stretched west of the Washington Monument for the first time, reaching to the banks of the Potomac River and incorporating the grounds known today as West Potomac Park. More improvements came in the 1930s, under the auspices of Roosevelt's New Deal-era Works Progress Administration (WPA), which also planted the now-famous elms. Meanwhile, the **National Park Service** was granted stewardship of the Mall and its monuments.

The erection of the Jefferson Memorial in 1943 completed the Mall's triumvirate of Presidential monuments. The same architect, John Russell Pope, designed the contemporaneous National Gallery of Art; the 1960s and 1970s contributed museums of American History and Air and Space, the Hirshorn art gallery and an East Building for the National Gallery; the 1980s, the Sackler Gallery and African Art museum. The dedication of the Vietnam Veterans Memorial in 1982 and the Korean War Veterans Memorial in 1995 proved that there's still space, too, for further **additions**. A memorial to Franklin Delano Roosevelt will be dedicated during 1997 a National World War II Memorial is in the design stage, and the last free block in the eastern Mall, next to the Air and Space Museum, is reserved for the National Museum of the American Indian, due to open in 2002.

Along the Mall: the buildings and monuments

On the face of it, the Mall presents the easiest of choices to visitors: **monuments and memorials** to the west and **museums** to the east, with the Washington Monument standing sentinel between the two. Most people, in fact, make a beeline for the Washington Monument and then plump for sightseeing on either side, which is no bad thing.

But there's an argument, too, for approaching the Monument **on foot from the east**, keeping to the central paths and resisting the temptation to dive into the museums. This way you get a flavour of the piecemeal development of the Mall, the landscaped grounds and buildings reflecting 150 years of architectural styles, while at the same time coming to a fuller appreciation of the sheer scale of the Washington Monument itself. It seems huge seen from the steps of the Capitol; by the time you reach 14th Street, your neck muscles are aching with the effort of keeping the top in view.

The museum buildings and grounds

All the museum buildings lie in the blocks between 3rd and 14th streets, on either side of the Mall, a distance of just under a mile.

For full reviews of each museum, turn to the relevant page numbers.

In the northeastern corner lie the two buildings of the **National Gallery of Art** (p.78–94). Built in 1941 by John Russell Pope, what is now known as the **West Building** (at 7th and Constitution) was DC's last great Classical construction. With its domed rotunda and sweeping front steps, it's a veritable palace of pink Tennessee marble, though one that was not to everyone's taste; one critic complained it was "hollow and pompous . . . an outdated extravaganza". This is not a charge that could fairly be levelled at I M Pei's **East Building** of 1978, which lies across 4th Street, connected to the main building by underground tunnel. Using the same pink marble as the original building, Pei fashioned a thoroughly modern interlocking triangular design – his hand partly forced by the shape of the block of land on which the building stands. A similar curtailment of space faced Douglas Cardinal, Canadian architect of the future **National Museum of the American Indian** which will lie directly opposite the East Building on a site bounded by Independence Avenue, Maryland Avenue and Jefferson Drive. Initial designs indicate that it will differ greatly from the Mall norm of lines and angles: influenced by Western landscapes (and by Cardinal's Native American ancestry), from the awkward plot will rise a curving, multi-layered stone-and-glass building with terraced facade and forest and wetland landscapes.

Work on the National Museum of the American Indian is due to start in late 1998 and to be completed by 2002.

There are no such space restraints immediately to the west, where the 700-foot-long **National Air and Space Museum** (p.73–77) fills

the land between 4th and 7th. All the adventure here is inside; the
building itself, designed by Gyo Obata, is a rather dull spread of
squat marble boxes split by glass frames. Sticking with the south side
and Independence Avenue, Gordon Bunshaft's cylindrical **Hirshorn
Museum** (p.71–73) of 1974 comes up next, a neat counterweight to
the angular gymnastics employed by Pei. Here, you're at possibly the
single most rewarding stretch of the Mall, with a further five museums and galleries imaginatively sited in the blocks between 9th
and 12th streets. Most prominent of all is the **Smithsonian
Institution Building** (p.105–106), the original home of the
Smithsonian and known more widely as the "Castle". Completed in
1855 by James Renwick, its Norman-style Gothic towers and battle-
ments jut out into the Mall, halfway between the Capitol and the
Washington Monument. It was mocked at the time by architect and
sculptor Horatio Greenhough as a "medieval confusion"*, though the
contemporary view of it is as a triumph in red brick – one to which
you're steadily drawn as you make your way down the Mall, since its
central tower is the only structure other than the Washington
Monument to rise above the trees. Between Castle and Hirshorn, the
Arts and Industries Building (p.67–68) was the Mall's second public construction, built in 1881 to house exhibits from Philadelphia's
1876 Centennial Exhibition. Architects Cluss and Schulze clearly
warmed to their brief, and it's positively jaunty in comparison with
the Castle, featuring playful polychromatic brick-and-tile patterns.

There's a century beween the Arts and Industries Building and the
two latest additions to the Mall, the adjacent **National Museum of
African Art** (p.94–96) and **Arthur M Sackler Gallery** (p.65–67).
Both designed by the same Boston architectural firm and opened in
1987, the twin embellished, granite-and-limestone cubes complement
each other in their interior and exterior thematic use of shapes (circles for the African Art, triangles for the Sackler). They're also connected by underground passage; indeed, all the gallery space at both
museums is underground, a reflection of the current shortage of room
along this part of the Mall. Outside, between the two, sits the flower-
filled **Enid A Haupt Garden** (daily June–Sept 7am–8pm, Oct–May
7am–5.45pm), where you'll find some strange topiary bison – live ani-

---

*Greenhough was singularly ill-placed to criticize the work of others, having
been on the end of a public lashing from Congress after he'd delivered his commissioned statue of George Washington in 1841, destined to be placed in the
Capitol. It was too big to get through the door into the Rotunda, which had to
be dismantled, and too heavy for the floor, into which it sank – when finally on
display, according to Washington historian E J Applewhite, "The seated, half-
naked figure . . . with a toga draped over his knees and right shoulder provoked
only derision and embarassment". The statue was eventually donated "in a gesture more desperate than generous" to the National Museum of American
History, where it remains today.

mals were once kept here in pens so that nineteenth-century Smithsonian boffins could study their expressions and posture before stuffing the beasts destined for their natural history collection. The museum grouping on this side is completed by Charles A Platt's **Freer Gallery of Art** (p.68–71), a granite-and-marble Italianate palazzo added to the corner plot at 12th and Independence in 1923. You can also reach this by underground passage, from the Sackler Gallery.

Across the Mall from the Castle, the north side buildings finish in some style with Hornblower and Marshall's domed, Neoclassical **National Museum of Natural History** (p.103–105), built in 1911 (though with two further wings added in the 1960s), and the symmetrical, Beaux Arts **National Museum of American History** (p.96–103) of 1964. The two are divided by 12th Street as it tunnels under the Mall and by fifty years of architectural tradition, but both in their lofty, virtuous way find their echoes in the splendid Federal Triangle buildings of the Great Depression, located across Constitution Avenue. Indeed, like the Federal Triangle buildings, the American History Museum comes laden with exterior inscriptions, with the sheer Mall-facing facade etched with improving quotations by such luminaries as Smithsonian founder James Smithson and John Quincy Adams. The **ice rink** on the east side of the Museum of Natural History (between 7th and 9th) seems incongruous, but it's a nice spot – with skates for rent in winter and shade, snacks and drinks in summer.

The Washington Monument

15th St NW at Constitution Ave ☎426-6841; Smithsonian Metro. Daily April–Aug 8am–midnight, Sept–March 9am–5pm. Admission free.

If there's one structure that symbolizes Washington, it surely is the **Washington Monument**, an unadorned marble obelisk built in memory of the first US president. Simple, elegant, majestic and, above all, huge, it's immediately recognizable from all over the city (and from a fair distance beyond), providing the Mall and the capital with a striking central ornament.

There had been much early talk about honouring the achievements of George Washington with a commemorative monument. L'Enfant's original city plan proposed an equestrian statue at the intersection of the south axis of the White House with the west axis of the Capitol, an idea of which Washington himself approved. Yet even after Washington's death in 1799 virtually no progress was made save the placing of a small **stone marker** on the proposed spot by Thomas Jefferson in 1804; the "Jefferson Pier" is sitll visible today. Impatient at Congress' apparent lack of enthusiasm for the work, the **National Monument Sociey** was established in 1833 and fostered a design competition and subscription drive, from which emerged **Robert Mills**' hugely ambitious scheme to top a colonnaded base containing the tombs of Revolutionary heroes with a massive obelisk: L'Enfant's original idea received a nod by the addition of a statue of Washington driving a horse-drawn chariot.

George Washington (1732–99) *1st President, 1789–97*

The Washington family, originally from the north of England, emigrated to America in 1656 after the English Civil War, during which they had been fierce loyalists. On February 22, 1732, George Washington was born on the wealthy family plantation in Westmoreland County, Virginia. Though most of what is known about his early life is almost entirely the product of various fawning and fictitious nineteenth-century biographies, it is clear that he received intermittent schooling, learned to ride and excelled in most outdoor pursuits. He also displayed a talent for surveying, and in 1748, assisted in the surveying of the new town of Alexandria (see p.249).

At the age of 21, he was appointed by Virginia's governor to travel into the Ohio Valley to ascertain the strength of the French forces, which had been steadily encroaching on Crown British land. This experience led him to be appointed lieutentant-colonel in the Virginia Regiment and, later, aide-de-camp in the French and Indian War, in which he gained his first battle experience – a bad defeat, though Washington gained local respect for his leadership qualities. Finishing the war as regimental commander he was subsequently elected to the Virginia House of Burgesses in Williamsburg. Giving up his commission, in January 1759 he married the equally wealthy Martha Dandridge Custis – who came with two children from a previous marriage – and settled at Mount Vernon (p.254) to the agreeable life of a gentleman plantation owner, a lifestyle buttressed by the endeavour of a large number of slaves. George and Martha never had any children of their own, but later became guardians to the youngest two of Martha's grandchildren by her first marriage.

Washington continued to serve in the House of Burgesses throughout the 1760s, during the growing confrontation with Britain. Acquiring a reputation for honesty and judgment, Washington was one of the Virginian delegates at the Continental Congress in 1774; the following year, when British soldiers clashed with American volunteers at Lexington and Concord, confrontation turned into revolution. At a second meeting of the Continental Congress in June 1775, the 43-year-old Washington was appointed commander-in-chief of the nascent American forces – as much for the fact that he was from Virginia (Congress wanted to combine the existing New England army with a general who would also attract southern volunteers) as for his military experience, which was fairly modest.

Washington's achievements in the field during the Revolutionary War have been subsequently overplayed. He wasn't a great general: making early mistakes, his under-equipped Continental Army lost more battles than it won and it took seven years to defeat a largely incompetently led British force fighting far from home. There was often insufficient money to pay, clothe or supply the American militia-men, who regularly deserted; the locals and often Congress, too, proved unsupportive, and to top it all

The Society took one look at the meagre collected subscriptions and settled for the obelisk on its own. In retrospect – given the trouble in getting even this built – it proved to be a wise decision. Early excavations revealed that L'Enfant's chosen spot was too marshy to build on and when the cornerstone was finally laid on July 4, 1848, it was on a bare knoll 360ft east and 120ft south of the true inter-

he was ill-served by traitors in his camp. But Washington was a dogged figure, determined to impose order and hierarchy onto the fledgling army. He also retained the respect of his forces during trying times, not least by sharing their hardships – throughout the war years, he stayed away from his Mount Vernon estate, Martha spending the winters encamped with George in his northern redoubts.

After Yorktown in 1781 and the winning of independence, Washington resisted military demands to assume an American "kingship", resigned his commission in 1783 and returned to Mount Vernon. However, four years later, at the Constitutional Convention in Philadelphia, Washington was back in the political frame. Called to safeguard the Revolution by devising a permanent system of government for the nation, the Convention unanimously elected Washington its presiding officer, as the only man to command universal respect. Once the Constitution had been drawn up and ratified, there was only one realistic choice for the post of first President of the United States – indeed, there's evidence that the powers outlined in the Constitution concerning the presidency were specifically tailored with Washington's character and probity in mind. In February 1789, George Washington was unanimously elected president for the first time.

Washington defined the uncharted role of president, bestowing upon it an hauteur that became almost monarchical, while developing the relationship between the executive and the other branches of government. It's doubtful anyone else could have contained the subtle machinations of various members of his cabinet as the Federalists and Republicans skirmished for influence. Luckily, he presided over an early economic boom; skilfully, and despite severe provocation by both sides, he kept America out of the war between England and France. During his first term, he even negotiated the political minefield that was deciding upon the site of the new federal capital (see p.36). The city was promptly named after him, and the president laid the cornerstone of the US Capitol in 1793 (though he never lived in Washington or the White House – which wasn't finished until 1800 – shuttling instead between New York, Philadelphia and other northeastern cities).

Washington was elected to a second term in 1793 and would undoubtedly have been granted a third, but in 1797 he was 65 and wanted nothing more than to retire to his farm. Delivering a farewell address to both houses of Congress, he went home to Mount Vernon, where he died two and a half years later on December 14, 1799, from a fever induced by being caught out in a snowstorm on his estate. Congress adjourned for the day, and even the British and French fleets lowered their flags in respect. Martha lived on until May 1802 (and on her death, Washington's will freed all their slaves); they're both buried together in the grounds at Mount Vernon.

section – which explains why the monument looks off-centre on the map. By 1853, when funds ran out, the monument was just 152ft high, and stayed that way for almost 25 years – grievously truncated, bordered by the foetid Washington Canal, the site roamed by cattle awaiting slaughter at a nearby abattoir. Mark Twain likened it to a "factory chimney with the top broken off", while the *New York*

Tribune, in a fairly universally held opinion, condemned it as a "wretched design, a wretched location".

After the Civil War, Congress finally authorized government funds to complete the monument and appointed **Lt Colonel Thomas Casey** of the Army Corps of Engineers to the work. He suffered his own tribulations, not least the discovery that the original marble source in Maryland had dried up; you can still see the transition line at the 150-foot level where work resumed with marble of a slightly different tone. At long last by December 1884 the Monument was finally ready and, at a shade over 555ft, stood unchallenged as the tallest building in the world; it's still the tallest all masonry structure on the planet. Fifty-five foot wide at the base, tapering to 34ft at the top, where it's capped by a small aluminium pyramid, it was originally accessible by a steam-powered elevator, which took twenty minutes to reach the top. Women and children were forced to toil up the 897 steps because the elevator was considered too dangerous.

The views of the city are, arguably, even better from the Old Post Office on Pennsylvania Avenue; see p.175.

Today, the **elevator** up takes seventy seconds and deposits you at the 500-foot level from where the views, naturally, are tremendous, glimpsed through surprisingly narrow windows on all four sides. The view aside, the only other diversion is provided by the bronze **statue of Washington** at ground level, which faces east towards the Capitol. Almost 7ft high, this is a faithful copy of the renowned statue by eighteenth-century French master sculptor Jean-Antoine Houdon*, which was commissioned for the Virginia State Capitol in Richmond and placed there in 1796. Washington, wearing the uniform of Commander-in-Chief of the Continental Army, holds a cane in one hand and is flanked on the other by a bundle of bound rods and a ploughshare, signifying authority and peace respectively.

To visit the monument, you must pick up a free **ticket** from the 15th Street kiosk (on the Mall, south of Constitution Ave), which allows you to turn up at a fixed time later in the day. You can also reserve with *TicketMaster* (☎ 1-800/505-5040; $1.50 per ticket).

The Lincoln Memorial

West Potomac Park at 23rd St NW ☎ 426-6841 or 6895; Foggy Bottom-GWU Metro or #13A/B bus from Constitution Ave. Daily 24hr; staffed 8am–midnight. Admission free.

Proposals to erect a monument to the revered sixteenth President were raised as early as 1865, the year of his assassination (see

---

*Houdon was the first major European artist to visit America, travelling to George Washington's home at Mount Vernon in 1785, where he stayed long enough to make a life mask and other studies. Washington had to lie flat on his back, his face covered with grease and then slapped with plaster of Paris, breathing through tubes while the facemask set – at which point, so the story goes, his step-granddaughter, Eleanor, came into the room and fled in tears, thinking him dead.

p.196): the problem was always to pinpoint a suitable structure and appropriate site. There was certainly no shortage of ideas: one early plan suggested building a Lincoln Highway between Washington and Gettysburg, while arch Neoclassicist John Russell Pope submitted four designs (including a vast pyramid and a stone funeral pyre), all of which were rejected. In 1901 the McMillan Commission grasped the nettle and finally approved the construction of a Greek temple in the marshlands of the newly created West Potomac Park. This, the **Lincoln Memorial**, has stood the test of time to become the best-loved of all DC's commemorative structures: solemn, inspirational, and providing a proportioned Classical counterpoint to the grandeur of both the Washington Monument and, beyond, of the US Capitol.

The Lincoln Memorial is pictured on the back of every $5 bill and penny coin.

Work began on the memorial in February 1914 under the aegis of New York architect **Henry Bacon**, who erected a bastardized Doric temple on a small rise in the park. Its 36 columns symbolize the number of states that made up the Union at the time of Lincoln's death, while bas-relief plaques on the attic parapet commemorate the 48 states of the Union that existed when the memorial was completed in 1922 (Alaska and Hawaii get a mere inscription on the terrace). But for all its restrained beauty, the temple is upstaged by what lies inside, the seated **statue of Lincoln** by Daniel Chester French (1850–1931), which faces out through the colonnade – one of America's most enduring images. French certainly succeeded in his intention to "convey the mental and physical strength of the great war President": full of resolve, a steely Lincoln clasps the armrests of a thronelike chair with determined hands, his unbuttoned coat falling to either side; the American flag is draped over the back of the chair. It's a phenomenal work, one which took French thirteen years to complete, fashioning the nineteen-foot-tall statue from 28 blocks of white Georgia marble.

An earlier statue of Lincoln (1909), jointly undertaken by French and by memorial architect Henry Bacon, stands in front of a wall inscribed with the Gettysburg Address in the Capitol grounds, in Lincoln, Nebraska.

Climbing the steps to the memorial is one of DC's more profound moments, as first you meet Lincoln's gaze and then turn to look out over the Reflecting Pool (see over) and down the length of the Mall. Turn back and you'll notice **murals** on north and south walls, painted by Jules Guerin, representing Fraternity, Unity of North and South, and Charity (north) and Emancipation and Immortality (south), directly under which are carved inscriptions of Lincoln's two most celebrated **speeches**. On the north wall is the Gettysburg Address of November 19, 1863 – the speech that Lincoln himself thought a "flat failure" – while on the south is the measured eloquence of Lincoln's Second Inaugural Address of March 4, 1865, in which he strove "to bind up the nation's wounds" caused by the Civil War.

The Memorial wields an emotional influence far beyond its commemorative function. In many ways, it's as much a memorial to the preservation of the Union as to Lincoln himself, as the inscription behind the statue makes clear: "In this temple as in the hearts of the people for whom he saved the Union the memory of Abraham

Along the
Mall: the
buildings
and
monuments

Lincoln and the Gettysburg Address

Four score and seven years ago our fathers brought forth on this continent, a new nation, conceived in Liberty, and dedicated to the proposition that all men are created equal . . .

Abraham Lincoln's Gettysburg Address astonished observers with its brevity – the official photographer hadn't even got his equipment ready before the President sat down again. At events such as the dedication of the war cemetery of Gettysburg orators were expected to expound lengthily, as indeed did Edward Everett (former senator and one-time Secretary of State), who was first to speak at the ceremony. Everett later claimed he wished he had even come close in two and a half hours to what Lincoln had managed to encapsulate in two and a half minutes. Yet the president's speech was poorly received: Lincoln himself was convinced that the audience had failed to appreciate its fine nuances, while the *Chicago Times* lambasted it as "silly, flat, and dish-watery utterances". Other newspapers had a keener sense of history – *Harper's Weekly* thought it "as simple and felicitous and earnest a word as was ever spoken".

Lincoln is enshrined forever." Ironic, then, that on its dedication day in May 1922, while President Warren G Harding and Lincoln's surviving son Robert could watch proceedings from the comfort of the speakers' platform, Dr Robert Moton, president of the Tuskegee Institute – who was to make the principal address – was forced to watch from a roped-off area since the crowds were segregated by colour. From this point on, the memorial became a focus for demonstrations in the name of **civil rights**: Spanish Civil War veterans from the Abraham Lincoln Brigade marched here in 1938; a year later, on Easter Sunday 1939, black opera singer Marian Anderson performed from the steps to a crowd of 75,000 having been refused permission to appear at the nearby Constitution Hall – pointedly dedicating the event to "the ideals of freedom for which President Lincoln died". Groups from the American Nazi Party to the Black Panthers have exercised their First Amendment rights at the memorial (as anyone can, provided they don't climb on the statue or hang banners from the building); but its brightest day saw the appearance of Dr **Martin Luther King Jr** who chose the memorial to the Great Emancipator from which to make his "I have a dream" speech to the 200,000 people who gathered here on August 28, 1963 during the March on Washington for Jobs and Freedom. Five years later, in June 1968, after King's assassination, his successors brought the ill-fated Poor People's March to the memorial (see "Resurrection City" below); while Jesse Jackson addressed a 50,000-strong crowd here in 1988 on the twenty-fifth anniversary of King's celebrated speech.

The memorial's lower lobby exhibit fleshes out its history; there are also restrooms here.

The Reflecting Pool and Constitution Gardens
The view from the memorial would lose a significant part of its attraction were it not for the 2000-foot-long, 160-foot-wide

Resurrection City

At the time of Dr Martin Luther King Jr's assassination, the Civil Rights' leader was planning a second march on the capital, an idea which his successors saw to fruition. Under the auspices of the Southern Christian Leadership Conference, the **Poor People's March** of May 1968 converged on Washington from Mississippi, its organizers determined to force Congress to take a serious stand against poverty and unemployment. The three thousand marchers set up camp around the Reflecting Pool, in view of the US Capitol, and called their shantytown structures **Resurrection City**. Water and electricity was supplied, and churches and charities brought in food, but rain was heavy that June and the mud-caked camp soon lost its momentum. Many residents left early; those that stayed were joined at the Lincoln Memorial by a crowd of 50,000 on June 19, Solidarity Day, to listen to a Peter, Paul and Mary concert and hear various fiery speeches. However, the turnout was much lower than expected and with an ebbing of public support, the dispirited camp was dissolved a week later as city police cleared away the tents.

Reflecting Pool which reaches out from the steps towards the Washington Monument. Supposedly inspired by the pools and canals at Versailles, and by the landscaping at the Taj Mahal, the mirror images of memorial and monument captured in the water have the capacity to bring strollers up short with a gasp. It's particularly affecting at night, when both pool and memorial are lit.

The pool was established at the same time as the memorial, in 1922. Though it was envisaged that the surrounding area – **West Potomac Park** – would be landscaped, "temporary" cement-board munitions and office buildings erected around the Reflecting Pool during both world wars proved hard to shift. Reconstruction was only considered seriously when President Nixon suggested the grounds might benefit from being turned into a Tivoli Gardens-style park in time for the Bicentennial. Money worries and aesthetic considerations produced the less flamboyant **Constitution Gardens** in 1976, a fifty-acre area of trees and dells surrounding a kidney-shaped lake. A plaque on the island in the centre commemorates the 56 signatories of the Declaration of Independence.

Every September on Constitution Day, the signing of the Constitution is celebrated in the gardens by, among other things, an outdoor naturalization service for foreign-born DC residents.

The Vietnam Veterans Memorial

Constitution Gardens, Henry Bacon Drive and Constitution Ave at 21st St NW ☎634-1568; Foggy Bottom-GWU Metro or #13A/B bus from Constitution Ave. Daily 24hr, staffed 8am–midnight. Admission free.

The polished, black, V-shaped granite walls of the **Vietnam Veterans Memorial** cut straight into the green lawns of Constitution Gardens and straight into the psyche of a country scarred by a war it tried to forget. Here, the names of the 58,191 American casualties of the war in Vietnam are recorded in chronological order (1959–75), etched into an east and west wall which each run for 250ft, slicing deeper

The movie To
Heal a Nation
*tells the story
of Vietnam vet
Jan Scruggs
(Eric Roberts),
prime mover
in collecting
donations to
build the
memorial.*

into the ground, until meeting at a vertex 10ft high. It's a sobering experience to walk past the ranks of names and the untold experiences they represent, not least for the friends and relatives who come here to take rubbings of the names and leave memorial tokens at the foot of the walls. Many of these artefacts – dog tags to teddy bears – end up at the National Museum of American History (see p.103). Directories list the names and their locations for anyone trying to find a particular person, and a ranger is on hand until midnight to answer questions.

In so much as it commemorates human life rather than US involvement in the war, this extraordinary memorial serves its purpose with distinction. Indeed it coincides perfectly with the wishes of the Vietnam vets who first conceived the idea of a contemplative memorial in Washington: their sole intention was to record the sacrifice of every person killed or missing in action without making a political statement.

Once the grounds had been earmarked, a national competition was held in 1980, open to all US citizens, to determine the memorial's design; it was won by Maya Ying Lin, a 21-year-old Yale student from Ohio. Determining that the names would become the memorial, she chose to record them on walls of reflective black granite which point to the city's lodestones, the Lincoln Memorial and Washington Monument, and which gradually draw visitors into a rift in the earth. Each **name** has appended the date of casualty and either a diamond (a confirmed death) or cross (missing in action and still unaccounted for – around 1100 names).

In the end, the memorial's non-political stance came to be seen as a political act itself by some ex-soldiers. Concerned that these sombre, dignified walls made no overt reference to military (as opposed to personal) sacrifice, successful lobbying led to the commissioning of a separate martial statue to be added to the site. This, the **sculpture** of three servicemen by Frederick Hart, stands at the west end, heralded by a sixty-foot flagpole flying the Stars and Stripes. These three young men, despite bulging with weaponry and ammunition, have an air of vulnerability all too easy to understand in the bewildering maelstrom that was Vietnam. More lobbying led to the establishment of the **Vietnam Women's Memorial** in 1993, which stands in a grove of trees at the eastern end of the main site. Few realize that 11,000 women served in Vietnam (eight were killed); the sculpture, in bronze by Glenna Goodacre, shows one on her knees, exhausted; one tending a wounded soldier, and a third raising her eyes to the sky in trepidation.

The Jefferson Memorial and the Tidal Basin

West Potomac Park, south bank of the Tidal Basin near 15th St SW and Ohio Drive ☎426-6821; Smithsonian Metro or #13A/B bus from Constitution or Independence Ave. Daily 8am–midnight. Admission free.

The last of the McMillan Commission's specific proposals was for a memorial to be erected to Thomas Jefferson, third President of the

United States, prime drafter of the Declaration of Independence (see p.180) and the closest thing to Reniassance Man yet produced in America. When the **Jefferson Memorial** was finally completed in 1943 it was long overdue: Jefferson had died in 1826, yet was well beaten to national memorials by both Washington and Lincoln. It wasn't for the want of inspiration, for with Jefferson there was more than enough to honour. The speaker of six languages, he practised law, studied science, mathematics and archeology, was an accomplished musician and keen botanist, a lucid writer and self-taught architect of considerable prowess – the only surprise is that he didn't build the memorial himself*.

Along the Mall: the buildings and monuments

The Jefferson Memorial is undergoing longterm restoration to combat the effects of fifty years of pollution. Scaffolding will be in place for several years, though the memorial remains open for visits.

With the US Capitol, Washington Monument, White House and Lincoln Memorial already in place, the obvious site lay on the southern axis, south of the Washington Monument, but it proved contentious. Many bemoaned the destruction of some of the city's famous cherry trees when the ground around the Tidal Basin was cleared (a few zealots even chained themselves to the trunks), others argued that the memorial would block the view of the river from the White House; more practically it proved difficult to reach, since the basin blocked direct access from the north. This, in fact, provides much of its charm today, as the sinuous walk around the tree-lined basin makes for a fine approach.

If the site had its critics then so did the memorial, when John Russell Pope – architect of the National Gallery of Art – revealed his plans for a Classical, circular, colonnaded structure with a shallow dome housing a nineteen-foot-high bronze statue. However, while for some it was too similar to the Lincoln Memorial, it was at least a design in-keeping with Jefferson's own tastes. Not only was it influenced by the Neoclassical styles which he had helped popularize in the United States after his stint as ambassador to France in the 1780s, but also it echoes closely the style of Jefferson's own (self-designed) country home at Monticello, in Charlottesville, Virginia.

It's one of the most harmonious structures in the city: a white marble temple, reminiscent of the Pantheon, with steps down to the water's edge and framed by the cherry trees of the Tidal Basin. The determined standing bronze **statue of Jefferson** (by Rudulph Evans) gazes out of the memorial, while the inscription around the frieze sets the high moral tone, trumpeting "I have sworn upon the altar of

---

*The genius Jefferson suffered a number of prejudices that put his achievements into perspective. The man who publicly strove to abolish slavery did nothing to free his own slaves whose labour kept him in the luxurious style to which he was accustomed. He was permanently in debt (spending $3000 on wine alone during his first year in the White House), fondly asserted that women should be kept in the home, and enjoyed a severely isolationist view in which immigrants were feared since they would dilute the virtues of the hardworking, independent farmers who formed his American Arcadia.

God eternal hostility against every form of tyranny over the mind of man". Inside, on the walls, four more texts flank the statue, most notably the seminal words from the 1776 Declaration of Independence (for Jefferson's role in which, see p.180).

Around the Tidal Basin

The **Tidal Basin** fills most of the space between the Lincoln and Jefferson memorials. This large inlet, formerly part of the Potomac River, was created in 1882, primarily to prevent flooding, while the famous **cherry trees** – a gift from Japan – were planted around the edge in 1912; the annual Cherry Blossom Festival each spring (usually early April) celebrates their blooming with concerts, parades and displays of Japanese lanterns.

*Tidal Basin
paddle boats
are for rent
(daily
10am–8pm, 2-
seaters $7/hr,
4-seaters
$14/hr).*

South of the Jefferson Memorial, the long spit of **East Potomac Park** has more cherry trees, while if you walk around the western side of the basin, following Ohio Drive, you pass the site of the FDR Memorial (see facing page) before reaching the **statue of John Ericsson**, south of the Korean War Veterans and Lincoln memorials. Ericsson, the Swedish-born inventor of the screw-propellor, also designed the ironclad warship *Monitor* – known in its day as a "tin can on a raft" – which in 1862 held its own in battle against the Confederate vessel *Virginia*; the first naval conflict between iron ships.

The Korean War Veterans Memorial

West Potomac Park, south of Lincoln Memorial Reflecting Pool ☎619-7222; Smithsonian Metro or #13A/B bus from Constitution Ave to Lincoln Memorial. Daily 24hr, staffed 8am–midnight. Admission free.

Latest martial memorial on the Mall is the **Korean War Veterans Memorial**, south of the Reflecting Pool just a few minutes' walk from the Lincoln Memorial. Dedicated in July 1995 (and, again, largely funded by private contributions), its main component is a Field of Remembrance in which nineteen life-size, heavily armed combat troops sculpted from stainless steel advance across an open field towards the Stars and Stripes. It's an affecting ensemble, which rather overshadows the flanking, reflecting black granite wall, inscribed "Freedom is not free" and etched with a mural depicting military support crew and medical staff. A plaque at the flagstand proclaims "Our nation honors her sons and daughters who answered the call to defend a country they never knew and a people they never met".

And what a call it was: between 1950 and 1953, when the war ended, almost 55,000 Americans were killed in Korea (with another 8000 missing in action and over 103,000 wounded), a harbinger of the slaughter to begin in Vietnam a decade later. Unlike Vietnam, however, the American soldiers sent into battle by President Truman on behalf of the South Korean government went, however tenuously, in the name of the United Nations; the memorial lists the fifteen other countries who volunteered forces, with Britain, France, Greece and

Turkey in particular suffering significant casualties. Perhaps it's not the place, but the figure the memorial signally fails to record is that of the Korean civilian casualties. It's difficult to be certain but best estimates are that around three million (North and South) Koreans died – quite apart from half a million North Korean, 50,000 South Korean and possibly one million Chinese soldiers.

The memorial has a CD-ROM database; relatives and friends can type in the name of a veteran and call up and print out their rank, serial number, unit, casualty date and a photograph.

The FDR and World War II memorials

Work is still taking place on the **FDR Memorial**, south of the Korean memorial near the Tidal Basin. It's a grand project designed to honour Franklin Delano Roosevelt, president from 1933 to 1945, who himself favoured only a small stone memorial on Pennsylvania Avenue (see p.173). Others demurred and insisted on a far more impressive memorial, whose seven-acre site will incorporate a museum and a series of interlinking ornamental gardens and fountains, as well as statues of Roosevelt himself (including one with his dog, Fala) and one of his wife, the redoubtable Eleanor. Finally, a **National World War II Memorial** has been allocated a site at the eastern end of the Lincoln Memorial Reflecting Pool. Although a design competition is underway, no completion date has yet been announced.

The museums and galleries

There are nine **museums and galleries** along the Mall, most of them national in name and scope and all but one (the National Gallery of Art) coming under the umbrella of the Smithsonian Institution. Quite apart from anything else, they're all free so there's little excuse not to look around at least one. Top of many lists, and with good reason, are the **National Air and Space Museum** and the two buildings of the **National Gallery of Art**; closest runners-up must be the **National Museum of American History** and the **Hirshorn Museum** of modern art and sculpture. Lesser-known standouts include the **Arthur M Sackler Gallery** of Asian art, and the **Freer Gallery of Arts'** peerless matching of Asian and American art, specifically the finest single display of the works of James McNeill Whistler.

The museums and galleries are reviewed below in **alphabetical order**.

Arthur M Sackler Gallery

1050 Independence Ave SW ☎357-2700; Smithsonian Metro. Daily 10am–5.30pm. Admission free.

The angular, pyramidal **Arthur M Sackler Gallery** conceals its artworks and devotional objects from Asia in comfortable, well-lit,

The museums and galleries

underground galleries. Around a thousand pieces were originally donated to the Smithsonian by research physician and art collector Dr Sackler, who also coughed up $4 million towards the museum's construction (the governments of Japan and Korea also weighed in with $1 million apiece). There's no doubting the quality of the entire collection. The problem – if such it be – is that most of the exhibitions are temporary, and occasionally draw from other museums' collections, so it's not possible to predict what is on display at any one time. We've covered the most permanent of the exhibitions below.

Underground galleries connect the Sackler to the Freer Gallery of Art (p.68) and the National Museum of African Art (p.94).

Temporary exhibitions might take in the Sackler's noted group of three-thousand-year-old Shang and Zhou dynasty Chinese bronzes, mostly ritual vessels found in royal burial sites; early Islamic texts from Iran, gorgeously coloured in gilt, silver, lapis lazuli and crushed stone pigments; or equally splendid fifteenth- to seventeenth-century illuminated Indian manuscripts. Of particular note is the *Vever Collection*, an unrivalled group of works related to the art of the Islamic book from the eleventh to the nineteenth centuries.

The **information desk** (daily 10am–4pm) at ground level should be your first stop; ask about the free daily **guided tours**. The gallery also has a decent **shop**, with a good range of prints, fabrics and artistic gewgaws (see p.304), and an Asian art research **library**, shared with the Freer and open to the public (Mon–Fri 10am–5pm).

The permanent exhibitions

Luxury Arts of the Silk Route Empires – taking up part of the underground walkway to the Freer – is designed to show the historic free-flow of artistic ideas between central, west and east Asia and the Mediterranean world. The decorative forms seen in medieval Western metalwork and ceramics are echoed in silver Syrian bowls, Persian plates and Central Asian swords and buckles. Here, too, is a limited selection from the museum's collection of Chinese Tang Dynasty (7th–10th century AD) ceramics, utilizing either simple white porcelain or vibrant tri-coloured glazes, as well as contemporaneous silverware – from everyday items like a ladle and stem cup to a fine mirror, inlaid with a winged horse and dragon motif. From the same period come the "Buddhist Heavenly Beings", floating angelic figurines of gold that once formed part of an altar set.

The main display is on the first floor, where *Sculpture of South and Southeast Asia* traces the spread of devotional sculpture across the continent. The earliest piece here is from ancient Gandhara (now part of Pakistan and Afghanistan), a third-century carved head of the Buddha whose features were directly influenced by images from Greece and Rome, with whom Gandhara traded. Later Hindu temple sculpture from India shows more pronounced eastern traits: among the bronze, brass and granite representations of Brahma, Vishnu and Shiva, you'll find a superb thirteenth-century stone carving of the elephant-headed Ganesha (the remover of obstacles) -- his trunk burnished by years of illicit, furtive touching by museum visitors. From India, Hinduism and Buddhism spread to the Khmer kingdom (Cambodia), which as well as adopting classical Indian styles also developed its own naturalistic artistic style – on a thirteenth-century temple lintel, male figures are shown entwined with vines, alongside an unidentified female goddess with conical crown and sarong.

Also on the first floor, *Metalwork and Ceramics from Ancient Iran* displays a conglomeration of vessels, weapons and ornaments made between 2300 and 100 BC. Many of the ceramic vessels here are animal-shaped, or painted with animal motifs, while a trio from northern Persia resemble metal, such was the craftsman's skill in firing. There's great dexterity, too, displayed in the metalwork, particularly the bronze and copper finials (ornamental pole tops) depicting demons (denoting magical powers) or vegetation (fertility).

The Arts and Industries Building

900 Jefferson Drive SW ☎357-2700; Smithsonian Metro. Daily 10am–5.30pm. Admission free.

America celebrated its centenary in 1876 by inviting its constituent states and forty foreign nations to display a panoply of inventions and exhibits that would celebrate contemporary human genius. The subsequent **Centennial Exhibition** in Philadelphia was a roaring success, though at its close the federal government was presented with an unforseen problem when most of the exhibits were abandoned by their owners, who couldn't afford to take or ship them home. Congress made the Smithsonian responsible for the objects and voted funds for a new "National Museum" – now the **Arts and Industries Building** – to house them.

Opened in 1881 in time to host President Garfield's inaugural ball, the building soon became rooted in people's consciousness as the "nation's attic", since quite apart from the Centennial exhibits – which included an entire American steam locomotive and Samuel Morse's original telegraph – the Smithsonian came to acquire ever more bequests and purchases, not all of a strict educational nature. Over the years, as the National Museum filled to bursting point, most of the Smithsonian holdings were farmed out to new, specialized museums on the Mall and elsewhere, which rather diminished the quirky appeal of the Arts and Industries Building: as Bill Bryson laments, with tongue only slightly in cheek, "At the old Smithsonian it could have been absolutely anything – a petrified dog, Custer's scalp, human heads adrift in bottles."

The building was restored completely for the Bicentennial celebrations of 1976. Only the central rotunda and four of the original exhibit halls remain as first envisaged, but these show off the Victorian interior to splendid effect – the colourful tiled floor, high windows and abundant use of natural light signal the involvement of Montgomery C Meigs, who went on to design the equally adventurous Pension Building (see p.184).

The Arts and Industries Building puts on a regular children's programme at its Discovery Theater (see p.297).

For twenty years after the Bicentennial, the Arts and Industries Building continued to house many of the items from the Philadelphia exhibition. Assorted bits and bobs of American Victoriana will probably remain on display for some time but in a recent switch of emphasis most of these have been dismantled and replaced by changing exhibitions sponsored by the African-American History Center, which may eventually make the building its permanent home.

Freer Gallery of Art

Jefferson Drive at 12th St SW ☎357-2700; Smithsonian Metro. Daily 10am–5.30pm. Admission free.

Opened in 1923, the **Freer Gallery of Art** was the first Smithsonian museum devoted exclusively to art. The airy Italian Renaissance palazzo of granite and marble, designed by Beaux Arts architect Charles Adams Platt, has long been considered one of the city's most aesthetic museums, with small, elegant galleries encircling an Italianate, herringbone-brick courtyard furnished with splashing fountain. Design appeal aside, the gallery's abiding interest lies in its unusual juxtaposition of Asian and American art, including over 1200 prints, drawings and paintings by James McNeill Whistler – the largest collection of his works anywhere.

The collection, and the impetus for the gallery, was the work of **Charles Lang Freer**, an industrialist who made a fortune from building railroad cars in Detroit and was content to spend it on what was then considered to be obscure Asian art. He bought his first piece, a Japanese fan, in 1887 and thirteen years later retired at the age of 44 to concentrate on his collection, adding Chinese jades and bronzes, Byzantine illuminated manuscripts, Buddhist wall sculptures and Persian metalwork during five trips to various Asian countries. Freer also began to put together a series of paintings by turn-of-the-century American artists whose work he considered complemented his Asian collection. Dwight William Tryon, Thomas Wilmer Dewing and Abbott Henderson Thayer benefited from Freer's patronage (indeed, the penurious Thayer was almost entirely dependent on him), though the most profitable relationship was with the London-based Whistler, practically all of whose works ended up in the hands of Freer. In 1912 Freer embarked upon a plan to endow and build a gallery to hold his collection. He was delighted with the plans drawn up by Platt but sadly never saw their fruition. Work began in 1916, but was interrupted by the outbreak of World War I; Freer died in 1919 and the gallery didn't open for another four years.

The museums and galleries

The **galleries** on the third level hold selections from the permanent collection, only a fraction of which is on display. It's grown since Freer's original bequest to around 28,000 works, but even when planning his gallery Freer wanted only to exhibit small samples of the works at any one time. Chinese and Japanese art are in separate galleries on opposite sides of the building, while entering from the Mall, stairs lead up to the American Art galleries, with Whistler's famous Peacock Room diametrically opposite.

On the S level, a shared underground gallery leads through to the Arthur M Sackler Gallery (p.65).

Whistler

Not unnaturally, it's **James Abbott McNeill Whistler** (1834–1903) who dominates room 1. Born in Lowell, Massachusetts, he moved first to Paris as an art student, from which time dates a *Self-Portrait* (1857), with flat-brimmed hat, very much the man at ease in Left Bank life. Moving to London in the early 1860s, Whistler not only began to collect modish Japanese prints and *objets* but embraced their influences wholeheartedly in a series of vibrant works, starting with *The Golden Screen* (1865), depicting a seated woman in Japanese dress in front of a fine painted screen. Freer, attracted by the oriental flavour of Whistler's art, made a special journey to London to introduce himself, returning on several occasions over the years to buy more of the painter's work. There's an unfinished portrait of Freer (1902), started on his last visit just before Whistler's death. Other works include studies incorporating a red Oriental fan, a prop dear to Whistler's heart, and various examples of the tonal experiments that fascinated the artist, who constantly repeated and developed shades of colour – purple and gold, blue and gold, rose and brown, red and pink – to harmonious effect. *Arrangement in White and Black* from 1873 contrasts the ghostly white dress and parasol of Whistler's mistress, Maud Franklin, with the dark shades of the background; *The Little Red Glove* harmonizes glove and bonnet with the subject's auburn hair. These and many other of Whistler's works in the Freer are signed with a butterfly monogram, a typically Japanese device (though one which the London *Times* of the day thought simply a "queer little label").

Besides the works in room 1, Whistler is also represented by the magnificent **Peacock Room** (room 12), which started life as a mere commissioned painting, *The Princess From the Land of Porcelain* (1864). It hung above the fireplace in the dining room of Frederick Leyland, a Liverpudlian shipowner who had commissioned interior designer Thomas Jeckyll to add a framework of latticework shelves and gilded leather panels to the room's walls so that he might display his fine collection of Chinese porcelain. Whistler happened to be working on another project in Leyland's house at the time and, taking advantage of his absence on business, took it upon himself to restyle Jeckyll's work. Using a technique similar to Japanese lacquerware, he covered the leather-clad walls, shelving and furnishings with rich blue- and gold-painted peacock feathers, gilt relief decor and green glaze, while above the sideboard he placed two golden painted peacocks trailing a stream of feathers. The idea, according to Whistler, was to present his art as a harmonious whole (the room's full title incorporates the phrase *Harmony in Blue and Gold*), much as the Japanese did; the room was at once a framed picture and an object of applied art, like an Oriental lacquer box. This artistic hijack outraged Leyland, who refused to pay Whistler for the work (his over-riding gripe was the cavalier way that Whistler had entertained visitors in the room without his permission). Completed in 1877, the room met a mixed critical reception, though Whistler's friend, Oscar Wilde, for one, thought it "the finest thing in colour and art decoration the world has known". After Leyland's death, the room passed into the hands of a London art gallery, which later sold it to Freer. Recent cleaning and conservation have restored the iridescent colours to their nineteenth-century best, the framed shelves filled with blue-and-white porcelain to show what Leyland's original dining room might have looked like.

Other American artists

The other **American art** rooms are less gripping, though it is interesting to trace what attracted Freer to many of the works. Note the Oriental-style calligraphic brush strokes of the trees in the foreground of *Winter Dawn on Monadnock* (room 2), just one of the Impressionist landscapes by **Abbot Henderson Thayer** (1849–1921), who was heavily influenced by Freer's Asian art collection, which he knew well. In room 3, **Thomas Wilmer Dewing** comes closer to Whistler's mood with *The Four Sylvan Sounds* (1896), a folding painted screen clearly of Asian influence. Contemporaries considered Dewing to be elitist and Freer didn't have much competition for his works, though he doubtless had to bid higher for paintings by the more popular John Singer Sargent, whose *Breakfast in the Loggia*, a scene in the arcaded courtyard of a Florentine villa, was bought to remind him of the gallery he planned to build in DC.

Oriental art

Rooms 5–8 contain examples from the Freer's collection of **Japanese art**, in particular the painted folding screens that so delighted Whistler. Called *byobu* (protection from the wind), these tend to depict the seasons or themes from Japanese literature and range from two to ten panels long. Other choice items include the nineteenth-century porcelain dish shaped like Mount Fuji or, one of the oldest pieces in the Japanese collection, a twelfth-century standing Buddha of wood and gold leaf. **Korean ceramics** in room 9 – wine bottles, tea bowls, ewers – date mostly from the tenth to the fourteenth century and show a uniform jade-like glaze. They're remarkably well preserved, many having been retrieved from aristocratic tombs or simply survived as venerated objects, handed down through the generations.

The next half-dozen rooms (10–16) are devoted to **Chinese art**, ranging from ancient jade burial goods to a series of ornate bronzes (1200–1000 BC), including ritual wine servers in the shape of tigers and elephants. There's also a stunning series of ink-on-paper handscrolls, though the calligraphy (literally "beautiful writing") isn't just confined to paper – jars and tea bowls, even ceramic pillows, are painstakingly adorned. Freer also spread his net to incorporate pieces from **Buddhist, South Asian and Islamic art**. A remarkably well-preserved Pakistani stone frieze (room 17) from the second century AD details the life of Buddha, while the South Asian art in room 18 sports some of the most delicate pieces yet: temple sculpture, colourful devotional texts, and gold jewellery set with rubies and diamonds. In the last room (19), Turkish ceramics (many repeating garden motifs) are displayed alongside a fine inlaid Persian pen box (thirteenth century), emblazoned with animal heads and engraved with the name of the artist and the owner.

Hirshorn Museum and Sculpture Garden

Independence Ave at 7th St SW ☎357-2700; L'Enfant Plaza Metro. Daily 10am–5.30pm; Sculpture Garden, daily 7.30am–dusk. Admission free.

Gordon Bunshaft's windowless, cylindrical **Hirshorn Museum**, balanced on fifteen-foot stilts above a sculpture-littered concrete plaza, has been likened to everything from a monumental doughnut to a spaceship poised for takeoff. Inside – where, incidentally, you barely notice that the building is round – is contained the Smithsonian's extensive collection of late nineteenth- and twentieth-century art, based on the mighty bequest of Joseph H Hirshorn, Latvian immigrant, stockbroker and uranium magnate. Hirshorn's vast fortune enabled him to collect art on a positively excessive scale: the original bequest in 1966 was of 4000 paintings and 2600 sculptures; by the time of his death in 1981, the overall number had risen to over 12,000 pieces, which Hirshorn was happy to see go to the country ". . . as a small repayment for what this nation has done for me and others like me who arrived here as immigrants".

It's both impossible for the museum to display more than a fraction of its collection at any one time and for the visitor to get much impression of what is on show in just one visit. If you have the time, separate tours of the permanent art and sculpture collections are worthwhile; you can also enjoy changing **exhibitions** of contemporary art, thematic shows, and a **Sculpture Garden**, which together with the *Full Circle* outdoor **café** (summer lunch only) provides respite when it all gets too much. There are free **guided tours** (Mon–Sat 10.30am, noon & 1.30pm, Sun 12.30pm), and highly rated **films** shown in the evenings (☎357-1300 for details).

The museum

The museum's remarkable **sculpture** collection is displayed on the second and third floors. Although there's little apparent consistency – quite simply, Hirshorn bought what he liked – if there's a recognized strength it's in nineteenth-century French sculpture, considered to be the best collection of its kind outside France.

Chronologically, the collection starts on the **second floor** where, with a bit of backtracking, it's possible to trace the transition from nineteenth-century naturalism to twentieth-century abstraction. Jean-Baptiste Carpeaux, principal French sculptor of his day, is represented, along with Auguste Rodin, whom he directly influenced; for sheer panache, however, seek out Honoré Daumier's raffish, crumpled, bewhiskered gent, *Ratapoi*. By the turn of the century, developments in sculpture and art were hand-in-hand, often literally so since painters became enamoured of the possibilities of working in another medium. Of various bronzes by Henri Matisse, most notable is *The Serf*, a stumpy portrait of downtrodden spirit, while alongside Edgar Degas' usual muscular ballerinas are energetic studies of women washing, stretching and emerging from a bath. Usually on display, too, are masks and busts by Picasso tracing his (and sculpture's) growing alliance with Cubism: contrast the almost jaunty bronze *Head of a Jester* (1905) with the severe *Head of a Woman*, produced just four years later.

Up on the **third floor** (sculpture from the rest of the twentieth century), you can spot Hirshorn's favourites a mile off. There's lashings of 1950s' Henry Moore, from the rather gentle *Seated Figure Against a Curved Wall* to the more imposing *King and Queen*, a regal pair of seated five-foot-high bronze figures whose curved laps and straight backs look as inviting as chairs. Look, too, for the nastiest piece by far, *General Nuke* (1984), Robert Arneson's snarling general's head with an erect missile for a nose, the neck sitting on a totem of entwined corpses. Also on the third floor, the **modern art collection** is a roll-call of the twentieth-century great and good, with several strengths (de Kooning, Bacon) and some weaknesses (few women, no Kandinsky paintings and, despite his sculpture on display, no Matisse). American art makes a particularly good showing: there are portraits by John Singer Sargent, Mary Cassatt and Thomas Eakins (including a strong study of Eakins' wife), and representative works by Winslow Homer, Albert Bierstadt, William Merritt Chase, Marsden Hartley and Edward Hopper.

Hirshorn's collection of work by abstract-expressionist Willem de Kooning is one of the most impressive anywhere, although changing displays, loans and special exhibitions play havoc with formal viewing plans. Two or three are usually on display, though, like the elaborate swatch of lines and colour that reveals itself to be *Two Women in the Country*. It's a fair bet, too, that you"ll see at least some of the earlier European Surrealists; among them Max Ernst, Joan Miró, Yves Tanguy and Rene Magritte. In addition, there's a changing selection of paintings by Georgia O'Keeffe, Robert Motherwell, Ellsworth Kelly, Louise Bourgeois, Clifford Styll, Piet Mondrian, Jasper Johns, Roy Lichtenstein, Gene Davis and Kenneth Noland – in short, just about anyone in the twentieth-century art world to whom Hirshorn could hand over money.

The Sculpture Garden

Much of the Hirshorn's monumental sculpture is contained in the **Sculpture Garden**, a sunken concrete arbour across Jefferson Drive on the Mall side of the museum. In May and October, there are special **free tours** (Mon–Sat at 12.15pm). Masterpieces come thick and fast: casts of Rodin's *Monument to the Burghers of Calais* and of Matisse's four human *Backs* in relief (1919–30) attract regular admirers. Many of those artists represented inside the museum appear in the garden, too – Henry Moore, naturally, but also Aristide Maillol (in particular, a graceful *Nymph* of 1930) and Henri Laurens, Joan Miró and David Smith. Of the lesser-known works, several stand out: Gaston Lachaise's proud, bronze *Standing Woman (Heroic Woman)* from 1932 is particularly fine, and nearby, there's great humour in Jean Ipousteguy's *Man Pushing the Door*. The pond, featuring a small Carl Milles' fountain, is fronted by Alexander Calder's static *Stabile-Mobile*; for a more impressive Calder, make for the Independence Avenue entrance to the museum, where his *Two Disks* (1965) sit on five spidery legs, tall enough to walk under.

National Air and Space Museum

Independence Ave and 7th SW ☎357-2700; L'Enfant Plaza Metro. Daily Sept–May 10am–5.30pm; June–Aug 10am–6.30pm. Admission free.

If there's one museum people have heard about in DC, and just one they want to visit, it's the **National Air and Space Museum**. Since it

Most of the artists on the third floor of the Hirshorn get another crack of the whip in the National Gallery's East Building; see p.92–93.

The museums and galleries

opened in 1976, it's captured the imagination of almost ten million people every year, making it easily the city's most popular attraction. The frisson of excitement begins in the entrance gallery, which flirtatiously throws together some of the most celebrated flying machines in history, prompting even the most steadfast Luddite to consider a brief technological romance. Twenty-three monstrous galleries on two floors containing objects the size of, well, spaceships means that even on the busiest days, it's not too much of a struggle to get close up to the exhibits; you may have to wait a while to get into the IMAX theatre, but otherwise the worst lines are in the cafeteria.

However, there are disappointments. With some very honourable exceptions, many of the explanatory background displays are lacklustre and too reliant on a photo-video-text storyboard approach, which palls somewhat after an hour or two. Many of the most frequented exhibits are also physically worn, giving parts of the museum a tired air. With children in tow, if you get no further than the huge lobbies, take in the *Apollo to the Moon* exhibit and catch a movie, you'll have seen the best of the museum in an afternoon.

Visiting the museum

The **information desk** is at the Independence Avenue entrance; **free tours** leave from here (daily 10.15am & 1pm). If you want to visit the *Einstein Planetarium* or see a **movie**, buy tickets ($4; ☎357-1686 for times) when you arrive. Come early to **eat** in the *Flight Line Cafeteria*, since by noon the place is a madhouse; the adjacent *Wright Place Restaurant* is more civilized. Finally, don't even think of entering the **museum shop** without wads of cash or the stamina to withstand repetitious demands from companions and kids for model spaceships, Klingon T-shirts and florid stunt-kites.

The first floor

Hanging from the rafters in the **Milestones of Flight** gallery, which confronts you upon entry, is the machine that started it all – the *Wright Flyer*, the handmade plane in which the Wright Brothers made the first powered flight in December 1903, at Kitty Hawk, North Carolina. They were an unlikely pair of pioneers, church-going, bicycle shop-owning bachelors who just happened to make themselves aerodynamic experts. The first flight – 20ft above the ground – lasted twelve seconds and covered 120ft, and within two years they were flying over twenty miles at a time, but there was curiously little contemporary interest in their progress. In part this was snobbery: in the rush for the skies, the Smithsonian Institution itself was supporting the efforts of a noted engineer (and, completely coincidentally of course, its third Secretary), Samuel Pierpoint Langley, who conspicuously failed to fly any of his experimental planes. It was forty years before the churlish Institution formally recognized the

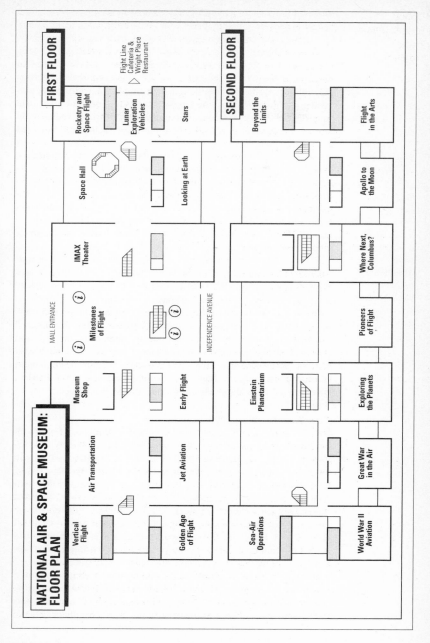

NATIONAL AIR & SPACE MUSEUM: FLOOR PLAN

FIRST FLOOR

Vertical Flight
Air Transportation
Museum Shop
Milestones of Flight
IMAX Theater
Space Hall
Rocketry and Space Flight

Golden Age of Flight
Jet Aviation
Early Flight
Looking at Earth
Stars
Lunar Exploration Vehicles

Flight Line
Cafeteria & Wright Place Restaurant

MALL ENTRANCE
INDEPENDENCE AVENUE

SECOND FLOOR

Sea-Air Operations
Einstein Planetarium
Beyond the Limits

World War II Aviation
Great War in the Air
Exploring the Planets
Pioneers of Flight
Where Next, Columbus?
Apollo to the Moon
Flight in the Arts

brothers' singular achievement, while the original *Wright Flyer* was only accepted into the Smithsonian fold in 1985.

Powered flight quickly caught the public imagination and prompted individual daring: on May 20, 1927 the 25-year-old Charles Lindbergh made the first solo transatlantic crossing in the moth-like *Spirit of St Louis*. He took off from Long Island and landed near Paris almost 34 hours later: when he wanted to see where he was headed Lindbergh either had to use a periscope or bank the plane since his gas reserve tank was mounted where the windscreen should have been. Just 59 years after the very first controlled, powered flight John Glenn became the first American to orbit the earth with the launch of *Friendship 7* in 1962. Glenn went round three times in five hours and saw four sunsets, in a craft barely big enough to swing an astronaut – his spacesuit is preserved upstairs in **Apollo to the Moon**, as are the toothpaste tubes used to squeeze food into his mouth. Three years later, an American, Edward H White, was walking in space for the first time, from the two-seater *Gemini 4*; while in July 1969, space travel came of age when the minuscule *Apollo 11* command module journeyed to the Moon.

The museum's first director was Michael Collins, the often-overlooked "third man" in Apollo 11: *he got to orbit the Moon while* Armstrong *and* Aldrin *made history by walking on it.*

For more space bravado, head to the right where the **Space Hall** traces the development of space flight with machines as diverse as a *V2* rocket, Hitler's secret weapon and the world's first ballistic missile system, and the pioneering *Skylab Orbital Workshop*. Just 120ft long, this was base during 1973–74 for a three-person crew which stayed for up to three months at a time – the confined space can be seen better from a platform on the second floor. For relaxation, the astronauts played with velcro-covered darts and dartboard.

Lunar Exploration Vehicles displays the machines which in eight extraordinary years met President Kennedy's avowed aim of 1961 to land a man on the Moon and return him safely. Unmanned probes – *Ranger, Lunar Orbitor* and *Surveyor* – finally gave way to the ludicrously flimsy Lunar Module *Eagle*, in which Neil Armstrong and Edwin "Buzz" Aldrin made their historic descent to the Moon ("Houston . . .the *Eagle* has landed"). The *Eagle* itself isn't on display although the model that is, *LM-2*, was a back-up, built for the moon-landing programme but never used: if told it was made out of tin foil, cans and coathangers, you could believe it. **Rocketry and Space Flight** traces the history of rocketry from the black-powder rockets used in thirteenth-century China to Robert Goddard's experiments with liquid-fuel in 1926, which pointed the way to eventual space flight. Light relief is offered by coverage of sci-fi stalwarts Jules Verne and Buck Rogers, and examples of spacesuit development (including details of exactly where the bodily waste goes).

If you were determined to see the museum chronologically, you'd need to start with the galleries on the left-hand side of *Milestones of Flight*. None is essential – if time is limited, the most engaging is perhaps **Early Flight**, where you can see Otto Lilenthal's glider (1894), which first inspired the Wrights, whose success in turn provided the impetus for the resourceful Herman Ecker. Having taught himself to fly in 1911, a year later he built his *Flying Boat* using bits and pieces bought from hardware stores. The early technology explored by people like Ecker and the Wrights is covered in **How Things Fly**, one of the museum's few interactive rooms.

The second floor

Upstairs, you can look down to the exhibits in *Milestones of Flight* below, before stepping back to view the complementary **Pioneers of Flight** gallery. The *Fokker T-2* was the first airplane to make a non-stop American transcontinental flight in 1923, a journey that took 26 hours 50 minutes. Just twelve years earlier – and after just twenty hours of flying lessons – one Cal Rogers had attempted to pick up the $50,000 prize offered by William Randolph Hearst to the first pilot to fly coast-to-coast in less than thirty days. He eventually managed the journey in a patched-up bi-plane, but it took him two months, seventy landings and several crashes. Perhaps the museum's most poignant airplane is the bright red *Lockheed Vega* flown solo across the Atlantic in May 1932 by Amelia Earhart; she disappeared five years later over the Pacific attempting a round-the-world flight.

On either side of *Pioneers of Flight*, fairly uninspired rooms deal with **Exploring the Planets** and, in **Where Next, Columbus?**, the possibilities of future space travel. Most visitors make a beeline for **Apollo to the Moon**, perhaps the most fascinating room in the museum (and usually the most crowded). The main gallery centres on the Apollo 11 (1969) and 17 (1972) missions, respectively first and last: there's Neil Armstrong and Buzz Aldrin's spacesuits, a Lunar Roving Vehicle (basically a golf cart with a garden seat), *Apollo 17*'s flight control deck, tools, navigation aids, space-food, clothes and charts, and an astronaut's survival kit (complete with shark repellant). In a side room, each American space mission is detailed, from May 1961 onwards, when in *Freedom 7* Alan B Shepard Jr became the first American in space on a fifteen-minute flight to an altitude of 166 miles. A separate memorial commemorates the three men who died on the Apollo launchpad in 1967 – Virgil Grissom, Edward H White II and Roger Chaffee.

This is all stirring stuff and although there's heroism on display in other second-floor galleries – like **Great War in the Air**, bursting with dog-fighting bi-planes, and **World War II Aviation** – it's hard to see the Apollo gallery as anything but the apex of the museum. You'll certainly have trouble getting too excited by the last two galleries: **Flights and the Arts** shows art displays of little distinction, while **Beyond the Limits** details how computers have affected flight. This, at least, has the advantage of being as up-to-date as the museum gets, featuring touch-screen work stations and a cockpit simulator.

The other great US space disaster, the explosion of the space shuttle Challenger, *is commemorated by a memorial plaque in Arlington cemetery;* *see p.244.*

National Gallery of Art

Constitution Ave, between 3rd and 7th St NW ☎737-4215; Archives-Navy
Memorial Metro. Mon–Sat 10am–5pm, Sun 11am–6pm. Admission free.

The genesis of the **National Gallery of Art** lay in the collection of
paintings and vision of just one man, **Andrew Mellon**. An industrialist and financier, Mellon began to buy European old masters in his
late twenties and his connection with central government in the
1930s – as Secretary to the Treasury and ambassador to Britain –
persuaded him that there was scope to create a national art gallery in
Washington. His own collection certainly begged to be seen by a
wider public: amongst the 121 paintings in Mellon's eventual
bequest to the gallery were a score of masterpieces bought in 1931
from the government of the USSR, which plundered the works in the
Hermitage to prop up its faltering economy.

The original National Gallery of Art, designed by John Russell
Pope, was opened by President Franklin D Roosevelt in March 1941.
It wasn't (and still isn't) a government (or even Smithsonian) institution, despite its name, but building and collection were at once perceived to be of national importance and scope. Now known as the
West Building, Pope's symmetrical, Neoclassical gallery is positively overwhelming at first sight, especially when approached up the
sweeping steps from the Mall. On the **main floor**, two wings without
external windows stretch for 400ft on either side of a central **rotunda**, whose massive dome is supported by 24 black Ionic columns.
The central vaulted corridor of each wing does duty as a sculpture
hall, both wings ending at an internal, skylit, fountain-and-plant-
filled garden court. The entire floor contains almost one hundred display rooms, full of masterpieces from thirteenth-century Italian to
nineteenth-century European and American art; down on the **ground
floor** are changing exhibitions from the gallery's virtuoso collection
of prints, drawings, sculpture and decorative art.

Remarkably, at its inauguration in 1941 the West Building was virtually empty, since Mellon's bequest – substantial though it was –
filled only five of the rooms. But such was the influx of gifts and purchases that by the 1970s it was clear that the original building
couldn't hope to hold them all. Consequently, I M Pei's thoroughly
modernistic, triangular **East Building**, as it became known, was
completed in 1978, utilizing a block of land between 3rd and 4th
streets that Mellon had earmarked from the very beginning as the
site of any future expansion. Pei's initial challenge was to deal with
the awkwardly shaped block of land (truncated by a slicing
Pennsylvania Ave), which he managed by making only the marble
walls permanent; the rest of the internal structure can be shaped at
will according to the dictates of the various temporary exhibitions.
The East Building has a separate main entrance on 4th Street,
although an underground **Concourse**, with a moving walkway, connects the two buildings: in here, there's more display space, a very

good bookstore, an espresso bar and a large cafeteria – topped by pyramidal skylights and bordered by a glassed-in waterfall.

Visiting the National Gallery of Art

It goes without saying that you can't hope to see the whole of the National Gallery in one visit, nor should you attempt to do so. However, it is surprisingly quick to move from West to East buildings using the Concourse, so visiting at least part of both collections in one go isn't out of the question. Note that the most popular galleries (like the nineteenth-century French or American rooms) tend to be busiest in mid-afternoon and at weekends. One way to make best use of limited time is to latch onto one of the informative daily **free tours and programmes**; pick up a schedule from any of the gallery's **Art Information Desks** – in the West Building on the main floor (Mall entrance), and on the ground floor (Constitution Ave at 6th St); in the East Building, at ground level central court.

It's vital to note that even in the permanent galleries of the West Building, certain paintings are **rotated or sent out on tour**. Consequently, a painting may not always be where we have said it should be. To track down the current location of a particular work, visit the **Micro Gallery** in the West Building (main floor, Mall entrance), in which an interactive computer system with touch-screen monitors allows you to locate and view around 1700 works in the gallery. The system can also access biographies of over 650 artists, and provide the historical and cultural background to an art work or artistic period – it can even print you a map of a self-selected tour.

The West Building is currently undergoing a **skylight and roof replacement project** in which rooms on the main floor will be closed in turn for renovation, with the relevant paintings and sculpture relocated to the ground floor. This process will last until at least 1999 so, whenever you visit, some major part of the collection will not be on show in its assigned place. Moreover, ground-floor space restrictions mean that not everything that was originally on show upstairs will be displayed in its temporary home. **Our accounts of the art on display** follow the room order in which the works were originally displayed on the main floor – and to which they'll be restored as each section is completed. For caveats about the permanent collections on display in the East Building, see p.92.

Special **exhibitions and installations** are detailed in a monthly calendar, which also lists the **free classical music concerts** (Sept–June, usually Sun 7pm) held in the serene West Building West Garden Court. Ask at the information desks.

Thirteenth- to fifteenth-century Italian

The gallery's oldest works are the stylized thirteenth-century Byzantine **icons** (holy images) in room 1, in which an enthroned

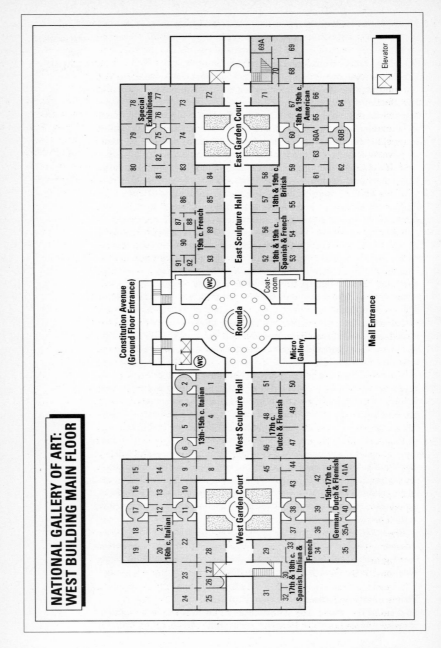

Elevator

69A
69
70
68
71
72
East Garden Court
18th & 19th c.
American
67
66
65
64
60A
60B
77
78
Special
Exhibitions
76
73
75
74
60
63
79
82
83
84
61
62
80
81
59
85
86
19th c. French
58
57
18th & 19th c.
British
55
87
88
89
56
18th & 19th c.
Spanish & French
54
52
53
90
91
92
93
East Sculpture Hall

Constitution Avenue
(Ground Floor Entrance)
WC
WC
Rotunda
Coat-
room
Micro
Gallery
Mall Entrance

2
1
3
13th-15th c. Italian
4
51
50
5
6
7
West Sculpture Hall
48
17th c.
Dutch & Flemish
49
46
47
15
14
9
8
45
44
16
13
12
11
10
43
42
15th-17th c.
German, Dutch & Flemish
41A
17
18
21
22
20
16th c. Italian
37
38
39
40
41
35A
40
19
23
24
25
28
26
27
30
32
31
29
33
37
36
34
35
17th & 18th c.
Spanish, Italian &
French
West Garden Court

Mary, Queen of Heaven, holds the Christ-child who – as medieval art dictated – is a small adult figure. Not until the early fourteenth century did a certain amount of naturalism and emotional range begin to manifest itself in religious art. The Sienese artist **Duccio di Buoninsegna** was one of the first to move beyond the strict Byzantine forms and in his *Nativity* you can trace genuine feeling in the faces of the subjects; the panel was taken from the base of Duccio's masterpiece, the great *Maesta* altarpiece of Siena Cathedral. But while Duccio continued to work within flat Byzantine forms, his contemporary in Florence, **Giotto**, was producing artistic innovations that, a century later, would kickstart the Renaissance. His *Madonna and Child* (completed by 1330) marks an extraordinary departure, with the representations of Mary and child typical of the artist's attempt to create believable human figures.

The emphasis switches in room 4 to fifteenth-century Florence, the city in which the Renaissance got its first and most enduring toe-hold. In Europe's pre-eminent banking and trading centre, rich families – like the Medicis – had sufficient money to sponsor a new band of innovative artists. The prominent *tondo* (circular painting) depicting the *Adoration of the Magi* (c.1445) was probably commissioned by the Medicis, and though started by the monk **Fra Angelico** was substantially completed by **Fra Filippo Lippi**, who invested the biblical scene with his full range of emotive powers. In the same room, **Domenico Veneziano**'s youthful, naked *Saint John in the Desert* (c.1445) would have been considered blasphemous before the Renaissance, when nudity was almost exclusively associated with the concept of sin. However, for dynamic realism there's nothing to touch the decorative shield painted by **Andrea del Castagno** showing *The Youthful David* (c.1450) preparing to fling his sling. This shows David in a natural stance, muscles tensed, hair flowing – with Goliath's decapitated head at his feet to complete the story for Florentine viewers, who would have understood the picture to contain a warning to the city's squabbling neighbouring states.

In room 6 (Florentine Portraiture) all eyes are drawn to **Leonardo da Vinci**'s *Ginevra da' Benci* (c.1474), the only work by the artist in the United States. Painted when he was only 22, its subject is a sixteen-year-old Florentine beauty with alabaster skin sitting before a spiky juniper bush – not only symbolizing chastity (this was commissioned as an engagement portrait) but also a visual pun on her name, Ginevra, and the Italian word for juniper, *ginepro*. Masterpieces by **Sandro Botticelli** include his devoutly religious rendering of the *Adoration of the Magi* from the early 1480s, which was one of the paintings Mellon appropriated from the Hermitage. The scene here is set in the ruins of a Classical temple from which the frame of a new structure, representing Christianity, is rising.

Among the Florentine sculpture in room 9 is the stern bust of Lorenzo de Medici by Andrea del Verrocchio, commissioned from the

The collection starts in room 1 of the West Wing of the West Building and proceeds chronologically.

Medicis' favourite sculptor to commemorate a failed assassination attempt. The **della Robbia** family and related artists (1475–1525) dominate room 10 with glorious glazed terracotta works that were popularly used as devotional images. Other Renaissance developments come to light in room 13 where **Andrea Mantegna**'s bluntly posed *Judith and Holofernes* – a calm Judith clutching the severed head of the Assyrian leader – is of less note for its quality than for the obvious influence Mantegna had on his brother-in-law, Giovanni Bellini.

Sixteenth-century Italian

By the beginning of the sixteenth century new artistic ideas were being explored in other wealthy Italian cities, though not until the work of the accomplished Bellini family did Venetian art thoroughly shake off its erstwhile Gothic influences and produce its own Renaissance styles. Nowhere is this seen better than with room 17's *The Feast of the Gods*, a powerful painting of mixed provenance. Commissioned by an Italian duke, it was started by the great **Giovanni Bellini** between 1511 and 1514 (virtually his last work) and depicts deities feasting to bawdy excess in a bucolic setting – among others, little Bacchus in his blue tunic pouring wine and a predatory Priapus lifting a nymph's skirt. Bellini died in 1516 and in 1529 Titian, his former pupil, was engaged to restyle the painting, removing a grove of trees and adding the brooding mountain in the background. Bellini's contemporary in Venice, **Giorgione**, made a similar use of colour and shadow to accentuate his subjects – his *Adoration of the Shepherds* neatly contrasts the blackness of the cave with the light-bathed garb of the doting family. This is one of the few of Giorgione's works that survive: he died of the plague at the age of 33, though like Bellini he had already managed to teach and inspire Titian, who would later eclipse them both to become the finest Venetian painter of all.

Before Titian, though, the gallery switches back to Florentine forms, with painting of the early and high Renaissance periods culminating in several works by **Raphael** in room 20. Prime piece here is the renowned *Alba Madonna*, another of Mellon's purchases from the Hermitage, which Raphael painted in 1510. Unusually, the Virgin and child are seated on the ground, leaning against a tree-stump, emphasizing humility: the perspective is breathtakingly accurate, while the figures of Jesus and John the Baptist suggest that Raphael had studied the cherubic sculpture of Michaelangelo.

The sixteenth-century Italian collection continues in rooms 23–28, with large-scale Venetian work to the fore. No one was more prominent than **Titian**, whose revealing portraits and visually seductive mythological scenes made him one of the most famous artists in Europe and eventually court painter to Charles V of Spain. His superbly strong *St John the Evangelist on Patmos* forms the roof panel of room 24, while around are hung works by **Jacopo Tintoretto** who, once Titian had died (aged 89, during a plague epidemic), assumed the mantle of chief Venetian master.

The 17th and 18th century: Spanish, French and Italian

The crossing of the lobby off the West Garden Court to room 29 is marked by a shift to **Spanish** works of the late sixteenth and seventeenth century. In the grip of the Counter-Reformation, Spanish art – its themes and parameters laid down by a zealous Catholic Church – remained deeply spiritual in character, with individual works designed to inspire devotion and piety. Paramount among these were the paintings of **El Greco**, "the Greek", the Cretan painter who moved to Spain in the mid-1570s (and is also said to have trained under Titian in Venice, which explains his often startling use of colour). A lively *Christ Clearing the Temple* (c.1570) warms to its subject, portraying Jesus with leather whip in hand laying into assorted traders and moneylenders. Perhaps more typical, though, is the dour *Laocoön* (1610–14), in which the eponymous Trojan priest and his two sons are attacked by serpents sent by the Greek gods. A storm rages above the city of Troy in the background (suspiciously reminiscent of El Greco's home, Toledo). From the same period, *Saint Jerome* – in retreat in the desert and about to beat his chest with a rock – expresses perfectly the emphasis the Spanish Church placed on the concept of penance.

El Greco's proper name was Domenikos Theotokopoulos; the National Gallery has the most important collection of his work outside Spain.

In room 30, **Francisco de Zubaran**, well known for his religious portraits, was responsible for *Saint Lucy*, a typical, spiritual study, though one with an accompanying shock as your eyes are drawn to hers – plucked out and laid on a dish which she holds in her hand. In this room you'll also find Zubaran's contemporary, **Diego Velázquez**, the finest Spanish painter of the seventeenth century. So precocious was his talent, he was court painter to Phillip IV by the time he was 24 and spent the rest of his life executing powerful court and royal portraits for his patron. He did return, however, now and then to domestic scenes; *The Needlewoman* from 1640 is a fine (unfinished) example, a gently lit study of concentration at work.

There are a limited number of **French** works from the same period on show, especially in room 32, where *The Repentant Magdalene* by **Georges de la Tour** (1640) is almost photographic in its quality – the pensive subject's face lit by the light of a candle hidden behind a skull. Work by popular seventeenth-century landscapist **Claude Lorrain** includes a typically ethereal *Landscape With Merchants* (c.1630). French he may have been, but Claude's ideas of natural beauty (as represented in this picture) were firmly Italian – he spent much of his life in and around Rome.

The emphasis is strictly **Italian** for the final few rooms, and in room 33 you come to *River Landscape* (c.1590) by the Bolognese artist **Annibale Carracci**, an example of early Baroque art in which nature itself was the subject of the painting, rather than the backdrop. From here, the jump into the eighteenth century is fairly abrupt, ending with a stream of interiors and landscapes. Italian painters were still much in demand throughout Europe and artists like Bernado Bellotto could make a handsome living producing commissioned works, like *The Fortress of Königstein* which he executed for Augustus of Poland. Meanwhile, back in Venice, highly accomplished artists were producing *vedutas*, or view paintings, for sale to the travelling gentry who wanted a memento of their Grand Tour. **Giovanni Antonio Canaletto** was the first acknowledged master of this genre, and in room 37 are paintings of the entrance to the Grand Canal and of St Mark's Square.

Early German, and Dutch and Flemish: 15th- to 17th-century works

Head for room 35 and you'll find a tranche of work by early German masters of the Northern Renaissance. Principal among these is **Albrecht Dürer**, whose visits to Italy had a direct influence on his art, something which can be seen in his splendid *Madonna and Child* (1496–99) which grafts realistic Renaissance figures – including a veritable squirming child – onto a landscape backdrop typical of northern European religious paintings of the time. Dürer's contemporary, **Matthias Grünewald**, had less time for the Italian niceties of proportion and perspective but there's no doubting the power behind his agonized *Crucifixion*, completed a decade or so later – the only painting by Grünewald in the US (indeed, there are only twenty left in the world). The same scene is presented from an entirely different perspective by **Lucas Cranach the Elder**, whose small panel, *The Crucifixion with the Converted Centurion* (1536), emphasizes the ideas of faith and salvation which made him such a Reformation favourite. You'll also find portraits by **Hans Holbein the Younger**, who as an artist in Germany couldn't adapt to the religious turmoil of the Reformation and moved to England where he became court painter to Henry VIII. In this guise he undertook the task of painting the pudgy *Edward VI as a Child*, Henry's heir and son of his third wife Jane Seymour: finished in 1538, it's thought it was given to Henry as a present on New Year's Day 1539, complete with added Latin inscription judiciously encouraging Edward to emulate the myriad virtues of his father.

Cut through room 40 to reach the early Flemish and Netherlandish works (rooms 39, 41 and 41a), many of which show the new techniques made possible by the revolutionary change from painting with quick-drying egg-based tempera to using slow-drying oil, which allowed artists to build up deep colour tones. Acclaimed fifteenth-century artist **Jan van Eyck** was one of the first to adopt the new technique – his *Annunciation* (1434) shows a remarkable grasp of colour and texture. Even more striking is the tiny panel by **Rogier**

van der Weyden of *Saint George and the Dragon* (room 39), also
executed in the mid-1430s, which followed the realism pioneered by
van Eyck and applied it to a medieval subject with incredible attention to detail: the artist probably used a magnifying glass to paint
individual tree branches and pin-prick windows. Also notable is
Hieronymous Bosch's *Death and the Miser* (1485–90) in room 41,
a gloriously ghoulish *tour-de-force*.

Come rooms 42 and 43 and the mood changes with a swathe of
Anthony van Dyck portraits of assorted Italian, English and Flemish
nobility, covering the period from 1618 to 1635. He was an
immensely popular portraitist, perhaps due in part to his flattery of
his subjects – elongating their frames, painting them from below to
enhance their stature, idealizing their features. He was duly knighted
for his efforts in England by Charles I, but his inherent artistic skill
shines through even the most overblown of his portraits; the earliest
one here, *Portrait of a Flemish Lady* from 1618, was painted when
he was just nineteen. Van Dyck's teacher, **Peter Paul Rubens**, is
responsible for the one real masterpiece in this section, *Daniel in
the Lions' Den* (1613–15), in room 45, in which virtually life-sized
lions bay and snap around an off-centre Daniel. Rubens used North
African lions from a private zoo in Brussels as his models; they're
now extinct in the wild, though you'll find some in DC's zoo if you
want to check the accuracy of the dimensions.

The raffish gentlemen in white collars and tall hats (room 46)
were bread-and-butter work for a talented portrait-painter like **Frans
Hals**. Not that, ultimately, it did him much good – in his dotage, Hals
was virtually on the breadline, supported only by handouts from an
almshouse whose governors liked the portrait he'd once painted of
them. For portraiture it's hard to touch **Rembrandt van Rijn** (room
48), amongst whose works the gallery numbers a prized painting of
his wife, Saskia. Begun in 1634, but not completed for almost five
years, it shows a remarkable contrast between the unearthly shine of
her face, headdress, neck and necklace, and her black dress which
virtually disappears into the canvas. After Saskia died in 1642,
Rembrandt fell into debt and was eventually declared bankrupt; a
second partner and his only son also died, though a mournful
Rembrandt lived on until he was 63. *The Mill* is a typical later work,
from 1650, a brooding study of a cliff-top mill, backlit under black
thunderclouds. It's a famous image, with its dark and light connotations of good and evil, and one which later influenced nineteenth-
century British artists like J M W Turner.

*Genre paint-
ing: Peter de
Hooch, Jan
Steen and
Johannes
Vermeer.*

The final rooms in this wing before the Rotunda, 50 and 51, are
devoted to other seventeenth-century Dutch artists, and although
most show flashes of brilliance, few can compete with the scope of
Rembrandt. Where he ranged far and wide across many forms, most
of his contemporaries settled for making a living from **genre painting**, depicting people in everyday social and work situations. These

The museums and galleries

quickly became popular in seventeenth-century Holland, partly because the paintings allowed the newly independent Dutch to celebrate a nascent national identity. Each artist had his particular specialization: as Hals (a Flemish immigrant to Holland) produced portraits, so **Peter de Hooch** depicted quiet domestic households – like *A Dutch Courtyard* or the tidy *The Bedroom*. With **Jan Steen**, the genre was typically festive: witness his bacchanalian *The Dancing Couple*. Many of Steen's paintings are of similar rustic scenes, doubtless inspired by his experience as an innkeeper.

Of all the genre artists, only **Johannes Vermeer** still commands mass appeal, the painstaking producer of just 45 refined paintings in his career, of which only 35 remain in existence. Of these, the gallery owns and displays in turn (usually in room 51) *The Girl With the Red Hat*, *Woman Holding A Balance* and *A Lady Writing*, contemplative scenes all set – like most of his works – in his parents' house, which he later inherited. A fourth, *Young Girl With a Flute*, may not be by Vermeer; the jury is still out.

18th- and 19th-century Spanish and French

Chronologically, the East Wing of the main floor starts at room 52; if you start over the corridor in 93 you're at the back end of nineteenth-century French works.

Back at the Rotunda, there's a last gasp for **Spanish** art in room 52, which principally means portraits by the flamboyant **Francisco de Goya**, Spain's greatest eighteenth-century artist, who after 1789 was court painter to Charles IV. The gallery owns several works, primarily the famous *Señora Sebasa García* in which he abandons background entirely to focus on the elegant *señora*.

With room 53 you're straight into eighteenth-century **French** painting and sculpture, announced back in 52 by the pair of marble busts of Voltaire by leading sculptor **Jean-Antoine Houdon**, sculptor of George Washington (see p.58). Attention is generally drawn straight to the portrait of *Napoleon in His Study* (1812) by Neoclassicist **Jacques-Louis David**. Arch imperial propagandist David meant the the sword, crisp uniform, military papers and imperial emblems to bolster Napoleon's heroic image, while his slightly dishevelled appearance, the dying candles and the time on the clock in the background point to the fact that he's been up all night working for the good of the country.

After this, head through to room 54 for the still lives and everyday scenes of **Jean Simeon Chardin**, who worked directly from the subjects, hardly ever making the prior detailed studies that contemporaries considered essential. *Soap Bubbles* (1733) is typically effusive. Works by **Antoine Watteau** include the delightfully absurd *Italian Comedians* (1720), a group portrait of clowns and players, whose characters and costumes he knew well having once worked as a scene-painter. Watteau's highly decorative rococo style is seen to best effect, however, in the oval panel depicting *Ceres*, the Roman goddess of the harvest, surrounded by the signs of the summer zodiac, Gemini, Cancer and Leo.

Room 55 is almost entirely dominated by **Jean-Honore Fragonard**, who knocked off his so-called "fantasy portraits" in as little as an hour. In *A Young Girl Reading*, a reflective study halfway between a sketch and a portrait, the neck ruff and bodice are etched in the paint using the wooden end of the brush while the lines of the book are mere blurred traces of paint. *The Swing* (1765) is a more artful, rococo work, whose images of sprayed dresses and petticoats had erotic connotations for contemporaneous viewers.

The museums and galleries

18th- and 19th-century British

The gallery's few **British** works are concentrated in rooms 57, 58, 59 and 61. There are individual pieces by William Hogarth, George Stubbs and George Romney, but the most interesting pieces are by contemporary eighteenth-century court rivals **Joshua Reynolds** and **Thomas Gainsborough**. Also usually hung here are works by two American artists who enjoyed great popularity during their time in England: Benjamin West, the first American artist to study in Europe, and Gilbert Stuart, pictorial chronicler of the first American presidents. During his time in London with West, Stuart put the cat among the portraiture pigeons by producing work with the sheer cheek of *The Skater* (1782), whose nonchalant, black-clad ice-skating gent was beyond compare in Britain at the time.

For West and Stuart in context, see "18th- and 19th-century American", below.

Other works stay firmly within the British tradition, particularly the harmonious landscapes by **John Constable** and the sea and river scenes of **J M W Turner**, which run the gamut from a gentle, hazy *Approach to Venice* – which John Ruskin rather zealously described as "the most perfectly beautiful piece of colour of all that I have seen produced by human hands" – to *Keelmen Heaving in Coals by Moonlight* (1835), a light-drenched harbour scene set in the industrial north of England.

18th- and 19th-century American

The enormously eclectic collection of eighteenth- and nineteenth-century **American art** takes up rooms 60 to 71, one of the most popular sections of the entire gallery.

Room 60a presents a line of portraits by **Gilbert Stuart** of the leading American men of his age. Born in Rhode Island where he first studied painting, poverty led him to London where he was taken on by fellow American Benjamin West. He quickly became a success and set up his own studio, but having got into debt, returned after seventeen years abroad to a new United States and resolved to make his fortune by painting the first President. He ended up painting the likeness of George Washington more than a hundred times during his career; the two examples here are the early *Vaughan Portrait* of 1795 and the more familiar *Athenaeum Portrait* (1810–15) – the latter eventually used as the model for the portrait on the dollar bill. Following his success with Washington, Stuart became in effect the

The Gilbert Stuart portraits.

American court painter and produced portraits of the next four presidents – Adams, Jefferson, Madison and Monroe – all of whom hang in the same room. Stuart produced over one thousand portraits (the National Gallery alone has 41), including private commissions such as in the beaky study of *Mrs Richard Yates*, whose crossed eyes are partly concealed by the expedient of having her looking sideways out of the picture.

For the most comprehensive display of American art in the city, see the National Museum of American Art (p.190); there are significant collections, too, in the National Portait Gallery (p.186) and the Corcoran Gallery of Art (p.155).

In contrast to the youthful Stuart, **John Singleton Copley** was already in his mid-thirties when he decided to study painting in Europe. The outbreak of the American Revolution kept him in England longer than he had planned and his family joined him instead in London, from which dates the *Copley Family*, celebrating their reunion; the artist is in the rear left of the painting. There are other Copley works in room 60b, which is also where you'll find work by **Benjamin West**. Born in Pennsylvania, West studied first in Rome in the 1760s before establishing himself as a history painter in England where he succeeded Joshua Reynolds as president of the Royal Academy in 1792, an office held for almost thirty years. Given this, it's debatable whether to consider him an American artist at all: certainly in his splendid historical scenes, which he helped popularize as an art form, West took subtle side with the British – in room 61's *The Battle of Le Hogue* (1778), which pits seventeenth-century English and French naval forces against each other, the heroic English admiral directs operations from close quarters while the French dandy is more concerned about losing his wig than about the hand-to-hand combat raging around him.

There's more portraiture in room 62, specifically works by two of West's former pupils, John Trumbull (who was later responsible for the murals in the Capitol) and Thomas Sully. Both were highly regarded, although the one painting here which most are keen to see, *The Washington Family* by Edward Savage, is by a much inferior artist – his formal group portrait shows George, Martha and grandchildren sat around a table at Mount Vernon in rather glum contemplation of a map of the new city of Washington DC.

American landscapes.

By the nineteenth century, American artists were tackling the theme of territorial expansion head-on. In room 64, *The Notch of the White Mountains* by **Thomas Cole** (1839) – leading light in the Hudson River School, in which human figures play second fiddle to their natural surroundings – is typical in its vibrant use of colour. The subject – settlers and (very distant) stagecoach passengers threatened by dark clouds and prey to an imminent avalanche – was based on an actual event. You'll see a similar awe of nature in Jasper Francis Cropsey's *Autumn – On the Hudson River* (1860), in which auburn, yellow and faded green conspire to suggest an autumnal brown. At around the same time, the German-born **Albert Bierstadt** brought his monumental eye to a grand study of a shimmering, turquoise *Lake Lucerne*, framed by mountains – the immediate progenitor of his startlingly successful American landscapes (the best are in the National Museum of American Art; p.190). Others, meanwhile, were recording the scale of human progess into the wilderness, like **George Inness**, whose *The Lackawanna Valley* (1855), in which a steam train puffs through a Pennsylvanian landscape of felled trees, was actually commissioned by a railroad company. Inness hadn't wanted the job, but needed the money; at the company's insistence he included the "roundhouse" building in which the trains were turned around, a technological innovation of which they were very proud.

Beyond, **American Still Life and Genre Paintings** (room 65) turns out to be a minor triumph. There's a real spark in Caleb Bingham's *The Jolly Flatboatmen* – the dancing, fiddle-playing subjects amusing themselves on a dull journey down the Mississippi River – an immensely popular picture in its day, reminiscent of a scene from a Mark Twain story. Take a look, too at the initially unassuming portrait of *Rubens Peale with a Geranium*, an early work by Rubens' brother **Rembrandt Peale**. The Peales were an extraordinary family of seventeen children, with most of the eleven who survived into adulthood named after notable figures by their artist father Charles Willson Peale, whose work also hangs in the gallery. No less than eight of them, male and female, became artists (including Titian, who travelled to and painted Western America), though Rembrandt was by far the most talented. The sickly Rubens was a keen botanist and the geranium he grips here is said to be the first grown in America (Jefferson had previously brought one back from France, but it died).

Room 68 ushers in the late nineteenth century, with a roomful of paintings by Philadelphia-based **Thomas Eakins**, from *Baby at Play* to the gentle *The Biglin Brothers Racing*. The light touch here is atypical of the post-Civil War period, which tended to bring out a darker element in the works of contemporaries. **Winslow Homer** is a case in point: trained as a graphic artist, he worked for *Harper's Weekly* during the Civil War recording battlefield scenes, which had a profound influence on his later work. In the typically stormy *Lost on the Grand Banks*, all hope seems to have been abandoned by the occupants of the wave-tossed skiff.

James McNeill Whistler dominates room 69. Stand-out work is *The White Girl* from 1862, subtitled *Symphony in White No.1*. The full-length study of his mistress is of secondary importance to his contrasting use of the various shades of white, from dress to drapes to flowers, all subtly different in tone. There's a similar idea behind his self-portrait of 1900, *Brown and Gold: Self Portrait*.

The century turns with the last two rooms in the section, taking American art up to World War I. In room 70 **Childe Hassam's** *Allies Day, May 1917* is a packed New York streetscape of flags and crowds, while the gallery also displays works by leading

The
museums
and
galleries

Rooms 73–79
are usually
devoted to
special
exhibitions.

Impressionist William Merritt Chase. In the same room, the first of the gallery's works by **George Bellows**, the assured *Portrait of Florence Davey*, in no way prepares you for his paintings in room 71, notably the brutal prizefight pictures *Club Night* (1907) and *Both Members of This Club* (1909), in which you can almost feel the heat as the crowd bays for blood. There's a similar energy in the brilliantly realized *Blue Morning* (1909), set on a New York construction site.

Nineteenth-century French

The most popular rooms in the West Building are those containing the National Gallery of Art's exceptional collection of nineteenth-century **French** paintings (80–91), with every Impressionist, post-Impressionist, Realist and Romantic artist of note represented.

Room 85 is the best place to start, with **Claude Monet** providing assorted, dappled European views, among them two facades of Rouen Cathedral. From 1892 onwards, he painted over thirty of these altogether, almost all from the same close-up viewpoint but at different times of the day and in varied conditions. They were reworked in his studio and a score of them finally exhibited in Paris in 1895, forming an integral part of Monet's experimentation with light and colour. Significant, too, is *The Japanese Footbridge* (1899), whose waterlily theme he was to return to with spectacular success again and again until his death in 1926.

Impressionism continues in room 86, with Monet's sparkling *Woman with a Parasol* (1875) – whose emphasis lies more on the vibrant summer light than its subjects, namely the artist's wife and child – and two of the dozens he made of the town of Argenteuil, where he had a floating studio on the river in the 1870s. Top honours go to **Edouard Manet**'s *Gare Saint-Lazare* (1873), showing two contrasting figures before the station railings. Altogether, it's a happy combination of pictures by artists who, in the summer of 1874, briefly all painted together at Argenteuil: Renoir was staying with Monet while Manet's parents lived nearby. Continue to room 87 for Impressionist landscapes, among them works by Degas, Camille Pissaro and Alfred Sisley, another faithful disciple of Monet.

You can keep vaguely in chronological order by backtracking to room 84 for more rustic Pissaro portraits. Paul Cézanne first crops up, too (though there's far more in room 80), with a portrait of his son and a set of still lives. But pick of the paintings here are easily those by **Vincent van Gogh**, notably *The Olive Orchard* and the rich honey and yellow tones of the *Farmhouse in Provence*, both portraying an intensity – like all his Provençal paintings – that echoed his ever-present mental turmoil. In room 83, it's portraiture by **Auguste Renoir**, where you can contrast the subdued *Girl with a Watering Can* and *Girl with a Hoop* with the rather more dissolute *Odalisque*, stretched out in abandon on floor cushions. Here, too, are female portraits by the American-in-Paris **Mary Cassatt**, whose work you can usually count on finding with the French Impressionists – a term she decried as not reflecting the careful technique and observations she employed. It's easy to agree when studying the flat blocks of colour and naturalistic models in *Mother and Child* (1905) and especially the earlier *Woman with a Red Zinnia* (1891) and *The Boating Party* (1894).

Symbolism and post-Impressionism is explored in room 81 and beyond. The powerful, even sinister *Self-Portrait* (1889) by **Paul Gauguin**, complete with halo, apple tree and serpent, resembles an early Salvador Dalí. Gauguin's declared aim to depict himself outside of society, as an "outlaw", was taken to its logical extreme with his move to Tahiti in 1891, where he dashed off dozens of paintings detailing its people, culture and religion: some of these are in room 80. Here, too, is the bulk of the gallery's collection of works by **Paul Cézanne**, with still lives, portraits and landscapes from most periods of his long life. Cézanne is often seen as the father of modern art, though he struggled to make an impression during his own lifetime, only ever selling around 50 of the 800 paintings he produced – hostile criticism forced him to stop exhibiting in 1877 and his first one-man show wasn't held for another eighteen years. The invective he inspired is now difficult to conceive: Evelyn Waugh thought him a "village idiot who had been given a box of paints to keep him quiet". Cézanne was 27 when he completed the handwringingly heartfelt *The Artist's Father* in 1866 – Cézanne *père* had no time for his son's desire to become an artist and opposed his move to Paris in the 1860s; Paul retaliated by perching his father uncomfortably in a high-backed chair in front of a representation of one of his own paintings.

Having a Break in the National Gallery of Art

At either end of the main floor in the West Building, the attractive Garden Courts are an ideal place to lounge, while the fountain steps in the Rotunda are usually busy, too. For food and drink, you need to head down a level or across to the East Building, noting as you go Salvador Dalí's *Last Supper*, which guards the escalators down to the Concourse.

Cascade Espresso Bar, Concourse (Mon–Sat noon–4.30pm, Sun noon–5.30pm). Coffee, desserts and salads; usually not too busy.

Concourse Buffet, Concourse (Mon–Fri 10am–3pm, Sat 10am–4pm, Sun 11am–4pm). Self-service breakfast (10–11am), salads, burgers, sandwiches and hot meals.

Garden Café, West Building, ground floor (Mon–Sat 11.30am–3pm, Sun noon–6.30pm). Lunch daily; later opening on Sunday for those attending the classical concerts in the Garden Court. Reservations on ☎789-3202.

Terrace Café, East Building, upper level (Mon–Sat 11.30am–3pm, Sun noon–4pm). Nicest lunch spot, with Mall views. Reservations on ☎789-3201.

You can pick up where you left off the Impressionists in room 88, lit low to protect varied works by **Henri de Toulouse-Lautrec**, portraying the dancers, madames and café patrons he observed in his peregrinations around the fleshpots of Montmartre. The last major room is 89, highlighting the multifarious talents of **Edgar Degas** as shown between 1850 and 1910. Most famous piece here is the dreamlike *Four Dancers* (1899), one of his last large paintings. It's a swirl of motion which could be four young ballerinas in different poses, or one single dancer moving through a routine – rather like a flick-book of sketches laid flat on the canvas.

Twentieth-century art

*Into the East
Building . . .*

Although the National Gallery's **East Building** was opened in 1978 to make room for the ever-expanding collection of **twentieth-century European and American art**, there still isn't anything like enough exhibition space to display the entire collection and most of it is usually in storage. This is partly due to I M Pei's audacious design, which places a generous premium on public areas – since the exhibition spaces, squeezed in like an afterthought, are often taken up with special shows, it means that the gallery's own twentieth-century holdings may not be on display at all when you visit. If any of the artists or works below form part of your reason for coming to the gallery (or even DC) in the first place, it's essential you call first.

Two or three items are always present, but that's only because they're too big to keep shifting around. Outside at the 4th Street entrance, **Henry Moore**'s bronze *Knife Edge Mirror Two Piece* is a male and female representation whose sensuous line and form contrast with the sharp angles of the building – Moore collaborated with Pei before deciding on its exact structure. Inside, dominating the atrium, a huge steel-and-aluminium mobile by **Alexander Calder** hangs from the ceiling, its red and black (and one blue) paddle-like wings moving slowly with the air currents. Also in the atrium, **Joan Miró**'s stunning tapestry *Woman* is usually on display.

*For more
Alexander
Calder on the
Mall, check out
Stabile, a
black, angular
piece at the
northeast
(14th and
Constitution)
corner of the
National
Museum of
American
History; his
Two Disks
stands outside
the Hirshorn
Museum on
Independence
Ave.*

When exhibitions from the twentieth-century collection *are* in place, they start chronologically on the upper level, which displays **pre-1945 art**, most of it European. The famous names are all here, none more so than **Pablo Picasso** who is represented by several diverse works, including the blue-period *The Tragedy* (1903) and *Family of Saltimbanques* (1905), itinerant circus performers captured in reflective mood in a stripped landscape. By 1910, when he completed *Nude Woman*, Picasso had turned fully to Cubism – this piece particularly challenged contemporary audiences with a dissection of anatomy reminiscent of X-ray photography.

There's a similar range in the gallery's collection of paintings by **Henri Matisse**, with restrained early works giving way to the exuberant *Pianist and Checker Players* (1924), pictured in Matisse's own apartment in Nice. Technically the most interesting pieces, however, are those kept behind light-sensitive doors down on the Concourse level (Mon–Sat 10am–noon, Sun noon–4pm), the so-called Matisse "Cut-Outs". These late works, completed during the 1940s and early 1950s when illness prevented him gripping a paintbrush, involved Matisse cutting painted primary-coloured sheets into assorted shapes which were then attached to a white background to form vibrant patterns.

There are also works by Piet Mondrian, Rene Magritte and **Wassily Kandinsky**, whose *Sea Battle* from 1913 buries the shape of the boats deep into swatches of primary colour; this is just one of a series of dozens of "improvisations" Kandinsky worked on in the years before World War I. If you were taken with the Miró in the atrium, you may also want to see if some of his typically bold early works are on show, like *The Farm*, a marvellous realist rendition of his family seat in Catalunya in Spain.

Post-1945 art (mostly American, though with several honourable exceptions) is usually shown downstairs in the Concourse level galleries. **Andy Warhol**'s works are as familiar as they come, with classic serial examples of *32 Soup Cans*, *Let Us Now Praise Famous Men* and *Green Marilyn*. Of **Roy Lichtenstein**, you may find *Cosmology*, notable mainly for its absence of the trademark speech bubbles; *Live Ammo* more than makes up, while his *Cubist Still Life* is a unique take on the still life guitar-and-bottle arrangement so beloved of the genuine Cubists. There's also usually work by Clifford Still and a manic *Woman* by **Willem de Kooning** (1949). Separate rooms are often set aside for the related works of those artists using huge colour swatches: the gallery owns large, primeval canvases by Mark Rothko, as well as the thirteen hessian-coloured *Stations of the Cross* by **Barnett Newman**, a series that took eight years to complete. There are various slabs of colour, too, by **Robert Rauschenburg** (his *Blue Eagle* is more diverting, a motor oil can, old T-shirt and blue lamp affixed to a black-and-white smear) and a wealth of **Jasper Johns**, whose *Field Painting* (1963–64) sports cans, cut-out alphabet letters, knife and paintbrush.

For more unexpected surprises you may need to strike lucky with a particular exhibition. *Cakes* (1963) by Wayne Thiebaud are fashioned from oil paint so thick they look edible, while **Chuck Close**'s *Fanny/Fingerpainting* (1985) is a mighty portrait of an elderly black woman realized from a brilliantly marshalled canvas of finger splodges. A more recent acquisition is the grim *Angel of History*, a warplane of lead and glass by the German expressionist **Anselm Kiefer** – 15ft long and embedded with dried poppy stalks. Much of Kiefer's work deals with the destruction of war; you can also look out for his landscape *Zim Zum*, which marries textured sheets of lead and a burned canvas marred by sand, ash and dust.

Sculpture, decorative arts, prints and drawings

Changing exhibitions of sculpture, decorative arts, prints and drawings take place on the **ground floor** of the West Building, and the

West Building: ground floor.

information desks can point out current highlights. It's worth noting, however, that the ongoing skylight restoration project (see p.79) means that for the next few years there will be less ground-floor exhibition space available, so it's even more difficult than usual to guess what might be on show. The gallery, for example, owns over two thousand pieces of **sculpture**: many Italian and French pieces from the fourteenth to eighteenth centuries, as well as pieces from the excellent nineteenth-century French collection, with works by Rodin, Degas, Maillol, et al. Among the **decorative arts** are Flemish tapestries, eighteenth-century French furniture, Renaissance maiolica, chalices and religious paraphernalia, Chinese porcelain, engraved medals, even stained-glass windows. Perhaps most impressive is the gallery's collection of **prints and drawings** – 65,000 works, from the eleventh to the twentieth century. Selections on show are necessarily limited and tend to be exhibited only for short periods, but if you're sufficiently clued up you can make an appointment to see particular works by calling ☎842-6380.

National Museum of African Art

950 Independence Ave SW ☎357-4600; Smithsonian Metro. Daily 10am–5.30pm. Admission free.

There's no café in the Smithsonian Castle, the Freer or Sackler galleries, or the African Art museum; and the outdoor café at the Hirshorn is open summer only. Nearest refreshments are in the Air and Space Museum – or from the vendors on the street outside.

The **National Museum of African Art** – the nation's foremost collection of the traditional arts of sub-Saharan Africa – occupies the underground levels of one of the Mall's most appealing new buildings, its circular motifs an architectural counterpoint to the triangular lines of the neighbouring Sacker Gallery. These are fine surroundings in which to view the collection, which runs to some six thousand diverse sculptures and artefacts from a wide variety of tribal cultures, displayed in a series of (more or less) permanent galleries and bolstered by special exhibitions.

In many ways, the museum is one of applied art, though the application of a particular piece is not always clear, not least to the curators. In part this is due to the techniques of early collectors, who tended not to concern themselves unduly with recording factual information about their loot. In most cases, even the artist's name isn't known, while dating a piece is fraught with difficulty, too. On the whole, most of the works are nineteenth or twentieth century – some are older, but because most African art is made from wood or clay, it tends not to survive for long.

For an overview of the collection, the free daily **guided tours** are an excellent introduction – pick up a schedule at the ground-floor **information desk**. It's also worth noting that the **gift shop** on the first level is one of DC's most intriguing, selling woven and dyed fabrics and clothes as well as the usual books and postcards. The permanent **galleries** are downstairs on the first level, heralded by a buffalo-shaped gong fashioned from a single piece of wood; push the button to hear the sound it makes when hit with sticks.

The Kerma and Benin collections

The Nubian trading city of **Kerma**, 180 miles south of the present
Egypt-Sudan border, flourished between 2500 and 1500 BC. Most of
what is known about the city is derived from the excavations of royal
tombs, discovered at huge cemeteries lost in the desert for centuries.
On display are ceramic bowls (perfectly round, despite being hand-
formed) and, more interestingly, carved legs and delicate ivory animal figures from the ceremonial beds used to carry the dead to the
cemetery for burial. As in Egypt, Nubian royalty were buried with
hundreds of what the museum likes to call "volunteers", who
"allowed themselves to be buried alive" to serve their masters in the
afterlife.

The adjacent gallery contains a more coherent display, that of
royal art from the **Kingdom of Benin**, home of Edo-speaking people
in what is now Nigeria. It's a small collection of highly accomplished
works relating to the rule of the *Oba*, or king, some dating back as
far as the fifteenth century. Best pieces here are the copper alloy
heads (made using the sophisticated lost-wax casting technique),
some of which depict an erstwhile *Oba*, although one is of a defeated
enemy – that he's not Edo is indicated by the four raised scars over
each eye; the other heads have only three. There's a picture of the
current *Oba* on the gallery wall, in resplendent orange, whose ceremonial headdress and neck-ruff echo those depicted on the copper
heads – evidence that the same royal style has prevailed for over five
hundred years.

The other galleries

The other galleries make valiant efforts to contextualize the objects
on show. In **Power and Identity**, the emphasis is on political, religious and ceremonial art – mostly from west and central Africa –
which by its nature includes some of the most elaborate of the museum's holdings. The section starts with the museum's two oldest
pieces – rounded, stylized, terracotta equestrian and archer figures
from Mali (13th–15th century) – and also includes the only work in
the museum where the artist is known. Olowe of Ise, an artist to royalty amongst the Yoruba people of Nigeria, was responsible for the
carved wooden palace door, 6ft high and depicting in relief a king
seated on a horse, his wives ranked above him, and soldiers and
daughters below. Remarkably, the door was carved from a single
piece of wood. Several works – fertility fetishes – represent woman
and child; note especially the worn wooden carving from Nigeria that
would have sat at one end of a ceremonial drum. Unlike Western tradition, where Jesus is the dominant figure in any carving of Madonna
and Child, here all the expressive power in the sculpture is with the
woman – giver of life. In other cultures power is expressed in more
abstract forms. From the Cameroons, a wooden sculpture of a regal
male figure holds his chin in his hand (a sign of respect), his decora-

tive bead **clothing** covered with symbolic representations of spiders (a wily opponent) and frogs (fecundity).

There's much to learn, too, about the varied African concepts of divinity or even beauty: a carved figure from the Ghanaian Asante people shows a seated male and female with disc-shaped heads, a form considered to be the aesthetic ideal. Not all concepts are completely alien to Western tradition, however. One of the most engaging works – a headrest from the Luba people of Zaire – is supported by two caryatid figures who (if you look round the back) have their arms entwined.

There's less to get to grips with in **Purpose and Perfection**, primarily a display of central African pottery, mainly from Zaire, collected by Belgian colonials. The bowls, jars and bottles date from this century and – like the bowls from ancient Nubia – were handbuilt, without using a wheel. This is probably the most remarkable thing about them, though several vessels also display enterprising decor, from incised strokes in the clay itself to the addition of glass beads, brass tacks, hooks and fibres. Finally, the **Art of the Personal Object** displays precisely that: chairs, stools and more headrests, mostly carved from wood using an adze; as well as assorted ivory snuff containers (two from Angola with stoppers shaped like human heads), beer straws (from Uganda), combs, pipes, spoons, baskets and cups.

National Museum of American History

14th St NW and Constitution Ave ☎357-2700; Smithsonian Metro. Daily 10am–5.30pm Sept–May; June–Aug 10am–6.30pm. Admission free.

If there's one single museum in the United States that can begin to explain what it is to be American, it's the **National Museum of American History**. Behind a rather staid title hides a bizarre melange of artefacts that goes some way to recounting the lives and experiences of ordinary Americans by displaying the very stuff of life – from eighteenth-century farming equipment to computer chips, juke boxes to washing machines, harmonicas to train engines. Each floor is a serendipitous delight: George Washington's wooden teeth, Jackie K's designer dresses and the ruby slippers Judy Garland wore in the *Wizard of Oz* are set among didactic displays tracing the country's development from colonial times. It's not so much a centre for scholarly study as a sanctuary for vanishing Americana, though the museum deftly looks forward, too, with its coverage of the white heat of information technology – where its hands-on approach sets its apart from any other "history" museum.

The museum's roots lie in the promiscuous bequests made to the original Smithsonian Institution (see p.105), starting with the exhibits left over from Philadelphia's 1876 Centennial Exhibition. Each item collected was destined for the "National Museum" (now the Arts and Industries Building), but since this meant displaying stuffed animals alongside portraits, postage stamps and patent models, the Smithsonian was soon forced to specialize. An attempt was made to direct part of the collection by founding a National Museum of History and Technology in 1954, for which this traditional Beaux Arts building – the last such on the Mall – was purpose-built a decade later. The emphasis proved important, since great parts of the museum are now devoted to the sweeping technological changes which helped mould modern America. But the final name change in 1980 was a belated acceptance of the constant underlying theme: that the museum of "American History" firmly relates its exhibits to the experiences of the American people. Not every item is domestic in origin – indeed, huge swathes of the museum deal in imported products and ideas – but each in its application has had both a personal and national effect.

You could easily spend a full day here; three to four hours would be a reasonable compromise, though to stick to this you'll have to be selective. There's an extremely good **museum shop and bookstore** on the lower level – the biggest of the Smithsonian stores (see p.304) – as well as the main self-service **cafeteria**. The ice-cream parlour is on the first floor, in the **Palm Court**, which is a table-service café – there's also a *Starbuck's* coffee bar just outside the Palm Court. Ask at the information desks for details of free **tours, lectures and events**, including demonstrations of antique musical instruments, printing presses, and machine tools.

Information desks at both Mall (second-floor) and Constitution Avenue (first-floor) entrances are staffed 10am–4pm.

Second floor

Entering from the Mall puts you on the second floor, where you are immediately confronted by a **Foucault Pendulum**, a seventy-foot-long swinging pendulum named for the French physicist who by these means in 1851 demonstrated that the earth rotates on its axis. Nearby is the battered red-white-and-blue flag that inspired the writing of the US national anthem – the **Star-Spangled Banner** itself, which survived the British bombing of Baltimore harbour during the War of 1812. With dimensions of around 30 by 42 feet, and weighing eighty pounds, it sports fifteen stars and fifteen stripes (eight red and seven white), representing the fifteen states in the Union at the time of the hostilities. In the early life of the new republic, there was no fixed design for the national flag, as arguments raged over the relative prominence to be given to existing and future states. Congress eventually settled on the more familar thirteen stripes (for the number of original colonies), while adding a new star to the flag each time a state joined the Union.

It's also difficult to miss Horatio Greenough's much-ridiculed **statue of George Washington**, commissioned in 1832 during the centennial of Washington's birth. He was paid $5000 by Congress and in 1841 came up with an imperial, seated, toga-clad Washington with swept-back hair, bare torso and sandals – mothers reputedly covered their children's eyes at its public unveiling. Look past the ill-

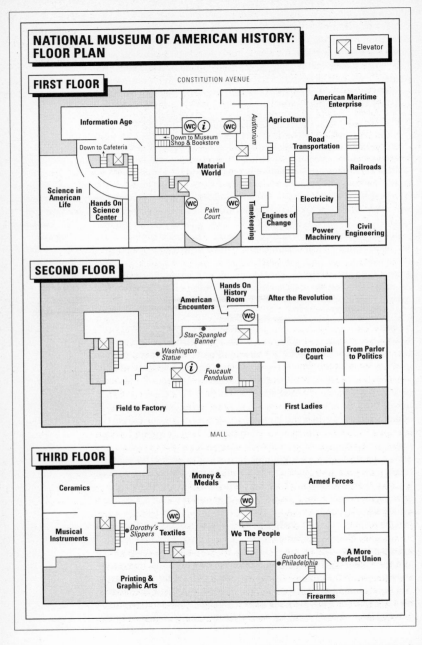

NATIONAL MUSEUM OF AMERICAN HISTORY: FLOOR PLAN

⊠ Elevator

FIRST FLOOR

CONSTITUTION AVENUE

American Maritime Enterprise

Information Age

WC (i) WC

Auditorium

Agriculture

Road Transportation

← Down to Museum Shop & Bookstore

Down to Cafeteria ↑

Railroads

Material World

Science in American Life

Hands On Science Center

WC

Palm Court

WC

Timekeeping

Engines of Change

Electricity

Civil Engineering

Power Machinery

SECOND FLOOR

Hands On History Room

American Encounters

After the Revolution

WC

Star-Spangled Banner

● Washington Statue

(i) Foucault Pendulum

Ceremonial Court

From Parlor to Politics

Field to Factory

First Ladies

MALL

THIRD FLOOR

Money & Medals

Armed Forces

Ceramics

WC

WC

Musical Instruments

● Dorothy's Slippers

Textiles

We The People

A More Perfect Union

Gunboat ● Philadelphia

Printing & Graphic Arts

Firearms

The Star-Spangled Banner

O say, can ye see by the dawn's early light
what so proudly we hail'd by the twilight's last gleaming?
Whose bright stars and broad stripes through the clouds of the fight,
o'er the ramparts we watch'd were so gallantly streaming?

After the burning of the Capitol and White House in Washington DC in
August 1814, the British turned their attention towards nearby Baltimore,
then America's third largest city, which was defended by the garrison at
Fort McHenry. To reinforce his defiance of the superior British force, the
commander ordered the making of a large American flag, which was
hoisted high above the fort in Baltimore harbour. The British finally
attacked on the night of September 13, subjecting fort and harbour
defences to a ferocious bombardment, which was witnessed among others
by **Francis Scott Key**, a 35-year-old Georgetown lawyer and part-time
poet. Attempting to negotiate the release of an American prisoner, Dr
William Beanes, Key was being held on board a British ship that night and
come "dawn's early light" was amazed to see not only that the flag was still
"so gallantly streaming" but that the cannons of the outnumbered
Americans had forced the British to withdraw.

Key may have been a mediocre poet but he was no slouch. Taking the
bombardment as his inspiration he rattled off a poem entitled "The
Defence of Fort McHenry", which he set to the tune of a contemporary
English drinking song. The first public performance of the song took place
in Baltimore a month after the battle and – in tune with its times if not itself
– it soon became an immensely popular rallying cry: Union troops adopted
it during the Civil War and it became the armed forces' anthem in 1916,
though not until a decreee by Herbert Hoover in 1931 did it become the
official **national anthem** of the United States. Despite Key's original title,
the song seems to have become known as the "Star-Spangled Banner"
almost immediately – indeed, the idea of the felicitous phrase had already
occurred to Key in an earlier poem celebrating the exploits of Stephen
Decatur against the Barbary pirates, which contained the words "the star-
spangled flag".

advised classic revivalism and the likeness actually isn't that bad;
perhaps hardly surprising since Greenhough based it on the far more
talented Jean-Antoine Houdon's earlier sculpture (see p.58).

Beyond here in the West Wing, the first main gallery covers
African-American migration from 1915 to 1940 in a display entitled
Field to Factory. The demand for unskilled labour stimulated by
World War I saw an unprecedented move from the fields of the South
to the factories of the North by hundreds of thousands of black
Americans. The "Great Migration" proved a momentous change,
establishing strong black communities in diverse northern cities – in
DC, the hub of settlement was the Shaw neighbourhood – and setting
the framework for modern demographic patterns. Most of the documents, photographs and exhibits tell of the experience of individuals, and there are re-creations of the new domestic situations they
encountered; on a farm in southern Maryland or in a Philadelphian

tenement row. **American Encounters** focuses on New Mexico, looking at how sixteenth- and seventeenth-century Hispanic invasions and, later, tourism have affected the native communities – in particular, the pueblo Indians of Santa Clara and Chimayo. Traditional and contemporary applied art, in the shape of ornate rugs, chests, figurines and ceramics, sit alongside photographs, videos and recordings of narrative stories, music and dance.

The museum's chief strength lies in creating compelling images of ordinary life for Americans of different backgrounds through the ages. Nowhere is this more apparent than in **After the Revolution**, whose walk-through displays detail the lives of three eighteenth-century families (of a Delaware farmer, a Virginia planter and Massachusetts merchant) as well as the wider concerns of three communities (African-Americans in Chesapeake, the Seneca Indians of New York State, and urban Philadelphia). Eager to efface difference and present a vision of consensus, the gallery tells of the same triumphs and difficulties in each community: the array of instruments and knives used for bleeding yellow fever victims in Philadelphia's 1793 epidemic is no more or less comforting than the brutal obstetrics equipment used on the Delaware farm.

The rest of the East Wing is devoted to Presidential life in and beyond the White House. Its fulcrum is the walk-through **Ceremonial Court**, designed to resemble the Cross Hall of the White House as it appeared after its 1902 renovation; the Smithsonian managed to purloin some of the original architectural bits and pieces which are incorporated here into the design, as are displays of glass, porcelain, tinware and silver from the White House collections. More satisfying is the cabinet displaying personal items of the presidents: Washington's telescope*, Grant's leather cigar case, Wilson's golf clubs, Jefferson's eyeglasses and Theodore Roosevelt's toiletry set.

Off the Ceremonial Court, **First Ladies** begins with portraits of each one, from Martha (who liked to be known as Lady Washington) onwards. Though there's game attempt to provide biographical padding, and exhibits exhort viewers to appreciate First Ladies as political partners (Eleanor), preservers of White House culture and history (Jackie) or advocates of social causes (Hillary), the real pleasure here is in the frocks themselves. Helon Herron Taft was the first to present her inaugural ball gown to the Smithsonian for preservation, starting a tradition that allows the museum to display a back-lit collection of considerable interest, if not always taste. Other outfits provide revealing historical snapshots: Jackie Kennedy's simple

---

*George Washington's wooden false teeth, also on display here, are in fact a facsimile: the originals, which he used to soak in wine to improve their taste, were stolen in the 1970s. Washington had several handmade denture sets, crafted from materials as diverse as elephant and walrus tusks, lead, and human teeth.

A-line brocaded dress and jacket raised hemlines in America almost overnight. There's access from the Ceremonial Court through to **From Parlor to Politics**, a worthy trawl through the history of women and political reform (1890–1925), with exhibits on women's clubs, the temperance movement and female suffrage.

First floor

Every technological change to affect America, from crop rotation to computers, is laid out with systematic and mind-bogglingly comprehensive clarity on the first floor. You know you're in for a treat when the central lobby, devoted to the **Material World**, throws up a veritable refuse tip of handcrafted and machine-made artefacts, designed to show what things are made of and why. There's a great half an hour or so to be spent here picking out favourite items: a steel slot machine from 1940, a brass US Army bugle, ornate nineteenth-century marble balusters from a Boston bank, a cast-iron toy train, an aluminium softball bat, even astroturf. Adjacent displays trace the development of items like washing machines, from the earliest wooden tub to the first electrically operated model of the 1960s; bicycles get the same treatment, with the oldest example (from 1869) made of hickory and wrought iron.

The Constitution Avenue entrance leads directly into the first floor.

Science in American Life fills in the background to many of the discoveries that made the artefacts possible in the first place. There's coverage of every scientific development you could think of, and several you've never even heard of; the interactive *Hands On Science Center*, contained within the gallery, explains many of them by letting you conduct basic experiments. The similarly interactive **Information Age** traces communications from Morse's first telegraph to modern information technology by way of a phalanx of radios, phonograms, telephones and computers of every age, shape and size. Among multifarious diversions, you can hear excerpts from early radio programmes, deal with a 911 emergency call, check out the state of contemporary communications in a re-created 1939 street scene, or sit in on a show in the *Bijou Theater* for archive newsreel and movie footage. The museum steps up a gear with its coverage of the development of computers: the thirty-ton ENIAC (Electronic Numerical Integrator and Computer) built for the US army during World War II could compute a thousand times faster than any existing machine but it takes up a thirty-by-fifty-foot room; by way of contrast, a dozen of its valves in a box are about the same size as the computer on which you can take part in an electronic opinion poll on recent government policies. There are up-to-the-minute computer-based presentations in the *Multimedia Theater*, and at the end of the section – if you can kick the kids off the consoles – you can explore the world of the "virtual Smithsonian".

The Palm Court on the first floor features functioning turn-of-the-century attractions: an ice-cream parlour, a Horn and Hardart automat, and a post office.

For all the interactive goodies, it's the east side of the floor which, for many, is the most affecting, since here in glorious profusion are

The museums and galleries

the artefacts and machines that have shaped America. Everyone will have their particular favourite, but the themes come thick and fast. **American Maritime Enterprise** is typical in its diversity, with the model boats and seafaring paraphernalia quite put in the shade by an entire ship's steam engine and a mock-up tattoo parlour; sea shanties warble away on tape in the background. The exhibits in **Road Transportation** are virtual icons of their various ages: a covered wagon from the mid-nineteenth century, a 1903 *Oldsmobile* (the first automobile to be built on an assembly line), a *Ford Model T* from 1913, Evel Knievel's *Harley Davidson*, and a solar-powered car which set a speed record of 75mph in 1988. In **Railroads**, an enormous *Pacific-type* locomotive from 1926 had to be shunted in through the museum window on a specially laid track, so vast is its bulk. Galleries like **Civil Engineering** (bridges and tunnels through the ages), **Power Machinery** (big drills) or **Timekeeping** (railroad pocket watches to the atomic clock) will have their particular devotees; of wider interest, perhaps, is **Electricity**, which celebrates not only the peculiar genius of Thomas Edison, who invented the light-bulb among other luminous discoveries, but concentrates, too, on Ben Franklin's early research on static electricity.

Third floor

Up on the top floor is everything else that had to go somewhere, and while the exhibits are divided into various themes, some items are simply unclassifiable, starting with **Dorothy's slippers** from the *Wizard of Oz*, on display at the top of the escalators in the West Wing. **Printing and Graphic Arts** shows temporary exhibitions from the museum's large collection of original prints alongside paper-making machines and printing presses. The west rooms then move around thematically, covering **musical instruments**, **textiles**, **ceramics**, and **money and medals**. Amid the eighteenth-century grand pianos, the racks of English and American porcelain or coins and notes from around the world, is the odd offbeat treat – President Clinton's first saxophone, say; a display devoted to the life and work of DC native and jazz legend Duke Ellington (see p.217); or the exhibit of *fai*, or circular stone money, of the West Pacific Yap Islands, which was up to 12ft in diameter and had to be carried around on poles. There were, needless to say, no very rich Yap islanders.

The East Wing is more consistently interesting, starting with **We the People**, which has sections on extending the franchise, and on the Constitution itself, though most people are content to pick over the roomful of mementoes from Presidential campaigns as far back as that for John Quincy Adams. Nineteenth-century straw boaters, pictures and commemorative plates give way to half-remembered button slogans – "LBJ: Light Bulb Johnson – turn him out in November" or "The Grin Will Win – Carter for President".

Note that Dorothy's slippers are currently out of the museum and won't be back on view until 1998.

Star piece of the various military-related collections is the oak gunboat **Philadelphia**, the oldest US man-of-war in existence. In 1776, in a campaign against the British on Lake Champlain, 63 men lived on this tiny ship for three months, suffering extraordinary privation – there was no upper or lower deck and only a canvas cover to protect them from the elements. Adjacent **Firearms** is a romp through weapons from the colonial era to modern machine guns, after which you'd do best to cross to **Armed Forces**, which combines model ship displays and artillery pieces with a sympathetic look at the experiences of the American GI (named for their "Government Issue" gear) in World War II, from shipping out to homecoming.

Two final sections change the mood quickly and are the most moving parts of the whole museum. **Personal Legacy: The Healing of a Nation** brings together some of the 25,000 items left by relatives and friends at the Vietnam Veterans Memorial in DC. These deeply personal mementoes tell of the strict human cost of a detached foreign policy: each child's letter, wedding band, dog tag or forage cap represents a host of other lives touched by the war.

After two decades, the Vietnam vets can stand up and recount their experiences without fear of rancour, but it took even longer to rehabilitate another group of Americans in the public's eye. Throughout the nineteenth century, racist laws were passed to restrict American citizenship for Asian immigrants and there was little public opposition during World War II when Roosevelt agreed to the "evacuation" of Japanese/American citizens into "assembly centers" – basically concentration camps where people were interned solely on the basis of their race. FDR's Secretary of War, Henry L Stimson, declared that "their racial characteristics are such that we cannot understand or even trust the citizen Japanese" – though no one ever suggested the containment of Italian- or German/Americans in the same period. **A More Perfect Union** deals with this shameful episode with commendable candour, pointing out for example that 25,000 Japanese-Americans served in the US forces, most of whom had family and friends in detention camps back home. Indeed, the largely Japanese 100th Infantry Battalion/42nd Regimental Combat Team was the most decorated military unit of its size at the end of the war. The displays contrast the dismal life in barracks at home with the valour of the combat units, who at the end of the war at least had their medals to prove their worth – the civilian Japanese-Americans, who had committed no crime other than to be born with the wrong "characteristics", got $25 and a ticket home.

National Museum of Natural History

10th St NW and Constitution Ave ☎357-2700; Federal Triangle Metro. Daily Sept–May 10am–5.30pm; June–Aug 10am–6.30pm. Admission free.

The imposing three-storey entrance rotunda of the **National Museum of Natural History** feels like the busiest and most boisterous crossroads in all DC, with troops of screeching school kids chasing each other non-stop around a colossal African elephant. Hundreds of other stuffed animals, tracing evolution from fossilized four-billion-year-old plankton to dinosaurs' eggs and beyond, are displayed on all sides. It's one of the oldest of DC's museums, founded in 1911, with its early collection partly based on the specimens that the Smithsonian commissioned from the game-hunting Theodore Roosevelt on his African safaris of 1909–10 – he collected (ie shot) hundreds, from lions to rhinos, many of which are still on display.

You'll need to go early to avoid the worst of the crowds, especially in summer and during school holidays; pick up floor plans at the **information desk** at the elephant's feet. Outside summer (daily Sept–June 10.30am & 1.30pm), **free guided tours** show you the highlights in around an hour; meet by the elephant. Several galleries are devoted to **temporary exhibitions**; check at the information desk.

The collection

Given that the museum owns forty million specimens, it can be forgiven for failing to exhibit some of them with sufficient gusto: there are only so many things you can do with a trayful of pinned butterflies and turning them into an attention-grabbing, interactive exhibit is not one of them. Much, then, is as you might imagine, with halls full of stuffed mammals and birds placed in lifeless dioramas.

To be fair, though, when the museum does connect – particularly in the Ocean to Dinosaur sections on the first floor – it's among the finest in its field. In **Exploring Marine Ecosystems**, videos, aquariums and the odd furry seal illustrate life on the temperate rocky shore of Maine and a tropical coral reef from the Caribbean. Free behind-the-scenes tours of the model ecosystems afford a closer look (Mon, Wed & Sat 2pm); tickets are available from the first-floor information desk. If you prefer your attractions macro rather than micro, a life-sized blue whale is on display along with a rare specimen of the giant squid; scientists don't know quite where it lives, but reckon it grows up to 50ft long. Naturally enough, the **Dinosaurs** section is the most popular part of the museum, with hulking skeletons reassembled in imaginative poses and accompanied by informative text, written with a light touch, accessible to children. The massive Diplodocus, the most imposing specimen, was discovered in Utah in 1923, at what is now Dinosaur National Monument. Stay in this section long enough to tour the related displays on the **Ice Age**, **Ancient Seas**, **Fossil Mammals** and **Fossil Plants** – each covering molluscs, lizards, giant turtles and early fish in exhaustive, engaging detail with the aid of diagrams, text and fossils.

Other highlights are upstairs on the second floor, where **Reptiles** and **Bones** give way to the splendid **Insect Zoo**, sponsored in a delicious irony by *O Orkin*, the pest control company. Here, many of the exhibits are actually alive, which may or may not be a recommendation: behind screens – with notices pleading, unsuccessfully, "Please do not tap the glass" – are imprisoned tarantulas, roaches, crickets, bird-eating spiders, worms, termites, even a thriving bee colony. A member of staff with the most unenviable job in the world sits in one corner with assorted creepy-crawlies wandering up and down his arms; kids generally can't wait to grab a bug, while cowering adults try hard not to flinch. There's more hands-on participation for children in the first-floor **Discovery Room** (Mon–Fri noon–2.30pm, Sat & Sun 10.30am–3.30pm), though this time it's rarely anything more alarming than old bones, pelts and stones to play with. You need a free pass to get in (available at the door); arrive early at peak times, since numbers are limited.

Since the museum's earliest days, "natural history" was deemed to embrace a broad remit. Today the exceptional **geological and mineral department** includes an array of renowned gemstones – the legendary 45-carat **Hope Diamond**, once owned by Marie Antoinette, is on display in the Geology, Gems, and Minerals Hall.

The museum has further to go before it deals successfully with its dated **ethnographical** collections; an early subtitle trumpeted it also as the "Museum of Man". There are moves to hive the ethnographical items off into their own new museum, but for now entire galleries on the first and second floors continue to raise hackles with their 1950s-style attitudes and assumptions. Displays on "Native Cultures of the Americas" include the Lucayans, said to have "vanished" shortly after encountering Columbus, and static dioramas of the "primitive" pueblos of the southwest stand alongside bison, bighorn sheep and other once-wild things. Occasionally, a token disclaimer notice, pointing out contemporaneous inaccuracies and prejudices, drags the exhibits into the late twentieth century. The way forward is perhaps shown by the more imaginative treatment of the Seminole of Florida, which portrays contemporary facets of tribal life, culture and activities alongside the museum's own historic objects.

The Smithsonian Institution Building

1000 Jefferson Drive SW ☎357-2700; Smithsonian Metro. Daily 9.30am–5.30pm. Admission free.

Easily the most striking edifice on the Mall, the **Smithsonian Institution Building** resembles nothing so much as an English country seat, with its ruddy brown sandstone, nave windows and slender steeples – little surprise, then, that it's widely known as the **Smithsonian Castle**. It's the headquarters of the **Smithsonian Institution** (see p.66), an independent trust holding 140 million artefacts in sixteen museums (and one zoo), which was curiously endowed by an Englishman. **James Smithson**, gentleman scientist and illegitimate son of the first Duke of Northumberland, had never even visited the US and yet on his death in 1829 left half a million dollars "to found at Washington, under the name of the Smithsonian

Less scary insects are on show in the Butterfly Garden, on the 9th Street side of the museum building.
There are wetland, wooded, meadow and urban habitats featuring – as the brochure has it – "plant-insect interaction"; it's on view at all times.

Institution, an establishment for the increase and diffusion of Knowledge" – provided, that is, his surviving nephew should die without an heir. Luckily for future generations he did (in 1835), though it took Congress until 1846 to decide, firstly, whether to accept the money and secondly, quite what establishment would fit the bill; John Quincy Adams, for one, favoured an astronomical laboratory. In the end, the vote was for a multi-purpose building that would encompass museum, art gallery and laboratory: the original Smithsonian Institution Building was duly completed in 1855.

For all its wealth, the **Smithsonian** had something of a shaky start, since it wasn't at all clear quite how it should diffuse the knowledge proposed by its benefactor. Even just a few years after its opening, the collections were too large and varied to be able to be displayed thematically in the Castle. Matters slowly improved under the stewardship of the Smithsonian's first Secretary, **Joseph Henry**, who tried to direct the institute primarily towards scientific research. Even the National Zoological Park had its origins here; a photograph inside shows buffalo grazing in the grounds in 1889.

As the Castle shed its collections and bequests to specific museums, it took up duty as the Smithsonian administrative headquarters and now houses the main **visitor centre**, whose fine marble-pillared Great Hall offers a foretaste of the Smithsonian attractions. Here, too, are scale models of all the major city plans, from L'Enfant onwards; twenty-minute video shows highlighting the role of the Institution; interactive touch-screen Smithsonian information displays and electronic wall maps. You can pick up the latest details on events at all the galleries at the information desk.

Incidentally, Smithsonian founder James Smithson, who never visited America in life, found a place here in death: his ornate, Neoclassical **tomb** stands in an alcove just off the Mall entrance, placed here in 1904, 75 years after his death in Italy. In a neat counterpoint to the patent uncertainties of his life – which, not aware of his true parentage, he started as James Lewis Macie – the tomb records his age incorrectly, since he was 64 and not 75 when he died. Out of the Mall itself, in front of the entrance, the resplendent robed **statue** is not of Smithson, as you might suppose, but of first Smithsonian Secretary, Joseph Henry.

Chapter 3

Capitol Hill

*Everyone knows that Washington has a Capitol; but the misfortune
is that the Capitol wants a city. There it stands, reminding you of a
general without an army, only surrounded and followed by a parcel
of ragged little dirty boys; for such is the appearance of the dirty,
straggling, ill-built houses which lie at the foot of it.*
Captain Frederick Marryat, 1839

Although there's more than one hill in Washington DC, when
people talk about what's going on on "The Hill" they mean
CAPITOL HILL, the shallow knoll at the eastern end of the
Mall topped by the giant white dome of the US Capitol. Home of both
the legislature – Congress – and the judiciary – the Supreme Court –
city planner L'Enfant's "pedestal waiting for a monument" is still the
place where the law of the land is made and refined.

Yet, as Marryat observed, the neighbourhood faced a lengthy
clamber to respectability. When L'Enfant and his surveyors first put
pen to paper, the cross drawn on what was then Jenkins Hill was the
focus of a grand, Baroque city plan. Duly the US Capitol building
was erected, and Congress moved in in 1800. But this marshy outpost was slow to develop: the Capitol froze in the bitter winters and
boiled in the harsh summers, and for an audience with the President
legislators had to trudge the muddy track of Pennsylvania Avenue
from their taverns and boarding houses. When the War of 1812
broke out the British weren't exactly spoiled for targets in
Washington, and the Capitol was the first to burn, prompting many
at the time to suggest abandoning the city altogether and setting up
somewhere more hospitable. Later, Marryat was only the first of a
long line of critics to point out the incongruity of the splendid ideal
of the Capitol building and its rather dismal surroundings – ironically, at the time of his visit the "dirty, straggling, ill-built houses" of
Capitol Hill comprised probably the most developed part of
Washington.

However, as the capital and federal government grew in stature, so
did the Hill. Over the course of the nineteenth century appeared the
rows of elegant townhouses that today form the keystone of Capitol

The following labels appear on the map:

Capital Children's Museum

Union Station

National Postal Museum · Columbus Meml Fountain · Union Station

NW · NE

Senate Office Buildings · Dirksen · Hart · Stanton Park

Taft Meml · Russell · Sewall-Belmont House

Peace Meml · US Capitol · Supreme Court · Folger Shakespeare Library · Lincoln Park

National Gallery of Art

Capitol Reflecting Pool · Grant Meml · Garfield Meml · Jefferson Bldg · Adams Bldg

The Mall

Botanic Gardens · Rayburn · Library of Congress · Eastern Market

Bartholdi Fountain · Longworth · Cannon · Madison Bldg

Federal Center SW · House Office Bldgs · Ebenezer Church · Eastern Market

Air & Space Museum

Capitol South · SW · Folger Square · Marion Park · SE

Christ Church

Navy Yard Metro · Navy Yard

Waterfront Metro

RFK Stadium

0 200 yds

Hill's status as a protected historic district. At least one, the **Sewall-Belmont House**, is open to the public. Eventually major federal institutions, housed since 1800 in the ever-expanding Capitol building, moved into suitable buildings of their own: first the **Library of Congress** in 1897, whose oldest building has recently been skilfully refurbished; then the **Supreme Court** in 1935, which – like all the Hill's federal institutions – remains open for public visits.

Today the federal buildings reach as far as the two C streets, on either side of the Capitol, and east to 2nd Street – for many, that is the extent of Capitol Hill. But beyond the buildings lie diverse residential neighbourhoods, where politicians, aides, lawyers, lobbyists and even real people live. The early stretches of **Pennsylvania Avenue**, around **Eastern Market**, provide a few distractions, not least the market itself. **Lincoln Park**, with its memorial to the Great Emancipator, marks the eastern limit of the neighbourhood, while to the north, the area around **Union Station** has been spruced up in the last decade or so.

The US Capitol

East end of the Mall, Capitol Hill ☎225-6827 for tour information, ☎224-3121 general information; Capitol South or Union Station Metro; bus #30, 32, 34, 36 from Pennsylvania Ave. Memorial Day–Labor Day daily 9am–8pm, rest of the year daily 9am–4.30pm. Admission free.

It's not mere chance that the dome of the **US Capitol** is visible from all over the city. Like the White House, it's both a workplace and a monument. In here meets Congress, the nation's law-makers and tax-takers, made up of the **Senate** and the **House of Representatives**; from here each President sets off on his inauguration parade, returning to give the annual State of the Union address. However, unlike the White House (where you get to see little more than museum pieces of rooms), the US Capitol, with its grand halls and statues, committee rooms and ornate chambers, is one of the few places in the District where you get a tangible sense of the immense power wielded by the nation's elected officials.

Even if most contemporary visitors are a touch too worldly to accept that the goings-on here truly represent democracy at work, the US Capitol has remained a powerful symbol for two centuries. As early as 1812, Thomas Jefferson was trumpeting it as "the first temple dedicated to the sovereignty of the people, embellishing with Athenian taste the course of a nation looking far beyond the range of Athenian destinies". The foot of the US Capitol has always been an obvious convergence point for **demonstrations**. In 1894, Jacob S Coxey led an "army" of unemployed from Ohio and points west to demand a public works programme; he was arrested for trespassing and the few hundred men with him slunk off home. Unemployed soldiers set up camp outside the building after World War I, as – fifty years later – did the weary citizens of the Poor People's March of May 1968, whose makeshift tents and shelters they called "Resurrection City" (see p.61). More recently still, in 1995, Nation of Islam leader Louis Farrakhan harangued white America from the terrace steps while addressing the Million Men March.

You can simply stroll into the Capitol for a look around (see "Visiting the Capitol" p.7). When Congress is **in session** (every year, from January 3, as prescribed in the Constitution, until close of business, usually in the fall) the lantern above the dome is lit, and flags fly above Senate or House wings.

History

A chaste plan, sufficiently capacious and convenient for a period not too remote, but one to which we may reasonably look forward, would meet my idea in the Capitol.

George Washington, 1792

In the best democratic fashion, the **design** of the US Capitol was thrown open to public competition in 1792. It was won by a dabbling amateur, **Dr William Thornton**, whose plan, it was agreed brought a certain pomp deemed appropriate for the meeting place of Congress. In particular, he dreamed up the domed rotunda, the feature that two centuries later grants the building its towering authority over the city skyline. The cornerstone was laid by George Washington on September 18, 1793, but by the time the government moved to Washington from Philadelphia seven years later, work was nowhere near completion. Not only did President John Adams move into an unfinished White House (see p.146), but on November 22, 1800 Congress assembled for the first time in the half-built brick-and-sandstone Capitol, which still lacked its rotunda and most of its offices: only a small north wing was ready, housing the Senate Chamber, the House of Representatives, Supreme Court and Library of Congress. What ceilings there were leaked, and the furnaces installed to heat the building produced intolerable temperatures. Adams' successor, Jefferson (the first president to be inaugurated inside the Capitol), appointed the respected **Benjamin Latrobe** as Surveyor of Public Buildings in an attempt to speed up work, and by 1807 a south wing had been built for the House of Representatives. In addition, Latrobe added a second floor to the north wing, allowing separate chambers for the Supreme Court and the Senate.

In **1814** the Capitol suffered the same fate as the President's house, as British troops burned the seat of government virtually to the ground. Indeed, with President Madison having fled the city, it was touch and go whether Washington – never a hugely popular choice as capital – would again house executive and legislative arms of the government. But with Madison later installed in The Octagon (p.163), Congress met for four years in a quickly built "Brick Capitol" – on the site of today's Supreme Court – while restoration work continued on what was left of the original Capitol.

It wasn't much. Latrobe found the interior gutted and the surviving exterior walls blackened by smoke; the British soldiers, it seemed, had stacked up all the furniture they could find in one of the rooms and lit a bonfire. Commissioned to rebuild and expand the Capitol, Latrobe's rather grandiose ideas found few admirers and in 1817 he was replaced by Charles Bulfinch. The reconstructed wings were re-opened in 1819 and, finally, in 1826 the Capitol appeared in a form that Thornton might have recognized, complete with central **rotunda**, topped by a low wooden dome wrapped in copper.

By the 1850s Congress had again run out of space and plans were laid to build magnificent, complementary wings on either side of the building and replace the dome with something more substantial. The new south wing, ready in 1857, now contained the **House Chamber**; two years later, the **Senate Chamber** moved to the new north wing. The Civil War threatened to halt work on the dome, but Abraham Lincoln was determined that the Capitol should be completed, recognizing the building as an enduring symbol of the Union he was pledged to defend. A cast-iron **dome** was painstakingly assembled, though the work was hampered by the presence of Union troops stationed in the Capitol; a company made up of enlisted fire fighters insisted on shinning up and down hundred-foot ropes draped from the Rotunda walls for amusement. But in December 1863 the splendid project came to fruition. Hoisted on top of the white-painted dome was a nineteen-foot-high **statue of Freedom** by sculptor Thomas Crawford, resplendent in feathered helmet and clutching a sword and shield (which gives it its alternative name of "Armed Liberty").

Give or take a few minor additions, the US Capitol building today shows little external change from this last burst of construction. The surrounding **terraces** were added after the Civil War and when extra office space was required this century, separate **House and Senate office buildings** were built in the streets either side of the Capitol, with tunnels to connect the legislators with their places of work. The Capitol's East Front was extended in 1962 and faced in marble to prevent the original sandstone from deteriorating further; thus far, the West Front – now the oldest original part of the building – has avoided modern accretions, though it, too, was restored in the 1980s.

Visiting the Capitol

The Capitol is the only building in Washington DC not to have an address, since it stands foursquare at the centre of the street plan: the city quadrants extend from the building, and the numbered and lettered streets count away from its central axis. For the same reason, the building doesn't have a front or a back, simply an "East Front" and a "West Front": the **public entrance** is at the East Front, where, from 1829 to 1977, all presidents were inaugurated.

From Memorial to Labor Day, there are free brass band concerts (Mon–Fri 8pm) on the East steps. And on the two holidays themselves, as well as 4 July, the National Symphony Orchestra performs on the West Terrace.

There's free, **walk-in access** all year to the Rotunda, Statuary Hall, the old Senate and Supreme Court chambers, and the Crypt. From April to September you can expect to have to **wait in line** for maybe one or two hours: lines are much shorter (or non-existent) in winter, and generally less busy on Sunday or between noon and 1.30pm most other days. Once inside the Rotunda, you can join a **free guided tour** (every 15min 9am–3.45pm), though there's nothing to stop you wandering off on your own. That said, it's hard to find your way around, even with the information desks, signposts and the omnipresent Capitol police officers to keep you on the right track. Note that there's a split between the House side (to the south) and Senate side (north) inside the Capitol; for details on visiting the House and Senate chambers, see p.114.

The Rotunda and National Statuary Hall

Standing in the **Rotunda**, you're not only at the centre of the US Capitol but at point zero of the entire city. It's a magnificent space:

180ft high and 96ft across, with the dome canopy decorated by Constantino Brumidi's almighty **fresco** depicting the *Apotheosis of Washington*. The painting took the sixty-year-old Brumidi almost a year to complete – like the Renaissance masters, he was forced to work lying on his back in a wooden cradle – and shows George Washington surrounded by symbols representing American democracy, arts, science, industry, and the thirteen original states; though they look lifesized from the floor, each of the figures is 15ft high. Brumidi had a hand, too, in the **frieze** celebrating American history that runs around the Rotunda wall, which starts with Columbus's arrival in the New World and continues clockwise, through the ages, finishing with Civil War scenes.

*US citizens
can contact
their represen-
tative or sena-
tor to arrange
a climb up to
the dome – not
available to
walk-in visi-
tors.*

From the floor, it's hard to see much detail of either frieze or fresco, and eyes are drawn instead to the eight large **oil paintings** that hang below the frieze. Four depict events associated with the "discovery" and settlement of the country – Columbus again, and the embarkation of the Pilgrims among them – though the most notable are the four of the Revolutionary War period by John Trumbull, who had trained under the celebrated Benjamin West. George Washington is represented with a fair accuracy; and so he should, since Trumbull once served as his aide-de-camp.

Consciously or not, William Thornton, the Capitol's first architect, had taken Rome's Pantheon as his model and it's fitting that busts and statues of prominent American leaders fill in the gaps in the rest of the Rotunda. Washington, Jefferson, Lincoln and Jackson are all here, along with a modern bust of Dr Martin Luther King Jr and a gold-and-glass facsimile of the Magna Carta (the original was loaned to the Capitol during the 1976 Bicentennial). In such august surroundings, 27 prominent members of Congress, military leaders and eminent citizens (including nine presidents from Lincoln to Johnson) have been **laid in state** before burial; the most recent was Claude Pepper (Florida congressman and senator), in 1989.

From the Rotunda, you move south into one of the earliest extensions of the building, the section that once housed the chamber of the House of Representatives. The acoustics are such that John Quincy Adams (a brass floor plate marks the site of his desk) was supposed to have been able to eavesdrop on opposition members on the other side of the room – something that is invariably demonstrated on the tour. When the House moved into its new wing in 1857, the chamber saw a variety of temporary uses – Anthony Trollope bought gingerbread from a market stall in here – until Congress decided to invite each state to contribute two statues of its most famous citizens for display in a **National Statuary Hall**. Around forty are still on show in the hall, with the others scattered around the corridors in the rest of the building; few are of any great distinction. That of suffragette Susan B Anthony (one of just six statues of women in the entire building) was recently dusted off after years hidden in the Crypt to be placed in the Rotunda – the only woman so honoured.

The Old Senate Chamber, Supreme Court and the Crypt

North of the Rotunda, there's access to the **Old Senate Chamber**, built in 1810 and reconstructed from 1815 to 1819 after the British had done their worst. The Senate met in this splendid semicircular gallery, with its embossed rose ceiling, until 1859 when it moved into its current quarters. The chamber then housed the Supreme Court (see over) until it, too, received a new building in 1935, after which the Old Senate Chamber lay largely unused until restored to its mid-nineteenth-century glory in time for the Bicentennial. Its furnishings are redolent of that period, during which the Senate's membership increased from 46 to 64 (two senators for each state) in step with the number of states admitted to the Union. In its heyday, the chamber made a formidable impression upon visitors, like Anthony's pioneering mother Fanny Trollope, whose travelogue, *Domestic Manners of the Americans*, published in 1832, amused Europe but outraged America with its trenchant observations. Sorely unimpressed with the goings-on in the House chamber, whose representatives were "sitting in the most unseemly attitudes, a large majority with their hats on", she was considerably more taken with the Senate, or at least the senators, who "generally speaking, look like gentlemen . . . and the activity of youth being happily past, they do not toss their heels above their heads". The members' desks today are reproductions, but the gilt eagle topping the Vice President's chair is original, as is the portrait of George Washington by Rembrandt Peale.

For more on Rembrandt Peale and his remarkable family, see p.89.

Contemporary engravings helped restorers reproduce other features of the original Senate chamber, like the rich red carpet emblazoned with gold stars. As Charles Dickens noted when he visited, the original carpet received severe punishment from "tobacco-tinctured saliva" despite the provision of a cuspidor by every desk – the universal disregard of which led to "extraordinary improvements on the pattern which are squirted and dabbled upon it in every direction". If visitors dropped anything on the floor, they were enjoined "not to pick it up with an ungloved hand on any account". Yet, doubtless squelching underfoot as they stood to speak, members of this Senate chamber participated in some of the most celebrated **debates** of the era: in 1830 the great orator Daniel Webster of Massachusetts fiercely defended "Liberty and the Union" in a famous speech lasting several hours; over two days in 1850 Henry Clay pleaded his succession of compromises to preserve the Union (brandishing a fragment of Washington's coffin for emphasis); while in 1856, Senator Charles Sumner of Massachusetts – having, unwisely perhaps, talked too forthrightly against the Kansas-Nebraska Bill (extending slavery, which Sumner branded a "harlot", into the Great Plains) – was beaten senseless at his desk by an incensed congressman from South Carolina.

The US Capitol

Before 1810, the Senate met on the floor below the Old Senate Chamber, in a room which architect Latrobe later revamped to house the Supreme Court. This sorely needed a permanent home: while the work was being carried out, sessions were often held in an inn opposite the Capitol, while once the British had delayed matters by burning the rest of the building, the nation's highest tribunal was forced to meet in rented townhouses on the Hill. However, by 1819 the Court was in residence in this chamber, where it remained until 1860, before moving again – confusingly, upstairs, to the chamber just vacated by the Senate. The **Old Supreme Court Chamber** served as a law library until 1950, after which it, too, was restored to its mid-nineteenth-century appearance, its dark, comfortable recesses resembling a gentleman's club – which, in many ways, it was. Again, some of the furnishings are original, including the desks, tables and chairs, and the busts of the first five chief justices.

Having viewed the historic chambers, spare a moment for the **Crypt**, on the same level as the Old Supreme Court Chamber, underneath the Rotunda. Lined with Doric columns, it was designed to house a tomb containing George Washington's body, a plan that was never realized; he's buried with his wife, Martha, at Mount Vernon (see p.254). The Crypt instead serves as an exhibition centre, displaying details of the plans submitted for the 1792 architectural competition and snippets about the Capitol's construction.

The House and Senate Chambers and Office Buildings

Both houses have their own unique lunch spots: Senate refectory *(Mon–Fri 8am–4pm),* House restaurant *(Mon–Fri 8–11am & 1.30–2.30pm), and* Dirksen Building buffet *(1st and C NE; Mon–Fri 11.30am–2.30 pm).*

To gain entrance to the **visitors' galleries** of either the House or the Senate, **American citizens** must apply to their representative's or senator's office well in advance for a pass valid for the entire (two-year) session of Congress. **Foreign citizens** need to present their passport either at the House or Senate appointments desk, both on the first floor; they'll be given a day pass for either body. To find out where a particular office or desk is, ask any Capitol police officer, or call Capitol **information** (☎224-3121), the House sergeant-at-arms (☎225-2456) or Senate sergeant-at-arms (☎224-2341).

The **House and Senate chambers** may well be empty, or deep in torpor, when you show up, which is fine if all you want is a flavour of either place. Both chambers are suitably grand, and if you've already glimpsed the Old Senate Chamber you'll know what to expect. The House chamber is the most imposing, with its decorative frieze and oil paintings; from here the President addresses joint sessions of Congress, including making the annual State of the Union speech. If you're lucky, you may coincide with members introducing legislation or even voting on various bills or issues (or at least hear the bells and see the flashing lights summoning the members to vote).

For more on the American system of government, see the Contexts *feature on p.319.*

However, most of the day-to-day fun and fireworks take place in committee rooms either in the Capitol or in the **House and Senate Office Buildings** on each side. The first of these six office buildings – named for past politicians – were built in 1908–09, the last in 1982, and they now house regular committee hearings, which have been open to the public since the 1970s. The buildings also contain the public and private offices of most representatives and senators. These follow the pattern of the Capitol in that the Senate Office Buildings (Russell, Dirksen and Hart) are to the north, the House Office Buildings (Cannon, Longworth and Rayburn) to the south: to reach them from the Capitol, head for the basement and ride the **Capitol subway** to the Senate offices or follow the pedestrian tunnels to the House offices. **Committee hearings** (usually held in the morning) are listed in the *Washington Post*'s "Today in Congress" section: unless you turn up early, you may not get in, especially to anything current-ly featured on the TV news. Of course, within reason you can simply wander around the buildings themselves, though there's little point unless you're a student of the minutiae of American politics, or have a wish to see the office of a particular senator or representative.

Only in the Senate **Hart Building** (on Constitution Ave NE at 2nd), is there anything to look at: dominating the atrium, Alexander Calder's monumental *Mountains and Clouds* was his last work – and the only one to combine a separate mobile and stabile. There are security checkpoints at the street-level entrances to the Hart Building, but visitors are free to pass through to see the sculpture.

The office buildings all have street access nearest Metros are Union Station for the Senate offices and Capitol South for the House offices.

West of the Capitol

Although, technically, the Capitol has no front (or at least no back), the **West Front** facade – facing the Mall – gets most photo calls, and from the terrace steps the views down the Mall to the Washington Monument are rightly lauded. Presidential **inauguration ceremonies** have taken place in the plaza here since 1981; before that, they were consigned to the more confined space at the East Front.

Two low-key memorials – to Peace and to assassinated twentieth President James Garfield (shot only four months after his inaugur-ation) – flank the **Capitol Reflecting Pool**, added in 1970, a stretch of water which mirrors in style that in front of the Lincoln Memorial, more than a mile away. But the most significant structure here is the 250-foot long **Grant Memorial**, a group statue honouring **Ulysses S Grant**, general-in-chief of the Union forces under President Lincoln (and the first since George Washington to hold the rank). Dedicated in 1922, it's an overbearing martial monument depicting a sombre Grant on horseback, facing the Mall, guarded by lions and oversee-ing an artillery unit moving through thick mud into battle (south side) and a charging cavalry unit (north side). Sculptor Henry Merwin Shrady took twenty years over the work, using uniformed soldiers in training as his models. The memorial is suitably single-tracked about Grant's achievements, focusing on his career as a sol-dier (as which he was formidable) rather than as twice-elected President (in which capacity he was undistinguished, verging on the corrupt; in the late nineteenth century, "Grantism" became a term synonymous with graft). In waging total war on the Confederate forces from 1864 to 1865 Grant secured final victory for Lincoln and the preservation of the Union, albeit at the cost of thousands of lives. Contemporaries talked of his personal shortcomings – he was once described as "an ordinary scrubby-looking man with a slightly seedy look" – and of his drinking habits: only Mrs Grant could keep him in check and when the general went on a drinking bout too far his aides would summon her to the front to sober him up. But Lincoln knocked back all complaints, recognizing his incalculable military worth: "You just tell me the brand of whisky Grant drinks", thundered the President, "I would like to send a barrel of it to my other generals".

South of the Reflecting Pool, there's quiet relief in the **United States Botanic Gardens**, at 245 1st St SW, at Independence Ave (daily 9am–5pm; free; ☎225-8333); guided tours (10am & 2pm) lead you past colourful ranks of tropical, subtropical and desert plants. While you're here, cross the avenue for a closer look at the marine-style **Bartholdi Fountain** (between Canal and 1st), the work of French sculptor Frédéric Auguste Bartholdi, who submitted it to the Centennial Exhibition in Philadelphia in 1876 – there's no hint here that Bartholdi would go on to create, just a decade later, one of America's most enduring icons, the Statue of Liberty.

East of the Capitol

All the other notable buildings and institutions of Capitol Hill – like the Supreme Court and the Library of Congress – lie on the east side of the Capitol, within half a dozen blocks of each other. Unlike the Capitol, you have to choose your day to tour these places: the Supreme Court is closed at weekends, while other buildings are closed on all or part of Sunday.

The Supreme Court

1st St and Maryland Ave NE ☎479-3211; Union Station Metro. Mon–Fri 9am–4.30pm. Admission free.

*For an
account of the
various homes
occupied by
the Supreme
Court in
Washington,
see p.114.*

First stop after the Capitol for most visitors is the pseudo-Greek marble temple that houses the **Supreme Court of the United States**, the nation's final arbiter of what is and isn't legal. Since it was established at the Philadelphia Constitutional Convention of 1787, the court has functioned as both the guardian and interpreter of the Constitution, flexing its muscular, judicial arm of government in favour of "Equal Justice For All" – the legend inscribed upon the architrave above the double row of eight columns facing 1st Street.

Oddly, for such a crucial pin in the American political system, the Supreme Court was forced to share quarters in the US Capitol until 1935, when on the prompting of William Howard Taft (then chief justice and formerly president – the only man to hold both offices) it was finally granted its own building. The architect, **Cass Gilbert**, seventy years old at the time, was perhaps an odd choice, known primarily for his tongue-in-cheek Gothic Woolworth Building in New York. But in Washington he behaved himself and in the dazzling Corinthian harmony of the Supreme Court – completed after his death – Cass' building shares its influences with those of the contemporaneous Federal Triangle. So well did it fit with the spirit of the age that Cass was unnerved by the compliments bestowed upon him – "It is receiving so much favourable praise [he wrote in 1933] that I am wondering what is wrong with it".

Absolutely nothing. **Outside**, the building positively glistens as natural light bounces back off the bright, white marble, while the wide steps down to 1st Street are flanked by **sculptures** (by James Earle Fraser) of the Contemplation of Justice and the Guardian of Law. Solemn, if not pompous, their effect is lightened somewhat when you cast your eyes up to the sculpted **pediment** over the main entrance; here, among allegorical Greek figures are relaxed representations of chief justices Taft (far left, portrayed as a Yale student) and Marshall (far right, reclining), while clad in togas are Gilbert (third from left) and sculptor Robert Aitken (second from right).

Inside, the main corridor – known as the **Great Hall** – features a superb carved and painted ceiling of floral plaques, while its echoing white walls are lined with marble columns, interspersed with busts of all the former chief justices. At the end of the corridor is the surprisingly compact **Court Chamber**, flanked by more marble columns and decorated with damask drapes and a moulded plaster ceiling picked out in gold leaf. A frieze runs around all four sides, its relief panels depicting various legal themes, more allegorical figures and lawgivers ancient and modern. When in session, the chief justice sits in the centre of the **bench** (below the clock), with the most senior justice on his right and the next in precedence on his left; the rest sit in similar alternating fashion so that the most junior justice sits on the far right (left as you face the bench); almost interestingly, the chairs for each justice are made in the Court's own carpentry shop.

Visiting the Supreme Court

The court is **in session** from October to June. Between the beginning of October and the end of April, oral arguments are heard every Monday, Tuesday and Wednesday from 10am to noon and 1pm to 3pm for two weeks each month. The cases to be heard are listed in the day's *Washington Post* (or call the Supreme Court for information) and the sessions, which last one hour per case, are open to the public on a first-come, first-served basis. They are rarely particularly illuminating for lay persons, but if you really want to witness an entire session arrive by 8.30am to be assured of getting one of the 150 seats. Most casual visitors simply join the separate line, happy to settle for a brief, three-minute stroll through the standing gallery. In May and June on Mondays, fifteen- to thirty-minute public sessions deal with

The Supreme Court

*The duties of the Supreme Court are the simplest and best
defined of any part of government. The Supreme Court justices
have to do nothing but sit and let others make ugly fools of themselves in front of the Supreme Court bench.*

P J O'Rourke

The Constitution established the **Supreme Court** in an attempt to oversee
the balance between the federal government and the states, and between
the legislature and the executive; the Court itself (and the associated system of district courts) convened for the first time in February 1790. At the
end of the following year, the ratification of the Bill of Rights in effect gave
the Supreme Court a further role – it was to defend the liberties enshrined
in the Bill, directing the country as to what was and wasn't constitutional.
However, it wasn't until 1803 and the case of *Marbury v Madison* that
the Court's power of judicial review – the ability to declare a law or action
of Congress or President unconstitutional – was established. Since then,
the Supreme Court has repeatedly directed the country's political debate
by declaring on the constitutionality of subjects as diverse as slavery (as in
the 1857 *Dred Scott* case), civil rights (1954 *Brown v Board of
Education*, which outlawed school segregation), abortion (*Roe v Wade* in
1973) or political freedom (Pentagon Papers and Watergate tapes cases in
the early 1970s).

Because of the vagueness of parts of the Constitution, and the fact that
the country relies on an eighteenth-century document as the basis of its
twentieth-century political structure, the Supreme Court has its work cut
out providing interpretative rulings. In practice, as O'Rourke points out,
this leads to a great deal of arguing in front of the Supreme Court justices.
That said, even though it's the country's final court of appeal, the Supreme
Court takes only about five percent of the seven thousand cases a year it's
asked to hear by lower courts (choosing which to take by the so-called
"Rule of Four" – the agreement of four justices to hear a case). These it
grants *certiorari* – the prospect of making a case "more certain" – and
then proceeds to hear written and oral arguments. After the deliberations,
one justice is made responsible for writing the **opinion**, which then forms
the latest interpretation of that particular constitutional issue. The justices
don't all have to agree: they can **concur** in the majority decision even if
they don't accept all the arguments; or they can produce a **dissenting
opinion**, which might be cited in future challenges to particular laws.

the rather less interesting reading of orders and opinions. When court
is not in session, guides give informative **lectures in the Court
Chamber** (Mon–Fri 9.30am–3.30pm; hourly on the half-hour).

On the **ground floor**, which has its own Great Hall overseen by a
mighty statue of Chief Justice John Marshall lounging in his chair,
there's a permanent **exhibition** about the Court: a free, short movie
fills you in on the political and legal background while architectural
notes, sketches and photos trace the history of the building itself.
You'll also find toilets, a gift shop, snack bar (10.30am–3.30pm) and
cafeteria (7.30–10.30am & 11.30am–3.30pm) on this level.

Contributing to these opinions are nine judges, or **justices**, who are appointed by the President, though their positions have to be confirmed by the Senate. One is named **chief justice**, though the position is not necessarily reserved for the most senior figure on the bench (or even for a justice already on the Supreme Court – a chief justice can be appointed from outside). Once appointed, they're in for life ("during good behaviour" as the Constitution has it) and can only be removed by impeachment. And, at $160,000 a year ($170,000 for the chief), the justices are pulling in a federal salary second only to the President.

Given the system, it's obvious that the make-up of the Supreme Court is of the utmost relevance to the opinions it might produce. Not surprisingly, presidents down the years have thought it useful to have **politically sympathetic** justices on the bench and have made appointments accordingly. But the process is tinged with an element of luck, depending on the longevity of the existing crop: both Dwight D Eisenhower and Richard Nixon, for example, got to appoint four justices, Jimmy Carter none. Controversial Supreme Court nominees can be rejected by the Senate – two of Nixon's were, as was Reagan's pet conservative judge, Robert Bork; Bush's second appointee, Clarence Thomas, only scraped through after the highly publicized hearings following allegations of sexual harassment against Anita Hill. And even when presidents do get the justices they want, they don't always want what they get: Earl Warren, appointed by the staunchly conservative Eisenhower, turned out to head the most liberal Court this century, his interpretation of the constitutional definition of "civil rights" facilitating presidents Kennedy and Johnson with their radical domestic programme.

Whichever way the Court leans, and despite its firm roots in the Constitution, it depends ultimately on the mood of the people for its authority. If it produces opinions that are overwhelmingly opposed by inferior courts, or by President or Congress, there's not much it can do to enforce them: indeed, Congress actually has the constitutional right (Article 3, Section 2) to restrict the Court's jurisdiction – a notion proposed by FDR when he tired of the Court's constant interference with his New Deal legislation. Strangely perhaps, and virtually unique among federal institutions, the Court has retained the respect of most of the population, not necessarily for the decisions of its justices (which are often viewed as confused or conflicting) but for its perceived impartiality in defending the Constitution against encroachment by that most hated of species – the politicians.

Sewall-Belmont House

144 Constitution Ave NE ☎546-3989; Union Station Metro. Tues–Fri 11am–3pm, Sat noon–4pm. Admission free.

North of the Court, across Constitution Avenue at 2nd Street, the redbrick townhouse known as the **Sewall-Belmont House** is among the oldest private residences in the city. Overwhelmed by the surrounding Senate Office monoliths, parts of the dainty building date back an astonishing – for Washington – three hundred years. However, like most of historical Capitol Hill its aspect is firmly early nineteenth century, dating from the restructuring carried out in 1800 by its owner Robert Sewall. He was succeeded in the house by Albert Gallatin, secretary of the Treasury under Jefferson. Gallatin took part in the negotiations for the Louisiana Purchase (1803), which was signed in one of the front rooms – and which, acquiring all land west of the Mississippi to the Rockies, at a stroke roughly doubled the size of the country for a mere $12 million. In 1814, while the Capitol was burning, a group of soldiers under Commander Joshua Barney retreated to the house and fired upon the British. It was virtually the sole act of resistance in Washington itself, but only stirred the British to have a go at setting the house ablaze too. Unlike the Capitol, it wasn't too badly damaged; intact enough, in fact, for Gallatin later to negotiate the Treaty of Ghent here which ended the war.

Although negotiated in the Sewall-Belmont House, the Treaty of Ghent was signed in The Octagon; see p.163.

In 1929, the house was sold to the **National Woman's Party** and was home for many years to Alice Paul, the party's founder and author of the 1923 Equal Rights Amendment. The house is still the party headquarters, and maintains a museum and gallery relating to the country's women's and suffrage movements. If the door's closed, ring the bell and you'll be escorted around on a short tour which makes much of the period furnishings. There are portraits, busts and photographs of all the best-known activists, starting in the lobby with suffragist sculptor Adelaide Johnson's formidable busts of Susan B Anthony, Elizabeth Cady Stanton and Lucretia Mott; Alice Paul is here, too, while nearby hangs the banner used to picket the White House during World War I as the clamour for universal suffrage reached its loudest pitch.

Folger Shakespeare Library

201 E Capitol St SE ☎544-4600; Union Station or Capitol South Metro; bus #40, 44 or 96. Mon–Sat 10am–4pm. Admission free.

On the south side of the Supreme Court, the renowned **Folger Shakespeare Library** provides an unexpected burst of Art Deco architecture, with a sparkling white marble facade, split by geometric window grilles and panel reliefs depicting scenes from the Bard's plays. Inside, however, the expansive 1930s mood is immediately transformed by a dark oak-panelled Elizabethan Great Hall, featuring carved lintels, stained glass, Tudor roses and a fine, sculpted ceiling. Founded in 1932, the Folger now holds over 300,000 books, manuscripts, paintings and engravings, accessible to scholars, and has also evolved over the decades into a celebration of Shakespeariana. The Great Hall displays changing exhibitions about the playwright and Elizabethan themes; the reproduction Elizabethan Theatre hosts lectures and readings, as well as medieval and Renaissance music concerts by the Folger Consort (see p.295); there's even an Elizabethan garden outside on the east lawn, growing herbs and flowers popular in the sixteenth century.

For more background, aim to coincide with one of the free **guided tours** (Mon & Wed–Sat 11am, Tues 10am & 11am; 90min); every third Saturday, from April through October (10am & 11am), a guide also expounds upon the intricacies of the garden. You should be able to take a quick look inside the theatre on most days; the library itself – another masterfully reproduced sixteenth-century room – is open to the public during the Folger's annual celebration of Shakespeare's birthday (usually the Saturday nearest April 23). Finally, as you'd expect, the **gift shop** sells everything from the Stratford lad's books to jokey T-shirts based on Shakespearean quotations, Elizabethan garden seeds, prints and postcards.

The Library of Congress

Jefferson Building, 10 1st St SE; Madison Building, 101 Independence Ave SE
☎707-5000 or 707-8000; Capitol South Metro. Mon–Fri 8.30am–9.30pm, Sat 8.30am–6pm, Sun 1–5pm. Admission free.

With Congress established in Washington in 1800 in its new, if incomplete, Capitol building, it was considered imperative to fund a library for the use of the members. Five thousand dollars were made available to buy books for a **Library of Congress**, which was housed in a small room in the original north wing. Calamitously, the carefully chosen reference works were all lost when the British burned the Capitol in 1814, an act which prompted Thomas Jefferson to offer his considerable personal library as a replacement. This was no empty gesture – at his retirement home at Monticello Jefferson was surrounded by over six thousand volumes, which he had accumulated during fifty years of service at home and abroad, picking up, he said, "everything which related to America". But neither was it an act of selfless charity: Jefferson's extravagant lifestyle always left him short of money so he was doubtless delighted when, in 1815, Congress voted to buy this stupendous private collection for almost $24,000, a massive sum for the age.

Jefferson's sale laid the foundation for a rounded collection, but another fire in 1851, this time accidental, caused severe damage. From that point, the library was forced to rely on donations and select purchases until it received two major boosts. In 1866, it acquired the thousands of books hitherto held by the Smithsonian Institution, and in 1870 was declared the national copyright library – adding to its shelves a copy of every book published and registered in the United States. Almost overnight, the Library of Congress was transformed into the world's largest library, and with time and technological progress books became the least part of its unimaginably large collection. Today, 98 million items (from books, maps and manuscripts to movies, musical instruments and photographs) are kept on 600 miles of shelving; it's said that on average ten items a minute are added to the library's holdings.

Hardly surprisingly, the library soon outgrew its original home and in 1897 the exuberantly eclectic **Thomas Jefferson Building** opened across from the Capitol, complete with domed octagonal Reading Room and flourishing hundreds of mosaics, murals and sculptures. This was projected to have enough space to house the library until 1975; by the 1930s it, too, was full, and in the surrounding blocks the **John Adams Building** was erected in 1939, followed by the **James Madison Memorial Building** in 1980. These three buildings today comprise the Library of Congress, which is open to the public either as readers and researchers or as visitors, who can see the best parts on guided tours.

Touring the library

Quite apart from the buildings – of which the Jefferson Building is one of the finest in the city – the Library of Congress attracts visitors to attend its changing exhibits of historic documents, concerts and lectures. From 1997 a permanent exhibition of its more renowned artefacts will include Jefferson's letter of 1814 to President Madison offering to sell his personal library to Congress.

Start in the massive marble **Madison Building** (Independence Ave between 1st and 2nd), picking up a *Calendar of Events* from the information desk in the lobby. In the hall to the left, beside the statue of fourth president James Madison, is displayed a treasured copy of the **Gutenberg Bible**. In the first-floor **Visitors' Orientation Theater**, you can watch a short film about the library (Mon–Fri 9am–9pm, Sat 9am–5.30pm; every 30min); while up on the fourth floor the **Copyright Office** maintains a rather dull exhibition about its work. Two floors up is the **cafeteria** (Mon–Fri 9–10.30am & 12.30–3pm).

The best way to see the buildings is on one of the free **library tours** (Mon–Fri 11am & 2pm, subject to change), which start at the **Jefferson Building** (West Front entrance, on 1st St). Taking the buildings of the Italian Renaissance as their model, architects John L Smithmeyer and Paul J Pelz produced a peach, centred on a domed reading room and flaunting a **Great Hall** that, after a decade of restoration, is again looking its best: marble walls and floors that were once blackened by the smoke from coal fires and the cinders from Union Station are now pristine, with the medallions, inscriptions, murals and inlaid mosaics as clear as the day they were fashioned. Upstairs, the visitor's gallery overlooks the octagonal marble-and-stained-glass **Main Reading Room**, a beautiful galleried space whose columns support a dome 125ft high. The mural in the dome canopy, the *Progress of Civilisation*, represents the twelve nations supposed to have contributed most to world knowledge.

Using the library

For research advice, call ☎ 707-6500; for reading room hours and locations, call ☎ 707-6400.

Anyone over high-school age carrying photo-ID can use the library, and around a million readers and visitors do each year; to find out what's where, head for the information desk in the Madison Building

lobby. The Main Reading Room in the Jefferson Building is just one
of 22 reading rooms; the rules are the same in each. It's a research
library, which means you can't take books out; in some reading
rooms you have to order what you want from the stacks. You can also
access papers, maps, and musical scores, many in machine-readable
format – the desks in the Main Reading Room are wired for laptops
and there are CD-ROM indexes. Major exhibitions, as well as prints,
photographs, films and speeches, are also available on-line.

Union Station and around

The Hill's northern limits incorporate **Union Station**, which stands
at the centre of a redevelopment plan designed to revitalize a formerly neglected part of the city. In addition to the station, a sight in
its own right, you should try to make time for the **National Postal
Museum** – the latest outpost of the Smithsonian Institution.

Union Station

The city's main railroad station, **Union Station**, at 50 Massachusetts
Ave NE, was built here in 1908 after the McMillan Commission
decreed an end to the chaos caused by the separate lines and stations
that criss-crossed the city. Its architect, Daniel H Burnham, a member of the commission, produced a classic Beaux Arts building of
monumental proportions to house the train sheds and waiting rooms,
alive with skylights, marble detail and statuary, culminating in a 96-
foot-high coffered ceiling covered in gold leaf. The model was no less
than the Baths of Diocletian, the relaxation spot of the militarily bold
and resolute third-century Roman emperor; the immense main waiting room is certainly imperial in scale if not in bathing appointments.
For five decades, the station sat at the head of an expanding railroad
network that linked the country to its capital: hundreds of thousands
of people arrived in the city by train, catching their first glimpse of
the Capitol dome through its great arched doors – just as the wide-
eyed James Stewart does at the beginning of Frank Capra's *Mr
Smith Goes to Washington*.

Come the 1960s, though, and the gradual depletion of train services, Union Station was left unkempt and underfunded. An ill-conceived scheme turned it into a visitor's centre during the
Bicentennial in 1976, and it wasn't fully **restored** until 1988. The
exterior is of a piece with much of monumental Washington, the
facade studded with allegorical statuary and etched with prolix texts
extolling the virtues of trade, travel and technology. Enter through
the main, triple-arched portico and you're immediately confronted
by the soaring vastness of its dimensions – the only other single-
roofed space in America to touch it is New York's Grand Central
Station, which is over 20,000 square feet smaller.

*Union Station
services:
Arrivals p.138
Car rental
agencies p.7
Cinema p.294
Departures
p.309
Food court
p.270
Restaurants
p.273*

Although you can still catch **trains** at Union Station – there's a Metro station on the east side of the building as well as *Amtrak* and *MARC* departures – the renovation project wouldn't have succeeded without its commercial adjuncts: the lower-gallery food court and cinema, and upper-floor stores, restaurants, money-exchange offices, car rental agencies, ticket counters and parking garage. Take a look at the statue near Gate C honouring **A Phillip Randolph**, founder of the Brotherhood of Sleeping Car Porters union and one of the prime movers in the 1963 March on Washington (see p.60).

It's also worth taking a turn outside in **Union Station Plaza**, the landscaped approach to the station that stretches all the way down to the Capitol grounds. In the middle, slap bang in front of the station (and destroying the sight lines to the Capitol), the **Columbus Memorial Fountain**, dedicated in 1912, features a statue of the old mercenary standing on the prow of a ship, between two lions and male and female figures representing old world and new; a replica of Philadelphia's Liberty Bell stands nearby.

The City Post Office: National Postal Museum

*For city post
office
locations, see
p.20.*

Having unwrapped the design for Union Station, Burnham turned his attention to a new **City Post Office** opposite the station (at Massachusetts Ave and N Capitol St); built between 1911 and 1914, it was used until 1986, when it was renovated at a cost of $200 million, in part to house a fascinating new National Postal Museum. Before you descend to the lower-level galleries, spare time for a quick look at the **building** itself, whose white Italian marble reaches are some of the most impressive in the city. In the style of the day, it is adorned with improving texts for the edification of the public: look up and strain to read how the postal service is "Messenger of Sympathy and Love . . . Consoler of the Lonely . . . . Enlarger of the Common Life" and "Carrier of News and Knowledge" among other treacly attributes. **Inside**, the main lobby has been restored to its 1914 appearance, full of burnished marble.

The museum

The **National Postal Museum** (daily 10am–5.30pm; free; ☎357-2700) is one of the Smithsonian's quiet triumphs. The collection, from the National Museum of American History, includes sixteen million artefacts, though since many of these are stamps, only a few of which are displayed, it's not that daunting a show. Indeed, the museum's strength is its selectivity, judiciously placing the history of the mail service within the context of the history of America itself.

Escalators down to the galleries dump you in **Moving the Mail**, basically an excuse to stack up some rattling pieces of machinery, from a Concord mail coach to a bi-plane. Beyond here you follow the first postal route, the seventeenth-century King's Best Highway between New York and Boston, while tracing the development of the

postal system – interactive video panels allow you to create your own
route between two towns in the 1850s, your choices determining
whether the mail gets through or not. It was soon clear that established overland mail routes helped attract commerce and settlers,
with President Buchanan envisaging a "chain of living Americans"
along the roads from east to west. Yet some of the most famous of
the pioneering stories turn out to be more hype than substance. The
relay-rider system of the famed *Pony Express* lasted for only two
years (1860–61), and although it cut mail delivery times in half –
from San Francisco to New York in thirteen days – the founding partners lost $30 on every letter carried; in the end, without government
backing, the private enterprise collapsed.

It was seventh president Andrew Jackson who first realized the
political importance of being able to rely on the mail, which could
disseminate information – and propaganda – quickly and efficiently
to even the most isolated communities; for a century after him,
whenever the party in power lost a presidential election, the employment patronage system led to a huge turnover in postal workers.
Photos and text trace the early racial make-up of the service, from
the opportunities offered to blacks during Reconstruction to the segregation measures introduced in 1913, which in DC led to the establishment of a post office on T Street in Shaw, staffed only by black
workers.

Elsewhere, there are examples of weird and wonderful rural mail-
boxes, including one made from car mufflers in the shape of a tin
man; while in a section devoted to **Postal Oddities** you'll find a paddle punch used to fumigate letters during Philadelphia's yellow fever
outbreak of 1890, as well as the uniform of the supremely annoying
Cliff Clavin, bar-fly and postie in *Cheers*. Only in **Stamps and
Stories** does the philatelic collection finally get a look-in – before
now, there's been barely a stamp to be seen. Along with some splendid rarities, you learn among other things about the research that
went into producing a gum that could be licked by those following a
vegetarian or kosher diet.

Before leaving (allow 90min or so), print out your free personal-
ized postcard at the machines in the lobby and buy a stamp from the
stamp store in order to mail it home.

East to Lincoln Park

East Capitol Street, one of the city's four axes, runs off between the
Supreme Court and the Library of Congress' Jefferson Building. One
of the first streets on the Hill to be settled, its wide tree-lined reach
presents a fine aspect for the first ten blocks or so, studded with
frame and brick townhouses, some dating from before the Civil War,
others sporting the trademark turrets and "rusticated" (roughened)
stonework so beloved of DC's turn-of-the-century builders.

East to Lincoln Park

Close to the Supreme Court, the typical row house at 316 A St NE was home to black orator and writer **Frederick Douglass** when he first moved to the capital in 1870 to take up the editorship of the *New National Era*, a newspaper championing the rights of African-Americans. His family owned no. 318, too, and Douglass lived here with his first wife Anna until 1877 when they moved to the rather grander Cedar Hill in Anacostia, which is where you'll have to go to discover more about his life (see p.139).

From here, it's just a few blocks north to **Stanton Park**, centred on its equestrian statue of Revolutionary General Nathanial Greene, though there's more interest in **Lincoln Park** further east along East Capitol Street, between 11th and 13th. In 1876, on the eleventh anniversary of Lincoln's assassination and in the presence of President Grant, Frederick Douglass read out the Emancipation Proclamation to the assembled thousands as the "Freedom Memorial" was unveiled in the centre of the specially designed park. It was paid for by funds collected from freed men and women; the first contributor, Charlotte Scott of Virginia, gave $5, "being her first earnings in freedom". To contemporary eyes it seems a paternalistic work, the bronze statue portraying Lincoln – proclamation in one hand – standing over a kneeling slave, exhorting him to rise. But it was considered rather daring in its day: working from a photograph, sculptor Thomas Ball re-created in the slave the features of one Archer Alexander, the last man to be seized under the Fugitive Slave Act, which empowered slaveowners to recapture escaped slaves – under Lincoln's gaze Alexander is breaking his own shackles.

Bus #96 runs along East Capitol St to Lincoln Park, from 1st St NE (Union Station/ Supreme Court).

It was a century, however, before any monument was erected in DC specfically to honour the achievements of a black American, or, indeed, a woman. Facing Lincoln, across the park, a second memorial – dedicated in 1974 – remembers **Mary McLeod Bethune**, educationalist, black women's leader and special advisor to Franklin Delano Roosevelt. Just as significant as the Lincoln statue, it is possibly even more striking: Robert Berks (responsible for the head of JFK in the Kennedy Center) provides an inimitable study of a stout Bethune, leaning on her cane, reaching out to two children, passing on, as the inscription says, her legacy to youth.

For more on Mary McLeod Bethune, see p.219.

East of the park the neighbourhood degenerates. Come here in daylight, peer up East Capitol Street to the **RFK Stadium** in the distance (home of the Washington Redskins; see p.309), but don't head there on foot.

Along and around Pennsylvania Avenue

Along the first few blocks of **Pennsylvania Avenue**, between 2nd Street and Eastern Market (at 7th), lie a score of bars and restaurants, including some notable Hill institutions: they're reviewed on p.284 (bars) and p.273 (restaurants). **Eastern Market** itself (7th and C, south of N Carolina Ave SE; Tues–Sat 7am–6pm, Sun 9am–4pm) makes a grand target, a red-brick edifice constructed in 1873 by Adolph Cluss, with rather less flamboyance than his Arts and Industries Building on the Mall. What it lacks in visual stimulus outside, though, it makes up for inside, where the traders continue to do roaring business: at the weekend, the stalls spill onto the sidewalk, when you can buy produce and flowers (Sat), or antiques and junk (Sun). On either side, along 7th Street, delis, coffee shops with outdoor seating, antique stores and clothes shops make it one of the more appealing hang-outs on the Hill.

There are more restored townhouses in the vicinity of Pennsylvania Avenue, and green splashes at places like Folger Square, Seward Square and Marion Park, but on the whole, the district south of, say, E Street is not one you want to wander around on your own. Two churches stand out, though, and in daylight at least there should be no problem in visiting them. The utilitarian red-brick **Ebenezer United Methodist Church** at 420 D St SE (Mon–Fri 8.30am–3pm, Sun service 11am; ☎544-1415) is the oldest black congregation in the neighbourhood. Founded in 1805, the church was the site of DC's first public school for black people, a short-lived affair (1864–65) though a pioneering one since the teachers were paid out of federal funds; the current building dates from 1897 and if you call in advance someone will be on hand to show you around. On the 4th Street side stands a wooden model of "Little Ebenezer", the original frame church which stood on this site. Further south, but unlikely to be open, **Christ Church** at 620 G St SE is an early work (1806) by Capitol architect, Benjamin Latrobe.

Along and around Pennsylvania Avenue

Transport: Eastern Market Metro, or bus #30, 32, 34, 35, 36 down Pennsylvania Ave.

Chapter 4

Southwest, Waterfront and Southeast

The **Southwest** quadrant, cut into by the encroaching curve of the river and East Potomac Park, is the most compact in the city: it's easy to loop through on your way from the Capitol to the Jefferson Memorial. This is the least distinguished of the city's areas – locals know it as the home of various federal agenices, while most visitors are hardly aware of its existence. Indeed, the district's two principal sights, the **Holocaust Memorial Museum** and the **Bureau of Engraving and Printing**, sit just off the Mall itself, necessitating only the merest diversion.

Museums aside, the bright spots are all down at the district's southwestern edge, by the restored **Waterfront**. Modern waterside apartment buildings have replaced nineteenth-century slum housing, and the area today is defined by its smart marina, promenades and seafood restaurants – useful lunch stops before walking back to the Mall or on to the monuments and memorials. The original fish market still survives, though in a much more regulated and less offensively smelly fashion than its eighteenth-century predecessor.

It's more of an effort (involving Metro, bus or taxi rides) to explore the limited attractions of Washington's **Southeast**, which straddles both sides of the Anacostia River. In reality, there's no exploration possible of this most blighted of neighbourhoods: visitors head directly to the three individual sights – the Navy Museum, the former home of black orator and writer Frederick Douglass, and the neighbourhood Anacostia Museum – and then come straight back again. To do anything else would be fruitless and possibly dangerous.

Southwest: Independence Avenue to L'Enfant Plaza

In the early nineteenth century, **SOUTHWEST** was a fashionable residential area, thriving on its proximity to the Capitol. But the arrival

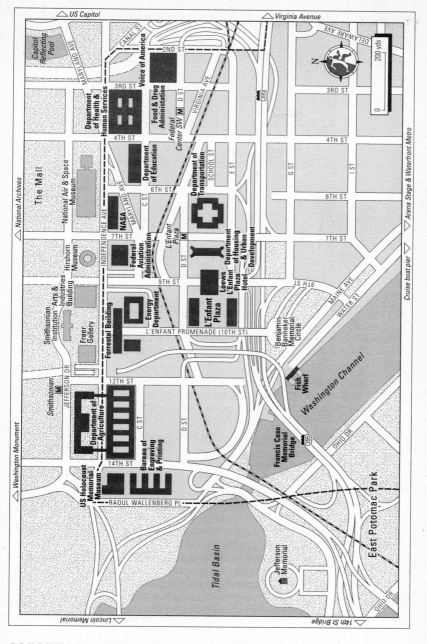

of the railroad in the 1870s, whose tracks cut right through the district – and still do – diminished its social cachet and the wealthy moved north of the Mall. Those left were mostly poor blacks, an influx of whom soon turned Southwest into the largest black neighbourhood in the city, its inhabitants working at the briefly flourishing goods yards, storage depots and wharves. As the work dried up, the swamp-ridden housing became ever more dilapidated, and by the 1920s the district had degenerated into a notorious slum. However, the federal government, looking for centralized office space, saw underutilized potential in the Southwest. The low-rent housing was demolished and families displaced to make room for federal **agencies**, including the Department of Agriculture and Bureau of Engraving and Printing, both of which still remain in situ; more agencies were added in the 1930s (to complement the work being undertaken across the Mall in Federal Triangle) and the 1960s. While these developments undoubtedly rescued Southwest from neglect, they also firmly stamped "federal" across its streets – there's little life here after 6pm on weekday evenings, even less at weekends, and few places to grab a coffee or sandwich that aren't brimming with office workers. There's a lack of architectural cohesion within the northern part of the quadrant too, certainly when compared to the public-works grandeur of Federal Triangle, just four blocks north.

Almost all the agencies are contained with a rectangle of land bounded by Independence Avenue, 3rd Street, E Street and 14th Street, and are served by two **Metro stations**, Federal Center SW and L'Enfant Plaza further west.

Voice of America

Heading west from the Capitol, you're not missing anything by sticking to **Independence Avenue** as far as 4th Street. The block between 3rd and 4th is taken up by the **Department of Health and Human Services**, whose imposing bulk makes it one of the few in Southwest to stand comparison with the classical entities of Federal Triangle; it dates from the same (late 1930s) period. It's the only federal building hereabouts open for public visits; part of the building houses the offices of the **Voice of America** (free 40-min tours Tues–Thurs 10.40am, 1.40pm & 2.40pm; ☎619-3919); the entrance is around the back, on C Street between 3rd and 4th.

Along with the BBC and Radio Moscow, the VOA is one of the world's three biggest international broadcasters, established in 1942 as part of the war effort and given its own charter in 1960 (as part of the US Information Agency) to disseminate overseas information radio programmes. In theory, the VOA Charter is as admirable as they come: "VOA will serve as a consistently reliable and authoritative source of news . . . [which] will be accurate, objective, and comprehensive." But, whichever way you cut it, its intention to "present the policies of the United States clearly and effectively" makes it a valuable propaganda tool for the government – which is why the VOA's broad-

casts have often been on the receiving end of jamming by various dis-
affected foreign powers. This, of course, is not something you hear too
much about on the tour, in which you're walked through the corridors
and studios from where broadcasts are made in 48 different languages
(including English) to 90 million listeners in 120 countries. It's only
really of interest if you've never been in a radio studio before, in which
case you'll be happy to get up close to broadcasters and journalists at
work (or at least reading the *Washington Post* and eating doughnuts).
The two most interesting discoveries are that you can call collect to
the *Talk to America* chatshow from anywhere in the world, a fact that
unsurprisingly isn't widely advertised; and that, as evidenced by the
photograph gallery of the personalities who've appeared on VOA over
the years, Telly Savalas once had a fine head of hair.

Other federal buildings

The other federal buildings – large, and largely unappealing structures – occupy a no-man's-land between 4th and 14th streets.
Presumably, it wasn't for want of trying that the area appears so
dreary: the Department of Transportation building (between D and E
at 7th) was designed by Edward Durrell Stone, who managed to
make the Kennedy Center stand out in similarly unpromising surroundings; while even I M Pei has had a hand in the regeneration of
the various plazas and streetscapes. But the only semblance of style
comes with the oldest (and westernmost) agency, the **Department of
Agriculture** (Independence Ave between 12th and 14th): sited here
since 1905, the original building on the north side of Independence
Avenue is connected by slender arches to the much larger, 1930s
classical structure across the avenue. The closest thing here to modern swagger is the curving double-Y-shaped concrete structure from
the late 1960s which holds the **Department of Housing and Urban
Development** (D St between 7th and 9th), whose architect, Marcel
Breuer, gave more than a nod to his Bauhaus origins.

L'Enfant Plaza

The main focus of development in Southwest in the 1960s and 1970s
was **L'Enfant Plaza**, at D Street between 9th and 10th, where there's
now also a useful Metro station. The buildings themselves, surrounding the plaza, are no more gripping than their neighbours, but
from the Metro station there's direct access into a huge underground
shopping mall and up into the luxurious **Loews L'Enfant Plaza
Hotel**, which occupies the entire east block of the plaza (see p.261).
Quite apart from being the one decent place in the district where you
can get a cup of coffee (in the *Café Pierre*), the outdoor terrace
which wraps around the hotel has great views. Nonetheless, it's easy
to feel a twinge of sympathy for Pierre L'Enfant – alone of the city's
spiritual founders, he gets not a monument but a windswept 1960s
concrete square and Metro station as his memorial.

Benjamin Banneker Memorial Circle

From the plaza, 10th Street is immediately accessible, forming a
landscaped mall (known as L'Enfant Promenade) which heads south
to the **Benjamin Banneker Memorial Circle**, where there's a viewpoint over the Washington Channel and Waterfront. The African-
American Banneker, born in Maryland in 1731 to a former slave and
a servant girl, was a remarkable figure. Almost entirely self-taught,
he distinguished himself as a mathematician, astronomer (he accu-
rately predicted a solar eclipse) and inventor (of, among other
things, a striking clock with every part made of wood) before, extraordinarily for the time and at the age of sixty, being invited to assist
in the surveying of the land for the new capital. He followed this coup
by publishing several editions of a successful almanac and spent his
last years (he died in 1806) in correspondence with Thomas
Jefferson, whom he hoped would abandon his "narrow prejudices"
against the native intelligence of African-Americans.

United States Holocaust Memorial Museum

100 Raoul Wallenberg Place SW; entrance on 14th St ☎ 488-0400; Smithsonian
Metro. Daily 10am–5.30pm; closed on Yom Kippur. Admission free.

Nothing in DC is more disturbingly unforgettable than the large and
symbolically sited **United States Holocaust Memorial Museum**. Just
a step from the Mall, and within the triangle formed by the city's three
great memorials to freedom, the museum commemorates in a uniquely provocative fashion the persecution and murder of six million Jews
by the Nazis. Upon entry, each visitor is given the ID card, containing
biographical notes, of a real Holocaust victim, whose fortunes are followed as the museum unfolds. This personalizes the fate of the affected individuals, while never losing sight of the wider historical machinations which allowed Hitler to assume power in the first place. The
detail throughout is perfectly pitched – highly informative and pulling
no punches, without being overly emotive. No knowledge of the
events of the Holocaust is assumed, and this too is deliberate: indeed,
however much you already know, nothing prepares you for this relent-
less, remorseless documentation of systematic brutality. The solemn
mood throughout is reflected by the museum's design, overseen in
part by noted Holocaust survivors. Half-lit chambers, a floor of ghetto cobblestones, an obscenely cramped barracks building, and an
external roofline which resembles the guard towers of a concentration
camp – all add to the overwhelming feeling of oppression. The themed
displays are a mix of personal possessions and photographs alongside
historical montages and video presentations, before which visitors
stand visibly moved. And on this level, certainly, the museum passes
the acid test: personal remembrance of an international horror.

Visiting the museum

Crowding can be a problem at the museum. To control the flow of people, **tickets** for fixed entry times are available free from 9am (limited to four per person). You can also book in advance through *Ticketmaster* (☎432-7328 or 1-800/551-7328; $4 fee). If you arrive without a ticket any later than mid-morning, you're unlikely to get into the permanent exhibition that day, but a certain number of temporary displays are usually open to all. Note that the main exhibitions were designed for **children** over eleven, though the less forbidding gallery, *Daniel's Story: Remember the Children*, is suitable for those over the age of eight.

The **permanent exhibitions** are on the second, third and fourth floors; you start at the top and work your way down. The 14th Street entrance is at first-floor level, where you'll find the information desk, children's exhibit and museum **shop**; stairs lead down to the auditoriums and **special exhibition** area at concourse level.

United States Holocaust Memorial Museum

The museum

The first rooms on the fourth floor chronicle the Nazi rise to power from 1933 to 1939 through story boards, newspapers, and film clips. The point that prejudice soon sweeps all before it is forcefully made: what started with the boycott of Jewish businesses and book-burning was swiftly followed by the organized looting of Jewish shops and the parading of German women who had "defiled" their race by associating with Jews. From there, anyone who didn't fit the Nazi ideal, like homosexuals (who were forced to wear a pink triangle), gypsies and even Freemasons were persecuted and imprisoned. Beyond a glass wall etched with the names of the hundreds of eastern European Jewish communities wiped off the map forever, a towering stack of photographs records the breadth of life in just one of them. Domestic life in the *shetl*, or community, of Eishishok (in what's now Lithuania) is vividly shown in street scenes, ceremonies, parties, family groups and portraits taken between 1890 and 1941.

There's a café in the Administrative Center, around at the Raoul Wallenberg Place (ie 15th St) entrance, open 9am–4.30pm.

The third floor covers the era of Hitler's **Final Solution**, beginning with the first gassing of Jews to take place at a death camp in Poland in December 1941. The Jews were transported to the camps from the **ghettos** in which they'd been incarcerated, most infamously at Warsaw. Even in the ghettos, there was **resistance** – although it's clear from the displays just how ultimately futile that proved to be. The slaughter at Babi Yar in Kiev (1941) claimed 33,000 Jewish lives in retaliation after Soviet saboteurs had blown up buildings in the city; in the Warsaw uprising of 1943, the resistance held out, remarkably, for a month but had no real weapons, no supplies and no hope. In the end, all the surviving ghetto Jews were taken to the camps in packed rail freight cars; the one that you can walk through in this section stands on railroad tracks taken from the camp at Treblinka.

The most harrowing part of the exhibition deals with life and death in the **concentration camps** themselves. There's an overwhelming poignancy in the pile of blankets, umbrellas, scissors, cutlery and other personal effects taken from the hundreds of thousands who arrived at the various camps expecting to be forced to work – most were gassed within hours. A re-created barracks building from Auschwitz provides the backdrop for the oral memories of some survivors, as well as concealing truly shocking film of gruesome medical experiments carried out on selected prisoners. At this point, many visitors, at least for a moment, are inconsolable; the survivors of course have lived with these memories all their lives.

Many histories claim that it was only after the war had ended that the full scale of these atrocities became apparent, but as the museum clearly – and uncomfortably – shows, the Americans knew of the existence of Auschwitz as early as May 1944 and yet refused to bomb it; Assistant Secretary of War John J Mclloy argued that its destruction "might provoke even more vindictive action by the Germans". It's a moot point now, though it's instructive that contemporary American Jewish organizations repeatedly demanded that the camps be bombed, while survivors later testified that they would have welcomed such terminal liberation – "Every bomb that exploded . . . gave us new confidence in life" records one witness. The third floor also ends with photographic coverage of the Eishishok *shetl*, this time relating it to the Final Solution. The pictures show a town and community that had existed for over nine hundred years completely destroyed, and its inhabitants (including two of the photographers) shot, in just two days.

As the Nazi front collapsed across Europe during 1945, many different groups became involved in efforts to save the Jews. The **Last Chapter** on the second floor recounts the heroism of particular individuals and the response of governments, among whom the Danes have most reason to feel secure that they did all they could to save their Jewish citizens. Much of the floor is taken up with details of the **liberation of the camps** by the Allied forces: film reels show German guards being forced to bury mountains of bodies in mass graves, while locals were made to tour the camps to witness the extent of the horror. If people later looked to the **war trials** in Nuremberg to draw a line under this evil, then there's little comfort offered here either. Despite the imprisonment and execution of various high-profile Nazis, and a continuing trickle of prosecutions over the years, most people responsible for the planning, maintenance and administration of the camps were never tried; thousands of others were treated leniently or acquitted altogether.

The sheer amount on display requires most visitors to spend at least three hours in the museum. There are rest areas throughout, and a contemplative **Hall of Remembrance** on the second floor. The **Wexner Learning Center**, on the same floor, has computer stations that allow you to access text, photographs, film and other sources.

The Bureau of Engraving and Printing

14th and C streets SW ☎ 622-2000; Smithsonian Metro. Mon–Fri 9am–2pm; closed Christmas to New Year. Admission free.

Half a million visitors a year wait patiently in line at the **Bureau of Engraving and Printing** before being led through narrow corridors for a tantalizing glimpse of the nation's money-making process. It must be the avaricious thrill of being close to so much money that drags in the crowds, because it certainly isn't the twenty-minute tour of what is, effectively, a large printing plant. The difference is that the presses here crank out millions of dollars in currency every day, $120 billion a year (95 percent of which is replacement currency for money already in circulation).

The Bureau is the federal agency for designing and printing all US currency, government securities and postage stamps (of which it produces 30 billion a year). It was established in 1862, when Abraham Lincoln empowered six employees to start up business in the attic of the Treasury Building (see p.153), sealing up blocks of $1 and $2 bills that had been printed by private banks. By 1877, all US currency was produced by the Bureau, which finally moved into this building in 1914. Nowadays, almost three thousand employees either work here or at a second plant in Fort Worth, Texas.

So much for the history, much of which is served up on video as you wait in line in the main corridor. What everyone wants to see is the cash, which is quickly revealed during the march through claustrophobic viewing galleries looking down upon the printing presses. It's a surprisingly low-tech operation: hand-engraved dyes are used to create intaglio steel plates, from which the bills are printed in sheets of 32, checked for defects and loaded into large barrows. On a separate press, they're then over-printed with serial numbers and seals, sliced up into single bills by ordinary paper cutters, and stacked into "bricks" of four thousand notes before being sent out to the twelve Federal Reserve Districts which issue the notes to local banks. Star facts, fired out amid lame jokes by the guides, include the Trivial Pursuit-winning knowledge that the notes aren't made from paper at all, but from a more durable fabric three-quarters cotton. Even so, the most-used note, the dollar bill, lasts only eighteen months on average. Those whose job it is to spot flaws in the currency get short shrift from federal-employee-baiting visitors, who see only a line of people with their heads in their hands gazing at bundles of notes. What you don't see in the two-minute gaze through the window is the rigour of the two-year apprenticeship that all undergo, or the eight-hour daily shift worked staring at one sheet a second, with just two twenty-minute breaks and a thirty-minute lunch. Yet they catch all but one in a thousand of misprinted bills. As a finale, guides deftly usher you in the **Visitor Center** (Mon–Fri 8.30am–3.30pm), which sells souvenirs like small bags of shredded currency – it's cheaper to provide yourself with two dollar bills and a pair of scissors from *WalMart*.

Despite the relative ordinariness of the process, the tour is immensely popular and between Easter and Memorial Day you must go first to the kiosk on the 15th Street side of the building to pick up **tickets**, which have often all gone by 11.30am. At other times, you can simply turn up, though you'll still have to wait in line.

The Waterfront

Downtown Washington has always been rather removed from the rivers (Potomac and Anacostia) on which the city stands. They meet at a Y-junction some considerable way from the Mall and the other central axes, and for a century after the city was founded, the nearest accessible riverbanks (in today's West Potomac Park) were too marshy and malarial to develop anyway. The only practicable wharves and piers were those built along the Washington Channel, the thin finger of water that sheers off from the Potomac, but this too had a tendency to stagnate – at least until the Tidal Basin was created this century, the opening of whose gates now serves to flush the channel clean after every tide. The rather hapharzardly developed commercial buildings and piers that lined the north bank of the Washington Channel were finally redeveloped during the 1960s as the **WATERFRONT**, a project designed to convince Washingtonians that they didn't have to go to Georgetown when they wanted a riverside stroll. Despite lacking Georgetown's natural advantages, the development has succeeded admirably, in part due to the proximity of so many office workers. Most people come here to eat seafood at one of the restaurants which line the waters of the Channel, along Maine Avenue or the parallel Water Street SW, west of 7th; all have terraces and patios providing views across to East Potomac Park. The district even has its own Metro stop, at 4th and M.

A couple of cruise boats sail out of Pier 4 at 6th and Water streets: see "City tours", p.46, for details. For reviews of the best Waterfront restaurants, see p.276.

The two main attractions are next to each other, near the bridge that crosses the Channel to East Potomac Park. The **Washington Marina** is the usual tangle of pricey nautical hardware, and provides a backdrop for various summer fairs and events. Adjacent lies the **Fish Wharf** (daily 7.30am–8pm), the oldest continuous fish market in America, conducted from permanently docked boats and trailers. This puts on a great spread, with huge trays of Chesapeake Bay fish, shrimp, clams, oysters and, especially, crabs, which you can buy live or steamed. There's nowhere to sit and eat, but there's nothing to stop you heading down the waterside promenade for a picnic.

Further down Maine Avenue, east of 7th Street, the **Waterfront Metro** station is closest if you're heading for the *Arena Stage* (see p.297). To the south, there's little to venture out for, save a clutch of restored eighteenth- and nineteenth-century townhouses within the **Harbour Square** development at 4th Street between N and O.

Channel and river collide just to the south of here, with the strategic spit of land occupied by the military (and subsequently off-limits) since the city's earliest days. Now known as **Fort McNair**, and originally fortified in 1791, the base became home to the **Washington Arsenal** in 1804, though its buildings were blown up by the British in 1814 and then later destroyed by an explosion which killed 21 people in 1864. At the US Penitentiary, built in the 1820s in the arsenal grounds, the conspirators in the Lincoln assassination (see p.196) were imprisoned, tried and executed.

Navy Yard

Run-down, impoverished Southeast Washington makes its presence felt just a few blocks south of the US Capitol; visitors shouldn't stroll around too far south of Eastern Market Metro or east of Waterfront Metro. Not that you'd have cause to: the only attraction north of the Anacostia River is the enclosed military campus of **Washington Navy Yard**, which can be reached directly by Metro or by bus (#90 or #92 down 8th St SE from Eastern Market Metro, #V6 along M St SE from Waterfront Metro). There's parking inside the compound.

Navy Yard is the US Navy's oldest shore establishment, building ships and producing weaponry for the fleet continuously from 1799 until 1961 – interrupted only in 1812 when the commander was ordered to burn the base to prevent the British capturing it. Since the 1960s the base has acted as a naval supply and adminstrative centre, and would be of no interest whatsoever were it not for its splendid Navy Museum. While you're within the confines of the Yard you'll probably also look into the Marine Corps Historical Center and the Navy Art Gallery, though both are very much an afterthought. You'll need **photo ID** to show the guard at the main gate at 9th and M.

Navy Museum

Bldg 76, Washington Navy Yard, 901 M St SE ☎ 433-4882; see above for transport. Mon–Fri 9am–4pm, June–Aug until 5pm, Sat & Sun all year 10am–5pm. Admission free.

Housed in the Navy Yard's former gun factory, the **Navy Museum**'s focused, illuminating collection traces the history of the US Navy, founded in 1794 in response to attacks on American ships by Barbary pirates – a painting illustrates the exploits of early naval hero Stephen Decatur (see p.152) who captured three boats during hand-to-hand fighting at Tripoli in 1804. Dress uniforms, ship figureheads and vicious cat o'nine tail whips, and a walk-through frigate gun-deck, illustrate the gradual development of the navy as a fighting force, while separate galleries deal with every conflict the US Navy has taken part in – from the War of 1812 to the Gulf War. The World War II displays are particularly affecting, featuring anti-aircraft guns in which you can sit, crackly archive film footage and an account of the sinking by a Japanese destroyer of a PT109 patrol boat on August 2, 1943: its commander, one John Fitzgerald Kennedy, his back badly injured, swam ashore towing the boat's badly burned engineer, an act for which he was later decorated.

The museum gets the balance just right, mixing informative text and glass-case displays with huge pieces of hardware which you're encouraged to explore – not least the *USS Barry*, a destroyer docked outside the museum, whose mess room, bridge and quarters are open to the public.

Anacostia

Washington's most notorious neighbourhood, **ANACOSTIA**, is also one of its oldest, the name derived from that of the area's original Native American inhabitants, the tobacco-growing Nacotchtanks. They were supplanted by nineteenth-century merchants seeking homes close to the Capitol, who in turn were displaced in the 1850s by a white working and middle class encouraged to settle in what the developers called Uniontown. Post Civil War Reconstruction saw the neighbourhood thrive, boosted by the building of the 11th Street Bridge which connected Anacostia with the rest of DC. But the white flight to the suburbs gathered pace in the 1950s and by 1970 over 95 percent of Anacostia's residents were black – and largely abandoned by investors and the city authorities. The 1968 riots did as much damage to infrastructure and confidence here as in Shaw, and it's been a long clamber back for the embattled community, which still suffers grievously from underfunding, poor housing, unemployment and crime – the latter fuelled by the city's spiralling drug problem.

Abraham Lincoln's assassin, John Wilkes Booth, escaped on horseback through Anacostia after shooting the President in 1865; see p.196.

None of which makes for a neighbourhood that you should visit lightly. There are, of course, handsome pockets of old houses, revitalized commercial areas and worthy community projects in Anacostia – people, after all, *do* manage to live perfectly ordinary lives here – but there's no reason to come as a tourist. Much of it is dangerous to outsiders who don't know where they're going; the two attractions reviewed below are best reached by cab from Anacostia Metro station.

Frederick Douglass National Historic Site

1411 W St SE ☎ 426-5961; Anacostia Metro and bus #B2 or taxi from there. Daily May–Sept 9am–5pm; Oct–April 9am–4pm. Admission free.

Frederick Douglass – former slave, abolitionist leader and blistering orator – was sixty when in 1877 he moved to the white, brick house in Anacostia he knew and loved as **Cedar Hill**. Its mixed Gothic Revival-Italianate appearance, 21 rooms and 15 acres were typical of the quality homes built in Uniontown twenty years earlier, though at that time they were restricted to whites. Douglass, newly appointed US marshal in DC, was the first to break the racial ban, paying $6700 for the property and living out the last eighteen years of his life here.

Tours (every 30min) of what is now known, rather cumbersome-ly, as the **Frederick Douglass National Historic Site** begin in the Visitor Center below the house, where a short docu-drama and a few static exhibits fill you in on his life. You're then led up the steep green hill for a tour around the house, the guides interrupting their rather dry narrative to keep visitors on the guide mats and off the furniture. It was a substantial property for the time, in which Douglass received all the leading abolitionist and suffragist lights of the day, talking in the parlours or eating in the dining room. Many brought him mementoes which are on display – President Lincoln's cane, given to him by Mary Lincoln, and a desk and chair from Harriet Beecher Stowe. Portraits of his family loom large: of his first wife Anna, who died in 1882; his second wife Helen, much younger and – more shockingly for hidebound DC – white; and his five chil-dren, two of whom served with distinction in the black Massachusetts 54th regiment during the Civil War.

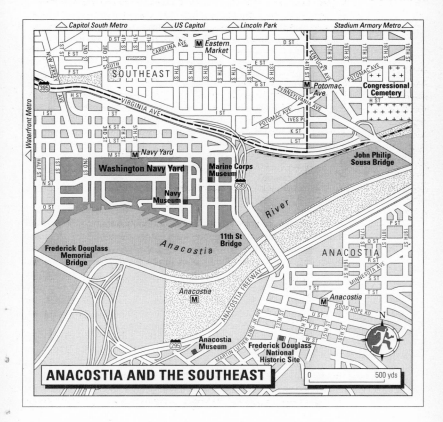

ANACOSTIA AND THE SOUTHEAST

A Life of Frederick Douglass (1818–95)

He stood there like an African prince, majestic in his wrath, as with wit, satire and indignation he graphically described the bitterness of slavery.

Elizabeth Cady Stanton, 1895

Frederick Douglass was born into slavery as Frederick Bailey on a Maryland estate in 1818; the exact date is unknown, as is the identity of his father (Bailey was his mother's name), though it was rumoured to be a white man, perhaps his owner. At the age of eight, he was sent to work as a house servant in Baltimore, where, although it was illegal to educate slaves, the owner's wife taught him to read, and he secretly taught himself to write. By 1834 he had been hired out to a nearby plantation where he was cruelly treated; his first attempt to escape, in 1836, failed. Later, apprenticed as a ship caulker in Baltimore docks, Frederick attended an educational association run by free blacks, where he met his first wife, Anna Murray. With money borrowed from her and equipped with a friend's passbook, he fled to New York in 1838 disguised as a free seaman. Anna followed him and they were married later that year, moving to Massachusetts where Bailey – now working as a labourer – became Douglass (after a character from Sir Walter Scott's *Lady of the Lake*) so as to confound the slave-catchers.

Douglass became active in the abolition movement, lecturing about his life for the Massachusetts Anti-Slavery Society during the 1840s and risking capture when, aged just 27, he published his early autobiography, *Narrative of the Life of Frederick Douglass, an American Slave*, in 1845. It was a resounding success, forcing the increasingly famous Douglass to leave for England (which had a strong abolitionist movement) for fear he'd be recaptured. After two years on the lecture circuit, friends raised the money to buy his freedom and Douglass returned home. His views were slowly changing and in a break with pacifist white abolitionists (particularly William Lloyd Garrison), he founded his own newspaper, the *North Star*, in Rochester, New York, in 1847 (later renamed *Frederick Douglass' Paper*) – in this, Douglass began increasingly to explore the idea of political rather than moral reform as a means of ending slavery. His reputation grew as a

Most of the fixtures and fittings are original and give a fair idea of middle-class life in late nineteenth-century Washington. Douglass kept chickens and goats outside in the gardens and the only water source was a rainwater pump, but inside the kitchen the domestic staff had access to all the latest technology, like the cranky *Universal* wrangler ("giving universal satisfaction"). Frederick himself worked either in his study, surrounded by hundreds of books, or in the outdoor "Growlery" – a rudimentary stone cabin (reconstructed in the garden) he used for solitary contemplation.

Returning to the Metro **by bus**, the #B2 (which drops you right outside the door on the way *from* Anacostia Metro) heads back *to* the Metro from Good Hope Road SE, three blocks down 14th Street from the house; cross Good Hope Road and wait for the bus (every 15min) on the other side, outside the grocery-deli. Or simply arrange for a taxi to pick you up from the house.

compelling orator and writer; a second autobiography, *My Bondage and My Freedom*, appeared in 1855. Meanwhile, he extended his interests to women's suffrage (a bold move at the time), debating issues with such luminaries as Susan B Anthony, Lucretia Mott and Elizabeth Cady Stanton.

When Lincoln issued the Emancipation Proclamation during the Civil War, the country's most respected black leader turned his attention to urging "Men of Color" to join up, which backfired somewhat when it became clear that his fiery recruitment speeches promised black soldiers an equality in service and conditions that the Union Army didn't offer. With slavery abolished in 1865, and Reconstruction set in place, Douglass turned to pressing for black suffrage. He campaigned for Ulysses S Grant and the Republicans in 1868 and played a major role in pushing through the Fifteenth Amendment (granting all "citizens" the right to vote) – though this caused a temporary rift with his suffragist colleagues since "citizens" still didn't include women. Frederick and Anna moved to DC in 1870, buying a house on Capitol Hill, where Douglass continued to earn his living lecturing and writing and, for a while, editing the progressive *New National Era* newspaper. Appointed to the largely ceremonial position of marshal of Washington DC in 1877, his last move was to Cedar Hill in Anacostia the same year.

He was made recorder of deeds for the city in 1880 and in 1881 published his third autobiographical work, the *Life and Times of Frederick Douglass*. Anna died a year later, but Douglass quickly remarried – Helen Pitts, a quick-witted white secretary almost twenty years his junior, whom he had met in the records office. More controversy followed as Douglass was accused of cosying up to successive political administrations that had been deemed to betray the aspirations of black Americans ever since Emancipation. Quitting his post as recorder, Douglass regained his reputation with a series of searing attacks on injustice and, in 1889, at a time when others might have considered retirement, he accepted the post of consul-general in Haiti, where he served for two years. Back at Cedar Hill, but by now in ill health, he continued to write and speak publicly until his death from a heart attack on February 20, 1895, at the age of 77. His funeral, effectively a state occasion, was held at the Metropolitan AME Church in downtown DC (see p.207); his writings continued to inspire a new generation of black leaders who took his fight into the twentieth century.

Anacostia Museum

1901 Fort Place SE ☎357-2700; Anacostia Metro and #W1 or #W2 from Howard Rd, or taxi. Daily 10am–5pm. Admission free.

The Smithsonian's least-known outpost, the **Anacostia Museum**devotes itself to recording African-American history and culture, with particular reference to the life of blacks in the upper South (DC, Maryland, Virginia and the Carolinas). There's no permanent collection and instead the museum holds renowned temporary exhibitions on themed topics: either call to see what's on or ask for details at the Smithsonian Castle on the Mall (p.105). The museum is well worth an hour or two of your time, but don't even think of walking here from the Metro; the bus stops outside, though it's less unnerving by far to come by taxi. As it's not far from the Frederick Douglass home, you could even combine the two on one visit.

Chapter 5

The White House and Foggy Bottom

T here are few residences in the world as recognizable as the patrician outline of the **White House**. With an impeccable lineage – oldest public building in Washington DC, home of the President since 1800, and, with the Capitol, one of the two original cornerstones of L'Enfant's masterplan for the city – it stands as perhaps the most enduring symbol of democracy in the nation, a symbol bolstered by the extraordinary public access granted since the time of Thomas Jefferson. Around the White House are genteel squares and streets fashionable since the early nineteenth century; to the west, in the high ground of **Foggy Bottom**, the chattering classes entertained the political elite in houses like **The Octagon**. Washington's first art gallery opened just a block from the White House in what is now the Smithsonian's **Renwick Gallery** of decorative arts and crafts; later, the art collection was moved into the larger **Corcoran Gallery of Art**, still one of the most respected art foundations in the country.

Today, the rest of Foggy Bottom – basically, the leafy area north of Constitution Avenue and west of the White House to the river – is best known for the federal institutions which have their headquarters here. However, the students of **George Washington University**, set bang in the heart of Foggy Bottom, add a certain life to the otherwise nine-to-five flavour of the streets, and there are a handful of minor museums and galleries. The biggest draws, though, are the **Kennedy Center**, the city's major cultural complex, and – though there's little actually to see – the nearby **Watergate** building, scene of the infamous burglary that toppled President Nixon.

The White House

1600 Pennsylvania Ave NW ☎ 456-7041; McPherson Square or Farragut West Metro. Continuous tours Tues–Sat 10am–noon; additional tours in summer; closed some holidays and official functions. Admission free.

For two centuries, the **White House**, 1600 Pennsylvania Avenue NW, has been the most famous house at the most famous address in

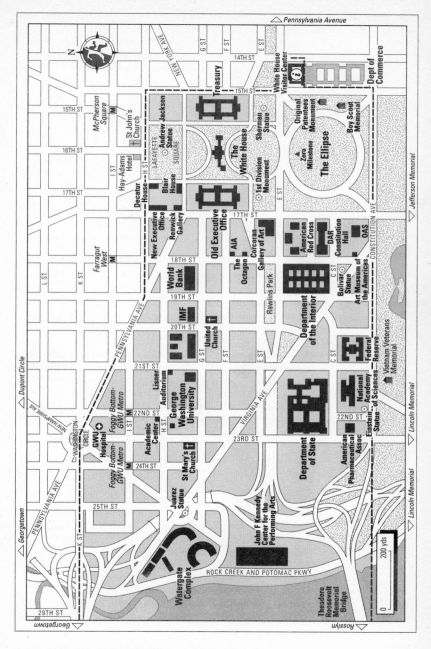

The White House

For a roll-call of US presidents, see p.323. For an account of the role of the President within the American political system, see p.148–149.

America. For millions, the notion of touring the White House, residence and office of the **President of the United States**, has an almost totemic quality. Quite apart from relishing the freedom to stand in the same building, for a moment at least, with the chief executive of the nation, the person with their finger on the button, there's the undeniable thrill of nosing around the home of the closest the country has to royalty.

In the end, however, if it's domestic curiosity that brings you to the White House, you're likely to go away disappointed. Many are surprised by how small it is – "I think I may say that we have private houses in London considerably larger" sniffed Anthony Trollope in 1862 – while tours tend to consist of a lot of waiting around followed by a quick shuffle past railed-off rooms filled with portraits of ex-presidents.

Public access (see "Visiting the White House" opposite) isn't affected except during official functions, but **security** is every bit as tight as you'd imagine. In 1995 the stretch of Pennsylvania Avenue immediately outside the White House was permanently closed to vehicles, following two incidents in which shots were fired at the house and a light aircraft crashed into one of the outer walls; the Oklahoma City bombing shortly afterwards only served to heighten the fear of terrorist attack. Balancing security requirements with the historic right of access is not a new problem: in the nineteenth century, though there were armed sentries at every door, and plain-clothes policemen mingling with the visitors, virtually anyone could turn up at the President's house without an introduction: in his diary, naval novelist Captain Frederick Marryat deplored the way a visitor might "walk into the saloon in all his dirt, and force his way to the President, that he might shake him by the one hand while he flourished the whip in the other". As late as the 1920s, the general public was allowed to saunter across the White House lawns and picnic in the grounds. President Warren Harding even used to answer the door himself.

History

From the outset, the White House – or **President's Mansion** as it was first known – was to be the focal point of executive government, connected to the proposed Capitol building by the broad diagonal sweep of Pennsylvania Avenue. L'Enfant was fired before he could make a start on the house, however, and its design was thrown open to an architectural competition in 1792. The winner, Irish immigrant and professional builder **James Hoban**, picked up a $500 prize for his Neoclassical design, which was influenced by the Georgian manor houses of Dublin. It coincided exactly with President Washington's requirement for a mansion that would command respect without being extravagant and monarchical – attributes the leader of the new republic was keen to avoid. A stone house, moreover, would give the crucial appearance of permanence and stability,

Visiting the White House

We entered a large hall, and, having twice or thrice rung a bell which nobody answered, walked without further ceremony through the rooms on the ground-floor, as diverse other gentlemen (mostly with their hats on, and their hands in their pockets) were doing very leisurely. Some of these had ladies with them, to whom they were showing the premises; others were lounging on the chairs and sofas; others, in a perfect state of exhaustion from listlessness, were yawning drearily. The greater portion of this assemblage were rather asserting their supremacy than doing anything else, as they had no particular business there, that anybody knew of. A few were closely eyeing the movables, as if to make quite sure that the President . . . had not made away with any of the furniture, or sold the fixtures for his private benefit.

Charles Dickens, *American Notes* (1842)

Long gone are the days when you could simply stroll into the White House. Now you must call first for tickets at the **White House Visitor Center** on Pennsylvania Avenue (see p.150). In **high season** (April–Sept), the line snakes right around the outside of the building by 7am; from the 15th Street edge the wait averages thirty to forty minutes. You'll be given free tickets (maximum of six per person) for a tour at a fixed time later that morning; the 4500 tickets available have usually all gone by 8.30am. Tours start at 10am: assemble in good time at the bleachers on the Ellipse and wait for the number to be called, at which point park rangers lead your group to the northeast gate on East Executive Avenue. In winter, when there are fewer visitors, advance tickets are not required – simply join the line at the northeast gate – though you'll still need to get there early. **American citizens** can arrange special tours by writing to their congressperson *at least six months* in advance. If you get a ticket this way, you'll be given a more in-depth VIP tour. Finally, whenever your visit, it's best to call the Visitor Center or the White House tour information line first – public access can be restricted at short notice.

Other parts of the White House are accessible on occasion throughout the year. In April and October, the **gardens** are opened for afternoon tours; at **Christmas** there are special evening tours of the festively decorated interior; while on **Easter Monday**, the traditional Easter Egg Roll takes place on the South Lawn, a ceremony introduced during the nineteenth-century administration of Rutherford B Hayes. The **flag** flies above the house when the President is in residence.

White House recorded information lines:

☎ 456-2200 *special events*

☎ 456-7041 *tours*

☎ 456-2343 *President's daily schedule*

though unfortunately for Hoban the city had few skilled masons and no quarries. Advertisements were even placed in European newspapers before Scottish masons from the Potomac region and local slaves were recruited for the work. Progress was slow: the masons downed tools in 1794 in the city's first pay strike and the house of grey Virginia sandstone wasn't completed in time for George Washington, whose second term in office ended in 1797.

John Adams was the first presidential occupant, moving into the unfinished structure on November 1, 1800: the family was reduced to hanging its laundry in the grand East Room while final touches were put to the mansion. East and west terraces were built during the administration of Thomas Jefferson, who, incidentally, had entered the original design competition under an assumed name; he also installed the first water closets and (true to extravagant form) introduced a French chef to the house. Under James Madison, the interior was redecorated by Capitol architect Benjamin Latrobe, who copied parts of Jefferson's earlier competition design with the defence that Jefferson's ideas were lifted in turn from "old French books, out of which he fishes everything". During the **War of 1812** occupying British forces burned down the mansion (Aug 1814), forcing Madison and his wife to flee; when the troops entered, they found the dining table set for forty, the wine poured in the decanters and the food cooked in the kitchen – they tucked in and then torched the building. Hoban was put in charge of its reconstruction after the war and it was again ready for occupation in 1817, but with one significant change: to conceal fire damage to the exterior, the house was painted white. Fitting, as – for obscure reasons – the mansion was already commonly known as the "**White House**".

Throughout the nineteenth century, the White House was decorated, added to and improved with each new occupant, though occasionally there were unforseen setbacks: to celebrate his inauguration in 1829, the populist Andrew Jackson invited back the rowdier campaigning elements of his fledgling Democratic Party who, in overexuberant mood, wrecked the place; Jackson was forced to spend the first night of his presidency in a hotel. He atoned by having the first indoor bathroom installed, in 1833; later improvements included gas lights in 1848, central heating and a steam laundry in 1853, the telephone in 1877 and electric lighting in 1891. During the Civil War, troops were briefly stationed in the East Room, cooking their dinner in the ornate fireplace, while the South Lawn was used as a field hospital; at the end of the war in 1865, following his assassination, Lincoln's coffin lay in state in the East Room (the first of seven presidents to be so honoured). When a second president, James A Garfield, lay dying from an assassin's bullet in 1881, enterprising naval engineers cooled his White House bedroom by concocting a prototype air-conditioner from a fan and a box of ice; full air-conditioning didn't follow until 1909.

Many of the house improvements were piecemeal and not until Theodore Roosevelt's administration (1901–09) was any serious attempt made to coordinate structural repairs and the expansion neccessary for family and staff. Elevators were added for convenience (Teddy once had a pony called Algonquin brought up in one

100 Rough Guides*

Southwest **USA**
THE ROUGH GUIDE
Greg Ward

India
THE ROUGH GUIDE
David Abram, Devdan Sen, Harriet Sharkey and Gareth John Williams

China
THE ROUGH GUIDE

Vietnam
THE ROUGH GUIDE
Jan Dodd and Mark Lewis

Peru
THE ROUGH GUIDE
Dilwyn Jenkins

Paris
THE ROUGH GUIDE
Kate Baillie and Tim Salmon

Spain
THE ROUGH GUIDE
Mark Ellingham and John Fisher

Norway
THE ROUGH GUIDE
Jules Brown and Phil Lee

London
THE ROUGH GUIDE
Rob Humphreys

Mallorca & Menorca
THE ROUGH GUIDE
Phil Lee

Indonesian
A ROUGH GUIDE PHRASEBOOK

French
A ROUGH GUIDE PHRASEBOOK

Mandarin Chinese
A ROUGH GUIDE PHRASEBOOK

Hindi & Urdu
A ROUGH GUIDE PHRASEBOOK

Thai
A ROUGH GUIDE PHRASEBOOK

The **Internet**
AND WORLD WIDE WEB
THE ROUGH GUIDE 2.0
Angus J. Kennedy from Internet

Jazz
THE ROUGH GUIDE

World Music
THE ROUGH GUIDE
Salsa to soukous, Cajun to Calypso... the complete handbook

Opera
THE ROUGH GUIDE
A COMPLETE GUIDE TO THE OPERAS, COMPOSERS, SINGERS AND RECORDINGS
Matthew Boyden

Rock
THE ROUGH GUIDE
MORE THAN 5000 CD RECOMMENDATIONS
THE DEFINITIVE GUIDE TO 1000 ARTISTS AND BANDS FROM THEN...TO NOW

100% Reliable

Stay in touch with us!

ROUGHNEWS is Rough Guides' free newsletter. In three issues a year we give you news, travel issues, music reviews, readers' letters and the latest dispatches from authors on the road.

I would like to receive ROUGHNEWS: please put me on your free mailing list.

NAME ....

ADDRESS ....

Please clip or photocopy and send to: Rough Guides, 1 Mercer Street, London WC2H 9QJ, England or Rough Guides, 375 Hudson Street, New York, NY 10014, USA.

Travel the world
HIV *Safe*

Travel *Safe*

HIV, the virus that causes AIDS, is worldwide.

You're probably aware of the dangers of getting it from unprotected sex, but there are many other risks when travelling.

Wherever you're visiting it makes sense to take precautions. Try to avoid any medical or dental treatment, but if it's necessary, make sure the equipment is sterilised. Likewise, if you really need to have a blood transfusion, always ask for screened blood.

Make sure your travelling companions are aware of the risks and the necessary precautions. In fact, you should take your own sterile medical pack, available from larger high street pharmacies.

Remember, ear and body piercing, acupuncture and even tattoos could be risky, because they all involve puncturing the skin. And although you might not normally consider any of these things now, after a few drinks - you never know.

Of course, the things that are dangerous at home are just as dangerous when you travel. So don't inject drugs or share works.

Avoid casual sex and always use a good quality condom when having sex with a new partner (and each time you have sex with them).

And it's not just a gay disease' either. In fact, worldwide, it's most commonly transmitted through sex between men and women.

For information in the UK:

Ring for the TravelSafe leaflet on the Health Literature Line freephone 0800 555 777, or pick one up at a doctor's surgery or pharmacy.

Further advice on HIV and AIDS: National AIDS Helpline: 0800 567 123. (Cannot be reached from abroad).

The Terrence Higgins Trust Helpline (12 noon–10pm) provides advice and counselling on HIV/AIDS issues: 0171 242 1010.

MASTA Travellers Health Line: 0891 224 100.

Travel *Safe*

Travel the world HIV *Safe*

to delight his sick son*) and an executive West Wing built, which incorporated the President's personal **Oval Office**. The famous **Rose Garden** was planted outside the Oval Office in 1913 on the orders of Ellen Wilson, and became used for ceremonial purposes. An entire residential third floor was added in 1927, an East Wing followed in the 1940s, while World War II saw additions as diverse as an air raid shelter, swimming pool (which the lame FDR used for exercise) and movie theatre. Roosevelt, though, refused to entertain the idea of painting the White House black in order to foil enemy bombers. . .

All these works were completed while the presidential family of the day was in residence. This meant that additions and expansions tended to be finished quickly, and by 1948 successive renovations had been so hurried that the entire building was on the verge of collapse. Harry Truman – who had already added a poorly received balcony ("Truman's folly") to the familiar south side portico – had to move into nearby Blair House (see p.152) for four years while the structure was stabilized; new foundations were laid, all the rooms were dismantled and a modern steel frame inserted. The Trumans moved back in 1952, since when there have been no significant alterations – unless you count Nixon's bowling alley, Ford's outdoor pool and Clinton's jogging track. Jimmy Carter contented himself with converting part of the house to solar energy.

The interior

Pick up a leaflet at the Visitor Center and you're set to steer yourself around the **self-guided tour**, which concentrates on the core of rooms on the ground and state (principal) floors. The Oval Office, family apartments and private offices on the second and third floors are off-limits; posted guards make sure you don't stray from the designated route. Once inside, your group is allowed to wander one-way through or past half a dozen furnished rooms. It's not exactly conducive to taking your time, though guards will answer questions if they can, and in many rooms you can't get close enough to appreciate the paintings or the furniture; caught up in the flow, most people are outside again well within thirty minutes. As if this wasn't enough, there's a paucity of quality fixtures and fittings on display, and not just because much of the best stuff is kept in private quarters. Until Jackie Kennedy and her Fine Arts Committee put a stop to the prac-

---

* Theodore Roosevelt's children were the last presidential kids permitted to impose themselves on the often stifling formality of the White House, sliding down the banisters and interrupting state dinners at the drop of a hat. They were encouraged by the prank-loving Teddy himself – "the very embodiment of noise" according to Henry James – who was happy to join in most of the rowdy pastimes, whatever the occasion. As the British ambassador at the time wrote home, rather wearily, "We must never forget that the President is seven years old".

tice, each incoming Presidential family changed, sold or scrapped the furniture according to individual taste, while outgoing presidents took favourite pieces with them – you're just as likely to come across White House furniture and valuables in places like Dumbarton House (p.239) or the Woodrow Wilson House (p.214).

Visitors enter the East Wing from the ground floor and traipse first past the Federal-style **Library**, paneled in timbers rescued from a mid-nineteenth-century refit and housing 2700 books by American authors. Opposite, you look into the **Vermeil Room**, once a billiard room but now named for its extensive collection of silver gilt; the portraits are of recent First Ladies. Regular tours don't go any further on this floor, while VIP tours head next to the **China Room** – used to display china and glass since Wilson's presidency, and the spot where Annette Bening and Michael Douglas first kiss in the movie *The American President*. Beyond, in the oval **Diplomatic Reception Room**, where panoramic wallpaper depicts American landscapes, new ambassadors present themselves to the President. Eight days after his inauguration in 1933, this was the room from which Franklin D Roosevelt made the first of his so-called "Fireside Chats", popularizing the New Deal. The adjacent **Map Room** was FDR's private retreat during World War II, where he and Winston

---

The Presidency

The executive Power shall be vested in a President of the United States of America.

Article 2, Section 1, Constitution of the United States

The President is simply chief enforcer of American financial interests.

Gore Vidal

When they created the role of **President of the United States**, the delegates at the Constitutional Convention in Philadelphia in 1787 had no intention of replacing a discredited, but all-powerful British monarchy with an American version. The federal system of government they devised separated executive, legislative and judical powers (see p.319 for more) and prescribed precisely the limits of their authority. The President was made chief executive, who – while no mere figurehead – would take his place within the uniquely balanced federal system and not above it. Indeed, the relative importance the Founding Fathers placed upon the position is clear from its place in the Constitution – presidential powers were detailed in Article 2, after full discussion of the more fundamental role of Congress in Article 1. At first, the President wasn't even directly **elected**, but chosen instead by an electoral college appointed by the states, the idea being to free the presidency from factional influence. The 12th Amendment (1804) opened up the ballot for President (and Vice-President) to popular election.

The President's place within the Constitution may be strictly defined, but the Constitution has very little to say about the presidency itself.

Churchill sank into the Chippendale chairs to chart the progress of
the war. It's now used as a private reception room for the President:
Bill Clinton taped his video testimony for the Whitewater trial here in
1996.

The regular tour moves upstairs to the State Floor, to the **East
Room**, the largest in the White House, which has been open to the
public since the days of Andrew Jackson. Used in the past for wed-
dings, various lyings-in-state and other major ceremonies, it's on a
suitably grand scale for once, with long, yellow drapes, a brown
marble fireplace and turn-of-the-century glass chandeliers. Between
the fireplaces hangs the one major artwork on general display:
Gilbert Stuart's celebrated 1797 portrait of a steely George
Washington, rescued from the flames by Dolley Madison when the
British burned the White House.

The last rooms on the tour are more intimate in scale. **The Green
Room**, its walls lined in silk, was Jefferson's dining room, and JFK's
favourite in the entire house. Portraits line the walls, Dolley
Madison's French candlesticks are on the mantelpiece, and a fine
matching green dinner service occupies the cabinet. The room is
now often called upon to host receptions, as is the adjacent, oval
Blue Room, whose ornate French furniture was bought by President

Specific, enumerated **powers** are few – to make treaties, appoint federal
officers, act as commander-in-chief, etc – and this may have reflected the
fact that the Constitution's authors couldn't agree themselves exactly what
the President's role should be. The subsequent elevation of the role is due
in part to the succession of extraordinarily able leaders that occupied and
enhanced the post in the late eighteenth and nineteenth centuries, from
George Washington to Abraham Lincoln. The presidency has subsequently
been moulded beyond recognition as incumbents have thrust themselves
forward as head of state, leader of their particular party and even national
symbol – in fact, the almost monarchical figure the Constitution's authors
desperately tried to avoid creating.

No longer simply chief executive, the President is the embodiment of
American power. Although the President's Constitutional powers have
barely expanded since the eighteenth century, the real influence available
to him has. For example, under the President, the government's work is carried out by fourteen **executive departments**, whose appointed secretaries
form the **Cabinet**. This is less a collective policy-making body than an advisory forum. Constitutionally, the President has sole executive responsibility, though is assisted in this by special advisors, private White House staff
and co-opted experts. Incoming presidents routinely change the staff at
scores of federal agencies and advisory bodies, from the Post Office to the
National Security Council, to ensure political consistency within the new
administration (and also, more deep-seatedly, to reward loyal camp follow-
ers); these days, something approaching two thousand people work directly or indirectly for the Executive Office of the President, providing great
scope for presidential patronage, while another 100,000 non-strategic federal posts are technically within the presidential gift.

Monroe after the 1814 fire. In 1886, Grover Cleveland was married in here, the only time a president has been married in the White House. The **Red Room** is the smallest of the lot, decorated in early nineteenth-century Empire style and sporting attractive inlaid oak doors. Finally, the painted-oak-panelled **State Dining Room** harks back to the East Room in scale and style, and hosts banquets for important guests. At one time, Theodore Roosevelt used to stick his big game trophies in here, though the most enduring item is the inscription engraved on the fireplace mantelpiece, part of a quotation from a letter by John Adams to his wife – "May none but honest and wise men ever rule under this roof". Some hope. You then loop back through the cross halls and exit on the north side of the White House, opposite Lafayette Square – wondering, perhaps, quite why you got up at 6am to queue for tickets.

The White House Visitor Center

US Commerce Dept Building, 1450 Pennsylvania Ave NW ☎208-1631; Federal Triangle or Metro Center Metro. Daily Memorial Day–Labor Day 7am–7pm; rest of year 8am–5pm. Admission free.

The **White House Visitor Center** (opposite Pershing Square, between 14th and 15th), where most of the year you must come to pick up tickets for the tour of the White House, is worth a visit in its own right – preferably after mid-morning when the lines have disappeared – to examine the displays concerning the history of the place and its occupants. These are housed in the imposing Great Hall of Federal Triangle's Department of Commerce (see p.178), whose nave is filled with photos and film footage of First Families and their distinguished guests. In one inaugural portrait after another, a drawn and exhausted president hands over power to his beaming successor.

The Ellipse

The **Ellipse** – the large grassy expanse south of the White House – forms an integral part of the city plan's symmetry: due north is the rounded portico and porch of the White House, with the axis of 16th Street beyond; south, the Washington Monument and Jefferson Memorial.

You'll probably have considerable time to kill in summer waiting for your White House tour – bleacher seats and occasional concerts help maintain the spirits, though the same can't be said of the group of nearby sights. On the northern edge of the Ellipse, at E Street opposite the South Lawn, the **Zero Milestone** marks the point from which all distances on US highways are measured. Here, too, is the rather stumpy **National Christmas Tree**, its lamps lit by the President every year to mark the start of the holiday season. If you can stand the excitement, keep to the east (15th St) side of the

Ellipse and walk south, passing the simple granite **Monument to the Original Patentees**, commemorating the eighteenth-century landowners who ceded land so that the city could be built; a few yards away a bronze boy scout marks the site of the **Boy Scout Memorial** – the flanking figures entirely unsuited to moral guardianship, at least until they put some clothes on. At the southeastern corner of the Ellipse, the stone **Bulfinch Gatehouse** at Constitution and 15th was one of a pair that once stood at the western entrance to the Capitol grounds. Its partner stands over the Ellipse at Constitution and 17th.

Around Lafayette Square

Pretty, spick-and-span **Lafayette Square** was formerly part of the White House gardens; in the earliest days of the nineteenth century it was known as President's Square, lined with period buildings erected for Cabinet members and other prominent citizens. Jefferson later turned it into a public park, at the same time as opening the White House to visitors, and since then it's remained the most attractive approach to the President's house beyond. **Redevelopment** has threatened many of the surrounding houses on several occasions, though ever since the Kennedys took a keen interest in their preservation in the 1960s, they have been safe from further interference. However, cosmetic changes are imminent in "America's Town Square", as it's referred to rather self-importantly. The banning of traffic on Pennsylvania Avenue outside the White House has prompted proposals to extend the square's parameters, introducing shops, galleries and cafés as part of a fully pedestrianized zone between H Street and the White House. In the meantime, roller-bladers take advantage of the lack of traffic by organizing scratch games of street hockey in front of the President's house.

The square

Regularly patrolled by the police, **Lafayette Square** is one of the safest places to stretch out on the grass in downtown DC. It's also the closest that protesters are allowed to get to the White House; there's a knot of banner-clutching citizens in place most days with various points to make.

For many decades in the nineteenth century, the only statue on show was the central figure of **Andrew Jackson**, astride a rearing horse and doffing his hat – soldiers encamped here during the Civil War used to hang their washing from it – though this was framed this century by the addition of four corner-statues, all of foreign-born revolutionary generals. Most famous of all, in the southeast corner, is the Frenchman, the **Marquis de Lafayette**, who – inspired by the Declaration of Independence and his friendship with Benjamin

Nearest Metro stations for Lafayette Square are Farragut North, Farragut West or McPherson Square.

Franklin, American minister in Paris – raised an army on behalf of the American colonists and was made a general at the age of nineteen. Later imprisoned in France as a "traitor" to his own country's revolution, he was never abandoned by America. He returned to the States an old man in 1824, a triumphal visit during which time he was feted on the Mall and received various honours, including the naming of this square. His statue shows him flanked by French admirals and being handed a sword by a female nude, symbolizing America.

The buildings

Built by the first surgeon-general in 1826, **Blair House**, in the southwestern corner of Lafayette Square, was where Robert E Lee was offered – and refused – the command of the Union Army (see p.245). It has served as the presidential guest house since the 1940s; both the Truman and Clinton families used it while White House renovations were underway, while at other times it hosts foreign dignitaries.

Oldest house on the square is **Decatur House** at 748 Jackson Place NW, at the corner with H St (Tues–Fri 10am–3pm, Sat & Sun noon–4pm; $4; ☎842-0920). This dates from 1819, built in red brick by Benjamin Latrobe (who had already worked on the White House) for Stephen Decatur, another precociously young American hero, who as a navy captain performed with distinction in the War of 1812. As things turned out, Decatur lived here for little more than a year, since he was killed in a duel with one Commodore Barron; the Federal-style first floor, studded with naval memorabilia, is decorated in the fashion of the day. Most of the other period rooms owe their inlaid floors, furnishings and decorative arts to the successive owners' penchant for heavy-handed Victorian style. Short guided tours run throughout the day; pick up tickets around the corner from the gift shop at 1600 H Street.

*For details of
the Hay-
Adams, see
p.261.*

Walking east along the top of the square, you pass the Renaissance splendour of the **Hay-Adams Hotel** (at H and 16th), fashioned from the former townhouses of statesman John Hay (once President Lincoln's private secretary) and his friend, historian and author Henry Adams. Their adjacent homes were the site of glittering turn-of-the-century soirées, attended by Theodore Roosevelt and his circle, an association which appealed to hotshot society hotel developer Harry Wardman (see p.222), who jumped at the chance to buy the properties in 1927. Since then, the hotel (which boasted the first air-conditioned dining room in the city) has been at the heart of Washington politicking – Henry Kissinger lunched regularly, Oliver North did much of his clandestine Iran-Contra fundraising here, while the Clintons stayed over before Bill's first inauguration.

Immediately across 16th Street the tiny, yellow **St John's Church** (Mon–Sat 8am–4pm; free tours after 11am Sun service) dates from 1816. Latrobe again did the honours, providing the neighbourhood

with a handsome domed church in the form of a Greek cross, with
appealing half-moon windows in the upper gallery of the intimately
proportioned interior. Unsurprisingly, St John's is commonly
known as the "Church of the Presidents"; all since Madison have visited – sitting in the special pew (no. 54) reserved for them (the
kneeling cushions are embroidered with their names) – and when an
incumbent dies in office the bells of St John's ring out across the
city.

Old Executive Office and Treasury buildings

The highly ornate, granite **Old Executive Office Building** at 17th
St and Pennsylvania Ave NW (free tours Sat 9–11.30am; ☎395-
5895) was built (1871–88) to house the State, War and Navy
departments. Its architect, Alfred B Mullet, claiming to be inspired
by the Louvre in Paris, in fact produced an ill-conceived French
Empire-style building, with hundreds of free-standing columns,
extraordinarily tall, thin chimneys, a copper mansard roof, pediments, porticos, and various pedantic stone flourishes. It was never
terribly popular – Truman thought it a monstrosity – but schemes
to renovate or rebuild came to nothing, mainly because of the
expense involved in tackling such a behemoth. These days its
gracefully ageing facade is loved a little more, and the roomy interior provides office space for government and White House staff:
notoriously, the building was the base of the White House
"Plumbers" and hosted several of the infamous tape-recorded
Watergate meetings (see p.166); it was also where the zealously
patriotic Colonel Oliver North shredded documents central to the
Iran-Contra affair. You need to call well in advance to tour the public rooms, rich in marble-and-gilt, stained glass, tiled floors and
wrought-iron balconies.

It's a similar story if you want to see inside the **Treasury Building**
on the other side of the White House, whose long facade interrupts
the line of Pennsylvania Avenue; ring at least a week in advance
(☎622-0896) to fix a free guided tour (Sat only). Built – or at least
started – in 1836 (by Robert Mills, of Washington Monument fame),
this is commonly judged to be the finest Greek Revival building in the
city: its thirty-column colonnade facing 15th Street is particularly
impressive. During the Civil War, the basement was strengthened
and food and arms stored in the building, since Lincoln and his aides
were determined to hole up here if the city was ever attacked. The
statue at the southern entrance, facing Hamilton Place, is of
Alexander Hamilton, first secretary of the Treasury (and the man on
the front of the $10 bill; the Treasury Building itself is on the back).
One of the most highly respected members of Washington's first
administration, Hamilton later died in a duel with Aaron Burr,
Jefferson's Vice-President and scheming Northern Confederalist, to
whom Hamilton was implacably opposed.

The Renwick Gallery

Pennsylvania Ave at 17th St NW ☎357-2700; Farragut West Metro. Daily
10am–5.30pm. Admission free.

The Second Empire flourishes of the Old Executive Office Building
were directly influenced by the earlier, smaller and much more harmonious **Renwick Gallery** of American arts and crafts, which lies
straight across Pennsylvania Avenue. Built by James Renwick (architect of the Smithsonian Castle) in 1859, the red-brick building was
originally destined to house the private art collection of financier
William Wilson Corcoran. Work was interrupted by the Civil War,
during which time the building was requisitioned for use by the
Union Army's quartermaster-general; Corcoran, a man with
Southern sympathies, had left for Europe in 1862, where he stayed
for the entire war. On his return, Corcoran finally got his gallery
back (and, having sued, $125,000 from the government as back
rent) and opened it to the public, but within twenty years his burgeoning collection had outgrown the site – which led to the building
of a new Corcoran Gallery, just a couple of blocks south (see facing
page). After several decades as the US Court of Claims, the now-
decrepit building was saved and restored in the 1960s by the
Smithsonian, which uses it to display selections from the National
Museum of American Art.

The building itself is a treat: an inscription above the entrance
announces it to be "Dedicated to Art", and the ornate design reaches
its apogee in the deep-red **Grand Salon** on the upper floor, a soaring
parlour preserved in the style of the 1860s and 1870s – featuring
windows draped in striped damask, period portraits (including one
of Corcoran), velvet-covered benches, marble-topped cabinets and
splendid wood-and-glass display cases taken from the Smithsonian
Castle. This was the main picture gallery in Corcoran's time; its lofty
dimensions meant that there was no difficulty in converting it into a
court room and judge's chambers during the Court of Claims' tenure.
Opposite, the smaller **Octagon Room** was specifically designed to
hold Hiram Powers' notorious nude statue *The Greek Slave* (now in
the Corcoran Gallery itself).

Between the two rooms on the same floor are galleries devoted to
American crafts, mostly modern jewellery and furniture but also
sculpture, ceramics, abstracts and applied art in all its manifestations. The first floor hosts **temporary exhibitions** of contemporary crafts (tours by appointment daily 10am, 11am & 1pm).

Along 17th Street

Having seen the major sights around the White House, you can stroll
south down **17th Street** towards Constitution Avenue, calling in at a
clutch of buildings along the way. Main port of call is the **Corcoran**

Gallery of Art, the city's earliest art gallery, and still among its finest, though there are smaller, more offbeat collections nearby.

The Corcoran Gallery of Art

500 17th St NW ☎638-3211; Farragut North or Farragut West Metro. Mon, Wed & Fri–Sun 10am–5pm, Thurs 10am–9pm. Suggested donation $3.

When the **Corcoran Gallery of Art** shifted premises at the turn of this century, moving from what is now the Renwick Gallery (see above), it took its collection and ideals with it. Ernest Flagg's Beaux Arts design is a beauty, of curving white marble with a green copper roof, the light and airy interior enhanced by a superb double-atrium. When an extension was required in the late 1920s, the trustees, seeking continuity, looked to Charles A Platt, who had done such a good job with the Freer Gallery of Art.

The Corcoran ranks with New York's Met and Boston's Museum of Fine Arts as one of the three oldest art museums in the US.

The Corcoran Gallery's American holdings are mighty: over three thousand paintings, from colonial to contemporary, alongside American Neoclassical sculpture and forays into modern photography, prints and drawings. Over the years, the permanent collection has expanded considerably to include European works (particularly seventeenth-century Dutch and nineteenth-century French), Greek antiquities and even medieval tapestries. The latest addition, though not yet fully displayed, is the important bequest by Olga Hirshorn (wife of Joseph of the eponymous gallery) of seven hundred works by two hunded nineteenth- and twentieth-century artists and sculptors, from Picasso to Calder.

Works from the permanent collection are rotated throughout the year; not everything mentioned below will be on display at any one time. Details of changing exhibitions of contemporary works are available at the **information desk**, inside the main entrance, which is also where you sign up for the **guided tours** of the permanent collection (daily except Tues 10.30am, noon & 12.30pm, Thurs also 7.30pm). The **gallery shop** has one of the city's better collections of posters, cards and books; the **café** (daily except Tues 11am–4.30pm, Thurs until 8.30pm) is decent, too, best during the gospel brunch (Sun 11am–2pm; $17), when the songs ring out through the gallery.

The first floor

Almost the entire first floor is devoted to **European art**, and a very mixed bag it is, too, being primarily comprised of the 1925 bequest of Senator William A Clark, an industrialist with more money than discretion. That's not to say there aren't some splendid pieces on display; rather that there's little overall cohesion, certainly in a gallery otherwise devoted to American art. Corcoran himself, though, had already blurred the edges of his collection by commissioning 120 animal bronzes by French sculptor **Antoine-Louis Barye** (1796–1875), a selection of which are shown in a special room.

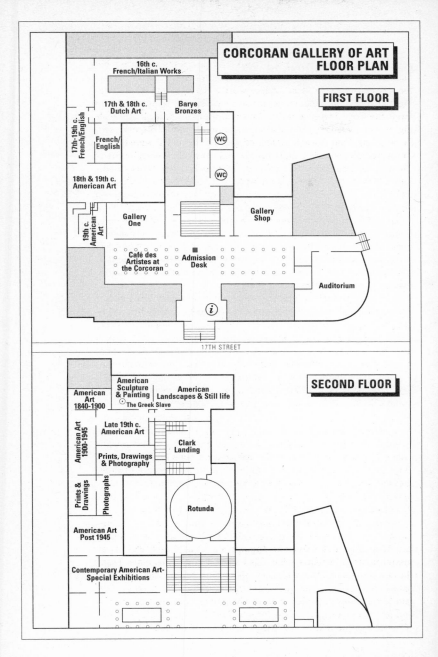

CORCORAN GALLERY OF ART FLOOR PLAN

FIRST FLOOR

16th c. French/Italian Works

17th & 18th c. Dutch Art

Barye Bronzes

17th-19th c. French/English

French/English

18th & 19th c. American Art

19th c. American Art

Gallery One

Gallery Shop

(WC)

(WC)

Café des Artistes at the Corcoran

Admission Desk

Auditorium

(i)

17TH STREET

SECOND FLOOR

American Sculpture & Painting
⊙ The Greek Slave

American Landscapes & Still life

American Art 1840-1900

American Art 1900-1945

Late 19th c. American Art

Prints, Drawings & Photography

Clark Landing

Prints & Drawings

Photographs

Rotunda

American Art Post 1945

Contemporary American Art- Special Exhibitions

These are graphic representations, often of snarling, fighting animals; a horse attacked by a lion, a python crushing a gazelle.

From here, you can stroll directly past the seventeenth- and eighteenth-century **Dutch** paintings – few of delaying interest – or double back through the parallel long gallery which holds a selection of sixteenth-century **French and Italian** works. Here are some outstanding Italian majolica plates depicting mythological scenes and two large, allegorical wool-and-silk French tapestries (1506), representing contemporaneous political and historical events. Beyond, two more rooms hold **French and English** paintings of the seventeenth to nineteenth centuries, most prominently perhaps the sympathetic Thomas Gainsborough portraits of Lord and Lady Dunstanville. You'll come across more French tapestries, too, this time early eighteenth-century, while an American connection is provided by Joseph Wright's 1782 portrait of a rotund Benjamin Franklin. The collection closes with eighteenth- and nineteenth-century **American** works, surprisingly uninspiring portraits by the usual suspects: Benjamin West, Gilbert Stuart and Thomas Cole. The one piece with any real spark is Rembrandt Peale's imperious, equestrian *Washington Before Yorktown* (1824), showing the general in the hours before the decisive battle for independence.

However, the main interest on this floor is not a painting, but the corner room known as the **Salon Doré** (Gilded Room), which originally formed part of an eighteenth-century Parisian home, the Hôtel de Clermont. Clark bought the entire room, intending to install it in his New York mansion: it came to the Corcoran after his death where it now stands as a supreme example of French design. Framed mirrors (flanked by medallion-holding cherubs) make it seem larger than it actually is; the floor-to-ceiling hand-carved wood-panelling, gold-leaf decor and ceiling murals are perfectly judged.

The second floor

There's a final European flurry on the second floor in the so-called **Clark Landing**, a two-tier, wood-panelled gallery accessed from the Rotunda. On the lower level, stacked on top of each other in nineteenth-century fashion, are works by Degas, Renoir, Monet and Pissarro; above, on the upper level, minor paintings by artists like George Innes and Benjamin West announce the start of the American collection proper.

Some of the gallery's finest **landscapes** are in the first room, starting with the expansive *Niagara* (1837) by Frederic Edwin Church and Albert Bierstadt's splendid *The Last of the Buffalo* (1889), both masterpieces of immense scale. While Church concerned himself with the power of nature, Bierstadt here celebrated human endeavour in the natural world, portraying the Native American braves, pursuing buffalo so numerous they darken the plain in their thousands. In marked contrast, Thomas Cole's *The Return* (1837), a mythical medieval scene of an injured knight returning to a priory glowing in the evening

Along 17th
Street

light, has little to do with America, though it does display the Hudson River School theme of ethereal natural beauty. An interesting historical note is provided by artist-cum-inventor Samuel F B Morse's *The Old House of Representatives* (1822), which the artist finished in a studio at the US Capitol so that he could observe his subjects at work. For all his efforts, he failed to convey any sense of the urgency of debate and Morse lost money when he exhibited the painting – which led him to conclude he'd be better off sticking with inventing.

Nineteenth-century sculpture and painting is next door, where you'll be waylaid by formal portraits by renowned artists like John Trumbull (who painted the Capitol murals) and Charles Bird King. Most prominent, though, are the presidential portraits by **George Peter Alexander Healy**, commissioned by Congress in 1857 for display in the White House: van Buren, Tyler, Polk, Taylor, Arthur and a highly sympathetic Lincoln. This seems an odd room to display the gallery's most notorious piece of sculpture, **Hiram Powers'** *The Greek Slave* (1846), originally on show in the Renwick Gallery up the road. Her manacled hands and simple nudity so outraged the sensibilities of contemporary critics that women visitors were prevented from viewing the statue while there were men in the room.

There are more Healy presidential portaits in the National Portait Gallery, see p.186.

Late nineteenth-century art occupies two more rooms on the floor, the gallery presenting changing selections of work by John Singer Sargent, Thomas Eakins and Mary Cassatt among others. Few are as robust as Winslow Homer's depiction of sea folk: the brawny arms of the woman swathed in fishing nets in *A Light on the Sea* (1897) suggest the realities of her life better than any storm-tossed fishing scene. Working women are rare subjects indeed in works of this period, while American blacks were hardly ever considered an enlightening contemporary subject – exceptions here include Richard Norris Brooke's beautifully lit family on the receiving end of *A Pastoral Visit* (1881).

Pre-World War II paintings throw up works by Childe Hassam, George Bellows, Thomas Hart Benton and, of course, Edward Hopper, whose yachting picture *Ground Swell* (1939) adds a real splash of colour. The remainder of the rooms on this floor are devoted to changing selections of prints, drawings and photographs from the permanent collection, as well as special exhibitions. Depending on space, post-war and contemporary American art gets a look-in too, and you can expect examples from all the big names, including Lichtenstein, Warhol and de Kooning.

Memorial Continental Hall: Daughters of the American Revolution

1776 D St NW ☎879-3239; Farragut West Metro. Mon–Fri 10am–4pm, Sun 1–5pm; tours Mon–Fri 10am–3pm, Sun 1–5pm; closed two weeks in April. Admission free.

The **National Society of the Daughters of the American Revolution** (DAR) has had its headquarters in Washington for over a century. Founded in 1890, its D Street address (no. 1776) has obvious significance since membership of this thoroughly patriotic (if unswervedly conservative) organization is open to women who can prove descent from an ancestor (male or female) who served the American cause during the Revolution. Fuelled by the motto "God, Home and Country", it busies itself with earnestly non-political good-citizen and educational programmes, including one designed to promote "correct flag usage" throughout America: the Stars and Stripes adorning the rostrums in the Senate and the House in the US Capitol are gifts from the DAR, just two of over 100,000 given away since 1909.

The organization's original meeting place was the 1905 Beaux Arts **Memorial Continental Hall**, facing 17th Street, whose main chamber hosted the world's first disarmament conference in 1921. Delegates now meet for their annual congress (the week of April 19, anniversary of the Battle of Lexington) in the massive **Constitution Hall** on 18th Street, designed with typical exuberance by John Russell Pope in 1929, but which you're unlikely to see unless you coincide with a concert (see p.295). It's one of the finest auditoriums in the city (indeed, until the Kennedy Center was built, the hall was the home of the National Symphony Orchestra), so it came as no surprise that when the peerless black contralto **Marian Anderson** (1902–93) was invited to sing in Washington in 1939, she was originally booked to appear here. What was shocking was that a racially hidebound DAR refused to allow her to perform at the hall: Eleanor Roosevelt resigned from the organization in outrage and Anderson gave her concert instead on Easter Sunday at the Lincoln Memorial to a rapt crowd of 75,000.

Visitors to the Memorial Continental Hall (entrance on D St) are shown first into the **gallery**, a hodge-podge of embroidered samplers and quilts, silverware, toys, kitchenware, glass, crockery and earthenware – in fact just about anything the daughters have managed to lay their hands on over the years. Although exhibits change, there's usually a particularly fine selection of ceramics, popular in the Revolutionary and Federal periods (from which most of the collection dates). On request, one of the docents will lead you through the rest of the building, starting off in the 125,000-volume genealogical **library** – once the main meeting hall, but now open to DAR members and the public ($5 a day) keen to bone up on such topics as *The History of Milwaukee* (in eight alarmingly large volumes) or *The Genealogy of the Witherspoon Family*.

What they're most proud of, however, are the **State Rooms**, a collection of no less than 33 period salons, mainly decorated with pre-1850 furnishings, each representing a different state. Few are of any historical or architectural merit, though occasionally, there's a glimmer of relief: the New England room containing a supposedly original laquered-wood tea chest retrieved from Boston harbour in 1773;

the Califonian adobe house interior; or the New Jersey room whose entire furnishings, panelling and furniture were fashioned from the wreck of a British frigate sunk off the coast during the Revolutionary War – the overly elaborate chandelier was made from the melted-down anchor.

Organization of American States Building

17th St at Constitution Ave NW ☎458-3000. Farragut West Metro. Tues–Fri 10am–5pm. Admission free.

Founded in 1890 "to strengthen the peace and security of the continent", the **Organization of American States** (OAS) is the world's oldest regional organization, with 35 member states from Antigua to Venezuela. Its headquarters occupy one of the more charming buildings in the city, a squat, white Spanish Colonial mansion built in 1910 and facing onto the Ellipse. From the main entrance on 17th Street – fronted by a gaunt statue of Queen Isabella of Spain, who sent Columbus on his New World voyage – you pass through fanciful iron gates to a cloistered lobby. The decor here turns almost to whimsy, with a fountain and tropical trees reaching to the wooden eaves and stone frieze above. Beyond the lobby, it's usually possible to catch temporary exhibitions of Latin American art; check in at the reception desk. Then climb upstairs, walk through the gallery of national flags and busts of OAS founder members, and take a peek in the grand Hall of the Americas.

A path leads from the Constitution Avenue side of the building through the so-called **Aztec Garden** to the smaller building behind. The **Art Museum of the Americas** – officially at 201 18th St NW (Tues–Sat 10am–5pm; free; ☎458-6016) – shows changing exhibits of Central and South American art, but again it's the interior that catches the eye. In the main brick-floored gallery, the walls are lined with lively Latin American ceramics reaching to a wood-beamed roof.

Foggy Bottom

Together with Georgetown, **FOGGY BOTTOM** – south of Pennsylvania Avenue to Constitution Avenue, between 17th and 25th streets – forms one of the oldest parts of DC. Settled as early as the mid-eighteenth century, the thriving town on the shores of the Potomac (which reached further north in those days) was known variously as Hamburg or Funkstown, after its German landlord Jacob Funk. Fashionable houses were built on the higher ground above today's E Street, though down by the river, in what is now West Potomac Park, it was a different story: filthy industries emptied effluents into the Potomac and the city canal, while workers' housing was erected on the low-lying malarial marshlands, blighted by plagues of rats, rampant poison ivy and winter mud and fog. It's not hard to see where the popular name originated.

The poor, predominantly black, neighbourhood changed radically once the low-lying marshlands were drained in the late 1800s. Families and industries were displaced by the new West Potomac Park; the neighbourhood's southern limit was now defined by the grand Constitution Avenue, which replaced the filled-in city canal. The smarter streets to the north formed the backdrop for a series of **federal and institutional organizations** which moved in during the years on either side of World War II, as the federal workforce rapidly expanded. Early city plans had made little provision for an influx of government support staff – in 1802, there were only 291 federal employees; by the 1970s the total number of civilians employed by US government had risen to over two million, and entire districts like Foggy Bottom were appropriated to house DC's burgeoning share.

The cultural activities at the **Kennedy Center** and the various offices and institutions rather set the white-collar tone, but you can visit enough of the buildings to make a walk through the neighbourhood worthwhile. The nearest Metro is **Foggy Bottom-GWU**, which is handy for George Washington University, Washington Circle and the Kennedy Center, but half a dozen blocks and fifteen minutes from Constitution Avenue. Consider, instead, approaching from the east, after touring the White House.

Constitution Avenue

From the OAS Building (see above) at the corner of 17th Street, **Constitution Avenue** – known as B Street until the 1930s – presents an attractive line of buildings framed by the greenery of Constitution Gardens across the way. First of any distinction is the enormous, eagle-fronted **Federal Reserve Building** of 1937, between 20th and 21st streets (Mon–Fri 11.30am–2pm; ☎452-3686), built by Paul Cret, who was responsible for the OAS and the Folger Shakespeare Library on Capitol Hill. It's the headquarters of the Federal Reserve System – which, basically, controls the money supply by tweaking financial policy and backing the system with government securities and gold. If you want to know any more than that, weekly tours of the building are available.

The Tourmobile *bus runs along Constitution Avenue and up 23rd Street to the Kennedy Center.*

The **National Academy of Sciences** (Mon–Fri 8.30am–5pm; free; ☎334-2000) is next, created by Congress in 1863 to provide the nation with independent, objective scientific advice. The motif here is Neoclassical, the facade adorned with Greek inscriptions, but its cold lines are tempered by a grove of elm and holly trees at the southwest (22nd St) corner, in which sits a large bronze statue of Albert Einstein, by Robert Berks. It's worth checking to see if there's an exhibition on in the academy, which also hosts chamber recitals (see p.295). Finally, the corner plot of the avenue, at 23rd Street, is occupied by the **American Pharmaceutical Association**, a severe Beaux Arts building by John Russell Pope, completed in 1933.

Department of State

Between 21st and 23rd streets NW, at C St ☎647-3241. Tours, by appointment only, Mon–Fri 9.30am, 10.30am & 2.45pm. Reserve several weeks in
advance. Foggy Bottom-GWU Metro. Admission free.

The **Department of State** received its own premises in 1947, following its move out of the Old Executive Office Building (see p.153),
and handsome they are, too, the long, white, unblemished building
occupying two entire blocks in the southwest corner of Foggy
Bottom. Effectively the federal Foreign Office, the State Department
is notoriously circumspect, and it's a wonder that visitors are allowed
in at all. As it is, it's all but impossible for foreign tourists, as the
hour-long tours must be booked several weeks in advance (up to two
months in summer) – effort that is rewarded by a glimpse of one of
the capital's more overblown interiors. During the 1960s, many of
the rooms were redecorated and refurnished to provide a series of
chambers suitable for the reception of diplomats and visiting heads
of state. In came a wealth of eighteenth- and nineteenth-century
paintings and furniture – including the desk on which the Treaty of
Paris was signed, which ended the War of Independence.

Department of the Interior

C St NW, between 18th and 19th Streets ☎208-4743; Farragut West Metro.
Mon–Fri 8am–5pm; call in advance for tours of the building and murals.
Admission free.

For a walk-in tour of a government department, head further east
down C Street to the **Department of the Interior**, the nation's principal conservation agency. One of the earliest federal departments to
take up residence in Foggy Bottom, the Interior Department moved
into Waddy Butler Wood's granite, square-columned building in
1937. Inside, grand WPA-era murals enliven the walls, including one
commemorating Marian Anderson's 1939 concert at the Lincoln
Memorial (see p.60).

*Inside the
Department,
the **National
Park Service
information
office**
(Mon–Fri
9am–5pm) has
free leaflets
about every
NPS park,
museum and
monument in
the country –
in DC, these
cover all the
major mem-
orials along
the Mall.*

Present ID at the reception desk and you'll be directed to the
Department of the Interior Museum, a little-visited nook which
throws some light upon the various agencies that come under the
department's auspices – notably fish, wildlife and geological services,
Bureau of Land Management and, most contentiously, the Bureau of
Indian Affairs. The wood-panelled museum, opened in 1938, is very
much of its time: then over 100,000 people a year toured the dioramas and exhibits; now you'll be on your own as you puzzle over fossil
and mineral samples and examine stuffed bison heads, old saddles
and paintings by nineteenth-century surveyors of the West. Like the
National Museum of Natural History, the museum has most trouble
with its ethnographical content, namely the coverage of the work of
the Bureau of Indian Affairs, which, unbelievably, holds Native
American property – "lands, forests, minerals, funds – in trust for the

Indian owners." But also like the natural history museum, the entire collection is being reviewed, so in the near future you can expect revitalized, revisionist, less rose-tinted displays. For now, probably the most arresting collection is the contemporary Native American paintings and crafts, much of it by women artists. There's more of this, for sale this time, across the hall in the gift shop.

The Octagon

1799 New York Ave NW ☎638-3105; Farragut West Metro. Tues–Fri 10am–4pm, Sat & Sun 1–4pm. Admission $3.

When Virginian plantation owner John Tayloe had his Washington townhouse built in 1800, he picked a prime corner plot just two blocks away from the new Presidential Mansion; in those days **the Octagon**, as it became known, was set amid fields and flanked by a line of fir trees. Today, dwarfed by the office buildings behind, it still serves as a fine example of the type of wealthy, private mansion that once characterized the neighbourhood. Tayloe, a friend of George Washington, was so rich and well-connected that he could afford to spend the colossal sum of $35,000 on his house, and engage no less an architect than William Thornton, winner of the competition to design the US Capitol.

The War of 1812 guaranteed the house its place in **history**. Spared the bonfire that destroyed the White House – possibly because the French ambassador was in residence at the time – the Octagon was offered to the Madisons, who had been forced to flee the city. For six months in 1814–15, President Madison conducted the business of government from its rooms; on February 17, 1815, the Treaty of Ghent, making peace with Britain, was signed in the study (on a table still kept in the house). For much of the latter part of the nineteenth century, the Octagon was left to deteriorate, but at the turn of this century it was bought by the American Institute of Architects (AIA), which used it as its headquarters until 1973. The AIA still maintains the building, which after a recent $5 million restoration is open as both an historic house and **museum of architecture**, with changing exhibitions devoted to architecture, decorative arts and city history.

The **building** itself is not, in fact, an octagon – forced into an acute street corner, it has only six sides; the name was mis-assigned by the Tayloes when it was built. The rather simple brick exterior hides an example of period American Federal architecture unsurpassed in the city. The circular entry hall sports its original marble floor, while beyond, a swirling, oval staircase climbs up three storeys; the house had two master bedrooms and five more for the Tayloe's fifteen children, most of which are now used as gallery space. In the dining and drawing rooms, period furnishings reveal how the house would have looked – light, with high ceilings, delicate plaster cornicing and Chippendale accompaniments. The two portraits in the dining room are of the architect and the owner; while the beautifully carved stone mantel in the drawing room is an original, signed and dated 1799.

GWU to Washington Circle

The L'Enfant city plan allowed for the building of a university in the Foggy Bottom district, and it was certainly a development that Washington himself was keen on; he even left money in his will to endow an educational establishment. A Baptist college founded by Act of Congress in 1821 was the precursor of today's **George Washington University** (GWU), which moved into the neighbourhood in 1912, where it's played a crucial role ever since, buying up townhouses and erecting new buildings on such a scale to make it the second biggest landholder in DC after the federal government. Famous alumni include Jacqueline Kennedy Onassis (who gets a building named after her), J Edgar Hoover, General Colin Powell and crime author (and Harry's daughter) Margaret Truman. The main campus spreads over several city blocks between F, 20th and 24th streets and Pennsylvania Avenue; there's an information desk in the **Academic Center**, 801 22nd St NW (Mon–Fri 10am–3pm, also Sat 10am–3pm Aug–Nov & Jan–April only; ☎994-6602), on the H Street side. You can pick up a map of the campus here and ask about **tours**: occasionally students lead historic walking tours of the neighbourhood.

Although the student presence certainly enlivens the district, few of the university buildings are worth more than a passing glance; some people have kind words for the **Law Library** (716 20th St NW), which at least makes an attempt to fit in with its surroundings. This backs onto perhaps the nicest part of the campus, **University Yard** (between G and H, and 20th and 21st), a green, rose-planted park surrounded by Colonial Revival buildings; the statue of George Washington here is yet another copy of the famous Houdon image (see p.58).

GWU's main entertainment hall is the Lisner Auditorium; see p.290 and p.295 for details.

Nearby, on the southeast corner of 20th and G, the redbrick Gothic, Lutheran **United Church**, built in 1889, provides a solitary reminder of Foggy Bottom's antecedents, erected for the descendants of the neighbourhood's Germanic immigrants. If you're heading back towards the White House, you may as well stick with G Street, which passes the concrete chicken-coop buildings of the twin peaks of international capitalism – the **International Monetary Fund** and, in the next block, the **World Bank**. For a glimpse of how modern development has encroached completely upon the remaining nineteenth-century pockets of Foggy Bottom, head instead up 20th Street to Pennsylvania Avenue. Between 20th and 21st, the **2000 Pennsylvania Avenue Complex** of offices, shops and cafés preserves the original pastel-coloured facades of a row of townhouses.

West of the university, en route to Foggy Bottom-GWU Metro station, you can swing by **St Mary's Church**, at 730 23rd St, between G and H (daily 9.30am–3pm), the first black episcopal church in DC. Established in 1886, the church was paid for by a wealthy band of

local citizens who stumped up $15,000 to hire the services of none
other than James Renwick (of the Smithsonian Castle and Renwick
Gallery), whose hand is clear in the church's careful Gothic proportions.

One block north of the Metro, the northern limit of Foggy Bottom
is marked by **Washington Circle**, L'Enfant's radial point for the
major thoroughfares of Pennsylvania and New Hampshire avenues
and K Street. In its centre sits Clark Mills' equestrian statue of
George Washington, erected at the outbreak of the Civil War and
looking towards White House and Capitol; not a thing of great splendour it's true, but quite how it aroused the particular ire of Anthony
Trollope is a mystery. He thought it "by far the worst" equestrian
statue he had ever seen, claiming "the horse is most absurd, but the
man sitting on the horse is manifestly drunk".

The Kennedy Center

2700 F St NW, at Rock Creek Parkway ☎467-4600; Foggy Bottom-GWU
Metro. Box office Mon–Sat 10am–9pm, Sun noon–9pm. Admission free.

Although government departments have been based in the capital for
two centuries, it wasn't until 1971 that Washington got its national
cultural centre, a $78-million white marble monster designed by
Edward Durrell Stone. Though the building has its detractors – travel
writer Jan Morris dismissed it as "a cross between a Nazi exhibition
and a more than usually ambitious hairdresser" – the **John F
Kennedy Center for the Performing Arts**, to give it its full title, continues to be the city's foremost cultural outlet. The National
Symphony Orchestra and Washington Opera have their homes here,
there are four main auditoriums, the American Film Institute, various
exhibition halls, and a clutch of restaurants and bars.

There's an **information desk** on your way in and you're free to
wander around; provided there's no performance or rehearsal taking
place, you should also be able to take a look inside the theatres and
concert halls (most are open to visitors 10am–1pm). Free 45-minute
guided tours depart daily (also 10am–1pm) from Motor Lobby A
(beneath the Opera House).

*For details of
performances
at the Kennedy
Center, see
Chapter 16.*

The **Grand Foyer** itself is some sight: 630ft long and 60ft high, it's
lit by gargantuan crystal chandeliers and features a seven-foot-high
bronze bust of JFK in the moon-rock-pimple style favoured by sculptor Robert Berks. You can also drop by the **Hall of States** (flags of the
states hung in the order they entered the Union) and **Hall of Nations**
(flags of nations recognized by the US); while each of the theatres and
concert halls has its own catalogue of artworks, from the Matisse
tapestries outside the Opera House or the Barbara Hepworth sculpture in the Concert Hall to the Felix de Welden bronze bust of
Eisenhower above the lobby of the Eisenhower Theater.

The **Roof Terrace Level** holds the **Performing Arts Library** of
scripts, performance information and recordings (Tues–Fri

11am–8.30pm, Sat 10am–6pm) and the centre's eating places: the none-too-good *Encore Café* and the much pricier *Roof Terrace Restaurant*. While you're up here, step out onto the terrace itself for scintillating **views** across the Potomac to Theodore Roosevelt Island, and north to Georgetown and the National Cathedral.

Watergate

I lied to protect the Presidency – until it became clear that the President was frantically trying to preserve himself, not his high office.

Howard Hunt, Watergate burglar

The burglars who broke into the headquarters of the Democratic National Committee at the Watergate were in effect breaking into the home of every citizen of the United States. And . . . what they were seeking to steal was . . . their most precious heritage, the right to vote in a free election.

Sam Ervin, chairman of Senate Investigating Committee

*The Watergate
Complex is
named for the
flight of steps
behind the
Lincoln
Memorial, to
the south,
which lead
down to the
Potomac.*

If there's a building that defines modern, political Washington, it's not the White House or the Capitol but the **Watergate Complex**, 25th Street NW, by Virginia Avenue, which gave its name to the most noxious political scandal ever to rock the country. This unassuming curving, Italian-designed mid-1960s residential and commercial complex has always been a much sought-after address for city top-brass (the Doles and Caspar Weinberger have maintained apartments here for years) and a base for various foreign embassies – among the shops, offices and businesses located here in 1972 was the headquarters of the Democratic National Committee, on the sixth floor. What started as the burglary of this office in June of that year by five men on the payroll of the campaign to re-elect Richard Nixon ended, two years later, with the resignation of a president.

The Watergate story

The 1972 presidential election campaign was well underway when five men were arrested at the Watergate Complex on June 17. Richard Nixon, running for re-election against the Democratic challenger Governor George McGovern, was determined to win a second term, elevating the election race into a moral, almost personal, struggle against encroaching liberal forces, who, crucially, were pushing the anti-Vietnam war message to the top of the political agenda.

After being spotted by a security guard on his rounds, the five men apprehended in the offices of the Democratic National Committee were caught in the act of tapping the phone of Lawrence O'Brien, the national party chairman. Once arraigned in court, it became clear that these were no ordinary burglars: one, **James McCord**, worked directly for the Committee to Re-Elect the President (known, delightfully, as **CREEP**), all had CIA connections, and some were later linked to documents which suggested that their escapade had been sanctioned by White House staffer **Howard Hunt** and election campaign attorney **Gordon Liddy**. To anyone who cared to look, the connections went further still: at the White House, Hunt worked for Charles Colson, Nixon's special counsel; while McCord's direct superior was the head of CREEP, John Mitchell, who also happened to be Attorney General of the United States.

Amazingly, at least in retrospect, no one looked further. The burglars, together with Hunt and Liddy, were indicted in September 1972 but continued to refuse to provide any collaborative detail. The Democrats, none more so than McGovern, complained loudly about dirty tricks, but the White House officially denied any knowledge. In the election in November, Nixon won a conservative **landslide**, carrying 49 out of the 50 states (only Massachusetts and, ironically, the District of Columbia, went for McGovern).

From such commanding heights, it was remarkable how quickly things unravelled. Initially the only people asking questions were *Washington Post* reporters **Bob Woodward** and **Carl Bernstein**. As the months went by, and aided by a source known to Woodward only as "Deep Throat", the pair uncovered irregularities in the Republican campaign, many of which had tantalizingly close, but so far unprovable, links with the Watergate burglary. To the FBI's annoyance, the stories often relied on verbatim accounts of the FBI's own investigations – someone, somewhere, was leaking information. However, it still proved difficult to generate much interest outside Washington in the matter, and it probably would have remained a marginal story but for the impetus provided by the trial of the defendants. All pleaded guilty to burglary, but before sentencing in January 1973 the judge made it clear that he didn't believe that the men acted alone; long sentences were threatened. Rather than face jail, some defendants began to talk, including James McCord who not only implicated senior officials like John Mitchell for the first time, but also claimed that secret CREEP funds had been used to finance an anti-Democrat smear campaign, which employed so-called "plumbers" – like the burglars – to work against domestic "enemies". This was precisely what Woodward and Bernstein had been trying to prove for months. As pressure on the administration for answers grew, Senate established a **special investigating committee** under Sam Ervin and appointed a special prosecutor, Archibald Cox. The trail led ever closer to the White House. In a desperate damage limitation exercise, Nixon's own counsel, John Dean, was sacked and the resignations accepted of White House Chief of Staff Robert Haldeman and domestic affairs advisor John Erlichman; all, it seemed, were involved in planning the burglary.

In June 1973, the **Watergate hearings**, now broadcast on national television, began to undermine Nixon's steadfast denial of any involvement. The Watergate burglars had been promised clemency and cash by the White House if they remained silent, it transpired;

the CIA had leaned on the FBI to prevent any further investigations; illegal wiretaps, dirty tricks campaigns and unlawful campaign contributions appeared to be commonplace. The President continued to stand aloof from the charges, but was finally dragged down by the revelation that he himself had routinely bugged offices in the White House and elsewhere, taping conversations which pertained to Watergate. It quickly became a matter of what the President knew, and when he knew it. The tapes were subpoenaed as evidence by Cox and the Senate committee, but Nixon refused to release them, citing his presidential duty to protect executive privilege. Soon after, he engineered the sacking of Cox, a move which led to the convening of the House Judiciary Committee, the body charged with preparing bills of impeachment – in this case, against the President for refusing to comply with a subpoena. To deflect mounting suspicion Nixon finally handed over edited transcripts of the tapes in April 1974; despite the erasure of eighteen minutes of conversation, rather than clearing Nixon of any involvement, the "smoking gun" transcripts simply dragged him further in. The President, it seemed, at least knew about the cover up and there was clear evidence of wrongdoing by key government and White House personnel. A grand jury indicted Mitchell, Haldeman, Erlichman, Dean and others for specific offences, while the House Judiciary Committee drew up a bill of **impeachment** against Nixon for committing "high crimes and misdemeanors".

On August 5, 1974, the Supreme Court ordered Nixon to hand over the tapes themselves. These proved conclusively that he and his advisors had known about the Watergate burglary within days and had devised a strategy of bribes and the destruction of evidence to cover up White House and CREEP involvement. The President, despite his protestations, had lied to the people, and it was inevitable that he should face impeachment. Urged on by senior Republican senators, in August 8, 1974, Richard Milhous Nixon became the first President to **resign**. Combative to the end, he made no acknowledgement of guilt, suggesting instead that he had simply made errors of judgement.

Nixon was replaced by his deputy, **Gerald Ford**, but though the President changed, little else did. Secretary of State Henry Kissinger – architect of the bombing of Laos and Cambodia and the My Lai massacre, campaigns hidden from the American public – kept his job, while Alexander Haig, a key figure in withholding and doctoring the Watergate tapes, was promoted to become head of NATO. To top it all, Ford formally pardoned Nixon with unseemly haste, allowing him to live out his retirement in California. In a bizarre twist, Richard Nixon slowly rehabilitated himself in the eyes of the political establishment and even in the eyes of the press; when he died in 1995 there was a full turn-out at his funeral by leaders of all political hues.

Chapter 6

Old Downtown and Federal Triangle

T he land between Capitol and White House, north of the Mall, was the only part of Washington in the nineteenth century that resembled anything like a city. In the diamond formed by Pennsylvania, New York, Massachusetts and Indiana avenues developed a convenient **downtown**, where just a few blocks' walk from the seats of legislative or executive power, fashionable stores and restaurants coexisted alongside printing presses and tailors' shops, shoeshine stalls, grocers, oyster sellers and market traders. Entertainment was provided by a series of popular theatres – not least, Ford's Theater, where President Lincoln was shot dead as he relaxed just days after the end of the Civil War.

By the 1960s, downtown was a shambling, low-rent neighbourhood, later to be badly affected by the riots of 1968 following the assassination of Dr Martin Luther King Jr. As established businesses fled to the developing area north of the White House, the old neighbourhood eventually became known, rather infelicitously, as **Old Downtown** (to distinguish it from the mushrooming buildings of New Downtown – see p.204).

In the nineteenth century, **Pennsylvania Avenue**, far from being the main artery it is today, marked the southern limits of civilized Washington society; the shops on its north side were as far as those of genteel sensibilities would venture. The area was given a new lease of life in the 1930s with the construction of the majestic buildings of **Federal Triangle**, though it wasn't until the 1980s that the avenue itself was finally rescued from years of neglect. An enormous amount of money has been pumped into renovation, especially in the easternmost area (south of G, between 3rd and 12th), now being trumpeted by the authorities as **Penn Quarter** – grafting a Left-Bank-like swatch of delis, restaurants, galleries and landscaping onto the existing historic buildings and cleaned-up streets.

Tours of Old Downtown start quite properly with the grand length of Pennsylvania Avenue and its landmark sights – **Navy Memorial**, **FBI Building**, **Old Post Office** and **Willard Hotel**. Adjacent Federal

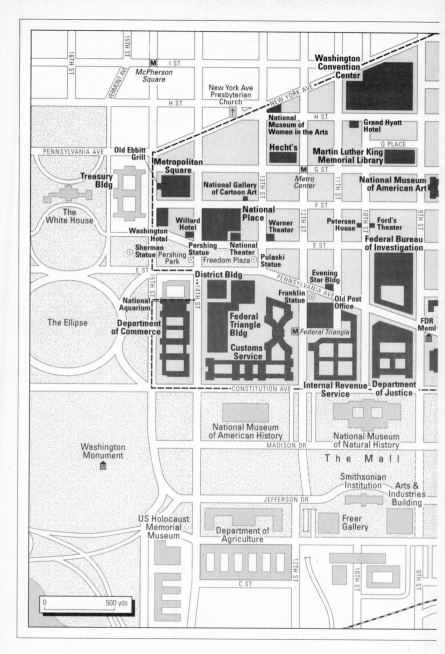

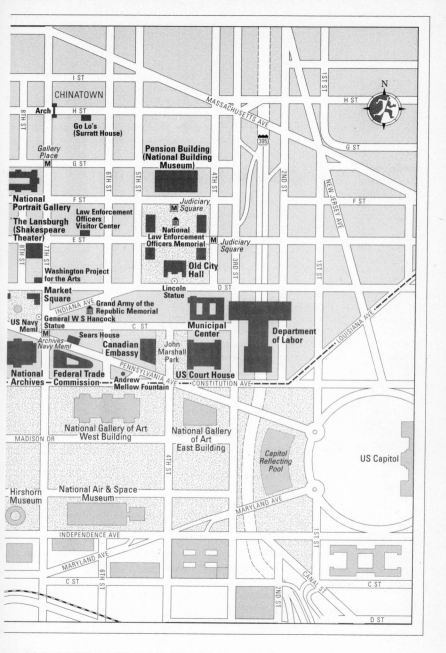

Triangle has less to show, since so many of the buildings are closed to the public, save for the outstanding collection of manuscripts in the **National Archives**. Elsewhere, many of the grander municipal buildings have been converted into fine museums – the exceptional Pensions Building now the **National Building Museum**, and the Old Patent Office split between the Smithsonian's **National Portrait Gallery** and **National Museum of American Art**. Other sights include **Ford's Theater** and a unique **Museum of Women in the Arts**; and you're only ever a short stroll from diminutive **Chinatown**, where you can lunch cheaply on noodles and *dim sum*.

Along Pennsylvania Avenue

A glance at the map shows **Pennsylvania Avenue** to be the backbone of the city, connecting Capitol to White House and, at its extremities, Georgetown to the Anacostia River. In its early days it was the only avenue in the city paved with federal funds, yet although it was the obvious focus for the new city's commercial life, it was hampered by the piecemeal development taking place all around. While fashionable shops traded along the north side of Pennsylvania Avenue, the swamp-ridden reaches to the south (today's Federal Triangle), close to the filth-ridden canal that isolated the city from the Mall, housed a notorious stew of slum housing, bordellos and cheap liquor joints. Often, the slurry washed onto the avenue itself; Anthony Trollope noted that in the 1860s there were "parts of Pennsylvania Avenue that would have been considered heavy ground by most hunting-men".

The account of the buildings along Pennsylvania Avenue starts from its south-eastern end at 6th St NW; nearest Metro is Archives-Navy Memorial

Turn-of-the-century additions to the avenue – notably the Post Office and the renowned *Willard Hotel* – formed part of an early attempt to transform the district's fortunes, but for much of this century Pennsylvania Avenue was in severe decline. In the 1970s the **Pennsylvania Avenue Development Corporation** (PADC) came into action, and it's become a much livelier area as a result, dotted with small plazas, memorials framed by newly planted trees and Victorian flourishes decorating lamp-posts and street furniture.

For the first time in years the avenue provides a suitable backdrop for that most Washingtonian of ceremonial processions – the triumphal **Inaugural Parade** that takes each new President from the Capitol to their residence for the next four years. Thomas Jefferson led the first impromptu parade in 1805; James Madison made the ceremony official; and every president since has trundled up in some form of conveyance or another – except Jimmy Carter who, famously, walked the sixteen long blocks to the White House.

From the Mellon Fountain to the Navy Memorial

The bronze, triple-decker **fountain** in the corner plot between 6th Street and Constitution Avenue commemorates former secretary of the Treasury and art connoisseur Andrew Mellon, fittingly sited across from the West Building of the National Gallery of Art which he funded and filled with paintings. It's overlooked by the ultra-modern stone-and-glass **Canadian Embassy**, on the north side of the avenue, a typical piece of contemporary braggadocio which cuts a neat bite out of its lower storey and then props up the overhang on a circle of columns forming a covered piazza. The gallery in the basement shows temporary Canadian art exhibitions (Mon–Fri 10am–5pm; free).

A little further up on the same side, the restored turreted, pink-stone **Sears House**, 633 Pennsylvania Ave, once contained the studio of nineteenth-century photographer Matthew Brady, whose graphic photographs of the slaughter at Antietam in 1862 first brought home the full horror of the Civil War to the American public. The small plaza here at 7th Street, Indiana Plaza, is taken up by the memorial to the victorious **Grand Army of the Republic**, a triangular obelisk adorned with figures representing Fraternity, Loyalty and Charity. Across 7th Street, the gruff equestrian statue is of **General Winfield Scott Hancock**, commander-in-chief of the Union forces – aged 74 at the outbreak of war and ridden with gout, he barely left the War Department offices close to the White House.

Across Pennsylvania Avenue from here, in the green plot in front of the Archives at 9th Street, a small marble memorial commemorates another war leader, **Franklin Delano Roosevelt**. It was his wish that any memorial to him erected after his death be "plain, without any ornamentation" and that's what he got: placed here in 1965 on the twentieth anniversary of his death, it's inscribed simply "In Memory of Franklin Delano Roosevelt 1882–1945".

Market Square

In 1801 the city's biggest outdoor market opened for business at the foot of 7th Street. Known as **Center Market**, it backed onto the canal along the Mall where goods barges could be unloaded; out front, top-heavy carts and drays spilled across Pennsylvania Avenue and up 7th Street on the way out of the city. It was a notoriously noxious spot – presidential secretary John Hay in Gore Vidal's novel, *Lincoln*, "was haunted by the ghosts of the millions of cats who had given their lives that the nearby canal might exude its distinctive odour" – and there was little clamour when it was demolished in 1870. The National Archives (see p.179) were erected on the site in 1935. The concave, colonnaded buildings of the development opposite, known as **Market Square**, frame the view up 8th Street to the Old Patent Office Building. The ground floors are given over to café-restaurants and outdoor seating, while upper-floor apartments provide sweeping views over the revitalized Penn Quarter.

The US Navy Memorial

Market Square's circular plaza is entirely covered by an etched representation of the world, circled by low, tiered, granite walls lapped by running water. These together make up the **US Navy Memorial**, complemented by the statue of a lone sailor, kit bag by his side, and inscribed naval quotations from the historic (Themistocles, architect of the Greek naval victory during the Persian Wars) to the tenuous (naval aviator Neil Armstrong's "That's one small step for man . . ."). Directly behind the memorial, in the easternmost Market Square building at 701 Pennsylvania Ave NW, the **Naval Heritage Center** (Mon–Sat 9.30am–5pm, Sun noon–5pm; ☎ 737-2300) can tell you more about the service with its changing exhibits and daily showing of the tub-thumping *At Sea* movie (Mon–Sat 10am, Sun 1pm; $3.75). Portraits honour the various presidents who have served in the US Navy: JFK famously commanded a motor torpedo boat and was awarded the Navy and Marine Corps medal for heroism (see p.138), but Johnson, Nixon, Ford and Carter all served with distinction, too, while George Bush, the Navy's youngest bomber pilot, received the Distinguished Flying Cross and three Air Medals for his endeavours.

There's a regular series of concerts by the Navy Band at the memorial (June–Aug Tues 8pm).

The Federal Bureau of Investigation

9th St and Pennsylvania Ave NW ☎ 324-3447; Federal Triangle Metro. Mon–Fri 8.45am–4.15pm. Admission free.

Disappointingly, the lightweight, partisan and ultimately tedious hour-long tour of the **Federal Bureau of Investigation** does not deserve its status as one of Washington's most popular attractions. The building itself sets the tone: a 1970s concrete excrescence ponderously named after the organization's most notorious red-baiting, cross-dressing chief, J Edgar Hoover, it's hardly the most inspiring structure in the city, and not one that provides any distraction for visitors who can expect to wait an hour (more in summer) before being ushered into what is effectively a PR job for America's most mythologized law enforcement agency.

Established in 1908 (motto: Fidelity, Bravery, Integrity) under the auspices of the Department of Justice, the FBI owed its early investigative techniques to those pioneered by the Pinkerton Detective Agency in the 1870s, and made its reputation in the 1920s and 1930s by battling gangsters and attempting to enforce Prohibition. Today, ten thousand Special Agents are employed to fight organized and white-collar crime, pursue drug-traffickers and lurk in the shadowy world of counter-intelligence.

After an introductory video, the walk-through tour continues with stilted presentations about FBI training and duties, led by guides who have swallowed the textbook whole. Thus you learn that the FBI discovered that "two Libyan terrorists were responsible" for the Lockerbie bomb, even though no trial has yet taken place. After a brief exposition about drugs (bad) and FBI agents (good) – note that the phials are filled with make-believe marijuana and crack, so as not to offend – it's off to the next exhibit: "Does anyone have a question about terrorism? OK, now let's look at violent crime". The whole set-up is rife with contradictions: while being led to condemn crimes of violence and their perpetrators, visitors are titillated with casefuls of confiscated, historic weaponry – "Pretty Boy" Floyd's Colt .45, John Dillinger's Winchester rifle – in a retrospective glorification of an age of cartoon villains. It is, if anything, even more problematic when looking to the future: systematic DNA sampling and the concept of a national fingerprint bank are championed as developments in the fight against crime, with not a mention of the encroachment upon civil liberties that each might bring.

The tour finishes down in the shooting range where an FBI agent fires semi-automatic handguns and assault rifles at a paper human target to approving gasps and whistles from the audience. The question-and-answer session afterwards tends to run, worryingly, along the lines of "how can I get one of those?", though to be fair the agent, when prompted, will claim that most FBI agents don't discharge their weapons during the entire course of their career. Neither, it turns out, do they have much contact with aliens, despite the high-profile exploits of the FBI's latest cult figures, the *X-Files'* Special Agents Mulder and Scully, who are often filmed running in and out of the building pursuing matters of life and death.

The Old Post Office

Built in 1899, the fanciful Romanesque **Old Post Office**, 1100 Pennsylvania Ave NW, at the junction with 12th Street, has survived various attempts to demolish it to become one of the most recognizable of downtown's monuments. For years, it served as federal offices, but since the mid-1980s it's been turned over to business. It's one of the city's great indoor spaces, with a glorious galleried interior, known as the **Pavilion** (Mon–Sat 10am–9pm, Sun noon–8pm; information ☎289-4224), whose glass roof throws light down onto the restored iron support beams, brass rails, balconies and burnished wood panelling. There's a large food court in the first-floor courtyard (where clerks once sorted mail), and gift shops and stalls on the second. Check out the period **post office counter** (Mon–Fri 9am–5pm), still in use at the Pennsylvania Avenue entrance.

Signs point the way to the **clocktower** (mid-April to mid-Sept daily 8am–11pm, closed Thurs 6.30–9.30pm; mid-Sept to mid-April daily 10am–5.45pm; free; ☎606-8691), where park rangers oversee short tours up to the observation deck, 270ft above Pennsylvania Avenue. The glass-elevator ride allows you to see the interior in all its glory, and the viewing platform itself boasts a stunning city panorama. On the way down, walk the three flights to the glass elevator to see the Congress Bells, a Bicentennial gift from London, replicas of those in Westminster Abbey and installed here in 1983.

Back outside on the avenue, **Benjamin Franklin** – "Philosopher, Printer, Philanthropist, Patriot", as his statue has it – gives a cheery little wave. You can park yourself on a bench and look across to the Neoclassical facade of the **Evening Star Building** (1898), whose attractive balconies, pediments and carvings provide virtually the only exterior relief on any building on the north side of the avenue as far down as the Sears Building.

Nearest Metro for the Old Post Office and Freedom Plaza is Federal Triangle.

Freedom Plaza to the Willard Hotel

Where Pennsylvania Avenue kinks into E Street (at 13th), you've reached the large open space of **Freedom Plaza**, site of various festivals and open-air concerts. Lined in marble, it's inlaid with a large-scale representation of L'Enfant's city plan, picked out in bronze and coloured stone, and etched with various laudatory inscriptions.

Freedom Plaza also offers an immediate view of the development going on along Pennsylvania Avenue. On the south side the sculpted capitals and pediments of the Beaux Arts District Building (see Federal Triangle, below) offer a sharp rebuke to the faceless behemoth which lines the plaza's entire north side. The *Marriott* hotel and restored facade of the **National Theater** (see *The Arts and Entertainment*, p.297) – on this site since 1835, though the current building dates from 1922 – both form part of the **National Place** complex, whose unexciting exterior hides a three-level shopping mall. There's access to the *Shops at National Place* (Mon–Sat 10am–7pm, Thurs until 8pm, Sun noon–5pm) through the hotel, as well as on 14th and F streets. At the northeastern corner of the plaza the historic **Warner Theater Building** (at 13th and E) forms part of the 1299 Pennsylvania Avenue development; the carved stone latticework facade shines pink in the sun and you can get a decent beer in the basement *Dock Street Brewing Co* (see p.285).

This section of the avenue ends at **Pershing Park**, named for the commander of the American forces during World War I whose statue stands alongside a sunken terrace that becomes a skating rink in winter. Just to the west, Hamilton Place marks the spot at which an earlier general, William Tecumseh Sherman (also honoured by a statue), presided over the **Grand Review of the Union armies** in May 1865; six weeks after Lee's surrender, the victorious troops marched proudly up Pennsylvania Avenue in the most stirring military parade ever seen in the capital. It was a show of Union strength tinged with sadness, since many at the time didn't think it appropriate to celebrate so soon after the assassination of Lincoln.

The Willard Hotel

Peering over the north side of Pershing Park at 14th stands one of the city's *grand dame* hotels, the **Willard**, a Washington landmark for 150 years. Though a hotel has existed on the site since the capital's earliest days, it was after 1850 when Henry Willard gave his name to the place that it became a haunt of statesmen, politicians and top brass – not least Abraham Lincoln, who was smuggled in before his first inauguration (during which snipers were placed on the roof). Its opulent public rooms attracted placemen and profit-seekers anxious to press their suit on political leaders; it's claimed, with a bare smidgen of proof, that this is whence the word "lobbyist" derives. Somewhat less apocryphal is the story that Julia Ward Howe wrote *The Battle Hymn of the Republic* while closeted in her *Willard* room during the Civil War – supposedly inspired by Union soldiers marching under her window belting out their favourite song, *John Brown's Body*.

Along
Pennsylvania
Avenue

In 1901, Henry Hardenbergh – architect of some of New York's finest period hotels – was engaged to update the *Willard* and produced the splendid Beaux Arts building which stands today; it went out of business after the riots of 1968, but a thorough restoration in 1986 has recaptured its early style. Drop by the galleried lobby and tread the plush carpets of the grand main corridor for a coffee in the Art Nouveau *Café Espresso* (see p.271); other browsing-and-sluicing spots are the *Nest* bar (p.291) and *Willard Room* restaurant (p.279).

While you're here, you may as well slip into the **Washington Hotel**, a little further along at 15th Street, less for its architectural attractions (though it's a decent enough building of 1917 with a fine lobby and handsome brown-and-white facade) than for its **rooftop café** (May–Sept only; see p.286 for more), from where there are splendid views across to the White House grounds.

For reser-
vation details
for both hotels,
see p.264.

Federal Triangle

The wedge of land between Pennsylvania and Constitution avenues – **FEDERAL TRIANGLE** – makes one of the most coherent architectural statements in the city. Grand Neoclassical government buildings follow the lines of the avenues, presenting imposing facades to the Mall on one side and Pennsylvania Avenue on the other; all were erected in the 1930s in an attempt to graft an instant "Imperial" look upon the capital city of the Free World. The district's nineteenth-century origins, however, were distinctly humble, as a canal-side slum known, graphically, as Murder Bay: hoodlums frequented its brothels and taverns, while on hot days the stench from Center Market drifted through the ill-fitting windows of the district's cheap boarding-houses. Few improvements were effected until the mid-1920s, when an increasing shortage of office space forced the federal government's hand. The triangle of land was bought and redeveloped in its entirety between 6th and 15th streets, following a Neoclassical plan with buildings opening onto quiet interior courtyards. Although never fully realized – the Old Post Office and the District Building intruded into the Triangle but were saved from successive attempts to knock them down – it's a remarkably uniform district, even today. Different architects worked on the buildings, but they all have the same characteristics: granite facades, stone reliefs, columns and worthy inscriptions.

Department of Commerce to the Federal Trade Commission

One of the first buildings completed was the thousand-foot-long **Department of Commerce** in 1931, which forms the western base of the Triangle, at 14th between E and Constitution. Its main interest today is as site of the White House Visitor Center (on the north side of the building; see p.150) and home of the **National Aquarium** (daily 9am–5pm; $2; ☎482-2825), tucked into the basement; the entrance is at the 14th Street side. Founded in 1873, it's the oldest aquarium in America, and even though it's had a home here since 1932 the grey federal corridors seem a strange environment for the fish; more surreal still are the dulcet tones of Dudley Moore drifting past the tanks from the aquarium theatre, where he narrates an introductory video. There are 1700 creatures from 260 species kept down here, forced to listen to Dud day in day out; the sharks (Mon, Wed & Sat) and piranhas (Tues, Thurs & Sun) get fed at 2pm.

Also at 14th Street, with a facade fronting Pennsylvania Avenue, the Beaux Arts **District Building** pre-dates the other Triangle edifices; walk down 14th for a view of its mighty caryatids and bold corner shield emblems. Erected as city council offices in 1908, it escaped demolition during the decade of Federal Triangle construction and clung on until 1992 when the mayor's office was shifted to Judiciary Square. Since then, the District Building has been undergoing restoration as part of the massive new adjacent development, which stretches right down 14th Street. The **Federal Triangle Building** will be the second largest federal building after the Pentagon when it's finished, though it hides its bulk well, behind a facade that's broadly sympathetic to its neighbours: mixed in with the federal offices will be shops, restaurants, theatres and galleries.

East along Constitution Avenue, between 14th and 12th streets, the large complex housing the **Customs Service Building** is as fussy as a building could be, its long colonnade and entablature of lazing nudes a stark contrast to the stripped facade of the National Museum of American History over the road. Across 12th Street comes the **Internal Revenue Service Building**, the earliest (1930) federal building to grace the area; while across 10th Street stands the **Department of Justice Building**, in whose (enclosed) courtyard stands a bust of former Attorney-General Robert Kennedy fashioned by Robert Berks – also responsible for the mighty bust of older Kennedy brother John Fitzgerald in the Kennedy Center (see p.165). The National Archives (see below) are next, across 9th Street, and the Triangle is completed by the suitably triangular **Federal Trade**

THE METRORAIL SYSTEM

Red Line
Wheaton / Shady Grove

Orange Line
New Carrollton / Vienna

Blue Line
Addison Road / Van Dorn Street

Yellow Line
Mt Vernon Sq-UDC / Huntington

Green Line
U Street-Cardozo / Anacostia
Greenbelt / Fort Totten

MARC Commuter Rail Services

For Metro information
call ☎202/637-7000

N

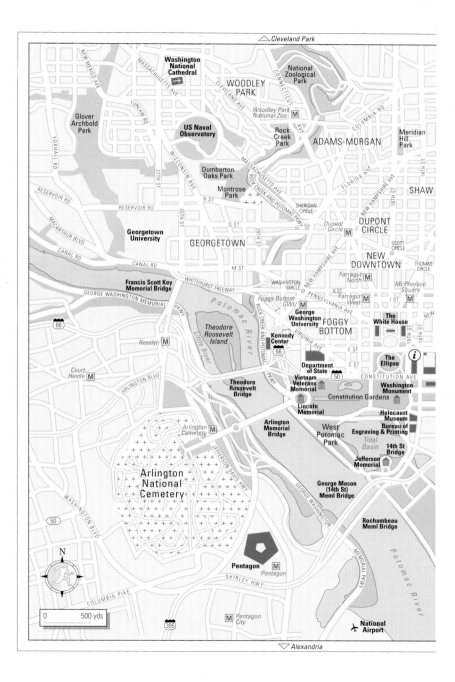

△ Cleveland Park

Washington National Cathedral

WOODLEY PARK

National Zoological Park

NEW MEXICO AVE

MASSACHUSETTS AVE

CLEVELAND AVE

CONNECTICUT AVE

COLUMBIA RD

Glover Archbold Park

TUNLAW RD

Woodley Park National Zoo Ⓜ

FOXHALL RD

WISCONSIN AVE

US Naval Observatory

Rock Creek Park

ADAMS-MORGAN

Meridian Hill Park

37TH ST

Dumbarton Oaks Park

FLORIDA AVE

NEW HAMPSHIRE AVE

16TH ST

14TH ST

SHAW

RESERVOIR RD

MACARTHUR BLVD

RESERVOIR RD

35TH ST

Montrose Park

R ST

ROCK CREEK AND POTOMAC PKWY

MASSACHUSETTS AVE

SHERIDAN CIRCLE

DUPONT CIRCLE

SCOTT CIRCLE

Q ST

Dupont Circle Ⓜ

CANAL RD

Georgetown University

GEORGETOWN

28TH ST

NEW DOWNTOWN

THOMAS CIRCLE

CANAL RD

M ST

WASHINGTON CIRCLE

NEW HAMPSHIRE AVE

Farragut North Ⓜ

McPherson Square

Francis Scott Key Memorial Bridge

WHITEHURST FREEWAY

Foggy Bottom-GWU Ⓜ

PENNSYLVANIA AVE

K ST

Farragut West Ⓜ

I ST Ⓜ

GEORGE WASHINGTON MEMORIAL

Potomac River

George Washington University

FOGGY BOTTOM

The White House

NEW

66

Little River

Theodore Roosevelt Island

VIRGINIA AVE

Kennedy Center

ROCK CREEK AND POTOMAC PKWY

E ST

The Ellipse

ⓘ

15TH ST

14TH ST

Rosslyn Ⓜ

66

Department of State

C ST

50

CONSTITUTION AVE

Washington Monument

Court House Ⓜ

ARLINGTON BLVD

Theodore Roosevelt Bridge

Vietnam Veterans Memorial

Constitution Gardens

Lincoln Memorial

Holocaust Museum

Arlington Cemetery Ⓜ

Arlington Memorial Bridge

West Potomac Park

Bureau of Engraving & Printing

JEFFERSON DAVIS HWY

Tidal Basin

14th St Bridge

Jefferson Memorial

Arlington National Cemetery

WASHINGTON BLVD

George Mason (14th St) Meml Bridge

GEORGE WASHINGTON

50

Rochambeau Meml Bridge

Potomac River

MEMORIAL PKWY

N

Pentagon Ⓜ

Pentagon

SHIRLEY HWY

COLUMBIA PIKE

0   500 yds

395

Pentagon City Ⓜ

✈ National Airport

▽ Alexandria

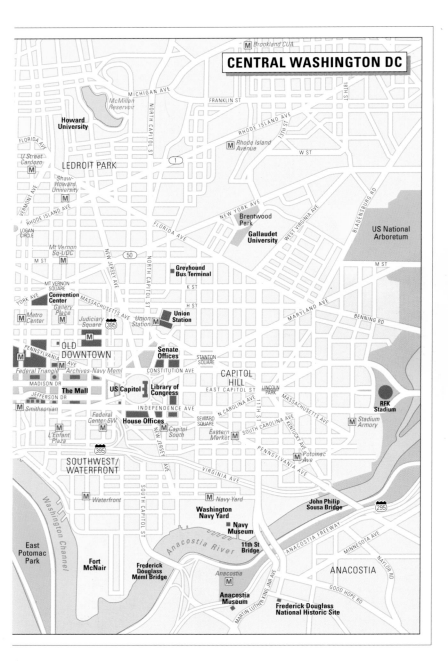

CENTRAL WASHINGTON DC

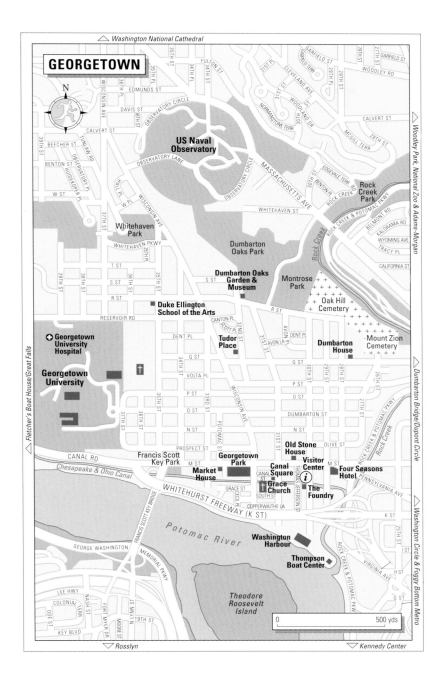

Commission Building, between 7th and 6th streets, where relief friezes over the Constitution Avenue doors depict Agriculture and Trade – and the control of trade, shown by the twin exterior statues of a muscular man wrestling a wild horse (at the rounded 6th St side).

The National Archives

7th St and Pennsylvania Ave NW ☎501-5000; for guided tours call ☎501-5205; Archives-Navy Memorial Metro. Daily 10am–5.30pm, until 9pm April–Labor Day. Admission free.

Almost as if John Russell Pope was bored with the restrictions of the brief, his **National Archives** building completely subverts the tenets of the Federal Triangle plan. Taller than the others, and refusing to follow the tapering lines of the flanking streets, this one is Neoclassical with knobs on, with 72 highly ornate Corinthian columns, each 50ft high, plain walls supporting a dome 75ft above floor level, and a sculpted pediment (facing Constitution Ave) topped by eagles. But then, unlike the other buildings, it was destined to hold a collection of national significance, namely the country's federal records dating back to the 1700s. When opened in 1935, the roll-call of the National Archives' holdings already made impressive reading; today they're of an almost unfathomable quantity. What everyone comes to see is the Holy Trinity of American historical record – the Declaration of Independence, the Constitution and the Bill of Rights – but the National Archives also encompass hundreds of millions of pages of paper documents, from war treaties to slave ship manifests, seven million pictures, 120,000 reels of cine film, almost 200,000 sound recordings, eleven million maps and charts, and a quarter of a million other artefacts.

The documents on permanent display are shown in the magnificent marble Rotunda, each in cases protected by bullet-proof glass, green light filters and a helium atmosphere; at night, they drop 20ft down into vaults for further protection. Visitors first file past the **Declaration of Independence**, rather faded now, but with its opening words and signatures still clear. The copy of the **US Constitution** is that signed at the Constitutional Convention in Philadelphia in September 1787 by twelve of the original thirteen states (Rhode Island signed three years later); the later amendments to the Constitution became the articles of the **Bill of Rights**, of which this is the federal government's official copy.

Murals on the side walls bang home the significance of the documents, with pictures of Thomas Jefferson handing the Declaration to John Hancock, and James Madison presenting the Constitution to George Washington (who chaired the Constitutional Convention). The other document on display is one of the few extant copies of the English **Magna Carta**, this specimen revised in 1297 after its initial agreement by King John in 1215. Written in Latin, it very much

The Declaration of Independence

*We hold these truths to be self-evident: that all men are created
equal, that they are endowed by their Creator with certain
unalienable rights, that among these are life, liberty, and the
pursuit of happiness . . .*

Declaration of Independence, Second Continental Congress, 1776

*We are the only nation in the world based on happiness. Search
as you will the sacred creeds of other nations and peoples, read
the Magna Carta, the Communist Manifesto, the Ten
Commandments, the Analects of Confucius, Plato's Republic, the
New Testament or the UN Charter, and find me any happiness
at all. America is the Happy Kingdom.*

P J O'Rourke

Revolutionary fervour was gaining pace in the American colonies in the
early months of 1776, whipped up in part by the publication of Tom
Paine's widely read, coruscating pamphlet, *Common Sense*, which casti-
gated monarchical government in general and George III of England in
particular. In May, the sitting **Second Continental Congress** in
Philadelphia advised the colonies to establish their own governments,
whose delegates in turn increasingly harried Congress to declare independence. The die was cast on June 7 when **Richard Henry Lee** of Virginia
moved in Congress that "these United Colonies are, and of right ought to
be, Free and Independent States". Four days later, while debate raged
among the delegates, Congress authorized a committee to draft a formal
declaration of independence.

Five men assembled to begin the task: **Thomas Jefferson, Benjamin
Franklin, John Adams, Roger Sherman and Robert Livingston.**

*For more on
the
Constitution,
see "The
American
System of
Government",
p.319.*

seems the odd one out, but the privileges and freedoms it guaranteed
(trial by jury, equality before the law, etc) were a precursor of those
enshrined in the Bill of Rights. Incidentally, it's owned (and permanently loaned to the National Archives) by businessman and failed
presidential candidate Ross Perot, who liked democracy so much he
tried to buy it.

Given that the Archives hold items as diverse as Napoleon
Bonaparte's signature on the Louisiana Purchase, the World War II
Japanese surrender document, the Strategic Arms Limitation Treaty
of 1972 and President Nixon's resignation letter, it's always worth
checking the **temporary exhibitions**. To hear selections from the
Watergate tapes (see p.166), which led to Nixon's downfall, a shuttle bus will take you to the Maryland depository where they're held
(call the Archives for details).

You can see much more of the holdings by signing up for one of
the excellent twice-daily **guided tours**, though you'll need to call well
in advance. The **Central Research and Microfilm Rooms** (Mon &
Wed 8.45am–5pm, Tues, Thurs & Fri 8.45am–9pm, Sat
8.45am–4.45pm) are also open to visitors, and are used for

Jefferson, an accomplished writer, was charged by the others to produce a draft, which was ready to be presented to Congress by June 28. Despite the evidence of most history books, though, Jefferson didn't simply rattle off the ringing declaration that empowered a nation. For a start, he lifted phrases and ideas from other writers – the "pursuit of happiness" was a common contemporary rhetorical flourish, while the concept of "unalienable rights" had appeared in George Mason's recent Declaration of Rights for Virginia. Moreover, his own words were tweaked by the rest of the committee and other changes were ordered after debate in Congress, notably the dropping of a passage condemning the slave trade in an attempt to keep some of the southern colonies on board. However, by the end of June, Congress had a document which spelled out exactly why Americans wanted independence, who they blamed for the state of affairs (George III, in 27 separate charges) and what they proposed to do about it. Read today, it's still a model of perfect clarity of political thought.

At this point, myths start to obfuscate the real chain of events. After a month of argument – not every delegate agreed with the proposed declaration – Congress finally **approved Lee's motion** on July 2, 1776. Technically, this was the day that America declared independence from Great Britain, though two days later, on **July 4, 1776**, Congress, representing the "thirteen United States of America", also approved Jefferson's explanatory declaration – and within a couple of years, and ever since, celebrations were held on the anniversary of the later date. The only man to sign the Declaration itself on July 4 was John Hancock (president of the Continental Congress) – hence the use of the colloquialism "John Hancock" for someone's signature; other signatures weren't added until August 2 and beyond, since many of the delegates had gone home as soon as the declaration was drawn up.

genealogical and research purposes – Alex Haley, author of *Roots*, spent a great many hours tracing his ancestry here.

Judiciary Square

East of 6th Street, between E and F streets, **Judiciary Square** – also a stop on the Metro – has been the focus for the city's judiciary and local government since 1800 when storehouses here served as rank jails for runaway slaves. Today, the mayor's new offices are at One Judiciary Square, while the unobtrusive **Old City Hall** on D Street, dating from the early nineteenth century, now houses courts and other offices – in 1881 it saw the trial for murder of Charles Guiteau, who shot President James Garfield in the back just four months after his inauguration. Within a few blocks are the US Tax Court, the District of Columbia Courthouse, the Municipal Center and the Federal Courthouse, all without exception uniformly bland – nineteenth-century workers in the nearby Pension Building (see p.184) had a vastly superior working environment. You could, were you determined to ruin your holiday, gain access to any of the public galleries and watch the proceedings: the Federal Courthouse has seen the most high-profile action, from the trial of Marion Barry to those of various Iran-Contra and Watergate defendants.

National Law Enforcement Officers Memorial

What you're more likely to come and see is Davis Buckley's impressive **National Law Enforcement Officers Memorial**, which occupies the whole of the centre of Judiciary Square; one of the Metro

Governing DC

Washington DC has always had an anomalous place in the Union. It's a **federal district** and not a state, with no official constitution of its own, and its citizens are denied full representation under the American political system: they have no senator to pursue their interests and only a non-voting representative in the House (a position the capital city shares, ingloriously, with Samoa, Guam and the Virgin Islands). Perhaps most incongruously, only since 1961, by virtue of the 23rd Amendment, have they been able to vote in presidential elections; the first they participated in was that of 1964.

Local powers have been similarly disregarded. There's been a city mayor and some sort of elected council since 1802 but in the early days, so many inhabitants were temporary visitors – politicians, lobbyists, lawyers and appointed civil servants – that there was no question of granting local tax-raising powers. Congress simply appropriated money piecemeal for necessary improvements. Under President Grant in 1871 the District was given **territorial status**: he appointed a governor and council, under whom worked an elected house of delegates, and boards of public works and health; all adult males (black and white) were eligible to vote. Many of the most significant improvements to the city infrastructure date from this period of limited self-government, with head of the Board of Public Works, **Alexander "Boss" Shepherd**, instrumental in sinking sewers, paving and lighting streets and planting thousands of trees. However, Shepherd's improvements and a string of corruption scandals put the city $16 million in debt. Direct control of DC's affairs passed back to Congress in 1874, which later appointed three commissioners to replace the locally elected officials.

And that was the way matters stood for a century, until 1973 when Congress passed the **Home Rule Act**. Small improvements had already been effected – the first black commissioner (for a city now predominantly black) was appointed in 1961; later, an elected school board was established. But only in 1974 with the advent of the District's first elected **mayor** for more than a century – the black Walter E Washington, supported by a fully elected thirteen-member council – did the city wrest back some measure of self-autonomy. However, Congress still retained a legislative veto over any proposed local laws as well as a close watch on spending limits.

Washington was succeeded as mayor by **Marion S Barry** in 1978, former Civil Rights activist and as picaresque a political leader as any city could wish for. At first, he was markedly successful in attracting much-needed investment; he also significantly increased the number of local

entrances emerges right by it. Dedicated in 1991, the walls lining the circular pathways around a reflecting pool are inscribed with the names of more than 13,500 police officers who have been killed in the line of duty, starting with US Marshall Robert Forsyth, shot dead in 1794. With symbolic bronze lions overseeing their cubs at the end of the memorial walls, it's a poignant spot in the oft-claimed Murder Capital of the nation (though the state with the highest number of police, as opposed to civilian, deaths is actually California). New names are added each May to the memorial, which has space for 29,000 – at the present rate (a murdered police officer every other

government workers, which gave him a firm support base among the majority black population. But longstanding whispers about Barry's turbulent private life – in particular, charges of drug addiction – exploded in early 1990, when he was surreptitiously filmed in an FBI sting operation, buying and using crack cocaine. Barry spent six months in prison, and was replaced as mayor by the Democrat **Sharon Pratt Kelly**, who signally failed to improve the city's worsening finances. In the mayoral election of 1994, Barry made an astounding **comeback**, admitting to voters the error of his ways. But a year later, Congress – influenced by the sweeping Republican gains in the previous year's general election – finally tired of the embarrassment of DC's massive budget deficit (standing at $700 million) and **revoked the city's home rule** charter.

Today, DC is effectively broke, but Congress (which subsidizes the District) can't afford to let the federal capital collapse. A Congressionally appointed **control board** has jurisdiction over the city's finances, personnel and various work departments until 2003; its principal task is to balance the budget, but the swingeing cuts and redundancies demanded are gradually stripping away what little responsibilty Barry (in office until 1998) has left. Only when the budget remains balanced will executive power be returned to the city.

However, DC's problems go far deeper than simple financial mismanagement. The heart of the matter is the shrinking **tax** base: two-thirds of DC's workers live (and pay local taxes) in Virginia and Maryland; the continuing middle-class flight to the suburbs has left the city population at its lowest since the 1930s. Thirty percent of those left are on welfare (which jacks up the deficit), while the rest face increased local income taxes in a doomed attempt to raise funds for put-upon city services. The obvious solution to this vicious circle – a commuter tax – is a non-starter for political reasons. Instead, some propose to exempt DC residents from federal and capital gains taxes, and freeze property taxes, to promote business and population growth in the city, but the outcry against self-serving politicians would be enormous. Granting **statehood**, with all the political, tax and jurisdictional rights that would entail, is another option (last considered and turned down by Congress in 1993), but here lies the crux of the whole matter of governing DC: **race**. The predominantly black city pays federal taxes but has no representation in predominantly white Congress, and as the prospect of home rule recedes into the distance there's a distinct whiff of distrust – locals, with some justification, feel that the last thing the government wants is a black city in charge of its own affairs on the nation's doorstep.

day on average), it will be full by the year 2100. There are directories
at the site if you want to trace a particular name, or call in at the nearby **Visitor Center**, two blocks west at 605 E St NW (Mon–Fri
9am–5pm, Sat 10am–5pm, Sun noon–5pm; free; ☎ 737-3400).

The Pension Building and National Building Museum

In the late 1860s the sheer number of Civil War casualties put a huge
strain on the government's pension system. New offices were
required in which to process claims and payments to veterans and
dependants; subsequently, in the 1880s, what became known as the
Pension Building was erected between 4th and 5th streets, framing
the entire north side of today's Judiciary Square. Emerging from the
Metro up the escalators brings you face-to-face with its imposing
redbrick facade.

Architect Montgomery C Meigs' concern was to honour veterans
of both sides with a building of distinction, and in this he succeeded
admirably. The Renaissance-style palazzo is handsome in the
extreme, its exterior enhanced by a three-foot-high terracotta **frieze**
that runs around the entire building (between the first and second
floors) and depicts the Union Army in all its manifestations: drilling
soldiers and the walking wounded, horses pulling wagons, marines
rowing in a storm-tossed sea, charging cavalry and thunderous
artillery.

Inside, Meigs maximized the use of natural light and freely
circulating air to produce a majestic **Great Hall**, a stadium-sized
interior centring on a working fountain. The eight supporting
columns are 8ft across at the base and more than 75ft high; each
is made up of 70,000 bricks, plastered and painted to resemble
Siena marble. Inspired by the generous proportions of Rome's
Palazzo Farnese, Meigs added every convenience for the Pension
Building workers. Above the ground-floor Doric arcade, the three
open-plan galleried levels, 160ft high, were aired by vents and
clerestory windows – opened each day by a young boy employed
to walk around on the roof. Hardly surprisingly, such a vast, sympathetic space has never been short of uses. Grover Cleveland
held the first of many presidential inaugural balls here in 1885
(when there was still no roof on the building); a century later, it
hosted President Reagan's second inaugural and then Clinton's
first; while every year the *Christmas in Washington* special is
filmed here.

The Pension Bureau moved out in 1926 and for a time the building served as a courthouse and various federal offices, although now
it's preserved as the **National Building Museum**, 401 F St NW
(Mon–Sat 10am–4pm, Sun 1–4pm; free; ☎272-2448), presenting
changing exhibitions on all aspects of architecture and building history. The permanent exhibition on the second floor, *Washington:*

Symbol and City, usefully concentrates on the construction of the city itself. Free **tours** (Tues–Fri 12.30pm, Sat & Sun 1pm) give you access to the otherwise restricted third floor (the best spot to view the towering column's curlicued capitals) and to the former Pension Commissioner's Suite on the second floor.

Old Patent Office Building

Three blocks west of the Pension Building, the older **Patent Office Building** houses two of the city's major art displays, the **National Portrait Gallery** and the **National Museum of American Art**, both of which come under the aegis of the Smithsonian.

The building, begun in 1836 by Robert Mills, is among the oldest in the city, though its Greek Revival structure wasn't completed for thirty years. It was designed to hold offices of the Interior Department and the **Commissioners of Patents**, displaying models of all patents taken out in nineteenth-century America. Thus it became one of the city's earliest museums, featuring models of inventions by Thomas Edison, Benjamin Franklin and Alexander Graham Bell as well as Whitney's cotton gin, Colt's pistol and Fulton's steam engine. Charles Dickens remarked that it was "an extraordinary example of American enterprise and ingenuity", although Anthony Trollope, hard to please as usual, was put out that he couldn't see what many of the inventions were supposed to be and thought the building "no better than a large toy shop". During the Civil War the echoing halls were pressed into emergency service as a hospital with over two thousand beds. One of the clerks in the Patent Office, a certain Clara Barton, abandoned her clerical duties to work in the hospital, going on to found the American Red Cross in 1881. The poet Walt Whitman worked here, too, as an untrained volunteer, dressing wounds and comforting injured soldiers, an experience which led directly to the long series of poems known as *Drum-Taps*, which was included in the fourth edition (1867) of *Leaves of Grass*. In March 1865, just before the end of the war, Whitman's "noblest of Washington buildings" hosted **Lincoln's second inaugural ball** with four thousand people in attendance for a night of dancing and feasting. "Tonight", wrote Whitman later, "beautiful women, perfumes, the violins' sweetness . . . then, the amputation, the blue face, the groan, the glassy eye of the dying".

Despite its heritage, the building was scheduled for demolition in the 1950s, before the Smithsonian stepped into the breach; the double museum opened in 1968. The galleries occupy separate wings: American Art on the G Street side, Portrait Gallery on F Street. There are separate main entrances, but since you can cross into either museum from the other once you're inside, it can occasionally get a little confusing.

Orientate yourself in the building's Patent Pending *cafeteria (p.271), just off the courtyard, on the 7th St side.*

National Portrait Gallery

8th and F streets NW ☎357-2700; Gallery Place-Chinatown Metro. Daily
10am–5.30pm. Admission free.

Portraits of prominent Americans formed the basis of many early art
collections: Congress itself commissioned a series of presidential
portraits for the White House in 1857. But the country wasn't provided with a **National Portrait Gallery** until the 1960s, when the Old
Patent Office Building was converted for artistic use. The permanent
collection holds more than four thousand images of notables from
every walk of life, and there are certainly some excellent paintings on
show – Gilbert Stuart's celebrated "Lansdowne" portrait of George
Washington the best-known – but the strength of the collection is in
the people it honours, from politicians, novelists and inventors to
sports heroes, Civil Rights leaders and industrialists. The collection
isn't restricted to paintings, either: there's a wealth of **sculptures**
and **photographs**, including over five thousand plate-glass negatives
of the Civil War era alone by Matthew Brady.

The **main entrance** is on F Street at 8th; the **information desk** is
here, where you can pick up a schedule of events, as is the gallery
shop. Ask at the desk about **guided tours** of the permanent collection (usually on request Mon–Fri 10am–3pm, Sat & Sun 11.15am),
or arrange them in advance by calling ☎357-2920.

First floor

The pick of the gallery's **recent acquisitions** are presented down the
south corridor, which leads to one of the most popular sections in the
gallery. **Performing Arts** presents a starburst of portraits: Paul
Robeson as Othello by Betsy Graves Reyneau; a regal portrait of
Marian Anderson (see p.60); photographs of Gloria Swanson and
Boris Karloff; a bronze bust of Grace Kelly; and an almost three-
dimensional metallic study of Ethel Merman as Annie Oakley by
Rosemary Sloat. Perhaps most striking is Harry Jackson's terrific
polychromed bronze sculpture of a *True Grit*-era John Wayne. In
Champions of American Sport, beyond, the spot-the-personality
games continue, with studies varying from a pugnacious Joe Louis
(again by Betsy Graves Reyneau; see below) to a poignant Arthur
Ashe (Louis Briel), painted in the last few months of his life. There
are action paintings, too – Mickey Mantle watching as Roger Maris
hits another homer in the 1961 season and, best of all, James
Montgomery Flagg's depiction of the Jack Dempsey-Jess Willard
heavyweight championship fight of 1919. With Willard (in black
shorts) in trouble, the eager reporter sat to the right of his knee is
Damon Runyon, who was a sports reporter before embarking on his
humorous stories. The staircase here provides one route up to the
second floor, past the dramatic rendition of *Grant and His Generals*
(1865) by Norwegian Ole Peter Hansen Balling, who spent five
weeks during the Richmond campaign sketching officers in the field.

At the end of
Champions of
American
Sport, *there's
access to the*
Patent Pending
*café and
through to the*
National
Museum of
American Art.

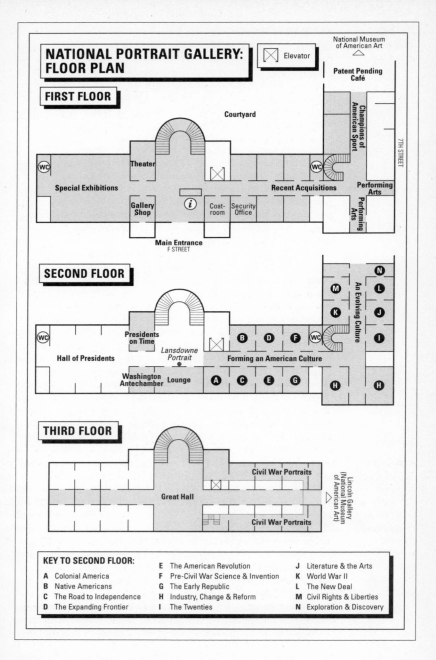

NATIONAL PORTRAIT GALLERY: FLOOR PLAN

⊠ Elevator

National Museum of American Art

FIRST FLOOR

Patent Pending Café

Champions of American Sport

7TH STREET

Courtyard

WC

Theater

Special Exhibitions

Gallery Shop

ⓘ

Coat-room

Security Office

Recent Acquisitions

WC

Performing Arts

Performing Arts

Main Entrance
F STREET

SECOND FLOOR

N

M

An Evolving Culture

L

K

J

WC

Presidents on Time

B

D

F

WC

I

Hall of Presidents

Lansdowne Portrait

Forming an American Culture

Washington Antechamber

Lounge

A

C

E

G

H

H

THIRD FLOOR

Civil War Portraits

Great Hall

Lincoln Gallery (National Museum of American Art)

Civil War Portraits

KEY TO SECOND FLOOR:

A   Colonial America
B   Native Americans
C   The Road to Independence
D   The Expanding Frontier

E   The American Revolution
F   Pre-Civil War Science & Invention
G   The Early Republic
H   Industry, Change & Reform
I   The Twenties

J   Literature & the Arts
K   World War II
L   The New Deal
M   Civil Rights & Liberties
N   Exploration & Discovery

For more on
Gilbert Stuart,
see The
National
Gallery of Art,
p.87.

The Hall of Presidents

First stop on the second floor should really be the celebrated **Hall of Presidents**, which you can reach straight up the stairs from the main entrance. You'll emerge in the Rotunda, face-to-face with **Gilbert Stuart**'s *George Washington* (1796), an Imperial study of an implacable man, head bathed in light, one hand clutching a sword-stick, the other outstretched. It's known as the "Lansdowne" portrait after the person for whom it was commissioned; the Marquis of Lansdowne, who had earned American respect by defending the rebellious colonies in the British Houses of Parliament. It's flanked by another Stuart portrait, of Thomas Jefferson, and a gentle study of Benjamin Franklin by eighteenth-century French court painter Joseph Siffred Duplessis.

On the west side of the Rotunda, the *Hall of Presidents* presents portraits and sculptures of every American President (there's a separate antechamber for studies of Washington). Some are most notable for the artists who were chosen to represent them: Norman Rockwell's overly-flattering *Richard Nixon* is the most striking, while the latest acquisition is a bust of *Bill Clinton* by Jan Wood, a sculptress otherwise best known for her depiction of horses. Other portraits illuminate the characters of the various presidents, starting with those of George Peter Alexander Healy who was first commissioned to produce presidential portraits in the 1850s. His pensive study of *Abraham Lincoln* manages to make the Great Emancipator rather more handsome than in virtually any other contemporaneous portrait. Balling, the Norwegian who made his name painting the Union Army during the Civil War, also managed portraits of presidents *Chester A Arthur* and, in what must have been a rush-job, *James Garfield*, who, inaugurated in March 1881, was shot in July and died in September. Other artists faced different problems. Edmund Tarbell's *Woodrow Wilson* had to be painted entirely from photographs since Wilson was always too ill to pose; while one critic noted of Joseph Burgess' stern portrait of *Calvin Coolidge* that the subject looked as if "without further provocation, he would bite the person . . . who, obviously, had been annoying him".

Before you cross the Rotunda for the rest of the collection, take a look in the adjacent **Presidents on Time** gallery. Here you get bitingly original artwork for which the covers of *Time* are renowned: Nixon and Brezhnev shaking hands, each concealing a fistful of armaments behind their backs; Ford as a prizefighter, rolling up his sleeves after Nixon's resignation; Jimmy Carter as a *High Noon* sheriff, preparing to take on the Iranians.

Second floor

The rest of the **second floor** is taken up with the major collections – the *Galleries of Notable Americans*. First come portraits of **Colonial America** (including one of Pocahontas in English dress) and **Native Americans**, with several studies of braves and chiefs by Western artist George Catlin (though there are better examples of his work across in the American Art museum; see p.191). There's a lithograph of Sitting Bull, and bringing the room up to date, a bust of Geronimo, sculpted by his distant relative, the Apache artist Allan Houser. In **Industry, Change and Reform**, industrialists, inventors and businessmen are pictured alongside churchmen and feminists, so together with Bell, Edison and Carnegie there's a Belva Ann Lockwood, the first woman to stand for President (in 1884; she got 4149 votes), a bust of Susan B Anthony by Adelaide Johnson (who sculpted many other suffrage leaders of the day) and a rather stuffy portrait of early feminist Elizabeth Cady Stanton.

There are more Adelaide Johnson busts on display in the Sewall-Belmont House, Capitol Hill; see p.120.

Other early rooms highlight personalities from the Revolutionary War and, more interestingly, from **Pre-Civil War Science and Invention**: in the latter, a group portrait by Christian Schussele depicts the nation's *Men of Progress* – effectively an 1862 year-book in which Samuel Morse, John Ericsson, Joseph Henry and Charles Goodyear figure among eighteen prominent scientists and inventors. The corridor meanwhile concentrates on portraits of those **Forming an American Culture** in the same period, and in *Washington Irving and His Literary Friends*, Schussele does the same for Oliver Wendell Holmes, Longfellow, Emerson, Fenimore Cooper et al. In **Literature and the Arts** there's a distinct qualitative jump. Gems include a touching early photograph by Man Ray of Ernest Hemingway and his young son, and the extraordinary, bulky terra-cotta figure of Getrude Stein, depicted by Jo Davidson as a tranquil, seated Buddha. Honours go, too, to Edward Biberman's creepy study of Dashiell Hammett in a horrible wool coat, and to the staring Samuel Clemens (better known as Mark Twain) portrayed by John White Alexander in 1902; the same artist painted Walt Whitman (1889) as a seated sage, with light streaming through his bushy beard. The most prized piece, however, is Edgar Degas' severe portrait of his friend, Impressionist Mary Cassatt (1880–84), hunched over a chair with a sneer on her face – the subject hated it so much she had it sold on the express understanding that it wouldn't be allowed to go to an American collection where her family and friends might see it.

With **The Twenties** come photographs and prints of names that defined an era, from executed anarchists Saccho and Vanzetti, to Babe Ruth – the "Sultan of Swat" – depicted as a baseball in *Vanity Fair*. A further selection elaborates on Roosevelt's **New Deal**. FDR is here, of course, in a portrait by Henry Hubbell, as is a rather kindly Eleanor, alongside most of their contemporaries. In particular (and also elsewhere in the gallery) you'll find portraits by Betsy Graves Reyneau, commissioned in the 1940s by the Harmon Foundation to paint prominent African-Americans: in this room alone, there's a sympathetic portrayal of Mary McLeod Bethune (see p.219), and of

A Phillip Randolph, president of the Brotherhood of Sleeping Car Porters and once regarded as the "most dangerous Negro in America", following his 1941 call for 50,000 blacks to march on Washington to protest against employment discrimination. Over the corridor, the **World War II** room mixes its portraits of generals with some interesting recruitment posters, like that of Private Joe Louis in uniform from 1942.

Final rooms take in **Exploration and Discovery**, in which Albert Einstein makes his mark as a kindly, twinkly uncle in a wonderful portrait by photographer Fred Stein, and **Civil Rights and Liberties**, which contains one of the strongest of all the gallery's sculptures. Marshall D Rumbaugh chose to represent Rosa Parkes manacled between two law enforcement officers after she had taken her seat on the bus in Montgomery, Alabama – their small heads and shade-clad eyes contrasting with the seamstress' defiant gaze as her handbag dangles beneath her handcuffs.

Third floor

*From the
Great Hall,
there's direct
access through
to the Lincoln
Gallery (mod-
ern art) of the
National
Museum of
American Art.*

Up on the third floor, the main staircase leads you straight into the beautifully restored Victorian **Great Hall**. This was originally used as a display area for the Patent Office, and the Declaration of Independence was on show here from 1841 to 1871; a selection of models of patented inventions still occupies two glass cases (the National Museum of American History has the other 10,000 models).

The surrounding mezzanine brings together portraits of the **Civil War** era (Union and Confederate), centred on a full-length likeness of Lincoln in front of the Capitol by William Cogswell (1869) – notable mainly for its poor proportions. Far more striking is the facsimile of the notorious portrait of Lincoln taken in February 1865 by war photographer Alexander Gardner. A crack in the plate runs right across Lincoln's forehead – after the President's assassination, many observers saw this, in retrospect, as a terrible omen.

National Museum of American Art

8th and G streets NW ☎357-2700; Gallery Place-Chinatown Metro. Daily 10am–5.30pm. Admission free.

The **National Museum of American Art** holds one of the more enduring of the city's art collections. Even before the founding of the Smithsonian, the federal government had its own art collection which, together with pieces loaned by prominent Washington citizens, was displayed for a time in the 1840s in the Patent Office Building. These works were later transferred to the Smithsonian, who had yet to find premises for a planned "National Gallery" of its expanding art collection. In the end the Smithsonian resorted to displaying its paintings in the Natural History Museum, receiving a second blow when Andrew Mellon's bequest to the nation resulted in the foundation of a quite separate National Gallery of Art. Not until the

Patent Office Building became available did the Smithsonian finally find a home for its 35,000 paintings, prints, drawings and sculpture, photographs, folk art and crafts – the largest collection of American art, colonial to contemporary, in the world.

Not everything, of course, is on permanent display in this building, large though it is. Many of the museum's decorative arts and crafts, for instance, are shown in temporary exhibitions at the Renwick Gallery (see p.154). "American" here includes significant selections of African-American and Hispanic-American art, though despite what some of the floor plans say, there's no permanent exhibition of African-American works. You're also unlikely to see the museum's New Deal-era WPA murals or its unrivalled collection of portrait miniatures – a happy consequence of the early Smithsonian's lack of space, which at one point forced the directors to acquire ever-smaller paintings.

The **main entrance** is on G Street, marked by Luis Jiménez's bucking, multi-coloured fibre-glass *Vaquero* sculpture. There's an **information desk**, at which you can pick up a floor plan and ask about the free daily **guided tours** (Mon–Fri noon, Sat & Sun 2pm), and a gallery **shop** (daily 10am–5.15pm) just across the corridor.

First floor

The museum scores an early success with its presentation of the nineteenth-century **Art of the American West**. The collection includes almost four hundred paintings by George Catlin, who spent six years touring the Great Plains, painting portraits and scenes of Native American life, later displaying them as part of his "Indian Gallery". Catlin received no formal training, and certainly had his critics as an artist, but as an early anthropologist, he was invaluable. This was the first contact many white settlers had with the aboriginal peoples of America, and viewers were fascinated by his lush landscapes of buffalo herds crossing the Missouri, or those showing Indian tribes at work and play. The contrast between cultures is best seen in Catlin's 1832 painting of a warrior named Pigeon's Egg Head arriving in Washington DC in full traditional dress, only to return to his tepee encampment in frock coat and top hat, sporting an umbrella and smoking a cigarette. Perhaps Catlin is most interesting for recording civilizations and habitats that survived only briefly after the onslaught of the pioneers – soon after he visited and painted the Plains Mandan tribes, they were wiped out by a smallpox epidemic introduced by white settlers. Not all the Western scenes are of warriors or hunts: Catlin produced endless keenly observed domestic studies, like that of the woman with child in an elaborately decorated cradle, while Joseph Henry Sharp has a later picture (1920) of Blackfoots making medicine by burning feathers over an open fire.

Changing displays of **Folk Art** on the first floor include some traditional pieces, notably Native American ceramics, but it's the contemporary works that stand out. Malcah Zeldis' *Miss Liberty Celebration* is typically exuberant – here, the Statue of Liberty surrounded by a family group of Elvis, Einstein, Lincoln, Marilyn and Chaplin was completed to celebrate the artist's recovery from cancer. Less easy to categorize are items like the painted swordfish bill (in a room of Maritime Folk objects) and the varied, modernistic animals, including a giraffe made entirely from bottle tops. Most extraordinary of all, though, is the room devoted to the so-called **Hampton Throne**, a mystic, cryptic cluster of foil- and gilt-covered lightbulbs, boxes, plaques, wings, altars and furniture capped by the text "Fear Not". The work of James Hampton, a solitary figure who referred to himself as "Saint James" and worked in a garage on N St NW between 1950 and his death in 1964, it's full of obscure religious significance. It's also thought that it was unfinished at the time of his death, though quite how anyone could tell is a mystery.

The Hampton Throne's full title is The Throne of the Third Heaven of the Nations' Millennium General Assembly.

Second floor

Climb the staircase from the *American West* section and you're in for a highly enjoyable romp through paintings by the heavyweights in **nineteenth- and early twentieth-century** American art. The rooms aren't labelled too clearly, and paintings are occasionally replaced, but working your way around to the main staircase should guarantee a view of most of the following.

*There's more about the life and work of the following American artists in the National Gallery of Art account.
See: Mary Cassatt, p.91.
John Singleton Copley, p.88.
Winslow Homer, p.89.
Gilbert Stuart, p.87.
J M Whistler, p.89.*

An early picture by James McNeill Whistler of *Valparaiso Harbour* (1866) stands in the same room as a still life by his friend, Abbott Henderson Thayer; for the best of both men, though, you'll need to visit the Freer (p.68). There are significant chunks of work by Albert Pinkham Ryder, whose dark, often-nightmarish paintings are full of symbolism, though there's more general appeal in those of Winslow Homer, whether it's the rural studies of his *Bean Picker* or *A Country Lad* or the leisurely antics of female models in his dappled *Sunlight and Shadow* and *Summer Afternoon*, all executed in the same prolific period during the 1870s. In the corner rooms, the paintings are mixed with sculpture: the only work in the gallery by accomplished society portraitist John Singer Sargent, his direct study of the beautiful, taffeta-clad *Elizabeth Winthrop Chanler* (1893), vies with such ephemera as Daniel Chester French's *The Spirit of Life* (1914), a winged sprite with laurel wreath fashioned by the man who produced the powerful statue in the Lincoln Memorial. You may see a couple of other single works by renowned artists – Mary Cassatt's *Spanish Dancer* (1873), portraying little of her later Impressionist flair, and colonial master John Singleton Copley's infinitely more striking portrait of *Mrs George Watson* (1756).

The museum excels when the emphasis changes from portraits and genre painting to American **landscapes**. *Among the Sierra Nevada Mountains* (1868) is a superb example of the dramatic power of **Albert Bierstadt**, whose three long trips to the American West between 1858 and 1873 provided him with enough material for the rest of his career – the detail is typical, with the ethereal light picking out distant waterfalls, ducks in flight and high snow-capped peaks. People rarely intruded into these romanticized, highly popular landscapes: nowhere is this seen better than in the enormous, startlingly coloured **Thomas Moran** landscapes at the top of the main staircase – two sweeping studies of Yellowstone Canyon, fully 12ft across, and *Chasm of the Colorado*, alive with multifarious reds. Elsewhere on the floor you'll find similar, though smaller, expressions of grandeur in scenes from Lake Placid, the Colorado River and the Niagara Falls, painted by Hudson River School artists (see p.88) like Jasper Francis Cropsey and John Frederick Kensett who cast their sensuous eye across what Americans soon came to regard as their own backyard. There is the odd portrayal of the original inhabitants of these landscapes; look for **Charles Bird King**'s powerful picture of five Pawnee braves sporting red face-paint and ceremonial bead earrings. King had studied in London under Benjamin West (see p.88) before moving to Washington DC, where he earned a comfortable living painting portraits of high society. The steady flow of Native Americans through the capital in the 1820s – there to sign away their land in a series of ultimately worthless treaties – prompted him to divert his attentions to recording their likenesses instead.

Beyond the Moran landscapes, the corridor contains examples from the noted collection of sculptures and models by **Hiram Powers**. The surface of *America* (1848), a plaster model of crowned Liberty, is punctured by the tips of a series of metal rods, inserted to act as a guide for carving the eventual marble version. *Thomas Jefferson* (1860) shows the same technique, unfortunately making it look as if the frock-coated President has a severe case of acne.

Old Patent Office Building

Hiram Powers' most famous work in DC, The Greek Slave, is in the Corcoran Gallery of Art; see p.158.

Third floor

On the third floor, the museum moves into the **twentieth century**, most spectacularly in the 260-foot-long **Lincoln Gallery**, which runs down the east side of the building. It was here, amid the white marble pillars, that Abraham Lincoln and his entourage enjoyed his second inaugural ball. Now, in what can be seen as an adjunct to the Hirshorn and the National Gallery of Art's East Building, a kaleidoscopic selection from the Smithsonian's modern and contemporary art collection is perfectly placed in this wonderful space.

Mostly, it's an exercise in name-spotting. Robert Motherwell, Willem de Kooning, Robert Rauschenberg, Louise Nevelson, Clyfford Styll, Ellsworth Kelly and Jasper Johns all battle for attention. Often you're delayed by less high-profile names and works, like that of Leon Golub whose red, raw *Napalm Head* is painted onto a torn canvas sack; or Marisol's comical *Charles de Gaulle* (1967), which depicts the great French President as a rectangular wooden box and head atop a small cart. The Hispanic-American sculptor whose work stands outside the museum – Luis Jiménez – is represented here by the alarming, moulded fibreglass *Man on Fire*, a red-and-orange human figure slowly losing shape as the fire takes hold.

Finally, although not always on display, the museum owns a decent selection of abstract works by the artists of the **Washington Color School** – primarily Gene Davis, Morris Louis, Kenneth Noland, Thomas Downing, Paul Reed and Howard Mehring. All tended to stain their canvases with acrylic paint to give greater impact to the colour and to the abstract form, methods that first came to public attention in 1965 at a ground-breaking modern art exhibition in the city.

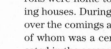

Chinatown to Metro Center

At the Old Patent Office Building, you're on the fringes of Washington's skimpy **Chinatown**, which marks downtown's north-eastern edge. From here, it's an easy eight-block walk back towards the White House past historic **Ford's Theater** (where President Lincoln met his end) and the former Masonic Lodge housing the excellent **Museum of Women in the Arts**. There are **Metro stations** at beginning, middle and end of the walk, at Gallery Place-Chinatown, Metro Center and McPherson Square.

Chinatown and around

*For reviews of
Chinatown's
best restau-
rants, see
p.277.*

Washington's **Chinatown** is not a patch on those in San Francisco, New York or even London, stretching no more than a few undistinguished city blocks along G and H streets NW, between 6th and 8th. The vibrant **triumphal arch** over H Street (at 7th), paid for by Beijing in the 1980s, looks hopelessly at odds with the rather listless, run-down neighbourhood. Come here to eat, by all means – restaurants are particularly thick on H Street – but don't expect much else, other than dodging the attentions of panhandling drunks at night. Washington DC's first Chinese immigrants, in the early nineteenth century, lived not in today's Chinatown (which only became such at the turn of this century) but in the gloriously named slums of Swampoodle, north of the Capitol. At that time, H Street and its environs were home to small businesses and modest, respectable rooming houses. During the 1860s, in one of these, Mary Surratt presided over the comings and goings of her son John and his colleagues, one of whom was a certain John Wilkes Booth – all subsequently implicated in the assassination of Abraham Lincoln (see p.196). A plaque records the affair at the **site of the house** (then no. 541 H St), now *Go-Lo's* restaurant at 604 H St NW.

North and west of Chinatown, big business is slowly reviving the area – or rather tearing it down and starting again. Among more typical developments – such as the colossal **Washington Convention Center** (H St, between 9th and 11th) and the multi-storey **Grand Hyatt** – the occasional remnant of former days survives: walk past the Convention Center and up to 1100 New York Ave to see the sprightly Art Deco facade of the avenue's former bus terminal.

Chinatown to Metro Center

Southeast, heading back towards Gallery Place-Chinatown Metro, a stroll along the pedestrianized section of G Street at 9th brings you up hard against the **Martin Luther King Memorial Library**, at 901 G St NW (Mon & Thurs 9am–9pm, Tues, Wed, Fri & Sat 9am–5.30pm; ☎ 727-1111), whose sleek lines of brick, steel and glass announce it immediately as the work of Mies van der Rohe. Opened in 1972, it's the city's main public library and you can walk in to see the large mural of the life of the assassinated Civil Rights leader, painted by Don Miller.

Along 7th Street

The most remarkable downtown transformation has been along **7th Street**, between F and D, whose spruced-up buildings form the focus of a nascent arts district studded with galleries. The **Washington Project for the Arts**, 400 7th St, is the best-known; see p.298 for more. New cafés and restaurants (like *Jaleo*, see p.276) bolster the area's growing appeal, which is perhaps best exemplified by the residents of 7th Street's finest building, **The Lansburgh**, at no. 420 (between D and E). Once a department store, the building's soaring Neoclassical facade now provides a grand frame for the **Shakespeare Theater** (see p.298) and the swish apartments above it – home to (or at least Washington mailing address of) celebs including Betty Friedan and Joe Kennedy Jr. Nearby **F Street** meanwhile, between 7th and 10th, still awaits its facelift. Once a prime commercial hub, this stretch has largely been abandoned to parking lots, T-shirt stalls and boarded-up buildings: businesses that moved west include *Hecht's* (see p.198), whose forlorn old store premises at 7th and F, with its beautifully carved facade, cries out for rescue.

Ford's Theater and the Petersen House

The district north of Pennsylvania Avenue has featured several theatres since the founding of the city; it was little more than a stroll from the White House and mansions of Lafayette Square when Washington's notables fancied a night's entertainment. In 1861, the *National* (see p.297) was joined by **Ford's Theater**, at 511 10th St NW, opened in a converted church by theatrical entrepreneur John T Ford. It proved just as popular as its near neighbour, until on April 14, 1865 – during a performance of *Our American Cousin* – it witnessed the dramatic **assassination of Abraham Lincoln** by John Wilkes Booth, actor and Southern sympathizer. During the play, which Lincoln was watching with his wife from the Presidential box,

Nearest Metro stations are Gallery Place-Chinatown, Metro Center or Federal Triangle.

Booth shot the President once in the head before escaping; pandemonium broke out and Ford lost his theatre in one fell swoop. Initially draped in black as a mark of respect, it was closed while the conspirators were pursued, caught and tried; Ford later abandoned attempts to re-open the theatre after he received death threats. The theatre was converted into offices and only in the 1960s was it decided to restore it to its previous condition.

Today it's a rather heavyhanded period piece, furnished in the style of 1865, but while still serving as a working theatre (see p.297)

The Assassination of President Lincoln

Five days after General Ulysses Grant received Robert E Lee's sword and surrender at Appomattox, effectively ending the Civil War, President Abraham Lincoln went to the theatre. There was a celebratory mood in the city and on the evening of Good Friday, **April 14, 1865**, President and Mrs Lincoln opted to go and see top actress Laura Keene perform in the comedy *Our American Cousin* at Ford's Theater, a play about a yokel who travels to England to claim his inheritance. The President's advisors were never very keen on him appearing in public, but Lincoln, as on several previous occasions, overrode their objections. The Lincolns were accompanied by their acquaintances Major Henry Rathbone and his fiancée Clara Harris; they all took their seats upstairs in the Presidential box, just after the play had started.

The conspirators had been planning for weeks. **John Wilkes Booth**, a 26-year-old actor with Southern sympathies and delusions of grandeur, had first conceived of a plan to kidnap Lincoln during the war and use him as a bargaining chip for the release of Confederate prisoners. Booth drew others into the conspiracy, notably John Surratt, whose mother owned a rooming house on H Street, where the conspiracy was hatched; John Surratt was already acting as a low-level courier for the secessionist cause. George Atzerodt from Maryland was recruited because he knew the surrounding countryside and its hiding places, as was David Herold, a pharmacist's clerk in DC; Lewis Powell (or Paine as he was sometimes known) was hired as muscle. With Lee's surrender in April, Booth decided to assassinate the President instead; Herold, Atzerodt and Powell were to kill Secretary of State William Seward and Vice-President Andrew Johnson. Surratt had already left the group when the talk turned to murder, and the other attacks came to naught: Johnson was left alone by a fearful Atzerodt while Seward, although injured by Powell, later recovered.

During the third act, at about 10.15pm when only one actor was on stage and the audience was laughing at a joke, the assassin struck. Lincoln's bodyguard had left the box unattended and Booth took the opportunity to step inside and shoot Lincoln in the back of the head. Major Rathbone grappled with Booth but was stabbed in the arm with a hunting knife and severely wounded. Booth then jumped the 12ft down onto the stage, catching one of his spurs and fracturing a bone in his left leg as he fell. But he was on his feet immediately – most of the audience still thought it was part of the play – and shouted "Sic semper tyrannis!" ("Thus ever to tyrants": the motto of the state of Virginia) before running off backstage, where in the alley he had a horse waiting for him.

it's more notable as a museum dedicated to the night that Lincoln died. Provided rehearsals or matinees aren't underway (usually Thurs, Sat & Sun), entertaining **talks** (hourly 9.15am–4.15pm; free) take place in the theatre itself, setting the scene and recounting the events of the fateful night. You can then file up to the circle for a view through glass of the damask-furnished Presidential box in which Lincoln sat in his rocking chair; most of the items inside are reproductions. In the basement, the **Lincoln Museum** (daily 9am–5pm; free; ☎426-6924) puts more flesh on the story. The actual weapon –

First into the box was Charles Augustus Leale, a young army doctor. Lincoln was unconscious and labouring badly and it was decided to carry him to the nearest house to better care for him. Once inside the Petersen House, Lincoln was placed in the small back bedroom, where Leale and the other doctors strived to save him. Soon the house was bulging at the seams, as Mrs Lincoln, her son Robert, Secretary of War Edwin Stanton, various politicians and army officers and, eventually, Lincoln's pastor, all arrived to do what they could. Lincoln never regained consciousness and died at 7.22am the next morning, April 15; Stanton spoke for all, declaiming "Now he belongs to the ages" (or, as some historians assert, to the "angels"). Lincoln's body was taken back to the White House, where it lay in state for three days before the funeral.

Booth, meanwhile, had fled on horseback through Maryland with David Herold, stopping at a certain Doctor Mudd's to have his injured leg treated. The pair hid out for several days, but after crossing into Virginia were eventually surrounded by Union troops at a farm. Herold surrendered and on the same day, April 26, Booth was shot dead while holed up inside. All the other alleged conspirators were soon captured and sent for trial on May 10 in a military court at Fort McNair (see p.137). They were kept chained and hooded and, after six weeks of evidence, Herold, Powell, Atzerodt and Mary Surratt were sentenced to hang, the punishment carried out on July 7, 1865. A last-minute reprieve for Mary Surratt – who, although she housed the conspirators probably knew nothing of the conspiracy – was refused, and she became the first woman to be executed by the US government. Dr Mudd received a life sentence, while the stage hand who held Booth's horse at the theatre got six years, though both were pardoned in 1869 by Andrew Johnson, Lincoln's successor. John Surratt, who had fled America, was recaptured in 1867 and also stood trial, but was freed when the jury couldn't agree on a verdict.

Much has been written about the effect on the country and its future of the assassination of Lincoln, who was at the start of his second term as President when he died. Many have held that the slavery question would have been settled with more skill and grace under his leadership. It's impossible to say, though it is interesting to note the personal effect that the close-quarters assassination may have had on the three other occupants of the Presidential box that night: ten years later Mary Lincoln – never the most stable of people – was judged insane and committed; in 1883 Clara Harris (later Clara Harris Rathbone) was herself shot, by her husband, Henry Rathbone, who died in an asylum in 1911.

a .44 Derringer – is on display, alongside a bloodstained piece of Lincoln's overcoat, Booth's knife and keys, and his diary, recording "I hoped for no gain. I knew no private wrong. I struck for my country and that alone").

The Petersen House

Having been shot, the President – now unconscious – was carried across the street and placed in the back bedroom of a house belonging to a local tailor, William Petersen. Lincoln never regained consciousness and died the next morning. Built of the same red brick as the theatre, **Petersen House**, at 516 10th St (daily 9am–5pm; free), has also been sympathetically restored and you can troop through its gloomy parlour rooms to the small bedroom to see a replica of the bed on which Lincoln died (laid diagonally, since he was too tall to lie straight). Period furniture aside, there's little to see – in a concession to taste, the original bloodstained pillow that used to be laid on the bed has been moved to the theatre museum. However, it's interesting to note just how small the room is: Lincoln's immediate family and colleagues were present in the house during his last night, but not all could cram into the room at the same time – something ignored by contemporaneous artists who, in a series of mawkish deathbed scenes popular at the time, often portrayed up to thirty people crowded around the ailing President's bed.

Around Metro Center

The downtown hub of the Metro system is **Metro Center**, with separate exits along G and 12th streets. From either you emerge by the **Hecht Company Department Store**, in stunning new premises on G Street (between 12th and 13th), but with decades of tradition behind it. Other aged department stores haven't done quite so well: a block east, at 11th and F, the venerable *Woodward and Lothrop* closed in 1995, while *Garfinkel's* lost its fight for survival in 1990, though its location at 14th and F forms part of the new **Metropolitan Square** development. This retains various historic Beaux Arts facades along 15th Street (facing the Treasury Building) – notably the turn-of-the-century *B F Keith's Theater* and the *National Metropolitan Bank*; there's also access to the historic **Old Ebbitt Grill** (see p.276).

Around the corner on the south side of F Street, there's an entrance to *The Shops at National Place* (see p.303); the facade incorporates the original, highly decorative half-rotunda entrance of the National Press Club. The newest addition to the street is the National Gallery of Caricature and Cartoon Art, 1317 F St NW (Tues–Sat 11am–4pm; free; ☎ 638-6411), a little further east, on the opposite side, detailing the history of the art and festooned with pungent political examples dating from 1747.

National Museum of Women in the Arts

1250 New York Ave NW ☎783-5000; Metro Center Metro. Mon–Sat 10am–5pm, Sun noon–5pm. Suggested donation $3.

Chinatown to Metro Center

The **National Museum of Women in the Arts** houses the world's most important collection of art of its kind – over 1500 works by 400 artists, from the sixteenth century to the present day. Incorporating silverware, ceramics, photographs and decorative items, as well as paintings, the museum opened in 1987 and proved an instant hit. This is partly to do with the building itself, converted from – of all things – a former Masonic Lodge built by Waddy Butler Wood.

The **permanent collection** is on the third floor. Contemporary works are rotated in the mezzanine level, and there are **temporary exhibitions** on the ground, second and fourth floors. The **information desk** and **shop** are on the ground floor as you enter.

The museum's airy Mezzanine Café (Mon–Sat 11.30am–2.30pm) is one of the most appealing lunch spots in the city.

The collection

The collection runs chronologically, starting with works from the **Renaissance** period, like those of Sofonisba Anguissola (1532–1625), who was considered the most important woman artist of her day. From a noble family, she achieved fame as an accomplished portraitist before becoming court painter to Phillip II of Spain; her well-judged *Double Portrait of a Lady and Her Daughter* is on show, as is the energetic *Holy Family with St John* by her contemporary, Lavinia Fontana (who had a head start by being the daughter of a successful Bolognese artist). A century or so later, **Dutch and Flemish** women like Clara Peeters, Judith Leyster and Rachel Ruysch were producing still lives and genre scenes that were the equal of their more famous male colleagues – witness the vivacity of Peeters' *Still Life of Fish and Cat*. Women broke out of their restricted environment on occasion, too. The superbly crafted natural science engravings of German-born Maria Sybilla Merian were the result of her intrepid explorations in Surinam in 1699, while eighteenth-century English women **silversmiths** produced tea sets, kettles, sugar tongs, goblets and cups of great refinement. Meanwhile, in France, women like Elisabeth-Louise Vigé-Lebrun (1755–1842) held sway as court painters, depicting the royalty fluttering around Marie Antoinette. But as a woman artist she was marginalized, her paintings not afforded the same respect as those of her male contemporaries – who kept her out of the Academie des Beaux-Arts until the 1780s.

In the **nineteenth century**, American women artists were coming into the fray. Lilly Martin Spencer was inordinately popular as a producer of genre scenes: *The Artist and Her Family at a Fourth of July Picnic* (1864) is typically vibrant. As Impressionism widened the parameters of art, painters like Berthe Morisot (1841–95) and particularly **Mary Cassatt** (1844–1926), produced daring (for the time) scenes of nursing mothers, young girls and mewling babies.

*Cassatt
befriended
Edgar Degas
in Paris– his
portrait of her
hangs in the
National
Portrait
Gallery (see
p.189).*

Cassatt, like many of her contemporaries, was intrigued by the forms and colours of oriental art; *The Bath* (1898), an etching of mother and baby using crisp swatches of pale colour, was influenced by an exhibition of Japanese woodblocks she had seen in Paris, where she lived from an early age. Cecilia Beaux (1863–1942), also inspired by her stay in Paris, was sought after for her rich, expressive portraits – so much so, she was honoured with a commission to paint Theodore and Mrs Roosevelt in 1903.

Twentieth-century artists and works include the Neoclassical sculpture of Camille Claudel (1864–1943), the odd painting by Georgia O'Keeffe and, most boldly, a cycle of prints depicting the hardships of working-class life by the socialist and feminist **Käthe Kollwitz** (1867–1945), part of her powerful *A Weaver's Rebellion* (1893–98). Self-portraits add some interesting insights into character: Kollwitz appears drained by her work in an etching of 1921, while Frida Kahlo, dressed in a peasant's outfit and clutching a note to Trotsky, dedicates herself to the Revolution. The last gallery brings you into modern times with pieces by sculptor Dorothy Dehner, minimalist Dorothea Rockburne and abstract expressionists Helen Frankenthaler and Elaine de Kooning among others: should these appeal, you'll need to set off for the Hirshorn, National Gallery East Wing and National Museum of American Art, whose holdings are all more substantial.

The New York Avenue Presbyterian Church

Half a block west of the museum, at 1313 New York Ave at H St, the red-brick **New York Avenue Presbyterian Church** (daily 9am–1pm; guided tours Sun after 9am & 11am services; ☎393-3700) is a clever 1950s facsimile of the mid-nineteenth-century church in which the Lincoln family worshipped. The pastor, Dr Gurley, was at Lincoln's bedside at the Petersen House (see p.198) when he died and gave the funeral service four days later at the White House. Ask in the office on the New York Avenue side and someone should be on hand to show you the President's second-row pew, while downstairs in the "Lincoln Parlour" you can see an early draft of his Emancipation Proclamation and portraits of Lincoln and Dr Gurley.

Chapter 7

New Downtown to Adams-Morgan

W hile tourists zig-zag back and forth through the cultural triangle formed by the Mall, White House and US Capitol, the business brain and artistic heart of the city tick away in a series of very different neighbourhoods to the north. Not all will be high on everyone's vacation agenda, many locals visit parts infrequently if at all, and some districts probably shouldn't be investigated by anyone with a desire to live a long and fruitful life. But to go home without sampling downtown Washington outside the Mall would be a mistake.

Closest to the centre, **New Downtown** – for the want of a better label – has least to recommend it, though visitors, perversely, often end up seeing more of these few blocks between K Street and Scott Circle than any others, since they contain most of the city's central mid-range hotels. Here, L'Enfant's grid is at its dullest, the architecture at its least inspiring, and although as many political and economic decisions are made in these white-collar offices as in Congress, a stately hotel, a church or two and a couple of offbeat museums are about the limit of New Downtown's interest. Things pick up at nearby **Dupont Circle**, DC's major arts corridor, where a score or more of private galleries are trumped in style by the **Phillips Collection**, the first modern art museum in America. There's enough to keep you in the neighbourhood for a day at least – avenues of imposing turn-of-the-century mansions, several open to the public, the buildings of **Embassy Row** and townhouse museums of neighbouring **Kalorama**, and some of the city's best shopping and nightlife. To the north, ethnically mixed **Adams-Morgan** has more soul and less pretension, and is one of the few areas in the city with a safe, democratic and inexpensive nightlife; dine out at least once here, since the run of ethnic restaurants is unbeaten in the city. Only in **Shaw**, to the east, do you have to pick your spot carefully. Once *the* thriving black neighbourhood, and home of a vibrant 1920s and 1930s music scene, the area is still feeling the effects of its rapid

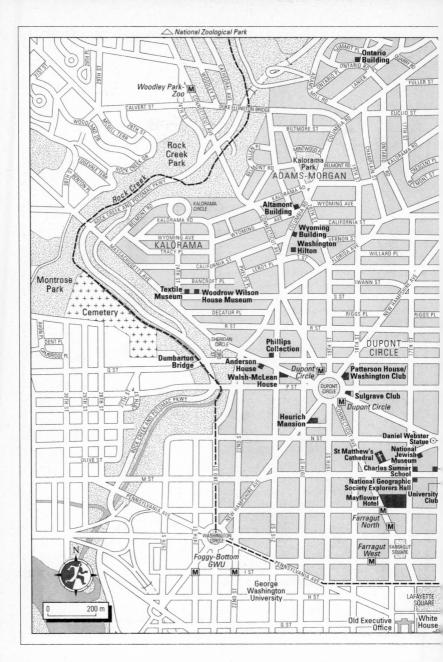

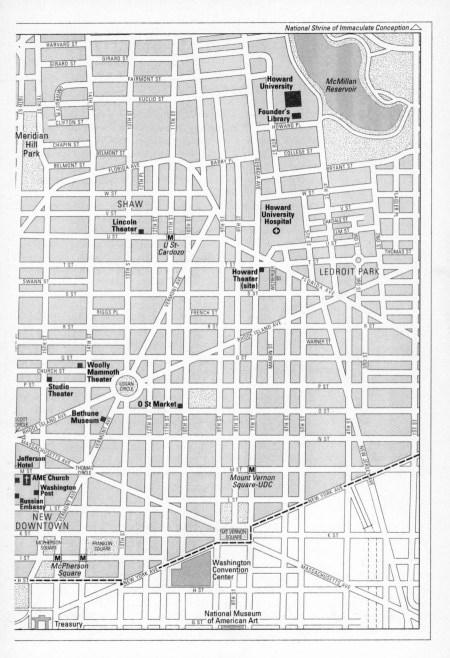

Meridian
Hill
Park

Howard
University

McMillan
Reservoir

Founder's
Library

HARVARD ST

GIRARD ST

GIRARD ST

FAIRMONT ST

EUCLID ST

CLIFTON ST

CHAPIN ST

BELMONT ST

BELMONT ST

HOWARD PL

FLORIDA AVE

BARRY PL

COLLEGE ST

BRYANT ST

SHAW

Lincoln
Theater

U St-
Cardozo

M

Howard
University
Hospital

LEDROIT PARK

W ST

V ST

V ST

U ST

T ST

T ST

Howard Theater
(site)

FLORIDA AVE

SWANN ST

S ST

S ST

RIGGS PL

FRENCH ST

RHODE ISLAND AVE

WARNER ST

R ST

R ST

R ST

Q ST

Woolly
Mammoth
Theater

CHURCH ST

Studio
Theater

P ST

LOGAN
CIRCLE

Bethune
Museum

O St Market

P ST

O ST

O ST

SCOTT
CIRCLE

RHODE ISLAND AVE

MASSACHUSETTS AVE

N ST

Jefferson
Hotel

THOMAS
CIRCLE

M ST

M ST

M

Mount Vernon
Square-UDC

AME Church

Washington
Post

NEW YORK AVE

Russian
Embassy

L ST

L ST

NEW
DOWNTOWN

K ST

MT. VERNON
SQUARE

K ST

MCPHERSON
SQUARE

FRANKLIN
SQUARE

I ST

M

M

McPherson
Square

NEW YORK AVE

Washington
Convention
Center

MASSACHUSETTS AVE

H ST

H ST

Treasury

National Museum
of American Art

G ST

post-war decline, though pockets are slowly being dragged back towards respectability: the odd museum, a fringe theatre scene and booming bar-life on U Street offer rare diversions.

New Downtown

DC's business district, or **NEW DOWNTOWN**, is the off-centre diamond north of Lafayette Square formed by Pennsylvania, New Hampshire, Massachusetts and New York avenues. Some of the interior thoroughfares, like 16th Street and Connecticut Avenue, saw early development by businessmen, hoteliers and socialites who saw the advantage in being just a few blocks from the White House. But these streets really took off after the panicked flight from the old downtown areas to the east after the 1968 riots. In part the district has paid the price for this shotgun arrangement: there's little sense of history and virtually no sense of a meaningful neighbourhood. In this, of course, New Downtown isn't alone and if it resembles anything it's the anonymous downtown ghettos of other modern American cities – largely white, largely sterile and largely deserted after 6pm.

Along K Street

Use Farragut West and Farragut North Metros for Farragut Square, K St, 16th St and 17th St; McPherson Square Metro for McPherson Square, Franklin Square, K St and 16th St.

K Street – spine of New Downtown's corporate business and political lobbying district – is DC's Wall Street only in spirit. When the companies first moved in during the 1970s, local zoning ordinances prevented them from aping New York's soaring urban streetscape. Restricted to a maximum height of 130ft, the buildings are generally production-line boxes of little distinction in which lobbyists, lawyers, brokers and bankers beaver away from dawn till dusk. Between 13th and 20th streets there's barely a building to raise the pulse, though street traders do their best to inject a bit of life, hustling jewellery, T-shirts, hot-dogs and bath-salts from the wide sidewalks.

Of the trio of squares on the south side of K Street, **Farragut Square** (at 17th) is the least prepossessing, a small green stain under the eye of Admiral David Farragut, whose statue celebrates his reckless heroism ("Damn the torpedoes. Full speed ahead") during the Civil War Battle of Mobile Bay. Two blocks east, across 16th Street, **McPherson Square** is named for the commander of the Tennessee Army during the Civil War. Here, at least, late nineteenth- and early twentieth-century architects injected a modicum of style and wit into their buildings' facades. The Neoclassical Investment Building (15th and K), the Southern Railway Building (1500 K St, opposite the square), the decorative Bowen Building and, best of all, the scrupulously carved capitals and lion's head plaques of the adjacent Southern Building (805 15th St) – all show K Street's planners a thing or two.

The most agreeable space is another block over to the east, where paths, benches and a central fountain break up the large expanse of **Franklin Square** (between 13th and 14th). The sleek flanking buildings on I and K streets are very 1980s Manhattan, but under the tree canopy inside the square they're hidden from view.

New Downtown

At Franklin Square, you're just a block from the National Museum of Women in the Arts (p.199) and the New York Avenue Presbyterian Church (p.200); the Convention Center and Chinatown (p.194) are three blocks east.

Connecticut Avenue and 17th Street

North of K Street the business-oriented boulevards of **Connecticut Avenue** and **17th Street** strike four hefty blocks to Dupont Circle. Connecticut Avenue is the grander, graced since 1925 by the double bay-fronted **Mayflower Hotel** (no. 1127), whose first official function was President Coolidge's inaugural ball. Designed by the New York architects responsible for Grand Central Station, it has the same glorious height and space: inside, the remarkable 500-foot-long Promenade – effectively a lobby connecting Connecticut Avenue to 17th Street – could comfortably accommodate an army division or two. It's rich in rugs, oils, sofas, gilt and mirrors, as is the hotel's Grand Ballroom, in which a dozen incoming presidents have swirled around the dancefloor over the years. FDR even lived in the *Mayflower* for a while after his inaugural, while J Edgar Hoover lunched here every day during his tenure at the FBI.

Having cut through to 17th Street, head north for one block to M Street where the **National Geographic Society** maintains its **Explorers Hall** at 1145 17th St NW (Mon–Sat 9am–5pm, Sun 10am–5pm; free; ☎857-7588). Founded in 1888, the Society started off by funding important expeditions to various uncharted territories, but its greatest asset was Gilbert Hovey Grosvenor, founding editor of *National Geographic* magazine, who first conceived that geography could be presented in an exciting fashion, primarily by commissioning spectacular illustrations. The yellow-bordered magazine is now recognized the world over and the Society capitalizes on its reputation in its Washington headquarters by presenting a child-friendly geography exhibit, designed ultimately to encourage subscriptions. The walk-through **Geographica** exhibit features interactive panels and videos, which teach about weather systems, evolution, planet-forming and fossil finds, with subjects often highlighted by splendid photography from the magazine. In **Earth Station One** a giant video screen and revolving eleven-foot globe combine to present a fifteen-minute interactive show on the workings of the earth, its seas, atmosphere and natural features.

Across M Street, the **Charles Sumner School**, at 1201 17th St (Tues–Fri 10am–5pm; free; ☎727-3419), was named for the nineteenth-century senator beaten in the Old Senate Chamber by a pro-slavery congressman who violently objected to Sumner's more enlightened views (see p.113). To improve the education offered to black children, a separate public high school – the first in the country – was established in the city in 1870; for a period it was located here at 17th Street. An harmonious redbrick building of 1872 with a handsome central clocktower, the school is largely used today for conferences, but sign in at the desk and check the list of current exhibits, which range from temporary shows by African-American artists to displays relating to the city's school system.

Half a block further north, turn left down Rhode Island Avenue for princely **St Matthew's Cathedral**, 1725 Rhode Island Ave NW (Mon–Fri & Sun 6.30am–6.30pm, Sat 7.30am–6.30pm; tours Sun 2.30–4.30pm; free; ☎347-3215), where the slain JFK's funeral mass was held in 1963; there's a memorial in front of the altar.

*JFK was, of
course, buried
at Arlington;
see p.243.*

B'nai B'rith Klutznick National Jewish Museum

1640 Rhode Island Ave NW ☎857-6583; Farragut North Metro. Daily except Sat 10am–4.30pm. Admission $2.

On the corner of Rhode Island Avenue and 17th Street, the exemplary **B'nai B'rith Klutznick National Jewish Museum** presents a captivating look at Jewish life through historical, ceremonial and folk art objects. The galleries cover every aspect of the Jewish experience, from birth to Bar Mitzvah, marriage and death – eighteenth-century circumcision instruments and tax permits, painted Italian marriage contracts and linen *Torah* (liturgical scroll) binders are all on display. The oldest items are two-thousand-year-old incantation bowls, whose Hebrew inscriptions cast a protective spell over those to whom the words were dedicated. Other pieces show extraordinary workmanship, like the silver spice containers adorned with turrets or the micrographic writing on miniature bibles. Enthusiastic docents point out the significance of silver amulets, *Torah* crowns and various parchment scrolls; slender metal *Torah* pointers, for example, in the shape of a hand, are necessary to avoid a human hand touching the sacred scroll itself. The museum also displays changing exhibits of Jewish art, while a new venture celebrates the Jewish-American contribution to sport in a Hall of Fame.

*The shop in
the Jewish
Museum (see
p.304) is one
of the most
alluring of
DC's gallery
stores, full of
quality arts
and crafts.*

Along and around 16th Street

If New Downtown has a street to match the grandiloquence of Pennsylvania Avenue it's **16th Street**, the wide boulevard that starts at Lafayette Square and runs north to the border with Maryland six miles away. Most of the area above K Street was scantily populated well into the nineteenth century, but post-Civil War expansion changed 16th Street completely, replacing a ramshackle black neighbourhood with large mansions, gentlemen's clubs and patrician hotels, revelling in their proximity to the White House.

The best of the buildings in the lower reaches are between K Street and Scott Circle, starting with the imposing **Russian Embassy** (1125 16th St NW); across the street from here, the original mansion facade of the **National Geographic Society** is far more appealing than its modern 17th Street addition. Further up come the equally grand University Club and, opposite, the stately **Jefferson Hotel** (1220 16th St NW; see p.265), before you reach Scott Circle itself where the traffic tunnels under the road.

There was a time, at the end of the nineteenth century, when **Scott Circle** was a fashionable park at the centre of a residential neighbourhood. Now the traffic is too thick and the park is non-existent – the only diversion provided by the plume-hatted General Winfield Scott himself, the Union commander astride a prancing horse. The views, though, up and down 16th Street from this point are majestic, particularly south to the White House.

Off 16th: Metropolitan AME Church and the Washington Post

Half a block to the east at 1518 M St, the large Gothic redbrick **Metropolitan African Methodist Episcopal (AME) Church** – built and paid for in 1886 by former slaves – saw the funeral of statesman and orator Frederick Douglass in February 1895, brought to lie in state in the church in which he had often preached. On the day of the funeral, crowds swamped the street outside, black public schools closed for the day and flags in the city flew at half mast. The church isn't strictly open for visits, though you may be able to take a look around if the doors are open, or after a service.

Walk around the block onto 15th Street for the offices of the **Washington Post**, at 1150 15th St NW (tours Mon 10am, 11am, 1pm, 2pm & 3pm; ☎334-7969; reservations required). Together with the *New York Times*, the *Post* likes to imagine that it informs the informed in America, its reputation based squarely on the investigative coup of its reporters Bob Woodward and Carl Bernstein, who between them in the 1970s brought down a President (see p.167). Tours let you see how the paper is produced; this, it has to be said, is not a deeply exciting experience and unless you're hot on the Watergate trail, it's certainly one you can live without.

Dupont Circle, Embassy Row and Kalorama

Until the Civil War, Pacific Circle – as **DUPONT CIRCLE** was first known – marked the western edge of the city, beyond where the nation's capital petered out into a series of farms, slaughterhouses and barns. With the post-war boom, however, came something of a transformation, as streets were paved and a bridge run across Rock Creek to nearby Georgetown. The British Embassy built premises here in the mid-1870s, to be followed by lawyers and businessmen who installed their families in substantial brick Victorian houses. By the turn of the century, Dupont Circle was where any self-respecting industrial baron or high-flying diplomat chose to build his city man-

Dupont Circle, Embassy Row and Kalorama

sion, often in the favoured contemporary Beaux-Arts style. Massachusetts Avenue, northwest of the Circle, became so popular with foreign legations that it acquired the tag **Embassy Row**, while even more secluded, upper-class residences sprouted north of S Street in an exclusive neighbourhood known as **Kalorama** – after the "beautiful view" (in Greek) it afforded of the Rock Creek Valley.

Dupont Circle's golden age of soirées, socialites and selectivity ended at roughly the same time as World War II. Many of the wealthy residents had been hard hit by the 1929 stock market crash and sold up; other mansions were torn down or, the ultimate ignominy, turned into rooming houses for the post-war influx of federal workers. The Circle became solidly middle-class and, during the 1970s, even vaguely radical, as a younger crowd moved in, attracted by a dilapidated housing stock in which they could strip pine, throw down weave rugs and demonstrate against Vietnam to their heart's content.

Rampant gentrification has long seen off the Dupont Circle hippies and it's once more a very definitely upscale address, but the neighbourhood has managed to retain something of a cultural edge. There's a thriving **gallery district** (around Q and R streets, between 20th and 22nd), while Dupont Circle is also centre of the city's **gay scene** with bars and clubs along 17th Street (east of the circle) and P Street (west). Washington's influx of designer coffee shops began here and there are more impressive restaurants and bookshops than in any other part of DC. One of the best days to visit is the first Saturday in June when the **Dupont–Kalorama Museum Walk** (☏ 387-2151) sponsors free concerts and activities.

Dupont Circle

Dupont Circle itself is one of the city's major intersections, with New Hampshire, Massachusetts and Connecticut avenues converging at a large traffic island centred on an allegorical **fountain** whose frolicking nude figures – representing sea, stars and wind – were designed to honour the Civil War naval exploits of Admiral Samuel Dupont. The Circle looks a little ragged at the edges today, but it's an easygoing hang-out with chess-players hogging the permanent tables in the centre. Within a few minutes' walk are a multitude of cafés, bookstores and restaurants, and there are **Metro** entrances on either side. At a couple of points, steps lead down into tunnels once used by streetcars – the Metro's precursor – which have been renovated to hold a sterile food court known as **Dupont Down Under** (Mon–Thurs & Sun 10am–9pm, Fri & Sat 10am–10pm).

It's hard to imagine Dupont Circle in its prime since most of the surrounding mansions were razed by developers in the 1950s and 1960s. Two survivors are the the Beaux-Arts specimen at the corner with Massachusetts Avenue, and the Neoclassical building at no. 15 – once the Patterson House, where, famously, the Coolidges, camping out while White House renovations took place, hosted Charles Lindbergh fresh from his solo transatlantic crossing.

The Heurich Mansion
Built in 1894 for German-born brewing magnate Christian Heurich, the Romanesque **Heurich Mansion**, 1307 New Hampshire Ave NW, a block south of the Circle, makes its statement about its owner's origins and wealth loud and clear with its turret, castellated accretions and rich carved wood-and-plaster interior. The building is occupied by the **Historical Society of Washington DC** (Tues–Sat 10am–4pm; $3; ☎785-2068), which conducts informative guided tours on the hour through many of the restored rooms, dwelling on the materials, decor and household life of the occupants. Temporary exhibitions also highlight aspects of city history and architecture, and there's a good bookstore, devoted to works about the city.

Along Massachusetts Avenue: Embassy Row

Embassy Row – as it still likes to think of itself – starts in earnest a few paces northwest up Massachusetts Avenue, where the Indonesian Embassy at no. 2020 (opposite the *Embassy Row Hotel*) occupies the magnificent Art Nouveau **Walsh-McLean House**, built in 1903 for gold baron Thomas Walsh. It's a superb building, with colonnaded loggia and intricate, carved windows; inside, sixty ornate rooms were pressed into regular service as one of high society's most fashionable party venues, with soirées presided over by Walsh's daughter Evalyn, the last private owner of the Hope Diamond (now in the National Museum of Natural History; see p.105).

The Goodwill Embassy Tour (May; ☎636-4225) is a unique chance to see inside DC's embassies.

A block further up – past the stately redbrick *Ritz-Carlton* hotel – the **Anderson House** at 2118 Massachusetts Ave NW is a similarly impressive pile, a veritable palace built between 1902 and 1905 for Larz Anderson, who served as ambassador in Belgium and Japan. As a Beaux-Arts residence it has no equal in the city, its grey-stone exterior sporting twin arched entrances with heavy wooden doors and colonnaded portico. Inside, original furnishings – cavernous fireplaces, inlaid marble floors, tapestries, diverse murals and a grandstand of a ballroom – provide a suitably lavish backdrop for government receptions. Some of this you'll be able to see for yourself since the house was bequeathed in Anderson's will to the **Society of the Cincinnati** (Tues–Sat 1–4pm; free; ☎785-2040), which maintains a fairly pedestrian museum of Revolutionary memorabilia. The society is the oldest patriotic organization in the country, established in 1783 – Anderson's great-grandfather was a founder-member – and all its members are direct descendants of Revolutionary War officers. Probably the best time to come to the Anderson House is for one of the regular **free concerts** (see p.296).

This far up the avenue, virtually every building flies a national flag outside its front door and security is tight but discreet. With time on

Dupont Circle, Embassy Row and Kalorama

your hands, you may as well stroll the block or so further northwest to **Sheridan Circle**, whose equestrian statue of Union General Phillip H Sheridan was erected in 1909. It's quite a dainty representation of the general astride a boisterous horse – restrained in the extreme given that sculptor Gutzon Borglum went on to carve the sixty-foot-high heads of Washington, Jefferson, Lincoln and Roosevelt at Mount Rushmore. On the south side of the Circle, the **Turkish Embassy** (1606 23rd St) is awash with Near Eastern motifs – oddly, it wasn't commissioned by the Turks at all but by one Edward Everett, the man who patented the fluted bottle-top. Finally, from the Circle, duck briefly down 23rd Street to **Dumbarton Bridge**, guarded on either side by enormous bronze bison. The bridge provides the quickest route into northern Georgetown, emerging on Q Street by Dumbarton House (see p.239), about twenty minutes from Dupont Circle.

The Phillips Collection

1600 21st St NW ☎387-2151; Dupont Circle Metro. Mon–Sat 10am–5pm, Sun noon–7pm. Admission $6.50.

The **Phillips Collection**'s much trumpeted claim to be "America's first museum of modern art" is based on its opening eight years before New York's MOMA. It's often rated as one of the most congenial galleries in Washington: the oldest part of the brownstone Georgian-Revival building was the family home of founder Duncan Phillips, who lost his father and brother in little over a year and established a memorial gallery in the house in 1921 in their honour. Financed by the family's steel fortune, Phillips bought close on 2500 works over the years: during the 1920s, he and his artist wife Marjorie became patrons of young painters like Georgia O'Keeffe and Marsden Hartley, while there are works by everyone from Renoir to Rothko (and several by distinctly non-modern artists like Giorgione and El Greco, in whose work Phillips saw the sources of modern art). **Highlights** are picked out below, but note that not everything can be displayed at any one time: changes of paintings and temporary exhibitions are common, which can frustrate particular viewing plans but can also throw up unexpected delights.

The **main entrance** is in the Goh Annex, on 21st Street. The permanent collection (tours Wed & Sat 2pm; call in advance) is exhibited on the first two floors of the annexe and on the first and second floor of the original building, reached by an enclosed "skywalk" between the two; the annexe third floor is taken up by **special exhibitions**, while on the ground level of the main building is the **museum shop**. In keeping with Phillips' idea of the collection as a "life-enhancing influence", there's a full programme of cultural events: in particular, **classical music recitals** (Sept–May Sun 5pm; free with admission) and so-called **Artful Evenings** (June–Sept Thurs 5–8pm; $5) with live music, lectures and a cash bar.

The Goh Annex

The permanent collection on the **first floor** of the Goh Annex makes for a rather low-key introduction, usually featuring a handful of Abstract-Expressionist works from the 1950s, including a characteristically gloomy set in the Rothko Room. Things cheer up no end once you climb the stairs to the **second floor** and start picking out favourites from the colourful ensemble: a wistful Blue Period Picasso, Matisse's *Studio, Quai St-Michel*, a Cézanne still life and no less than four van Goghs, including the powerful *Road Builders* (1889). Pierre Bonnard gets a room to himself, where you have to stand well back to take in the expansive and assertive *The Terrace* (1918). Top billing in the **Renoir Room** goes to *The Luncheon of the Boating Party* (1891), where straw-boatered dandies linger over a long and bibulous feast in an outgoing work showing a typically generous use of light – Phillips bought the painting in 1923 for $125,000 as part of a two-year burst of acquisition that also yielded Cézanne's *Mont Saint-Victoire* and Honoré Daumier's *The Uprising*. There's an interesting spread of works in the **Degas Room**, too, from early scenes like *Women Combing Their Hair* (1875) to a late ballet picture, *Dancers at the Bar* (1900), in which the background and hair of the subjects collide in an orange frenzy.

The English landscapes of John Constable, considered coarse in their day, include the fine *On the River Stour* (1843), where a fisherman battles against the elements. This is found alongside earlier nineteenth-century works by artists like Eugène Delacroix, while Phillips' catholic taste comes to the fore with the juxtaposition of two paintings of the *Repentant Peter*: one, fat and bluff, by late eighteenth-century artist Francisco de Goya, the second – two centuries older – a more familiar, biblical study by El Greco. An odd pictorial choice on the face of it, this last was bought by Phillips for his modern art museum for the very good reason that he considered El Greco "the first impassioned expressionist".

Main building

Across the skywalk and down the stairs to the **first floor** of the main building brings you into the oak-panelled **Music Room**, where Cubist works by Georges Braque (a particular favourite of Phillips) and Pablo Picasso (including a vibrant *Bullfight*) vie for attention. Beyond here the collection begins to concentrate more on late nineteenth-century American artists, with Winslow Homer's bleak *To The Rescue*, James McNeill Whistler's gentle *Miss Lilian Woakes* and moody Albert Pinkham Ryder landscapes to the fore.

The **second floor** features artists who Phillips championed in the 1920s and 1930s when few others would, like Milton Avery (who influenced the young Rothko) and Jacob Lawrence – the latter represented by extracts from a powerful series known as *The Migration of the Negro*. Better-known names abound, too, notably Edward Hopper, whose works include the faintly menacing *Sunday* (1926) and the much later *Approaching a City*, viewed from the vantage point of sunken train tracks. A separate **Klee Room** displays a stunning collection of nine paintings by the Bauhaus teacher and artist, from the stick figures embellishing *Arrival of the Jugglers* (1926) to the abstract *The Way to the Citadel* (1937), where red arrows point the way through a kaleidoscopic maze of rectangles, triangles and trapezoidal shapes. With a final flourish, the rooms throw up a melange of Matisse, Kandinsky, Miró and Mondrian, not to mention Braque's *Round Table* (1929), piled high with guitar, dagger, apples, books, clay pipe and wallet – the sort of stuff lying around in the average Cubist's kitchen.

Kalorama

North of Sheridan Circle, in the high-rent district of **Kalorama**, quiet, crisp, lawned streets stretch out to meet Rock Creek Park.

Woodrow Wilson (1856–1924) *28th President*, 1913–21

He was the perfect prototype of the seventeenth-century Puritan reincarnated.

Alistair Cooke *America*, 1973

Born Thomas Woodrow Wilson in Stanton, Virginia, to a plain-living Presbyterian family, the future president dropped the "Thomas" at a very early stage, convinced that the new version would sound better when he was famous. He attended law school and, though he didn't take his final exams, practised law in Georgia for a year, discovering only that it wasn't his *métier*. Wilson returned to graduate school to take his doctorate (making him the only American president to have earned his PhD) and taught law and political economics for twelve years, eventually rising to become a reforming President of Princeton. Known and respected as an academic writer on political science and stern critic of government corruption, there he might have stayed but for the Democratic Party's need for progressive candidates to run against the splintering Republicans. In 1910 an ambitious Wilson won election as the governor of New Jersey and two years later received the Democratic nomination for president. The split in the Republican Party – with Theodore Roosevelt running against the incumbent William Howard Taft – gave the Democrats both houses in Congress and let Wilson into power.

A stirring orator (and the last president to write his own speeches), in his two terms of office Wilson saw a batch of reforming legislation that wouldn't be matched until the days of FDR: the Federal Reserve Bank was established to better regulate the banking system, anti-trust laws were strengthened, the 19th Amendment (for women's suffrage) passed and labour laws enacted that at least gave a nod to workers' rights. But, with Congress dominated at least at first by southern Democrats, Wilson also presided over rather darker deeds – not least the violent breaking of the Colorado coal strike, leaving 66 people dead, or the entrenchment of segregation in the federal system. Indeed, it's misleading to see Wilson as any kind of liberal; his reforms made capitalism safe in a period of consider-

---

Here, the city's diplomatic community sits behind lace curtains and bullet-proof glass in row after row of million-dollar townhouse embassies, private homes and hibiscus-clad gardens. If you wanted an immediate object lesson in the inequalities of life in downtown DC, just ten blocks to the east you can buy crack on the street in Shaw.

As in all rich American ghettos there is very little to see (the only similarity they have, in fact, with poor American ghettos). But for an agreeable stroll in quite the nicest neighbourhood this side of Georgetown, head up 24th Street towards **Kalorama Circle**, from where there are splendid views across Rock Creek Park. Just to the east, the **French Embassy** at 2221 Kalorama Rd NW is the most ambitious house hereabouts, a Tudor-style country manor built originally for a mining magnate and sold to the French in 1936 for the ludicrously expensive (for then) sum of almost half a million dollars.

---

able turmoil and sat firmly within the turn-of-the-century context of strengthening federal power at the expense of individual freedom. It's no coincidence that the 18th Amendment sanctioning Prohibition was passed during his presidency.

If Wilson was blind to the narrow concerns of workers and minorities, he had a keen political eye for the wider picture mixed with a high moral tone that brooked no argument. Inspired by his sound analysis of the mood of the American people, and, perhaps, by a gut pacifism, he managed to keep America out of World War I until 1917 – the machine politician in him happy to win re-election on the pacifist ticket. Within four months, however, the country was at war, prompted ostensibly by unprovoked German attacks on American shipping, though later critics would claim that the government wanted Allied war orders to stimulate the economy. Abandoning his pacifist stance, Wilson instead declared a war "for democracy" and devoted his considerable energies to ending it quickly and imposing a new moral order on the world. This manifested itself in his championing of a League of Nations, which idea he took to the peace conference in Paris, seeing it as a "matter of life or death for civilization". Returning in June 1919 to sell the idea to the American people (and more importantly to the Senate, which has to ratify any treaty by a two-thirds majority), Wilson undertook a draining speaking tour. After a series of blinding headaches he had to cut it short, returning to DC where, on October 2, 1919, he suffered a huge stroke that half-paralysed him.

His cherished treaty was finally rejected by the Senate in March 1920, but by then Wilson was almost completely incapacitated. Few people outside government were informed of this, and in what today looks suspiciously like a cover-up, his wife Edith – sixteen years his junior – took on many of the day-to-day decisions in the White House, prompting critics to complain of a "petticoat presidency". As inflation rose and the economy slumped, Warren Harding was swept into power in the 1920 presidential elections. Wilson and his wife left the White House for S Street, where crowds greeted him on the steps, old and infirm. There he died, three years later on February 3, 1924 and was buried in Washington National Cathedral (see p.226).

Woodrow Wilson House

2340 S St NW ☎387-4062; Dupont Circle Metro. Tues–Sun 10am–4pm.
Admission $5.

Many future and soon-to-be presidents have lived in Washington
DC before their stint in the White House; all but one of them left the
moment after passing on the presidential baton. Only Woodrow
Wilson, the 28th President, stayed on in the city, moving into a fine
Waddy Butler Wood-designed Georgian-Revival house on S Street
that is now open to the public as the **Woodrow Wilson House**. It's
a comfortable home – light and airy, with high ceilings, wooden
floors, a wide staircase and solarium – which, despite his incapaci-
tating stroke in 1919, Wilson aimed to use as a workplace where he
could write political science books and practise law. That his second wife Edith, a rich jeweller's widow, wanted to stay in DC near
her family and friends probably had something to do with the decision to stay on; she lived in the house for over 35 years after his
death.

Visitors are first ushered into the front parlour, where Wilson liked
to receive guests, to watch a hagiographical film narrated by Walter
Cronkite. There's plenty to see in the house itself, not least the elevator – powered from the nearby streetcar supply – installed to assist
the enfeebled President's movement between floors, and the bedroom, furnished by Edith as it had been in the White House. The can-
vas-walled **library** of this most scholarly of presidents once contained 8000 books, which were donated to the Library of Congress
after his death; those that remain are the 69 volumes of Wilson's own
writings (the only President to have written more were Theodore
Roosevelt – who, incidentally, Wilson used to impersonate, unflat-
teringly, to amuse his children). The silent-movie projector and
screen were given to him after his stroke by Douglas Fairbanks Sr.
Frozen in the 1920s, the fully equipped **kitchen** is a beauty, with
blacklead range and provisions stacked in the walk-in pantry.

Textile Museum

2320 S St NW ☎667-0441; Dupont Circle Metro. Mon–Sat 10am–5pm, Sun
1–5pm. Suggested donation $5.

*The museum
shop (see
p.304) is one
of the best in
DC for textiles
and fabrics.*

Next door to the Woodrow Wilson House, in two equally grand converted residences, the **Textile Museum** presents up to nine temporary exhibitions a year drawn from its 15,000-strong collection of
textiles and carpets. The museum had its roots in the collection of
George Hewitt Myers, who bought his first Oriental rug as a student
and opened the museum with three hundred other rugs and textiles
in 1925. Based in his family home, designed by no less an architect
than John Russell Pope, the museum soon expanded into the house
next door and today both buildings, and the lovely gardens, are open
to the public. Displays – in some of the most pleasingly presented
galleries in town – might take in pre-Columbian Peruvian textiles,

Near and Far East exhibits (some dating back to 3000 BC) and rugs and carpets from Spain, South America and the American Southwest.

It's best to call for a schedule of exhibitions; better still, aim to coincide with a free **tour** (Sept–May Wed, Sat & Sun 2pm) or the weekly **rug/textile appreciation** mornings (Sat 10.30am; free).

Shaw

East of Dupont Circle, the change in surroundings couldn't be more marked. In a few short blocks, the embassies, mansions and tended streets melt away until, past 15th Street, you're in **SHAW**, an historic district with an upbeat past and the stirrings of a future but still sorely affected by three intervening decades of neglect. The neighbourhood – roughly north of M Street between North Capitol and 15th – is one of the oldest residential areas in DC, its first settlers immigrant whites who built shanty housing along **7th Street** after the Civil War. The district thrived as one of the booming city's main commercial arteries and remained busy during the Depression when the low-rent housing in the alleys either side began to attract countless black immigrants from the rural southern states in search of work. Pool halls, churches, cafés, bars, theatres and social clubs sprang up; across on **14th Street**, a shopping strip developed; while U **Street** evolved into the "Black Broadway". For years the neighbourhood was simply known as "14th and U", taking the name Shaw at the turn of the century after Colonel Robert Gould Shaw, the (white) commander of the first black regiment in the Union Army. With the all-black **Howard University** prospering in its grounds at 6th Street and **Griffith Stadium** (now Howard University Hospital, 2401 Georgia Ave), one of the city's few integrated public buildings, attracting massive crowds to its black baseball games, there was a rare vibrancy to this corner of DC.

Segregation – entrenched in Washington since the late nineteenth century – only secured Shaw's prosperity, since the local blacks stayed within the neighbourhood to shop and socialize. Conversely, **desegregation** (starting with the Supreme Court's overturning of the "separate but equal" schools policy in 1954) opened up the varied attractions of downtown Washington for Shaw's black inhabitants and decline was swift. Black middle-class flight to the periphery had been taking place since the turn of the century, with larger Victorian properties bought from suburb-bound whites in fringe neighbourhoods like LeDroit Park, Logan Circle and the so-called "Striver's Section" of U Street (between 15th and 18th). By the 1960s, the older black streets in Shaw were feeling the pinch, while the **riots** of 1968 finished them off. News of the assassination of Dr Martin Luther King Jr sparked three days of arson, rioting and looting which destroyed businesses and lives along 7th, 14th and H streets. A dozen people were killed, millions of dollars of property lost and the confidence of nearby businesses in Old Downtown jolted so severely that within a decade that area, too, was virtually abandoned.*

The three decades since have done little for Shaw, much of which has become indistinguishable from the crack-infested neighbourhoods to the northeast and southeast. Signs of **revival** are there for those who look close enough – revitalized U Street has a Metro station and once again features on the city's nightlife scene, while 14th Street has blossomed as an alternative theatre district. There's no harm in a night out on U Street or a stroll around some of the peripheral historic sights and landmarks, but heed the fact that you're away from the safer parts of Northwest. Drugs (and the crime that goes with them) are still very prevalent, many buildings rundown, the street atmosphere often oppressive. Don't wander aimlessly and alone in the neighbourhood, which can change from borderline to downright threatening in a block or two; head straight for your destination, take cabs when necessary and keep your wits about you.

U Street

U Street-Cardozo Metro is named after Francis Cardozo Sr, renowned Washington educationalist and first principal of the M Street High School – successor to the Charles Sumner School on 17th St, the nation's first public high school for black students.

The only part of Shaw most visitors see is the thriving section of U **Street**, in the blocks near U **Street-Cardozo Metro**, where trendy bars and clubs wait in line for shop-front space. Between the wars, U Street – known locally as "You" Street – ranked second only to New York's Harlem as the centre of black entertainment in America. At the splendid **Lincoln Theater**, 1215 U St, built in 1921, vaudeville shows and movies were bolstered by appearances from the most celebrated jazz performers of the day: Count Basie, Billie Holiday, Cab Calloway, Ella Fitzgerald and DC's own Duke Ellington among them. The theatre now serves as a performing arts centre (see p.297). Next door, *Ben's Chili Bowl* (see p.280) is a forty-year-old institution frequented by the likes of Bill Cosby and Denzel Washington.

Of all the neighbourhood's theatres, the one with the proudest pedigree was the elegant **Howard Theater**, 624 T St, just a few blocks east of the U Street scene. Opened in 1910, it was the first theatre in DC built strictly for black patrons, though that didn't stop hep whites flocking here to see the shows – an unknown Ella Fitzgerald won an open-mike contest, 1940s big bands filled the place, while later artists like James Brown, Smokey Robinson, Gladys Knight and Martha and the Vandellas were queuing up to appear; in 1962 the Supremes played their first headlining gig at the *Howard*. The theatre survived

---

*The 1968 riots weren't the first to tear Shaw apart. Immediately after World War I, returning black servicemen were dismayed to find segregation forcefully applied in DC. In the summer of 1919, prompted by the violent antics of vigilante white ex-soldiers, five days of racial rioting left thirty people dead, after fierce fighting on U, 7th and T streets, as well as in areas of southwest Washington.

the riots in one piece but closed soon after and still stands abandoned today – sadly, it's hardly worth the walk.

Howard University and LeDroit Park

Perhaps the most prestigious black university in the country, **Howard University** – named for General Otis Howard, commissioner of the Freedmen's Bureau – was established in 1867 by a church missionary society to provide a school for blacks freed after the Civil War. Its first faculties were in law, music, medicine and theology, though now scores of subjects are taken by almost 13,000 students from over a hundred countries. Sadly none of the original campus

See p.288 for reviews of U Street's bars and clubs.

Duke Ellington (1899–1974)

Edward Kennedy Ellington was born in Washington DC (on 22nd St NW), and grew up in Shaw at 1212 T Street (not open to the public). A precocious child, nicknamed "Duke", at fifteen he was playing ragtime in scratch bands at local cafés; he wrote his first composition, *Soda Fountain Rag*, in 1914. Also an accomplished young artist, Ellington turned down a scholarship to New York's Pratt Institute to form instead "The Washingtonians", a trio with whom he played extensively in DC before making the big move to New York in 1923. By 1927, his band had expanded to become **The Duke Ellington Orchestra**; a year later, it was a permanent fixture at Harlem's Cotton Club, where Ellington made his reputation in five tumultuous years, writing early, atmospheric classics like *Mood Indigo* and *Creole Love Call*. Established as one of America's finest jazz composers and bandleaders, Ellington set off on his first European tour in 1933, where he went down a storm. The decade after saw the penning of his most celebrated works – from *Sophisticated Lady* and *Take the A Train* to *Don't Get Around Much Anymore*. The Ellington style was unmistakeable: melodious ballads and stomping swing pieces alike employed inventive rhythmic devices, novel key changes and fluid playing to devastating, creative effect. In 1943, he was the first popular musician to perform at Carnegie Hall (where he premiered the ambitious *Black, Brown and Beige*) and, despite a decline in big-band popularity after World War II, managed to keep both his band and personal following largely intact. He spent much of the 1950s and 1960s touring and diversifying his output – writing soundtracks for (and appearing in) movies, and composing extended pieces which mixed jazz with classical and even religious music. In 1969 he received the Presidential Medal of Freedom for his services to music and the arts; by the time of his death in 1974, Duke Ellington had arranged or composed over six thousand works.

In DC, the city remembers its favoured son with a week-long festival of his music each year around April 20 on the **Duke Ellington Birthday Celebration**. The Calvert Street Bridge between Woodley Park and Adams-Morgan was renamed Duke Ellington Bridge in his honour; while the city established the **Duke Ellington School of the Arts** in Georgetown (35th and R streets NW; ☎ 337-4022) as a public high school, with a four-year course for artistically talented youth; free tours are available once a month (except June–Sept) – call for details.

---

buildings remain; the earliest structure was replaced by the **Founder's Library** in the 1930s, which now maintains the Moorland-Spingarn Research Center (Mon–Thurs 9am–4.45pm, Fri 9am–4.30pm, Sat 9am–5pm) housing the country's largest selection of literature relating to black history and culture. This is open to the public, but as a casual visitor, you're more likely to come for a campus **tour** (call ☎ 806-6100 in advance); the **main entrance** is at 2400 6th St NW. Nearest **Metro** is Shaw-Howard University, half a dozen blocks south down Georgia Avenue – take a taxi to the gates.

Famous Howard alumni include Toni Morrison, Jessye Norman, Thurgood Marshall, David Dinkins and Andrew Young.

Short of money just a decade after its inauguration, the university sold a plot of land to the south (in the shallow angle formed by Florida and Rhode Island avenues) to developers who built an exclusive parkland-suburb of sixty detached houses. White university staff were the first to take up residence in **LeDroit Park**, as it was known, though the addition of brick row-houses in the 1880s and 1890s signalled the advance of well-to-do black families. By 1920 LeDroit Park was established as a fashionable black neighbourhood and though much of it has decayed over the decades, the area has been declared an historic district, with the best surviving group of original houses along the 400 block of U Street. Prominent black citizens continue to be associated with the area – the family of DC's first black mayor, Walter Washington, has owned a house here for years, while Jesse Jackson also maintains a property in the district. Perhaps it was LeDroit Park that blues musician Leadbelly had in mind when he wrote his *Bourgeois Blues* in the 1930s; to an ex-jailbird, these rarefied streets must have seemed miles away from the basement jazz and blues clubs on U:

> *Look a here people, listen to me,*
> *Don't try to find no home in Washington DC*
> *Lord, it's a bourgeois town, it's a bourgeois town.*

Logan Circle and 14th Street

At the same time as LeDroit Park saw a black middle-class influx, so too did the roomy Victorian houses around **Logan Circle**, at the southern edge of Shaw. Nearby 14th Street was the black community's swankiest shopping thoroughfare; in the 1930s, the blocks between P and U streets were known as "Auto Row" after the rash of car showrooms which opened up, eager to sell vehicles to the upwardly mobile incomers. Fashionable Iowa Circle, as it was then known, became Logan Circle in 1930, named after the Civil War general whose impressive equestrian statue still lords over it. The surrounding Victorian houses have miraculously survived the slow decline in the neighbourhood since the 1950s – turrets, terraces, balconies and pediments in various states of repair signal the fact that this, too, is a protected historic district.

Fourteenth Street, half a block west, was almost completely lost to the 1968 riots but recently its rough edges have been tamed by the arrival of various fringe theatre companies that have set up here and in the surrounding streets. It's still a bit dodgy in this area at night – don't wander around alone – but cutting-edge café-bars like *Dante's* (1522 14th St; see p.280) are probably symptomatic of the way the neighbourhood's going.

Shaw

The 14th Street theatres are reviewed on p.297.

The Bethune Museum and Archives

Just off Logan Circle, the **Bethune Museum and Archives**, 1318 Vermont Ave NW (Mon–Fri 10am–4pm; $1; ☎332-9201), based in one of the district's restored Victorian townhouses, serves as a fascinating memorial to one of DC's most prominent African-American inhabitants. **Mary McLeod Bethune** was born on a cotton farm in South Carolina in 1875 to poor parents, both ex-slaves; she was one of seventeen children. A bright, enquiring child, she was sent to a local school and later entertained thoughts of becoming a missionary in Africa, before moving to Florida in 1904 to found the Daytona Educational and Industrial School for Negro Girls (later the Bethune-Cookman College). Starting in a rented room, and using homemade materials, Bethune persevered with her intention to train teachers who would serve the African-American community. In 1935, recognition came with the award of a prize by the National Association for the Advancement of Colored People (NAACP), swiftly followed by a call from President Roosevelt to serve as special advisor on minority affairs. Later, as the director of the Division of Negro Affairs in the National Youth Administration, she became the first African-American woman to head a federal office, and was the only woman to work in the ad-hoc "Black Cabinet" which advised FDR on the implications for blacks of his New Deal policies. In 1945, under the aegis of the NAACP, Bethune was in San Francisco to attend the conference which established the concept of the United Nations.

The memorial to Mary McLeod Bethune in Lincoln Park (see p.126) records more of the "Legacy".

The house on Vermont Avenue was bought by Bethune in 1942 as her home (she lived there for seven years) and as headquarters for the National Council for Negro Women, which she had founded in 1935, bringing together various organizations in order to fight discrimination more effectively. Her work here formed the basis of her "Legacy", finished just before her death in 1955, in which she encapsulated the meaning of her life's work in a stirring series of messages for those who would follow: "I leave you a thirst for education. I leave you a respect for the use of power. I leave you faith. I leave you racial dignity".

The best way to the museum is the fifteen-minute walk straight up Vermont Avenue from McPherson Square Metro, past Thomas Circle.

Adams-Morgan

Nowhere is gentrification faster undermining the original, ethnic character of a Washington neighbourhood than in **ADAMS-MORGAN**, DC's trendiest district. With every passing month new designer restaurants, stylish bars and hip stores march confidently further into the area, if not – for the time being – displacing then at least beginning to outnumber the traditional Hispanic businesses which thrived here from the 1950s. Spanish signs and notices are still much in evidence, and the neighbourhood certainly celebrates its heritage fulsomely at the annual Latin American Festival (July) and Adams-Morgan Day (Sept) shindigs, but these days its character is better defined by the burgeoning number of cafés where asking for a *latte frappé* won't be met by a blank stare and a shrug. For a night out largely free from the braying collegiate antics of Georgetown, you'll find Adams-Morgan's 18th Street strip a refreshing change – laid-back, open-to-the-sidewalk bars, restaurants, cafés and clubs with an ethnically mixed, cross-class clientele.

Ironically, this middle-class influx into the neighbourhood is simply turning Adams-Morgan full-circle. In the last decades of the **nineteenth century**, its hilly, rural reaches were colonized by wealthy Washingtonians looking for a select address near the power-housing of Dupont Circle. Impressive apartment buildings were erected in the streets off Columbia Road, boasting fine views and connected to downtown by streetcar. Until World War II some of the city's most prominent politicians and business people lived here; many of their mansions still survive intact. After the war, the city's accommodation shortage meant that many buildings were converted into rooming houses and small apartments; the well-to-do families moved further out into the suburbs and were replaced by a growing blue-collar population, black and white, and, crucially, by an increasing number of Latin American and Caribbean **immigrants**, whose numbers grew rapidly in the 1960s. Concerned that the area was becoming too segregated, a local group fashioned a symbolic name from two local schools: one all-white (Adams), one all-black (Morgan).

Today, Adams-Morgan is regarded as the most racially mixed neighbourhood in the city and for the most part there's a good-natured atmosphere in streets where grocery stores and corner cafés rub shoulders with arty boutiques and sharp bars. Undoubtedly, the yuppies have "discovered" Adams-Morgan, or at least discovered that it's a relatively cheap, fairly groovy, reasonably central place to live; but they're not the only recent immigrants. As any quick glance at the shop-fronts will tell you, Adams-Morgan's **restaurant scene** is the most eclectic in the city – Ethiopian arrivals are responsible for some of the neighbourhood's most highly rated places, but you can eat anything from Argentinian to Vietnamese.

Adams-Morgan orientation

Adams-Morgan is generally thought of as being bounded by Connecticut and Florida avenues and 16th and Harvard streets, although in practice most visitors see little more than the few blocks on either side of the central **Columbia Road/18th Street** intersection, where most of the bars and restaurants are situated. The eastern boundary of the neighbourhood is marked by 16th Street and **Meridian Hill Park** – don't stray further east than 16th Street into Shaw. To the west, the boundary is formed by the National Zoological Park and Connecticut Avenue NW, which is where you'll find the nearest **Metro**: from Woodley Park-Zoo Metro on Connecticut Avenue, it's a fifteen-minute walk down to Calvert Street, across the Duke Ellington Bridge to the Columbia Road/18th Street junction. From Dupont Circle Metro it's a steep twenty-minute hike up 19th Street to Columbia Road. By **bus**, take the #L2 from McPherson Square, which travels up 18th Street to Calvert Street.

Adams-Morgan frequently pops up in establishing shots in the movies: look out for scenes in In the Line of Fire, Dave *and* A Few Good Men.

Adams-Morgan listings: bookshops, p.301 cafés, p.272 restaurants, p.280

A neighbourhood tour

Adams-Morgans' Hispanic legacy is at its strongest in Columbia Road northeast of 18th Street, a good place to check out the street stalls, tape and jewellery sellers, and thrift stores; 18th Street south of Columbia is lined with the best of the bars, clubs and restaurants. Where the two meet, a Saturday market occupies the southwestern plaza. For most visitors that's more than enough, though the streets east and west of the two main drags contain a fair amount of interest – walking tours leave from outside the *Wyoming* building, 2022 Columbia Rd NW (Sun 11am; reservations ☎301/294-9514; $5).

The **Wyoming** itself is a classic example of the marvellous apartment houses built early this century, its mosaic floor, moulded ceilings and marble reception room forming one of DC's loveliest private interiors. The Eisenhowers lived here between 1927 and 1935. Up the street the Italian-Renaissance-style **Altamont** (1901 Wyoming Ave NW, at 20th) is similarly well-endowed, with a baronial reception room and a top-floor that once incorporated its own roof-terrace restaurant. Often, the historical associations and **former occupants** are more diverting than a building itself: Admiral Robert Peary, first to reach the North Pole in 1909, lived at 1831 Wyoming Ave; Tallulah Bankhead spent her teenage years in the *Norwood*, 1868 Columbia Rd (her father was speaker of the House of Representatives); while Lyndon Baines and Mrs Johnson spent the early years of their marriage at the *Woburn*, 1910 Kalorama Rd. Ronald Reagan was shot in Adams-Morgan, surviving an assassination attempt in 1981 as he left the *Washington Hilton*, at the southern end of Columbia Road. Most glamorous of all the Adams-Morgan buildings is the cupola-topped **Ontario** (2853 Ontario Rd, at 18th), built between 1903 and 1906, whose roll-call of famous residents has numbered five-star generals Douglas MacArthur and Chester Nimitz, journalist Janet Cooke, whose Pulitzer Prize-winning story about youth and drugs was later discredited, and Bob Woodward, who could afford to live here once Watergate had made his fortune and his reputation. At the time of Watergate, his partner Carl Bernstein lived in Adams-Morgan, too, in a much less grandiose apartment in the *Biltmore*, 1940 Biltmore St, off 19th St, just a couple of blocks south.

Chapter 8

Upper Northwest

Bus #L2 runs up Connecticut Ave from McPherson Sq/Adams-Morgan (18th St) to Chevy Chase; #30, 32, 34, 35 and 36 run up Wisconsin Ave from Georgetown to Friendship Heights.

Ｎone of the fluctuating fortunes that have afflicted DC's other neighbourhoods have ever ruffled the well-to-do feathers of the districts of the **Upper Northwest**. The upper- and middle-class flight up Connecticut, Wisconsin and Massachusetts avenues began with a series of nineteenth-century presidents who made the cool reaches of rural **Woodley Park** – across Duke Ellington Bridge from Adams-Morgan – their summer home. Grover Cleveland later bought his own stone cottage a little further north in an area which, as a consequence, became known as **Cleveland Park**. Few others could afford the time and expense involved in living a four-mile carriage-ride from the city centre until the arrival in the 1890s of the streetcar; within three decades both Woodley Park and Cleveland Park had become bywords for fashionable, out-of-town living, replete with apartment buildings commissioned from the era's top architects. The tone is no less swanky today, with the red **Metro** line providing access on into a series of ritzy suburbs that stretch into Maryland. Politicians and media people choose to live in the safe streets of Cleveland Park; President Clinton sent Chelsea to school in neighbouring Tenleytown; and in the gleaming, upscale malls of Friendship Heights, on the DC/Maryland boundary, power-shoppers pause only to bemoan the fact they're not on Fifth Avenue.

This part of town, then, has pedigree aplenty but relatively little to offer visitors. You can only view the most celebrated mansions from the outside while the surrounding streets, though pleasing, are hardly exciting. The three major targets are the excellent **National Zoological Park**, the furthest-flung of the Smithsonian attractions; **Washington National Cathedral**, and the expanses of **Rock Creek Park**, largest and most enjoyable of the city's green spaces.

Woodley Park and Cleveland Park

Architect Harry L Wardman designed many of the apartment buildings and townhouses in **WOODLEY PARK**, his most adventurous construc-

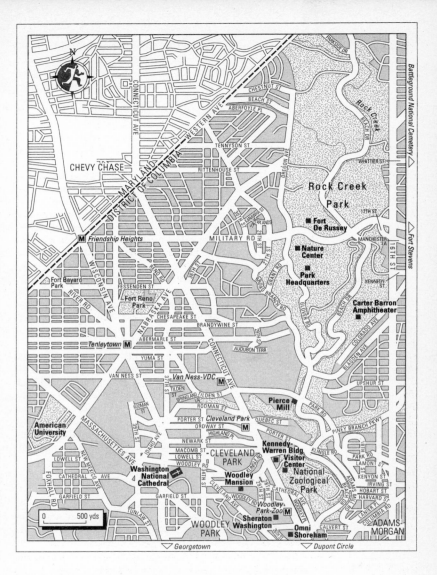

A map of the Upper Northwest area showing the following labels:

N (compass)

CHESTNUT ST
BEACH ST
ABERFOYLE PL
CONNECTICUT AVE
WESTERN AVE
TENNYSON ST
RITTENHOUSE ST
CHEVY CHASE
BEACH DR
Rock Creek
PARK SIDE DR
WHITTIER ST
Rock Creek Park
12TH ST
MARYLAND
DISTRICT OF COLUMBIA
M Friendship Heights
MILITARY RD
RENO RD
28TH ST
NEBRASKA AVE
OREGON AVE
Fort De Russey
MANCHESTER LA
16TH ST
Nature Center
Fort Bayard Park
WISCONSIN AVE
FESSENDEN ST
Fort Reno Park
RIVER RD
CHESAPEAKE ST
ABERMARLE ST
BRANDYWINE ST
Park Headquarters
KENNEDY ST
GRANT RD
27TH ST
BRANCH RD
GLOVER RD
BEACH DR
Carter Barron Amphitheater
COLORADO AVE
Tenleytown M
YUMA ST
VAN NESS ST
CONNECTICUT AVE
AUDUBON TERR
BLAGDEN AVE
UPSHUR ST
Van Ness-VDC M
TILDEN ST
SPRING RD
TILDEN ST
RODMAN ST
Pierce Mill
PARK RD
PINEY BRANCH PKWY
American University
MASSACHUSETTES AVE
39TH ST
IDAHO AVE
PORTER ST
Cleveland Park
ORDWAY ST
HIGHLAND PL
QUEBEC ST
PORTER ST
KLINGLE RD
34TH ST
NEWARK ST
MACOMB ST
LOWELL ST
Cleveland Park M
CLEVELAND PARK
Kennedy-Warren Bldg Visitor Center
LAMONT ST
National Zoological Park
KENYON ST
IRVING ST
HOBART ST
HARVARD ST
LOWELL ST
NEW MEXICO AVE
CATHEDRAL AVE
FOXHALL RD
Washington National Cathedral
WOODLEY RD
Woodley Mansion
34TH ST
CLEVELAND AVE
28TH ST
CATHEDRAL AVE
GARFIELD ST
GARFIELD ST
TUNLAW RD
Woodley Park-Zoo M
Sheraton Washington
CALVERT ST
ADAMS-MORGAN
0   500 yds
WOODLEY PARK
Omni Shoreham

▽ Georgetown   ▽ Dupont Circle

Battleground National Cemetery ▷
Fort Stevens ▷

tion being the massive **Wardman-Park** hotel (Connecticut Ave NW and
Woodley Rd) in 1918, whose tower dominated the local skyline (it's now
part of the 1500-room *Sheraton Washington*). It proved a resounding
success, attracting high-profile politicians and social gadflys who entertained guests in the grand public rooms and rented apartments for

**Woodley
Park and
Cleveland
Park**

themselves. Within a decade a second landmark followed, the hybrid Art Deco-Renaissance-style **Shoreham** on Calvert Street (now the *Omni Shoreham*), designed by Joseph Abel for owner-builder Harry Bralove. Built in 1930 at a cost of $4 million, this has held an inaugural ball for every president from FDR to Clinton; Truman played poker here, JFK courted Jackie, Nixon announced his first cabinet and, in the hotel's celebrated *Blue Room*, Judy Garland, Marlene Dietrich, Bob Hope and Frank Sinatra entertained the great and the good.

*For reviews of
the* Sheraton
Washington
and the Omni
Shoreham, *see
p.268; for
restaurants in
Woodley Park,
see p.281.*

For a view of where the generally more staid nineteenth-century presidents passed their summers, head up Connecticut Avenue to Cathedral Avenue and walk west past 29th Street to the white stucco Georgian **Woodley Mansion**. This was built in 1800 for Philip Barton Key, whose nephew Francis was later to compose the "Star-Spangled Banner" (see p.99). Its elevation meant it was a full 10° cooler in the summer than downtown and presidents Van Buren, Tyler and Buchanan needed no second invitation to spend their summers here; it's now a private school.

Back on Connecticut Avenue and heading north past the zoo (see below) you're soon, and imperceptibly, in **CLEVELAND PARK**. For sheer exuberance, the **Kennedy-Warren** apartment building (3133 Connecticut Ave NW) on the east side takes the local biscuit – this soaring Art Deco evocation of 1930s wealth is home today to P J O'Rourke, among others. A short way further north, just before the Metro station, the Art Deco movie house, the **Uptown** (3426 Connecticut Ave NW), which first opened in 1936, continues to show movies as part of the *Cineplex Odeon* chain (see p.294).

Backtracking a little from Cleveland Park Metro down Connecticut Avenue you can make your way through the broad streets to the cathedral (see p.226), picking a route along **Newark Street** and **Highland Place**. These hold the highest concentration of upper-class residences dating from the area's great turn-of-the-century expansion: Robert Head, Waddy Butler Wood and Paul Pelz all built houses here, and it was on Newark Street that Grover Cleveland's (long-demolished) summer house – the one that prompted the whole influx – once stood.

National Zoological Park

3001 Connecticut Ave NW ☎ 673-4800; Woodley Park-Zoo Metro, or bus #L2 from McPherson Square or 18th St (Adams-Morgan). Grounds daily mid-April to mid-Oct 8am–8pm; mid-Oct to mid-April 8am–6pm; buildings daily 9am–4.30pm. Admission free.

Few people realize that the enormously entertaining **National Zoological Park** forms part of the Smithsonian ensemble – which apart from anything else means that admission is free. Sitting between Woodley Park and Adams-Morgan, it sprawls down the steep slopes of the gorge cut by Rock Creek, with trails through lush vegetation leading past comparatively humane simulations of the home environments of over three thousand creatures. Although founded in 1889 as a traditional zoo, it likes to think of itself these days as a "BioPark", combining the usual menagerie of giraffes and elephants, birds and bees, and lions and tigers with botanic gardens, a wetlands zone, *Amazonia* (a re-creation of a tropical river and rainforest habitat), as well as aquariums and natural history displays.

The **main entrance** on Connecticut Avenue is ten minutes' walk north from the Metro station; just inside the gates, the **Visitor Center** has a map and list of the day's events (like feeding times). From here, two trails loop downhill through the park to Rock Creek itself: the **Olmsted Walk**, passing most of the indoor exhibits, and the steeper **Valley Trail**, with the major aquatic exhibits, birds and *Amazonia*. Head down one and back up the other, visiting the side exhibits on the way and you'll walk over two miles – give youself a minimum of three hours to do the park justice.

Café, restaurant, concessions stands, paid parking, police post and restrooms are scattered throughout the park.

Park highlights

The scales outside the **Cheetah Conservation Station** provide the first means of interaction between visitor and captive. Weigh yourself, check the chart to see with which animal your weight corresponds – and then read just how quickly the apparently somnolent cheetahs and hyenas in the paddock beyond would take to kill and eat you. The first celebrity is a little further on, the **panda** Hsing Hsing, one of a pair presented by the People's Republic of China during Richard Nixon's 1972 visit. His mate, Ling Ling, died in 1992; touching letters from children line the glass wall of her former enclosure. Hsing Hsing, meanwhile, has been left to mourn (though, admittedly, it's difficult to distinguish a mourning panda from a blissful panda) and you can usually only see him at feeding times. The path winds down past elephants, giraffes, hippos and rhinos to perhaps the saddest relic in the zoo, Hsing Hsing included. Before the European settlement of America, millions of **bison** roamed the country; now, along with the couple here, just 140,000 or so survive in scattered parks, refuges and private ranches, their numbers boosted by the modern success in breeding bison for its lo-cal and minimum cholesterol meat. The first of the zoo's garden areas, the **American Indian Heritage Garden**, celebrates the natural history knowledge of the Native Americans whose life was sustained by the bison herds before they and the animals became surplus to white American requirements. Here you learn about the healing properties of herbs and plants like the coneflower (used to treat insect bites, venereal disease and rabies) and the gloriously emetic Indian tobacco plant: should you ever be tempted to make cigarettes out of this, bear in mind that it's also known as vomitweed, pukeweed and gagroot.

Hsing Hsing the panda gets fed at 11am & 3pm.

Some of the zoo's most adventurous work is taking place with its primates. The orangutans are encouraged to leave the confines of the **Great Ape House** and commute to the **Think Tank** and back down the "O Line" – overhead cables strung from towers across public areas of the zoo, with only the depth of the fall (and some low-vault electric wires on the towers) to deter them from leaping off. At the Think Tank, scientists and orangutans come together to hone their communications skills and discuss world events: if in any doubt about the relative intelligence of monkey and human, take a look at the glass case in the Great Ape House which displays the ludicrous items visitors have thrown in the ape enclosures over the years – from cans of soda to plastic crocodiles.

Between Ape House and Think Tank is the excellent **Reptile Discovery Center** (opens 10am), with a full complement of snakes, turtles, crocs, alligators, lizards and frogs, and some enterprising interactive displays, though quite how interactive you want to be with said beasts is open to question. Ponder here on the remarkable komodo dragon, the first to be born in captivity outside Indonesia: it currently eats two rats a week, but will eventually grow to be over 9ft long and weigh over 200 pounds – at which point they'll have to start rat rationing. The adjacent **Invertebrate Exhibit** (Wed–Fri opens 10am, Sat & Sun opens 9am) covers the lives and loves of everything from ants to coral and octopus – admission to these two popular centres can be restricted at busy times; check first at the Visitor Center. Beyond here, the special moated island with the **lions and tigers** marks the end of the big animals, though you might want to duck in and out of the thoroughly unpleasant **Bat Cave** before heading back up the Valley Trail.

Best thing on the Valley Trail is undoubtedly **Amazonia** (opens 10am), the indoor tropical river and forest habitat. A cleverly constructed undulating aquarium gets you close to the fish – piranhas included – while bombarding you with informative notes; you then climb up a level into the humid, creeper-clad rainforest, above the water you've just walked along, familiarizing yourself with roots, leafmould, forest parasites and birdcalls.

Outside again, seals and sea lions splash at an outdoor pool, and then it's a slow pull uphill, past beaver dams, a **Bird House**, an artificial wetland replete with cranes and herons, and assorted eagles, bongos and tapirs. If there's some jiggery-pokery in the bushes as you go, it'll be the **golden lion tamarins**, or South American marmosets, the successful breeding of which is one of the zoo's quiet triumphs – they've been released into a cageless enclosure to prepare them for eventual return to the wild in Brazil.

Washington National Cathedral

Massachusetts and Wisconsin Ave NW ☎537-6200; Woodley Park-Zoo or Cleveland Park Metro; bus #30, 32, 34 or 36 from Pennsylvania Ave (downtown) or Wisconsin Ave (Georgetown), or #N2, N4 or N6 from Farragut Square. April–Sept Mon–Fri 10am–9pm, Sat 10am–4.30pm, Sun 12.30–4.30pm; Oct–March Mon–Sat 10am–4.30pm, Sun 12.30–4.30pm. Suggested donation $2.

The twin towers of **Washington National Cathedral** – the sixth largest cathedral in the world – are visible long before you reach the church itself. Turn the final corner and you're confronted by one of the city's most surprising edifices, a monumental building so medieval in spirit it should surely rise from a dusty European old town plaza rather than from a two-car-two-kid suburb. It comes as no surprise, however, in this planned city that the siting of the cathedral was intentional: here, on the heights of Mount St Alban, unaffected by the District's zoning restrictions, the architects could have free rein to produce their anachronistic Gothic masterpiece.

George Washington first proposed the establishment of a "national" church in the city, but it was a century before Congress finally granted a charter for what is officially known as the Cathedral Chuch of St Peter and St Paul. President Theodore Roosevelt graced the foundation ceremony in 1907 and architects George Bodley (a noted English church architect) and Henry Vaughan set to work, superseded after their deaths by **Philip Hubert Frohman**, who spent the next fifty years completing the design. Frohman died in 1972; the cathedral was finally completed only in 1990, though parts have been in use since the 1920s. It's a Protestant church, the seat of the Episcopal Diocese of Washington, yet conceived as a national church it also hosts services for other denominations.*

Built from Indiana limestone and modelled entirely in the medieval English Gothic style – its great spaces supported by flying buttresses, bosses and vaults – it's a supreme achievement. Unfortunately, there are more similarities with the hoary, crumbling relics of Europe than appearances alone suggest: although it looks brand new – and indeed, some parts are – the cathedral is already undergoing restoration. The decorative bosses have been attacked by lichen, while Washington's freezing winters have cracked the gutters and the roofing and damaged some of the exterior gargoyles.

Inside the cathedral

The centre portal in the west facade isn't always open and you may have to **enter** from the northwest cloister; for a floor plan and information, descend to the crypt floor, where there's an **information desk** and gift shop. **Guided tours** are available on request at the west entrance (Mon–Sat 10am–3.15pm, Sun 12.30–2.45pm; suggested donation $2); ask one of the purple-hatted docents.

Place yourself first at the west end of the **nave** (completed as late as 1976) to appreciate the immense scale of the building; it's more than a tenth of a mile to the high altar at the other end, and the only

Washington National Cathedral

From Woodley Park-Zoo Metro (20min), turn left from Connecticut Ave into Cathedral Ave and right into Woodley Rd to reach the lower-level information center; the west door is around the corner on Wisconsin Ave. The Tourmobile *runs here, too.*

Cathedral services: Mon–Sat 7.30am, noon & 4pm; Sun 8am, 9am (10am Sept–June), 11am, 4pm & 6.30pm.

*Thoroughly Roman Catholic but similarly immense in scale is DC's other major church, the **Basilica of the National Shrine of the Immaculate Conception** (4th St and Michigan Ave NE), a striking hilltop Marian shrine in NE, three blocks west of Brookland-CUA Metro. It's an architectural hodge-podge compared to the National Cathedral, but the majolica-tiled dome and mosaics are spectacular.

Washington National Cathedral

In size, Washington National Cathedral ranks behind St John the Divine (New York), St Peter's (Rome), the Duomo (Milan), the Anglican Cathedral (Liverpool) and La Catedral (Seville).

reason you can see the gold cross on the altar from this distance is because it's 6ft tall. Along the south side, the first bay commemorates **George Washington**, whose marble statue proclaims him to be "First Citizen, Patriot, President, Churchman and Freemason", while five bays down is the sarcophagus of **Woodrow Wilson** – the only president to be buried in the District (although Eisenhower's funeral was also held in the cathedral). Much of the work on the building took place during Wilson's presidency, a process which so fascinated him he used to visit the construction site in his chauffeur-driven limousine. In the adjacent bay, look up to the **Space Window**, whose stained glass incorporating a sliver of moon rock commemorates the flight of Apollo II, and resembles nothing so much as the cover of a Robert A Heinlein paperback. On the north side, across from Washington, the **Abraham Lincoln Bay** is marked by a bronze statue of Abe with Lincoln head pennies set into the floor. The next berth down is for cathedral architect **Philip Hubert Frohman**, a Catholic, whose family received special dispensation to have him buried in this Protestant church. Last bay before the North Transept features a small likeness of **Dr Martin Luther King Jr** above the arch, inscribed "I Have A Dream": on Sunday March 31, 1968, the reverend preached his last sermon here before heading for Memphis where he was due to lead a march of striking black workers; four days later he was dead, assassinated by a bullet fired by James Earl Ray.

At the **High Altar** there's a splendid view back down the Gothic carved vault, criss-crossing away to the west rose window. The beautifully intricate *reredos* features 110 figures surrounding Christ in Benediction. You'll also want to take the elevator from the south porch at the west end of the nave (near the Washington statue) to the **Pilgrim Observation Gallery**, which affords stupendous city views.

The 57-acre grounds or **Cathedral Close** – virtually a small fiefdom – hold cathedral offices, three schools, a college, sports fields and a swimming pool, not to mention a **Herb Cottage** selling dried herbs and teas, a **Greenhouse** and the attractive **Bishop's Garden**, a walled rose and herb garden laid out in medieval style.

Rock Creek Park

Most visitors and many Washingtonians overlook the attractions of the city's major park, **Rock Creek Park**, the bulk of which stretches between the quiet suburbs of the Upper Northwest. Established by mandate from Congress in 1890, its 1800 acres cut a generous six-mile-long swathe, tracing the line of the eponymous creek from its early meanderings through Georgetown and Woodley Park to the northernmost DC-Maryland border. Little more than a narrow gorge in its southern reaches, the park spreads out above the National Zoo to become a mile-wide tranche of woodland, west of 16th Street.

A road shadows the creek for much of its length, called the **Rock Creek Parkway** until the zoo, whereafter it's known as **Beach Drive**, and by car is certainly the easiest way to get in and around the park. By **public transport**, your only real choices are the Metro to Cleveland Park, which provides access to the section of the park just north of the zoo; or the Metro to Tenleytown-AU, from where buses #D31, #D33, #D34, #W45 or #W46 run up Nebraska Avenue NW and along Military Road through the middle of the park; for the east side of the park, buses #S1, #S2, #S3, #S4 and #S5 all run straight up 16th Street from anywhere north of K Street NW.

The park is open during **daylight hours**, which in practice means from around 7.30am: it's not a wise idea to come on foot, on your own, at night, though traffic is permitted 24 hours a day.

Inside the park

There are fifteen miles of **trails and paths** in the park, along both sides of the creek, including tracks and workout stations, bridleways (in the wooded, northern section) and a **cycle route** that runs from the Lincoln Memorial, north through the park and into Maryland; to the south, Arlington Memorial Bridge links the route to the Mount Vernon Trail in Virginia (see p.249). At weekends (7am Sat–7pm Sun), Beach Drive between Military and Broad Branch roads is closed to cars, when the **rollerblading** fraternity comes out to primp and preen. The park also features ballparks and thirty **picnic areas**, some of which have fireplaces – bring your own fuel, and take everything away with you afterwards.

There are a variety of summer concerts at the Carter Barron Amphitheater (16th St and Colorado Ave NW); see p.290.

The sights start at the southern end of the park, a mile above the zoo, where the serene, granite **Pierce Mill** (Wed–Sun 9am–5pm; free; ☎426-6908) stands in a beautiful riverside hollow on Tilden Street, near Beach Drive. One of eight nineteenth-century gristmills in the valley, and the last to shut down, in 1897, it has been restored by the National Park Service and today produces cornmeal and wheatflour for sale to visitors. You can observe the process, and even have a go yourself with small hand-grinders and sifters. Just across the way, the old carriage house serves as the **Rock Creek Gallery** (Wed–Sun 10am–5pm; ☎244-2482), which displays local art.

The **Nature Center** on Glover Rd, just south of Military Rd (Wed–Sun 9am–5pm; free; ☎426-6829), acts as the park visitor centre, with natural history exhibits and details of weekend guided walks and self-guided nature trails. Finally, just on the other side of

Military Road, the remains of **Fort DeRussey** stand as a reminder of the network of defences that ringed the city during the Civil War. Guarding against Confederate attack from the north, this was just one of 68 forts erected in the city. The sites of others – notably forts Reno, Bayard, and Stevens (see below) – have been appropriated as small parks on either side of Rock Creek Park proper.

Fort Stevens and Battleground National Cemetery

Drive east on Miltary Road from the park to 13th Street NW where **Fort Stevens** marks the spot at which the city came closest to falling to Confederate troops during the Civil War. An army of 15,000 men crossed the Potomac in July 1864 and got within 150yd of the fort before the hastily reinforced Union defence drove them back under a barrage of artillery fire. President Lincoln was in the fort during the attack and mounted the parapet for a better look at the Confederate line, drawing a stinging rebuke from a nearby soldier who is said to have shouted "Get down you damned fool" at his commander-in-chief. Lincoln, to his credit, heeded the advice, but not all his troops were so lucky. Seven blocks further north on Georgia Avenue you can visit **Battleground National Cemetery**, in whose restricted confines lie the remains of the Union soldiers killed in the battle to defend the fort. Buses #70 and #71 run here, up 7th Street (which becomes Georgia Ave NW) from the Mall.

Chapter 9

Georgetown

Socially, politically and culturally, **GEORGETOWN** sits at the centre of Washington high life. Geographically, of course, it's out on a limb, way to the west of downtown, off the Metro line and beyond the divide of Rock Creek. This relative isolation has engendered an elitism that isn't entirely imagined: a stroll around the steep, leafy, brick-lined streets past rows of million-dollar chocolate-box houses is to step inside what Jan Morris has called "the most obsessively political residential enclave in the world". The Kennedys moved here before Jack made it to the White House and were followed by a cocktail-party full of establishment figures who have counted Georgetown as their home (or, more usually, one of their homes): Bob Woodward, Katherine Graham (former *Washington Post* publisher), Benjamin Bradlee (executive editor of the *Post* during Watergate), Bill Clinton as a student, singer-Congressman Sonny Bono, art collector Paul (son of Andrew) Mellon, biographer Kitty Kelley, novelist Herman Wouk, even Elizabeth Taylor during her marriage to Senator John Warner – the list goes on and on.

There is, of course, more to Georgetown than its upper-crust inhabitants or no normal person would ever go there. The vibrant feel of the place brings most people to the neighbourhood, at its best along the spine of **Wisconsin Avenue** and **M Street** – here the **students** of Georgetown University rub shoulders with bright young things and staid old power-brokers in a series of enjoyable saloons, coffee shops, fashionable restaurants and antique book stores. Its history is diverting, too, since its **buildings** date back to the early eighteenth century, making it older than the capital itself. Genteel Federal-era and shuttered Victorian townhouses hung with flower baskets stud the streets, while north of Q Street lies a series of stately mansions and handsome parks, gardens and cemeteries. Down on the **C&O Canal**, which runs through Georgetown, below M Street, horse-drawn boats fill the waterway while the tree-shaded towpaths have been turned over to cyclists and walkers; to the east, the boardwalk, cafés and restaurants of the **Washington Harbour** development provide views down the Potomac to the Kennedy Center.

For a map of Georgetown, see the colour insert in the centre of this book.

Georgetown's most annoying anomaly is that it's not on the **Metro** (Rock Creek and its valley are in the way). And don't even think of driving: there's nowhere to park. The nearest Metro station is **Foggy Bottom-GWU**, from where it's a twenty-minute walk up Pennsylvania Avenue and along M Street to the junction with Wisconsin Avenue. Alternatively, approach from Dupont Circle, a similar-length walk west along P Street (or over the Dumbarton Bridge; see p.210), which puts you first in the ritzier, upper part of Georgetown – in which case you might want to start with the mansions, parks and gardens (see "Northern Georgetown", p.238). **Buses #30, #32, #34, #35 and #36** run up Pennsylvania Avenue from Washington Circle (and other points downtown), along M and Wisconsin; **#D2 and #D4** run from Union Station/Dupont Circle to Q Street; and **#G2** runs from Dupont Circle to P and Dumbarton. At night you'll find **taxis** relatively easy to come by on the main drags if you want to head back downtown in safety; it's a $5–7 ride to most destinations.

*Georgetown
listings:
art galleries
p.299
bars p.289
cafés p.273
restaurants
p.281*

History

In the early eighteenth century, when this area was still part of Maryland, **Scottish merchants** began to form a permanent settlement around shoreside warehouses on the higher reaches of the Potomac River (or Patowmack, as it was then known). Here they oversaw a thriving trade, exporting the plentiful tobacco from nearby farms and importing foreign materials and luxuries for colonial settlers. In 1751 the Maryland Assembly granted a town **charter** to the merchants, who named their flourishing port after their royal protector, George II. Within a decade, "George Towne" was a runaway success, attracting other merchants who built large mansions on estates to the north of the river, and by the 1780s, it was America's largest tobacco port.

Once George Washington had pinpointed the Potomac region as the site of the new federal capital (see p.36), it seemed logical that such a thriving port be included in the plans. In 1791, together with Alexandria in Virginia, the town was incorporated within the federal district. And while for many years the new city of Washington, to be built across Rock Creek, remained little more than a plan on paper, Georgetown itself continued to prosper – by 1830 it had a population of nine thousand, and boasted streets of Federal-style brick houses, fashionable stores, well-tended gardens and even a university (founded in 1789). By the time of the **Civil War**, Georgetown was distinct enough from Washington to be considered suspect in Union eyes. Many of the town's early landowners came from the South and during the war there was strong support for the Confederate cause. But its proximity to the capital (and the Union troops stationed in the town) kept the lid on any overt secessionist feeling.

The war and Georgetown's commercial prospects flickered and died at about the same time. The tobacco trade had already faltered due to soil exhaustion, while the steady growth of Baltimore and

Washington itself badly affected the town's prosperity. The **Chesapeake and Ohio (C&O) Canal**, completed in 1850, represented an attempt to revive trade with the interior and for a time Georgetown became a regional centre for wheat, coal and timber shipment. But the canal was soon obsolete: the coming of the railroads was swiftly followed by the development of larger steamboats which couldn't be accommodated by Georgetown's canal or harbour. After losing its charter in 1871, relegated to a mere neighbourhood in the District of Columbia, Georgetown was delivered another insult in 1895 when most of its old **street names** – some in use for over 150 years – were abandoned by order of Congress in favour of the numbers and letters of the federal city plan; there was even a suggestion that Georgetown become known as "West Washington".

For much of the late nineteenth and early twentieth century, Georgetown was anything but a fashionable place to live. Water-powered foundries and mills provided employment for a growing, predominantly black population, based in the neighbourhood of Herring Hill, south of P Street and close to Rock Creek. Gardens were lost to speculative row housing and many larger mansions were subdivided; a noisy streetcar system was installed; and M Street became a workaday run of cheap stores and saloons owned by immigrant families. However, a mass influx of white-collar workers to DC during the New Deal era and World War II reversed Georgetown's rather down-at-heel image. Black and immigrant families were slowly pushed out of the Victorian streets, apartments were knocked back into houses and Federal mansions renovated. Part of the charm for newcomers was that Georgetown's natural boundaries – southern river, eastern creek, western university grounds and northern estates – had prevented wholesale, indiscriminate development; despite the disruption, a certain smalltown character had survived the years.

Now, of course, this character is zealously preserved by Georgetown residents who, since the 1950s and 1960s, have included ever-increasing numbers of DC's most fashionable, politically connected inhabitants. Certain historic houses have been lost to developers and some of the streets are overwhelmed by traffic, but since 1967 Georgetown has been registered as a **National Historic Landmark** – new buildings and renovations have to be sympathetic to their surroundings, house facades are colour-coordinated, and the canal has been landscaped and preserved as a national historic park.

The canal, river and harbour

On a summer's day there's no finer part of Georgetown than the **Chesapeake and Ohio (C&O) Canal**, whose eastern extremity feeds into Rock Creek at 28th Street NW – overlooked on both sides by restored redbrick warehouses, spanned by small bridges, lined with trees and punctuated by occasional candy-coloured towpath houses.

The canal, river and harbour

The prettiest central stretch starts at 30th Street, where the adjacent **locks** once opened to allow through boatloads of coal, iron, timber and corn from the Maryland estates upriver.

The Potomac River had been used by traders since the earliest days of settlement in the region, but a series of rapids and waterfalls – like those at Great Falls, just fourteen miles from Georgetown – made largescale commercial navigation all but impossible. A canal was proposed (George Washington was one of the shareholders) that would follow the line of the river and open up trade as far as the Ohio Valley – hence the name – but when construction finally finished in 1850, the C&O reached only as far as Cumberland in Maryland, 184 miles and 74 locks away. Confederate raiding parties found the barges and locks easy targets during the Civil War and much of the traffic dried up for the duration – doubtless to the satisfaction of the Union troops stationed in Georgetown who used to swim naked in the canal, offending local sensibilities. Even after the war, the canal never attracted sufficient trade, mainly because of the economically devastating development of the railroads; the last mule-drawn cargo boat was pulled through in the 1920s, after which severe flooding from the Potomac destroyed much of the canal infrastructure. The C&O's historical importance was recognized in 1971 when its entire length was declared a national historical park, and today scores of visitors hike, cycle and horseride along the restored towpaths; canoeing and boating is allowed in certain sections, too.

Massive **flooding** in early 1996 washed away several stretches of the towpath. The fourteen-mile Georgetown to Great Falls section should be open by now, though it might take longer to restore the National Park Service passenger **canal boat** service (see opposite).

One of the most appealing stretches of the canal is the short section between **Thomas Jefferson Street** and 31st Street, where artisans' houses dating from the building boom of the mid-nineteenth century have been handsomely restored as shops, offices and, occasionally, private homes. Thomas Jefferson Street itself is lined with more attractive brick-built houses, some in the **Federal style**, featuring rustic stone lintels, arched doorways with fanlights and narrow top-floor dormers. On the south side, **The Foundry**, 1050 30th St, is just one of the many brick warehouses that line the canal, originally built as a machine-shop and later serving as a veterinary hospital to care for the mules that worked the boats. It's been sympathetically restored and expanded, and now houses a multi-screen cinema (see p.294), as well as shops and a restaurant (the *Music City Roadhouse*). Other warehouses have received similar treatment – like the shops and offices at **Canal Square**, 1054 31st St – and frame either side of the waterway as far up as Francis Scott Key Bridge, five blocks west. Various steps and paths from the towpath connect with the backstreets off M Street, and there's also direct access into Georgetown Park shopping mall (see p.237).

Canal Boats and Other C&O Activities

It is 184 miles from Georgetown to the canal terminus at Cumberland, MD,
passing through highly varied scenery, past waterfalls, through forests,
and skirting the ridges and valleys of the Appalachian Mountains.

Canal Boats

To sign up for trips on the ninety-foot, mule-drawn **canal boats*** – accompanied by park rangers in nineteenth-century costume who work the locks –
call at the Georgetown **Ranger Station/Visitor Center**, 1057 Thomas
Jefferson St NW (April–Oct daily 10am–4pm; ☎653-5190). Tickets cost $6
and there are usually three daily departures (Wed–Sun) from mid-June to
mid-September, with reduced services in April/May and October/November.
**Note that the service was suspended in 1996 due to flood damage.
Call for current information.*

Along the Canal

A number of outlets along the canal rent boats, canoes and bikes: there are
several in the first twenty-mile stretch from Georgetown (see p.44–45).
For a day-trip by **bike**, Great Falls (see below) – an easy, flat fourteen
miles away – should be far enough for most. You'll need to observe a
15mph speed limit on the towpath, wear a helmet and give way to all
pedestrians and horses. **Canoes** and **boats** are limited to specific areas
(visitors centres and rental outlets can advise) and should not venture onto
the Potomac River, which can be very dangerous; you also shouldn't **swim**
in the canal or river due to unpredictable currents. You can **picnic** anywhere you like, but only light fires in authorized fireplaces; first come-first
served basic campsites are dotted along the entire length of the canal;
closest to the city is at Swain's Lock, twenty miles from Georgetown.

Great Falls

At **Great Falls**, fourteen miles from Georgetown, the *Great Falls Tavern
Visitor Center*, 11710 MacArthur Blvd, Potomac, MD (April–Oct daily
8.30am–5pm; ☎301/299-3613), offers terrific views of the falls themselves,
along with a museum about the history of the canal. This is the starting point
for guided local tours, walks and canal boat trips (same prices and schedules
as in Georgetown – and the same caveat about the service after the floods).
There's a snack bar but no other eating or rental facilities. By car, take
MacArthur Boulevard from Georgetown or exit 41 off the Beltway; outside
rush hour, it's a twenty-minute drive; parking is $4 per vehicle. There's also
a visitor center on the Virginia side of the falls (☎703/285-2965) – though
no access between the two sides of canal and river – featuring more tours
and trails, though no boat trips. Get there by following Rte 193 (exit 13 off
the Beltway) to Rte 738, from where it's signposted (parking $4).

At **Wisconsin Avenue**, south of the canal, you're at the oldest part of
Georgetown. This was the first road built from the river into Maryland
during colonial times and was a major route for farmers and traders who
used the slope of the hill to roll their barrels down to riverside warehouses. Later, canal boatmen would be enticed into the Gothic Revival
Grace Church on South Street, just off Wisconsin Avenue, by promises
of salvation from the earth-bound drudgery of hauling heavy goods from

barge to warehouse. Others sought solace in nearby *Suter's Tavern*, where, it's claimed, George Washington met Maryland landowners to discuss the purchase of property so that work could start on the federal city; the inn was knocked down long ago, but there's a plaque marking its approximate site at 31st and K streets.

K Street itself was once known as Water Street for the very good reason that it fronted the Potomac River, though land reclamation has now pushed the water a hundred yards or so further south. Its most noticeable feature is what's above it, namely the **Whitehurst Freeway**, the elevated road built in the 1950s to relieve traffic congestion on M Street. Cross the road under the freeway and you reach the riverside development known as **Washington Harbour** (east of 31st), whose interlocking towers and capsules are set around a circular, terraced plaza with spurting fountains. From the heavily jogged, landscaped boardwalk there are views upriver to the Francis Scott Key Bridge, and downriver to Theodore Roosevelt Island and Bridge as well as the backs of the Watergate building and Kennedy Center. The restaurants and bars in the complex are all fairly high-ticket, but there's nothing more relaxing than a summer evening's drink on the terrace watching the boats sculling by.

Along and around M Street

Central artery of Georgetown for two centuries has been **M Street** – first known as Bridge Street – which cuts through the lower town and crosses Rock Creek into the city of Washington. As elsewhere in Georgetown, the street retains many of its original Federal-style and later Victorian buildings, though the ground floors have all long been converted to retail use. Where new buildings have filled in any gaps they've tended to follow the prevailing redbrick style, none more noticeably than the elegant and supremely luxurious **Four Seasons Hotel** (see p.268 for accommodation details), between 28th and 29th streets. Built in 1979, it regularly garners awards as one of the most exclusive hotels in America.

There's a colour map of Georgetown in the centre of this book.

Though the **Old Stone House**, 3051 M St (Wed–Sun 8am–4.30pm; free; ☎ 426-6851), facing Thomas Jefferson Street, has the very real accolade of being the only surviving pre-Revolutionary house in DC (it was built in 1764 by a Pennsylvania carpenter, Christopher Layman), the only thing that saved it from demolition in the 1950s was the fanciful suggestion that L'Enfant used it as a base while designing the federal city. Today it has been restored to the state it probably resembled in the late eighteenth century, and short guided tours lead you through kitchen and carpenter's workshop downstairs, panelled parlours and bedrooms upstairs.

Shops, restaurants and bars proliferate around the main M Street/Wisconsin Avenue junction, whose useful landmark is the gold dome of the *Riggs National Bank*. Just beyond, the late twentieth century imposes upon the late nineteenth in the shape of **Georgetown**

Park, a high-profile shopping mall at 3222 M St (Mon–Sat
10am–9pm, Sun noon–6pm). As a deskbound designer's idea of what
a Victorian architect might have come up with given the money, material and tools it's just about a success – wrought-iron fencing and balconies, glass lanterns and skylights, potted ferns, polished brass, tiles
and brickwork all add to the image, though no Victorian marketplace
was ever this clean. There's a food court inside, too, and one exit from
the mall leads directly to the canal towpath. The next block west, at
Potomac Street, has been the site of a public market since the 1860s
and the restored, triple-arched redbrick **Market House** building is
back in business. Admittedly, rather than butchered carcasses and
nineteenth-century patent medicines the offerings are as culturally
exotic as its inhabitants, deli entrepreneurs *Dean & Deluca*, can manage; conservatory-style sidewalk seating, decent coffee and a good
salad and pasta bar make it a favoured lunch spot.

Potomac Street is as good a point as any to detour briefly north to
N Street – known as Gay Street until the late nineteenth century –
which contains some of Georgetown's finest Federal-era buildings.
None are open to the public, but there are several particularly attractive facades between 29th and 34th streets. At 3014 N St, Robert
Todd Lincoln (President Lincoln's son) lived out the last decade of
his life, while four blocks along, JFK and Jackie owned no. 3307
from 1957 to 1961 – Jackie also moved briefly into no. 3017 after
the assassination. Other historic houses cluster on **Prospect Street**,
one block south, where early merchants built late eighteenth century
mansions like those at nos. 3425 and 3508; as the street name sug-
gests they were once masters of splendid views down to the river
from which they derived their wealth.

Back on M Street, aim for the junction with 34th Street, from
where the **Francis Scott Key Bridge** shoots off across the river to
Rosslyn. Francis Scott Key, author of the "Star Spangled Banner"
(see p.99), moved to Washington in 1805 and lived in a house here
at M Street which was demolished to make way for the Whitehurst
Freeway – an act of sacrilege only belatedly acknowledged by the
establishment of the **Francis Scott Key Park**, just off the street.
There's a bronze bust of the man, a sixty-foot flagpole flying the
Stars and Stripes, a wisteria-covered arbour and a few benches from
which to peer through the break in the buildings to the river.

Before you leave lower Georgetown you may as well swing by
Georgetown University, splendidly sited on the heights above the
river; the main gate is at 37th and O streets. Founded in 1789 as the
Jesuit Georgetown College (the oldest Catholic university in the US),
its 6000 students are what gives the neighbourhood much of its buzz.
No one will mind if you pop in for a look around, though apart from
treading in the footsteps of exorcized priests and excitable college
kids (see "Georgetown in the Movies", over), there's little incentive
to do so. The architecture is a bit of a hybrid, ranging from the plain

facade of the building known as Old North, which dates from 1795,
to the Romanesque niceties of Healy Hall, finished ninety years later.

Northern Georgetown

Set above the rest of Georgetown on "The Heights" (above Q Street),
the grand mansions and estates of **northern Georgetown** sat out the
nineteenth- and twentieth-century upheavals taking place below.
Owned by the richest merchants, the land here was never exploited
for new building when Georgetown was in the throes of expansion.
Today several of the fine mansions are open to the public, their
grounds and nearby cemeteries forming a pleasing backdrop.

*For details of
the annual
Georgetown
garden tour
(May; fee
charged), call
☎ 333-4953.*

In Georgetown, the easiest access is straight up Wisconsin Avenue
(bus #30, 32, 34, 35 or 36 from M St), but consider starting your
tour of Georgetown in these parts – crossing Dumbarton Bridge from
Massachusetts Avenue NW (Dupont Circle Metro) puts you directly
on Q Street.

Mount Zion Cemetery

Five minutes from the bridge, hidden away down an offshoot of 27th
Street (northern side of Q St), the headstones scattered through the
tangled undergrowth form part of **Mount Zion Cemetery**, the oldest
mainly black burial ground in the city. Formerly the Old Methodist
Burying Ground, the land was bought in 1842 by a women's association known as the Female Union Band for the burial of members of
the Mount Zion Methodist Church (whose fine redbrick church build-

ing still stands at 1334 29th St, at Dumbarton). The cemetery has been
neglected over the years, though a start has been made on tidying up
the grounds and restoring some of the monumental gravestones.
There's still a long way to go, though, before it mimics the pristine
grounds of the adjacent (white) Oak Hill Cemetery (see below), whose
tiered gravestones you can glimpse through the trees beyond.

Dumbarton House

Past 27th Street, **Dumbarton House**, one of the oldest houses in
Georgetown, built between 1799 and 1804, hoves into view at 2715 Q
St NW (tours Tues–Sat 10am–12.15pm; closed Aug; $3; ☎ 337-2288).
Known for a century as "Bellevue", its elegant Georgian proportions
housed Georgetown's first salon, as political leaders of the day came to
call on Joseph Nourse, registrar of the US Treasury, who lived here until
1813. The following year, as the British overran Washington, Dolley
Madison watched the White House burning from Bellevue's windows –
the house was the first sanctuary for the fleeing presidential couple. It's
a period that the guides from the National Society of Colonial Dames of
America (whose headquarters Dumbarton House now is) make much
of, and you'll be escorted slowly through period rooms, filled with
Federal furniture, early prints of Washington and less-than-accom-
plished portraits. If you don't have an hour to spare, or an insatiable
interest in decorative porcelain that once, possibly, adorned the White
House, content yourself instead with a seat in the restful garden and
contemplate perhaps the most remarkable fact about the house – the
building of the bridge over Rock Creek in 1915 necessitated its removal,
brick-by-brick, from further down Q Street to its present position.

Oak Hill Cemetery

Endowed by banker and art collector William Wilson Corcoran, the
exclusive **Oak Hill Cemetery** (Mon–Fri 10am–4pm; free) began burying
the wealthy dead of Georgetown in 1849. The brick gatehouse at 30th
and R streets dates from that period, which is where you enter the lov-
ingly kept grounds, which spill down the hillside to Rock Creek. Inside,
the diminutive brick-and-sandstone Gothic chapel is the sprightly work of
James Renwick (architect of the Smithsonian Castle, among other
works); just to the west stands a marble plinth with a bust of John Howard
Payne – author of the treacly "Home Sweet Home". Ask at the gatehouse
for directions to the cemetery's other notable inmates, among them
Corcoran and Edwin Stanton, secretary of war under President Lincoln.

Dumbarton Oaks

If one estate typifies both the success of the early Georgetown merchants and the durability of their property it's **Dumbarton Oaks**. In
1703 Scottish pioneer Ninian Beall was granted almost 800 acres of
land, stretching from the river to Rock Creek, and proceeded to make

Outside, in the
10 acres of for-
mal **gardens**
(daily
Nov–March
2–5pm;
April–Oct
2–6pm; $3),
the beech ter-
race, ever-
greens, rose
garden, brick
paths, pools
and fountains
provide one of
the quietest of
DC's back-
waters; the
garden
entrance is at
3101 R St.

himself a fortune from the tobacco trade. Although much of the land was later sold by his descendants, more than enough of the coveted northern reaches remained for incomer William H Dorsey to build a grand redbrick mansion in 1800, surrounded by gardens and woods. This was added to and renovated down the years, and then last acquired by diplomat Robert Woods Bliss in 1920 to house his significant collection of Byzantine and pre-Columbian art. In 1940 the house was handed on to Harvard University (the current owners) and in 1944 its commodious Music Room saw a meeting of American, Russian, British and Chinese delegates whose deliberations led directly to the founding of the United Nations the following year.

The house – restored to its Federal glory and entered at 1703 32nd St – contains a beautifully presented **museum** (Tues–Sun 2–5pm; suggested donation $1; ☎ 338-8278). Eight connected circular glass pavilions, added in 1963, display selected carvings, sculpture, jewellery and textiles of Olmec, Inca, Aztec and Mayan provenance – ceremonial axes, polychrome vases depicting palace scenes, jade pendants, goldwork recovered from graves and bluff stone masks of unknown significance. Bliss was equally fascinated by the Byzantine Empire; the silver Eucharist vessels, decorated ivory boxes and various painted icons stand out. Perhaps most extraordinary is the celebrated fourteenth-century mosaic icon of the Forty Martyrs, a miniature work so-called because it depicts – in cubes of enamel paste and semi-precious stone – forty Roman soldiers left to freeze to death because they refused to recant their Christian beliefs.

Tudor Place

Final mansion call is at stately **Tudor Place**, 1644 31st St NW, between Q and R streets, designed by William Thornton, who won the competition to design the US Capitol. Commissioned by Thomas Peter (descendant of one of the original Scottish tobacco merchants and son of Georgetown's first mayor) and his wife Martha Custis (granddaughter of Martha Washington), the house displays a pleasing incongruity, rare for the period – a fundamentally Federal-style structure which Thornton embellished with a Classical domed portico on the south side. The exterior has remained virtually untouched since and, as the house stayed in the same family for over 150 years, the interior is considered rather fine, too, saved from the constant "improvements" wrought in other period Georgetown houses by successive owners. **Tours** (Tues–Fri 10am, 11.30am, 1pm & 2.30pm, Sat on the hour 10am–3pm; $6; ☎ 965-0400) point out the highlights, including furnishings lifted from the Washington's family seat at Mount Vernon. You're supposed to reserve in advance for the tours, but by ringing the bell at the front gate you can gain access to the **gardens** (Mon–Sat 10am–4pm; free) during the day; walk up the path and bear to the right where a white box holds detailed plans ($2 donation) of the paths, greens, box hedges, arbours and fountains.

Chapter 10

Arlington

A cross the Potomac River from DC lies the Virginian county of **Arlington**, technically part of Washington itself until 1846 when Virginia demanded back the thirty square miles it had contributed to the capital city. The river here was always more than a geographical boundary: for many in the nineteenth century, Arlington was where the South started and it was to prove significant that Confederate commander Robert E Lee made his home for many years on the Arlington heights, overlooking the Potomac and the capital city beyond. In the 1930s, as a final act of reconciliation, **Arlington Memorial Bridge** was dedicated – symbolically connecting the Lincoln Memorial with the dead of both sides buried in Arlington National Cemetery.

It might be in Virginia, but to all intents and purposes modern Arlington is still part of Washington DC, with easy access by four bridges and Metro to the commuter and shopping belt that stretches from Rosslyn and Clarendon to Crystal City. Planes land at **National Airport**, closest airport to downtown DC, while locals descend on the mega-**malls** at Pentagon City or Crystal City, refuelling on Southeast Asian food in the burgeoning number of **restaurants** along Wilson Boulevard (see p.283). For most out-of-towners, though, the area is defined by two high-profile attractions: **Arlington National Cemetery**, burial place of John, Jackie and Robert Kennedy, and the **Pentagon**, the country's top military headquarters.

Note that the area telephone code for Arlington is ☎703.

Arlington National Cemetery

Across Arlington Memorial Bridge, Arlington, VA ☎692-0931; Arlington Cemetery Metro. Daily April–Sept 8am–7pm; Oct–March 8am–5pm. Admission free.

The grand monuments of the capital across the river are placed into sharp perspective by the vast sea of identical white headstones which

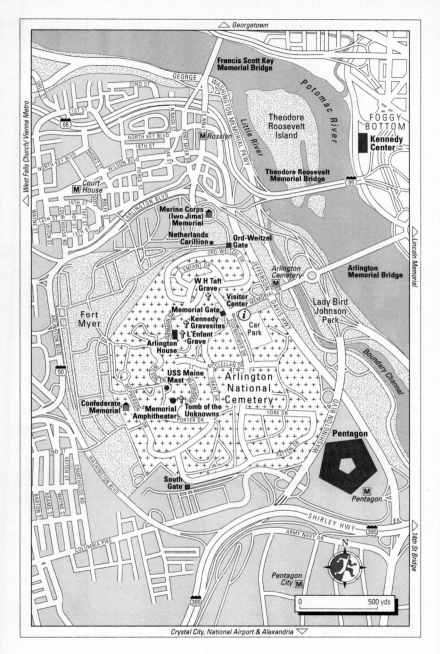

△ Georgetown

Francis Scott Key
Memorial Bridge

GEORGE
22ND ST
21ST ST
66
N NASH'S ST
N LYNN ST
N OAK ST
NORTH KEY BLVD
18TH ST
WILSON BLVD
M Rosslyn

FORT MYER DR

Little River

Potomac River

Theodore
Roosevelt
Island

FOGGY
BOTTOM
Kennedy
Center

◁ West Falls Church/Vienna Metro

UHLE ST
N NASH'S ST
NORTH KEY BLVD
RHODES ST
PIERCE ST
OAK ST
QUINN ST
WILSON BLVD
15TH ST N
14TH ST
COURT HOUSE RD
TAFT ST
NASH ST
13TH ST
M Court
House
ARLINGTON BLVD

WASHINGTON MEMORIAL PKWY

Theodore Roosevelt
Memorial Bridge
66

Marine Corps
(Iwo Jima)
Memorial
Netherlands
Carillion
Ord-Weitzel
Gate

ORD-WEITZEL DR

Arlington
Cemetery

Lincoln Memorial ▷

Arlington
Memorial Bridge

L'ENFANT DR

W H Taft
Grave

Visitor
Center

JEFFERSON DR

M

Lady Bird
Johnson
Park

Fort
Myer

ARLINGTON BLVD
50

SHERIDAN DR

Memorial Gate
Kennedy
Gravesites
L'Enfant
Grave
Arlington
House

MEMORIAL DR

Car
Park

EISENHOWER DR

i

DAVIS HWY

Boundary Channel

MCCLELLAN DR

USS Maine
Mast

MCPHERSON DR

Confederate
Memorial

Memorial
Amphitheater
Tomb of the
Unknowns

GRANT DR

PORTER DR

Arlington
National
Cemetery

YORK DR

PATTON DR

WASHINGTON BLVD

Pentagon

2ND ST
VEITCH ST
COURTHOUSE RD
WASHINGTON BLVD

South
Gate

M
Pentagon

ADAMS ST
WAYNE ST
BARTON ST

COLUMBIA PIKE

SHIRLEY HWY
395

ARMY NAVY DR

14th St Bridge ▷

395

Pentagon
City M

N

0   500 yds

▽ Crystal City, National Airport & Alexandria △

spreads across the hillsides of **Arlington National Cemetery**. The city's celebration of the life of a few prominent Americans – Lincoln, Washington and Jefferson – gives way at Arlington to the commemoration of the death of many thousands of others, including the assassinated Kennedy brothers, whose internment here elevates the cemetery to pilgrimage site. Primarily a military burial ground – the largest in the country – Arlington's 600 landscaped acres contain the graves of almost quarter of a million war dead and their dependants, as well as those of a panoply of other national heroes with military connections from boxer (and ex-GI) Joe Louis to the crew of the doomed Space Shuttle *Challenger*. In some ways it's America's pantheon, which partly excuses the constant stream of visitors on sightseeing tours, which elsewhere might be considered unseemly in a military cemetery. What saves it is partly its size – far too large to take in every plot on a single visit – though largely the dignity inherent in the democratically similar lines of simple markers and unadorned headstones. Paris's Père Lachaise it's emphatically not; there's a restrained, understated ambience here which honours presidents, generals and enlisted personnel alike.

The **Metro** takes you right to the main gates on Memorial Drive; by **car**, cross the Arlington Memorial Bridge (from 23rd St) and park in one of the signposted parking lots. The **Visitor Center** by the entrance hands out a sketch map that details some of the more prominent graves; the various guidebooks for sale are considerably more thorough in their coverage. The cemetery is absolutely enormous, so if you simply want to see the major sites without doing too much walking, buy a **Tourmobile** ticket ($4) from the booth inside the Visitor Center, for a narrated, shuttle-bus tour: you can get on and off as many times as you like.

Combined Tourmobile tickets are also available, including sights in DC and transport to Arlington; see p.46.

The cemetery

In good weather the cemetery is busy by 9am, with a good portion of the crowds heading straight for the Kennedy gravesites, though few realize they're bypassing Arlington's only other presidential occupant: through Memorial Gate, just to the right lies **William Howard Taft**, the poorly regarded 27th President (1909–13), who in a heartfelt outburst towards the end of his administration said "the nearer I get to the inauguration of my successor [Woodrow Wilson], the greater the relief I feel"; Taft – uniquely – enjoyed a second, much more personally rewarding, career as chief justice of the Supreme Court between 1921 and 1930.

The focus of attention, though, is the marble terrace further up the hillside where simple name plaques mark the graves of **John F Kennedy**, 35th US President, his wife Jacqueline Kennedy Onassis (laid to rest here in 1994), and a son, Patrick, and un-named daughter who both died shortly after birth. The eternal flame was lit at JFK's funeral by Jackie, who ordered the funeral decor to be copied

The drums and bugle played at JFK's state funeral are on show in the First Ladies room of the National Museum of American History; see p.100.

from that of Lincoln's, held a century earlier in the White House. When it's crowded here, as it often is, the majesty of the view across to the Washington Monument and the poignancy of the inscribed extracts from JFK's inaugural address – "Ask not what your country can do for you . . ." are sometimes obscured; come early or late in the day if possible. In the plot behind Jack a plain white cross picks out the gravesite of his brother Robert, assassinated in 1968 during the presidential primaries.

The **Tomb of the Unknowns**, a white marble block dedicated to the unknown dead of two world wars and Korean and Vietnam conflicts, is guarded 24 hours a day by impeccably uniformed soldiers, who carry out a sombre, clipped **Changing of the Guard** (April–Sept every half-hour, otherwise on the hour) on the sweeping steps; the circular, colonnaded Memorial Amphitheater behind is the site of special remembrance services. The cemetery's beginnings were as a burial ground for Union soldiers (see below), though as a national cemetery it was subsequently deemed politic to honour the dead of both Civil War sides. The **Confederate Section**, with its own memorial, lies to the west of the Tomb of the Unknowns; other sections and memorials remember every conflict from the Revolutionary War to the Gulf War. As for notable individual graves, the highest concentration is found in the myriad plots surrounding the Tomb of the Unknowns: with a map, and an eye for knots of camera-toting tourists, you'll find the graves of **Audie Murphy**, most decorated soldier in World War II and **Joe Louis** (born and buried here as Joe Louis Barrow), World Heavyweight Champion from 1937 to 1949. Elsewhere, among others and in no particular order, are buried Robert Todd Lincoln, the President's son; John J Pershing, commander of the American forces during World War I; Arctic explorer Robert Peary; civil rights leader Medgar Evers, shot in 1963; astronauts Virgil Grissom and Roger Chaffee of the ill-fated 1967 Apollo training exercise; actor Lee Marvin; thriller-writer Dashiell Hammett; and William Colby, former director of the CIA, who died in a canoeing accident in 1996.

Main Arlington services and ceremonies take place at Easter, Memorial Day and Veterans Day; see pp.306–307.

The most photographed of the many memorials is that to the **Space Shuttle Challenger**, immediately behind the amphitheatre; adjacent is the memorial to the **Iran Rescue Mission**, whose failure doomed Jimmy Carter at the polls. Both stand close to the **mast of the USS Maine**, whose mysterious destruction in Havana harbour in 1898 prompted the short-lived Spanish-American War – the war itself is commemorated by both a memorial and a monument to the **Rough Riders**, a devil-may-care cavalry outfit in which a young Theodore Roosevelt made his reputation. More controversial is the new memorial inscribed with the names of those killed over Lockerbie, Scotland, in the 1988 Pan Am 103 terrorist explosion; some felt its siting in a military cemetery inappropriate.

Arlington House

The entire cemetery stands on land that formerly belonged to George Washington Parke Custis, the grandson of Martha Washington by her first marriage. Custis built an imposing Georgian-Revival mansion known as **Arlington House** on the high ground above the Potomac, which passed to his daughter, Mary, on his death. Her marriage in 1830 to Lieutenant **Robert E Lee** (1807–70) of the US Army was later of enormous consequence: in 1861, Lee was at home at Arlington House when he heard the news of the secession of Virginia from the Union. Coming from a proud Virginian family, whose number included two signatories of the Declaration of Independence, the West Point-trained Lee was torn between loyalty to his native state and to the preservation of the Union which he served. His decision was made more acute when he was also offered command of the Union Army by Lincoln, who greatly respected his ability. But familial loyalty held out and Lee resigned his US Army commission and left Arlington for Richmond, where he took command of Virginia's military forces. Mary fled Arlington a month later as Union soldiers consolidated their hold on DC and the estate was eventually confiscated by the federal government. The Lees never returned to Arlington (though the family was later compensated for the estate's seizure) and as early as 1864 a cemetery for the Union dead of the Civil War was established in the grounds of the house. A year later, Lee – now general-in-chief of the Confederate armies – surrendered to General Grant at Appomattox.

Since the 1950s Arlington House has stood as a memorial to the Lee family, who lived here for the thirty years prior to the Civil War. The house is immediately above the Kennedy gravesites and you can look around during cemetery opening hours on a self-guided **tour** (information on ☎ 557-0613), though note that some rooms may be under restoration. Highlights include the principal bedroom, where Robert E Lee wrote his resignation letter, and the family parlour below, in which he was married from home. A fair proportion of the furnishings are original.

Outside, the views across the river to the Mall are exemplary, and fittingly, the grave of city designer **Pierre Charles L'Enfant** was belatedly sited here in 1909 after the city forgave his feuding about low pay for his services. No less a man than the Marquis de Lafayette, a guest at Arlington House in 1824, thought the aspect "the finest view in the world" and who's to say that's still not the case.

The Marine Corps Memorial and Netherlands Carillon

The final ports of call in the cemetery are a twenty-minute walk or so north of the main section, through the Ord-Weitzel Gate (or approach from nearby Rosslyn Metro). The hugely impressive, 78-

foot, bronze **Marine Corps Memorial** (24hr; free; ☎285-2601) is more popularly known as the Iwo Jima Statue, after the "uncommon valor" shown by American troops in the bloody World War II battle for the small Pacific island which cost 6800 lives. In a famous image – inspired by a contemporaneous photograph – half-a-dozen marines raise the Stars and Stripes on Mount Suribachi in February 1945; three of the survivors of the actual flag-raising posed for sculptor Felix W de Weldon.

The US Marine Corps presents a parade and concert at the memorial every Tuesday (June–Aug) at 7pm; and the annual Marine Corps Marathon starts here each October.

Nearby, to the south, rises the **Netherlands Carillon**, a 130-foot steel monument dedicated to the Netherlands' liberation from the Nazis in 1945. Given by the Dutch in thanks for American aid, the tower is set in landscaped grounds featuring thousands of tulips which bloom each spring. The 49 bells of the carillon are rung on Saturdays and holidays from April to August (call ☎285-2598 for times), when visitors can climb the tower for more superlative city views.

The most recent memorial (though not in the cemetery itself) is Rosslyn's **Journalists Memorial**, a few hundred yards from the Iwo Jima statue in the new Freedom Park. It's the world's first memorial to journalists killed in the line of duty, the 24-foot-high spiralling glass prism etched with the names of almost a thousand international journalists, beginning with James Lingan, trampled to death in Baltimore in 1812 during a mob attack on a printing press.

The Pentagon

Along I-395, Arlington, VA ☎695-1776; Pentagon Metro. Tours on the half-hour Mon–Fri 9.30am–3.30pm. Admission free.

The headquarters of the US military establishment, the **Pentagon** is one of the largest chunks of architecture in the world, with a total floor area of 6.5 million square feet (three times that of the Empire State Building) and five 900-foot-long sides enclosing 17.5 miles of corridors. Unfortunately, facts like these, churned out ad nauseum by tour guides and Pentagon pamphlets, are as much of the story as you'll ever get from a visit to this lair of the Department of Defense. While invisible tacticians in isolated Operation Rooms target Tripoli and Baghdad, they'd rather you heard about the 284 rest rooms and 1700 pints of milk used every day by the 25,000 employees.

The wonder is not that the Department of Defense allows visitors to the Pentagon, but why it bothers in the first place. Almost everyone bar statistics junkies goes away disappointed since, aside from a short introductory film and very brief stops at selected military portraits, model craft and memorial bays, the guided tour imparts next to no information worth having. What you do get for the ninety-minute investment of your time is the chance to walk very quickly through one of the famed seventeen miles of corridors behind a service personnel-guide who – in the one novel departure from norm – walks backwards the entire time to ensure that disguised foreign agents don't slip off into one of the aforementioned rest rooms.

Indeed, the most interesting thing about the Pentagon is the structure itself, thrown together in just sixteen months during World War II to consolidate seventeen different buildings of what was, in those days, known less euphemistically as the War Department. Efficiency dictated the five-storey pentagonal design: with so many employees, it was imperative to maintain quick contact between separate offices and departments – for someone versed in the arcane numbering system, it takes just seven minutes to walk between any two points in the building. Built on swamp- and wasteland, the building was constructed entirely of concrete (fashioned from Potomac sand and gravel) rather than the marble that brightens the rest of Washington; President Roosevelt thus neatly avoided boosting the Axis war effort since Italy was then the world's foremost supplier of marble. The design has barely been tampered with since, save for the oak cladding around some of the higher echelon offices. Naturally, modern technology has transformed communications within the Pentagon over the years and the 100,000 miles of telephone wires laid down since 1943 are gradually being replaced by fibre-optic cables – it's unclear whether this will hinder the 71 successful daily attempts to hack into the Pentagon's computer system (an alarming fact they have no intention of sharing as part of the general tour).

Crossing the Potomac by bridge, the yellow line Metro affords great views of the famous outline. The **Metro station** debouches right into the Pentagon lobby area where you sign up for the **tours**; you'll need photo ID. At peak times (generally, after 11.30am), there may be a thirty-minute wait for the next tour – before it leaves, the "security briefing" informs you that there are no cameras allowed and no rest-room stops during the ninety-minute tour.

The Pentagon

There are five armed forces of the United States. The one everyone forgets is the Coast Guard.

Chapter 11

Out of the City

Arlington aside, the other forays into northern Virginia made by virtually every visitor to Washington are to preservation showpiece **Old Town Alexandria**, six miles south of the capital, and to **Mount Vernon**, country seat of George Washington, another ten miles beyond. Virginia was the first and biggest British colony on the continent, generating the bulk of its wealth in a tobacco industry that relied on the forced labour of thousands of imported slaves. When Civil War came, Virginia declared for the Confederacy, its forces led by Robert E Lee, scion of one of the state's most venerable families. Alexandria – a solidly Southern town – was occupied by federal forces.

> All **area telephone codes** for numbers given in this chapter, unless otherwise stated, are ☎703.

A generation earlier, before the great divide, Alexandria had been a typical town in the heartland of Virginia's landed gentry. The state had a habit of producing great leaders and here the Lee family socialized with the Washingtons in the local churches and parlours. Tours of northern Virginia provide fascinating glimpses of their private lives: especially at Mount Vernon, where the daily experiences of George Washington, farmer, are laid bare.

Access to both places is easy, either by public transportation, car or the Mount Vernon Trail. You could see the best of either in half a day, though at Alexandria, in particular, you'll probably want to spend more time.

Old Town Alexandria

ALEXANDRIA, an historic port-town six miles south of Washington DC, predates the capital considerably and, in its preserved old town district, gives a good idea of what eighteenth-century life was like for

---

Mount Vernon Trail

The 18.5-mile **Mount Vernon Trail** – a biking-and-hiking route – runs parallel to the George Washington Memorial Parkway, from Arlington Memorial Bridge, south via Alexandria to Mount Vernon in Virginia. In DC, you can pick up the trail near the Lincoln Memorial; an offshoot runs north from here to Rock Creek Park. The trail sticks close to the Potomac for its entire length (diverting around the west side of National Airport) and runs past a number of sites of historic or natural interest. There are picnic areas en route. For more information, and a free trail guide, contact the National Park Service in Washington (☎202/619-7222).

---

its rich Virginia tobacco farmers. First settled by Scotsman John Alexander in 1699, Alexandria was granted town status fifty years later – according to tradition, a seventeen-year-old George Washington assisted in the preliminary survey (a claim bolstered by the existence of a contemporaneous parchment map with his name on it, in the Library of Congress). By the time of the Revolution, Alexandria was a booming port and trading centre (exporting wheat and flour to the West Indies), with a thriving social and political scene. With the establishment of the new capital in 1791, the town was incorporated into the District of Columbia very much against the wishes of its Southern, estate- and slave-owning inhabitants, and few were sorry when in 1846 Virginia demanded its land back from the federal government. Alexandria's Confederate sympathies led to it being occupied by Union troops during the Civil War, from which dated its decline: the new railroad tracks used to move troops and supplies throughout northern Virginia were later employed to carry freight, destroying Alexandria's shipping business at one fell swoop.

What's now known as **Old Town Alexandria** – the compact downtown grid by the Potomac – was left to rot for a generation. Many of the warehouses and wharves were abandoned, while other buildings became dirty munitions factories during both world wars. Today, after twenty years of spirited renovation, the preserved historic buildings, colonial-era streets and converted warehouses are hugely popular tourist attractions. Certainly, the glut of gift and antique shops, costumed guides and endless insistence on "authenticity" can become wearing, but for all that, it does have plenty of fascinating building interiors, museums, galleries and informative guided tours. It's also not preserved in theme-park isolation, but forms part of greater Alexandria, which has boomed as a commuter-belt town since the 1970s. Consequently, you can get here easily on the Metro, and there's more than a fair share of decent cafés and restaurants.

Arrival, orientation and information

The **Metro** station for the Old Town is King Street (yellow and blue line; 25min from downtown DC), a mile or so from most of the sights.

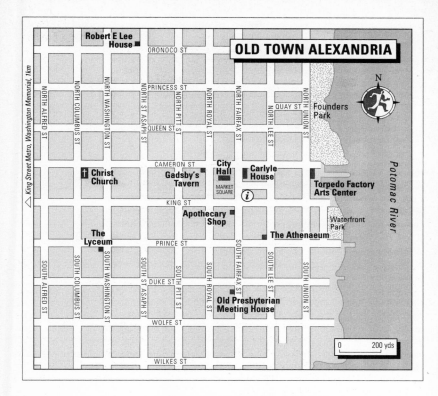

Outside the station, pick up local *DASH* bus #2 or 5, which runs down King Street, and get off at Fairfax Street. **Drivers** should follow the George Washington Memorial Parkway south from Arlington and take the East King Street exit. Metered **parking** in the Old Town is limited to two hours though a free 24-hour parking pass is available by taking ID and licence registration to the Visitor Center (see below) – insert enough money to cover the time between parking the car and returning with the pass. Cyclists or walkers can get here using the **Mount Vernon Trail** (see p.249).

Alexandria's restaurants are reviewed on p.283.

The Old Town is laid out in a grid and most of the sights lie within the same ten blocks. A good first stop is the **Ramsay House Visitor's Center**, 221 King St, at Fairfax St (daily 9am–5pm; ☎838-4200), where you can pick up dozens of leaflets and brochures and book various **tours** – conducted walks ($3), ghost tours ($5) or river cruises (from $7). There are **combination-museum** tickets available for the five most visited attractions ($12; valid indefinitely), or you can pay as you go. Note that many sights are **closed on Monday** and opening hours are limited on Sunday.

Alexandria's Festivals

Alexandria has a full **festival** calendar, many of its annual events based around its connection with the Scottish settlers or Washington and Lee families. Call the Visitor Center for exact dates.

January (3rd Sun): music, house tours and other entertainment to celebrate the birthday of Robert E Lee.

February (3rd weekend): George Washington's birthday, with a ball at *Gadsby's Tavern*, a parade, and mock battle at nearby Fort Ward.

March St Patrick's Day parade.

April Special homes and gardens tours in old town.

June Waterfront festival, with tours, cruises, stalls and entertainment.

July (last weekend): Virginia Scottish Games, featuring highland dancing and all manner of Celtic games, sports and pastimes.

December (1st Sat) Scottish Christmas Walk with more dancing and parades; (2nd Sat) candlelit tours of museums and historic houses, accompanied by traditional music.

Around the town

It's a relief, after the expansive boulevards and monuments of DC, to walk around a town built on a more human scale. Although Alexandria's main drags – particularly King Street – are top-heavy with traffic, it's not hard to find eighteenth-century peace and quiet. Cobbled, tree-lined streets with herringbone brick sidewalks are lined with pastel-washed houses featuring boot-scrapers and horse-mounting blocks outside the front door, and cast-iron drainpipes stamped "Alexandria, DC". The angled second-floor mirrors allowed the occupants to see who was calling.

You may as well start at the Visitor Center on King Street, which occupies **Ramsay House**, oldest in the town, built (though not originally on this site) in 1724 for William Ramsay, one of Alexandria's founding merchants and, later, its first mayor. It faces the river where Ramsay's ships loaded tobacco, though the water today is three blocks away: the bluff that the town was built on was excavated after the Revolution and the earth used to extend the harbour into the shallow bay – which is why Ramsay House stands so high above the street, its foundations exposed.

Ramsay's fellow merchant, John Carlyle, bought two of the most expensive land plots when the town was established and built Alexandria's finest colonial-era house. In the 1750s, when all the town's other buildings were of wood, the white sandstone **Carlyle House**, 121 North Fairfax St (Tues–Sat 10am–4.30pm, Sun noon–4.30pm; $3; ☎549-2997), made an ostentatious statement about its owner's wealth. Accounts of Carlyle's business dealings – he ran three plantations and traded slaves – inform the half-hour guided tours of the restored house. Contrast the family's draped beds, expensively painted rooms and fine Georgian furniture with the bare servants' hall, which has actually been over-restored – in the eighteenth century it would have had an earthen floor and no glass in the windows. In August 1755, the house was used as General Braddock's headquarters during the planning of the French and Indian War; George Washington was on Braddock's staff and, later, was a frequent guest in Carlyle's house when visiting from Mount Vernon.

Braddock's troops paraded across the way in **Market Square**, off King Street, heart of Alexandria since its foundation. The modern brick terrace sounds one of the few discordant notes in the Old Town, and the restored eighteenth-century **City Hall** which faces the square also fails to look its age, though a weekly **farmers' market** still sets up in the City Hall arcades (Sat 5–9am), as it has for over two hundred years.

Follow Cameron Street past City Hall to **Gadsby's Museum Tavern**, 134 North Royal St (April–Sept Tues–Sat 10am–5pm, Sun 1–5pm; Oct–March Tues–Sat 11am–4pm, Sun 1–4pm; $3; ☎838-4242), occupying two (supposedly haunted) Georgian buildings in a prime spot close to the market. Downstairs, *Gadsby's Tavern* still operates as a working restaurant (complete with "authentic" colonial food and costumed staff). Short tours by a knowledgable guide lead you through the old tavern rooms upstairs – in the galleried ballroom, Washington used to cut a rug at parties thrown for his birthday. Three blocks west up Cameron Street, at North Washington Street, the English-style **Christ Church** (Mon–Sat 9am–4pm, Sun 2–4pm; free), set in a beautiful churchyard, retains the Washington family pew.

The Washingtons weren't the only notable family with ties to Alexandria. A descendant of the Lees of Virginia, Phillip Fendall built his splendid clapboard mansion in 1785; in the **Lee-Fendall House**, 614 Oronoco St (Tues–Sat 10am–3.45pm, Sun noon–3.45pm; $3; ☎548-1789), distinguished Revolutionary War general Henry "Light Horse Harry" Lee composed Washington's funeral oration (in which, famously, he declared him "first in war, first in peace, and first in the hearts of his countrymen"). Henry Lee bought his own house over the road just before the War of 1812 and installed his wife and five children there. This, the **Boyhood Home of Robert E Lee**, 607 Oronoco St (Mon–Sat 10am–4pm, Sun 1–4pm; $3; ☎548-8454), makes much of the early years of Henry's son and future Confederate general, though the enthusiastic tours can't hide the lack of original Lee memorabilia; the house itself is a beauty, though, filled with period furniture.

*For more on
Robert E Lee,
see p.245.*

South of King Street, the **Lyceum**, 201 South Washington St (Mon–Sat 10am–5pm, Sun 1–5pm; free; ☎838-4994), houses the town's history museum in a Greek Revival building of 1839. The changing displays, film shows and associated art gallery can put some flesh on the town's history, highlighted in varied exhibits from old photographs and Civil War documents to locally produced furniture and silverware (the latter an Alexandrian speciality in the nineteenth century). Four blocks east down Duke Street to South Fairfax Street, you'll find the **Old Presbyterian Meeting House**, 321 South Fairfax St (Mon–Fri 8.30am–4.30pm; free; ☎549-6670), in whose quiet graveyard lies the tomb of John Carlyle. The Scottish town founders met regularly here, most prominently in December 1799 when they gathered in the cool, white pews for the memorial service to George Washington who had recently died on his estate at Mount Vernon. Patent medicines for Washington were made up at the nearby **Stabler-Leadbeater Apothecary Shop**, whose yellow bay windows jut out at 105–107 South Fairfax St (Mon–Sat 10am–1.30pm, Sun 1–5pm; $2; ☎836-3713). The shop was founded in 1792 and still displays its original furnishings, herbs, potions and medical paraphernalia.

The waterfront

Eighteenth-century Alexandria wouldn't recognize its twentieth-century **waterfront** beyond North Union Street, not least because the riverbank is several blocks further east, following centuries of landfill. Where there were once wooden warehouses and wharves heaving with barrels of tobacco, there's now a smart marina and boardwalk, framed by the green stretches of **Founders Park** to the north and **Waterfront Park** to the south. Forty-minute sightseeing **cruises** depart from in front of the *Food Pavilion* (several daily May–Oct; information from the *Potomac Riverboat Company*; ☎548-9000); longer trips run to DC and back.

Before this whole area was cleaned up, the US government built a torpedo factory on the river, which operated until the end of World War II. Restyled as the diverting **Torpedo Factory Arts Center** (daily 10am–5pm; free; ☎838-4565), its three floors contain the studios of over two hundred artists, all open to the public, and displaying sculpture, ceramics, jewellery, glassware and textiles in regularly changing exhibitions. Take a look, too, inside the centre's **Alexandria Archeology Museum** (Tues–Fri 10am–3pm, Sat 10am–5pm, Sun 1–5pm; free; ☎838-4399), where much of the town's restoration work was researched and carried out.

George Washington Masonic Memorial

In a town bursting with Washington mementoes, nothing is more prominent than the **George Washington Masonic Memorial** (daily 9am–5pm; free; ☎683-2007), whose 333-foot tower looms over town behind the King Street Metro station – it's best visited first or last thing. Washington was considered a "deserving brother" by the Virginian freemasons who built this memorial – a Greek temple with the Empire State stuck on top – in his honour in 1932. Inside, there's a tall bronze statue of the man, sundry memorabilia, and laughable dioramas depicting events from his life. To see this, and – more pertinently – the superb views from the observation platform, you'll have to wait for a forty-minute **tour**, which leaves from the hall (on the half-hour in the morning, on the hour in the afternoon). But even from the steps outside, the views are magnificent, across the Potomac to the Washington Monument and Capitol dome in the distance.

Mount Vernon

George Washington Pkwy, Mount Vernon, VA ☎ 780-2000; Metro Huntington, then Fairfax Connector bus #101. Daily March 9am–5pm; April–Aug 8am–5pm; Sept & Oct 9am–5pm; Nov–Feb 9am–4pm. Admission $8.

*For a life of
George
Washington,
see pp.56–57.*

Set on a shallow bluff overlooking the broad Potomac River, sixteen miles south of Washington DC, **MOUNT VERNON** is among the most attractive historic houses in America. The beloved **country estate of George Washington**, it was his home for forty years, during which time he ran it as a thriving progressive farm, anticipating the decline in Virginia's tobacco cultivation and planting instead grains and food crops with great success. When he died, it seemed only natural that he be buried in the grounds, as his will directed; America's first President lies next to his wife, Martha, in the simple family tomb.

His father, Augustine, first built a house on the Washington estate in 1735. When he died, the house and lands passed to George's elder brother Lawrence and, in turn, on Lawrence's death in 1752 (and his widow's in 1761), eventually to George. Not that he had much early opportunity to spend time here, since for much of the 1750s he was away on service with the Virginia militia, later fighting in the French and Indian War. He married in 1759 and it was during the years before 1775 – when he was next called away on service, as commander-in-chief of the Continental Army – that Washington came to know his estate. He tripled its size to eight thousand acres, divided it into five separate working farms, and landscaped the mansion grounds – rolling meadows, copses, riverside walks, parks and even vineyards, all laid out for the family's amusement.

Just 500 acres of the estate remain today, the rest split and sold off by the terms of successive wills, but there's more than enough to give an idea of the whole. The lifestyle of an eighteenth-century **gentleman farmer** was an agreeable one, in Washington's case supported by the labour of over two hundred slaves who lived and worked on the outlying farms. The modest house he inherited was enlarged and redecorated with imported materials; formal gardens and a bowling green were added; and the general bred stallions, hunted in his own woods, fished in the river and entertained visitors. But it would be unfair to view Washington as a dilettante. Daily at dawn he made a personal tour of inspection on horseback, sometimes riding twenty miles around the grounds. He studied the latest scientific works on farming, corresponded with experts, and, introducing new techniques, expanded the farms' output to include the production of flour, textiles and even whisky. His experimental methods often cost him financially and, once he was away fighting the Revolutionary War, he was forced to rely on others to run his estate – who were doubtless thrilled to receive his sixteen-page letters from the front directing the latest farm improvements.

Washington spent eight years away from Mount Vernon during the war, but still wasn't allowed to retire there for good, as was his wish, at the end of the fighting. By 1787, he was back at the head of the Constitutional Convention in Philadelphia and two years later was elected to his first term as president – news he heard first at Mount Vernon, from a messenger who had ridden all the way from Philadelphia. In the event, he only visited his house another dozen or so times during his presidency, often for just a few days. When he finally moved back in 1797, at the end of his second term in office, he and Martha had just two and a half years together before his death on December 14, 1799. Out on one of his long estate inspections, he got caught in the snow and succumbed to a fever which killed him.

Practicalities

The **Metro-and-bus** combination is an easy enough route to Mount Vernon, though it takes over an hour – more if you miss the bus at Huntington station (hourly, half-hourly after 3pm; call ☎339-7200 for schedules). A **cab** from the station costs around $15–20. **Drivers** should follow the George Washington Parkway from DC; there's free parking. The **Mount Vernon Trail** (see p.249) finishes here, too.

Potomac Spirit **cruises** from Pier 4, 6th and Water streets SW in DC (mid-March to Oct; $22 round-trip; ☎202/554-8000) take ninety minutes to reach Mount Vernon. The **Tourmobile** (see p.46) also runs out here, the Mount Vernon section taking four hours. Both boat and *Tourmobile* trips include admission to the house and grounds.

Mount Vernon is an extremely popular day-trip and summer weekends, especially, can be very busy. Come early, or midweek, if you can and allow at least two hours to see the house and grounds. You can't eat or drink on the estate, but just outside the gate – pass-outs allowed – is a snack bar (daily 9.30am–estate closing) and a more refined **restaurant**, the *Mount Vernon Inn* (Mon–Sat 11am–3.30pm & 5–9pm, Sun 11am–4pm), specializing in colonial food.

Washington's birthday celebration (around the 3rd weekend in Feb) sees free admission, wreath-laying and fife and drum parades.

The house and grounds

Pick up a map of the grounds at the entrance gate and, if you need historical background, sit in for a few minutes on the saccharine video, which ends with the treacly entreaty, "Thank you, George Washington, for being there when we needed you".

The path up to the mansion passes various outbuildings, including a renovated set of former **slave quarters**. Ninety slaves alone lived and worked in the mansion grounds and though there's evidence that Washington was a kinder master than most – refusing to sell children away from their parents, for instance, allowing slaves to raise their own crops, and engaging the services of a doctor – they still lived familiar lives of deprivation and overwork. His overseers were continually enjoined to watch the slaves like hawks and guard against theft and slacking. To his credit, Washington was quick to realize that the move away from tobacco cultivation to more skilled farming made slavery increasingly unprofitable. He stopped buying slaves in the late 1770s, allowing those he owned to learn occupations such as carpentry, bricklaying and spinning, and to be maintained once they had reached the end of their working lives. His will freed his remaining slaves a year after his death, making provision for them all.

Nearby, a small **museum** traces Washington's ancestry and displays porcelain from the house, medals, weapons, silver and a series of striking miniatures by Charles Willson Peale and his brother James, of Martha and her two children by her first marriage. The clay bust of Washington was produced by French sculptor Jean-Antoine Houdon, who worked on it at Mount Vernon in 1785 prior to completing his famous statue for the Richmond Capitol (see p.58).

Around the corner, fronting the circular courtyard, stands the **mansion** itself, with the length of the bowling green stretching before it. Join the line and walk through the wings and connecting colonnades into the house, where stationed guides answer questions. It's a handsome, harmonious wooden structure, reasonably modest, but sporting stunning views from the East Lawn. The wooden exterior was painted white, bevelled and sand-blasted to resemble stone; inside, the Palladian windows and brightly painted and papered rooms follow the fashion of the day, while the contents are based on an inventory prepared after Washington's death. Fourteen rooms are open to the public: portrait-filled parlours and cramped bedrooms, and the chamber where Washington breathed his last on a four-poster bed still in situ –

You can view the third floor (usually closed) on special Christmas tours, which re-create the Washingtons' yuletide celebrations.

his body was later laid out downstairs in the striking green dining room. Curiosities in his study give insights into his character – a wooden reading chair with built-in fan, and a globe he ordered from London – while in the central hall hangs a key to the destroyed Bastille, presented by Thomas Paine in 1790 on behalf of Layayette.

After touring the mansion there's plenty more to see in the grounds: the kitchen (set apart from the house because of the risk of fire), cluttered storehouse, stables, smokehouse, wash-house, overseer's quarters, kitchen garden and shrubberies. Take a stroll down to the **tomb**, too, where two marble sarcophagi for George and Martha are set behind iron gates, "interred here in a private manner, without parade or funeral oration", as his will stipulated. Washington's will also directed that a new brick vault be erected after his death since the original family vault on the grounds was in poor shape; the current structure was built in 1831. Nearby lies a slave burial ground, while beyond, you may catch one of the occasional demonstrations held on a special site growing crops and displaying farming techniques used by Washington.

Listings

Chapter 12

Accommodation

As you might expect, Washington DC possesses some of the most exclusive and pricey hotels in America: Georgetown's *Four Seasons* is top of the scale, while rates at the *Willard Inter-Continental, Omni Shoreham, Hay-Adams* and *Jefferson* reflect their standing as historic landmarks. However, you can find reasonably priced, central accommodation, though you'll need to plan ahead if you want to guarantee a room at a particular time. For a full list of properties contact the *DC Committee to Promote Washington* (☎724-4091, fax 724-2445) or one of the free **reservation services** listed below. All hotels reviewed here are marked on the **map** on p.262.

There are hotels in all the main downtown **areas**, though those near the White House, on Capitol Hill and in Georgetown tend to be business- (political or otherwise) oriented and pricey. The odd budget option exists in Foggy Bottom and Old Downtown (where you'll find the city's youth hostel), while most of the chain hotels and mid-range places are in New Downtown – specifically in the streets around Scott and Thomas cir-

cles. Outer neighbourhoods tend to have a wider selection of smaller, cheaper hotels and B&B-style guest houses, and it's no hardship at all to be staying in Dupont Circle, Adams-Morgan or Woodley Park – you'll probably be eating and drinking in these places anyway. You're also more likely to be able to **park** for free in the outer neighbourhoods; garage parking is available at most downtown hotels, but you'll be charged $10–20 a night for the privilege. Very occasionally, an inn or hotel we list is on the cusp of a slightly dodgy neighbourhood; where **safety** is an issue, we've said so, and you're advised to take taxis back to your hotel at night.

Standard room rates throughout the city start at around $100–120 a night, but there's plenty of scope for negotiation for canny travellers. Most hotels **discount** their rates at weekends (some by up to fifty percent), while rates also remain low throughout July and August, when Congress is in recess, and prices drop again in December and January. Always ask if the rate you've been quoted is the best available; often, dis-

---

B&B Agencies

Bed & Breakfast Accommodations Ltd ☎202/328-3510, fax 332-3885

Bed & Breakfast League ☎202/363-7767

Hotel Reservation Services

Capitol Reservations ☎202/452-1270 or 1-800/847-4832, fax 452-0537

Washington DC Accommodations ☎202/289-2220 or 1-800/554-2220, fax 483-4436

Accommodation

count information has to be ferreted out of desk clerks. Where places offer particularly good discount deals, we've said so in the review. Hotels also charge by the room, so three people can often stay in a double for the same (or a slightly higher) price as two. Although **breakfast** usually isn't included in the price at most hotels, it often *is* as part of the special weekend packages.

The **price codes** given in the reviews below reflect the **average price for a standard double room in peak season** (late March to early July); consequently you'll often be able to find a room for less. Groups and families should consider the city's **suite hotels**, where you'll get a kitchen and possibly a separate lounge-room, too. One other thing to keep in mind: DC in summer is hot and humid, and **air-conditioning** is essential for getting a good night's rest.

A number of **B&B agencies** offer rooms in small inns, private homes or apartments, starting from around $55–65 per night; luxury B&B, though, can be every bit as pricey as a hotel, reaching as high as $150–250. For rock-bottom alternatives, there's the international **youth hostel** (which is very central, but at its busiest in July and August) and a couple of similar places; **students** can try contacting one of the educational establishments listed in the box on p.268.

> Unless otherwise stated, all the hotels reviewed in this chapter have the DC-area **telephone code** ☎202, to be used when ringing from outside the city.

Note that all DC hotels add **13 percent room tax** to your bill, plus an extra $1.50 occupancy tax per room.

Capitol Hill and Union Station

Bellevue, 15 E St NW ☎638-0900 or 1-800/327-6667, fax 638-5132. Union Station Metro. Great 1930s building with panelled wood interior and splendid balconied lobby; rooms are modern and sound-proofed, with some very comfortable suites. There's also the incentive of the *Tiber Creek Pub* (where yards of ale are drunk with gusto), in a neighbourhood otherwise short on nightlife. Buffet breakfast included. ④.

Capitol Hill Suites, 200 C St SE ☎543-6000 or 1-800/424-9165, fax 547-2608. Capitol South Metro. Popular apartment conversions whose rooms all come with kitchen-diners, free morning coffee and daily paper. Busy when Congress is in session – at weekends and in August the price drops a category. ⑤.

Holiday Inn on the Hill, 415 New Jersey Ave NW ☎638-1616 or 1-800/638-1116, fax 347-1813. Union Station Metro. Revamped hotel, far cheaper than the nearby *Hyatt Regency*. Rooms are nothing special, but there's a pool and exercise room, and weekend rates can be a bargain. ④.

Hyatt Regency Washington on Capitol Hill, 400 New Jersey Ave NW ☎737-1234 or 1-800/233-1234, fax 737-5773. Union Station Metro. Monster (800-room) luxury hotel with multi-storey garden atrium, pool and health club. ⑥.

Accommodation Price Codes

① Under $50	④ $100–140	⑦ $250–300
② $50–70	⑤ $140–200	⑧ Over $300
③ $70–100	⑥ $200–250	

The price codes given in the reviews reflect the **average price** for a standard double room in peak season, **excluding** room and occupancy tax. Unless otherwise stated all rooms come with bathroom and breakfast is usually not included.

Name Changes and New Hotels

Hotels in Washington seem to **change names** at the drop of a hat, often because the parent companies change, go bust or acquire new properties. Add to this the number of similarly named hotels – a profusion of Hyatts, Ramadas, Holiday Inns and Doubletrees all want to call their properties "Downtown", "Capitol Hill", "Park" or "Plaza" – and you may have trouble tracking down the place you want. Always check, especially if you're booking with a chain, that the hotel you're paying for is where you think it is.

There are over one hundred hotels in DC alone and more than three hundred in the metropolitan area, but that doesn't stop demand for rooms increasing. The two latest downtown projects are the *Crowne Plaza Washington* (1375 K St NW), ready for business in 1997, and a new hotel at Washington Harbour in Georgetown, to be completed by 1998.

Accommodation

Phoenix Park, 520 N Capitol St NW ☎ 638-6900 or 1-800/824-5419, fax 393-3236. Union Station Metro. Pleasing, well-equipped rooms in a conveniently sited, Irish-owned hotel, across from Union Station. Popular with politicos and an after-work crowd, who frequent the associated *Dubliner* pub (see p.284). There's a good restaurant, too, with hearty breakfasts. ⑤.

South of the Mall

Channel Inn Hotel, 650 Water St SW ☎ 554-2400 or 1-800/368-5668, fax 863-1164. Waterfront Metro. The city's first waterfront hotel, a 1970s development down at the revitalized Washington Channel, with some rooms looking across to East Potomac Park. There's free parking, an outdoor pool-sundeck and a choice of good seafood restaurants nearby. ④.

Holiday Inn Capitol, 550 C St SW ☎ 479-4000 or 1-800/465-4329, fax 488-4267. L'Enfant Plaza or Federal Center SW Metro. Varied rooms within walking distance of the Capitol and Air and Space Museum, and a rooftop pool. As with all the city's *Holiday Inns*, weekend rates are attractive. ⑤.

Loews L'Enfant Plaza, 480 L'Enfant Plaza SW ☎ 484-1000 or 1-800/223-0888, fax 646-4456. L'Enfant Plaza Metro. Superbly appointed, modern hotel, a couple of blocks south of the Mall and with access from the Metro. Spacious rooms in nineteenth-century French style, most with river or city views, plus health club and rooftop pool. Special winter and weekend rates apply, and the hotel is kid- and pet-friendly – ask about specific deals. ⑥.

Near the White House

The Carlton, 923 16th St NW ☎ 638-2626 or 1-800/325-3535, fax 347-4758. A 1920s Italian Renaissance palace a couple of blocks north of the White House. Stylish rooms and perfectly judged service. ⑥–⑦.

Hay-Adams Hotel, 1 Lafayette Square NW ☎ 638-6600 or 1-800/424-5054, fax 638-3803. Farragut West or McPherson Square Metro. One of DC's finest hotels, fashioned from two historic townhouses in 1928 and ever since a byword for indulgence, from the gold-leaf and walnut lobby to the ornate, airy rooms and suites – with fireplaces and original cornicing, marble bathrooms, balconies and high ceilings. Splash out (a lot) for views of St John's Church or (from upper floors) the White House; 8th-floor rooms are best of all. Breakfast in the stylish park-facing restaurant. ⑦–⑧.

JW Marriott, 1331 Pennsylvania Ave NW ☎ 393-2000 or 1-800/228-9290, fax 626-6991. Metro Center or Federal Triangle Metro. Flagship *Marriott* property in one of the best locations in the city,

Price categories:
① *Under $50*
② *$50–70*
③ *$70–100*
④ *$100–140*
⑤ *$140–200*
⑥ *$200–250*
⑦ *$250–300*
⑧ *Over $300*

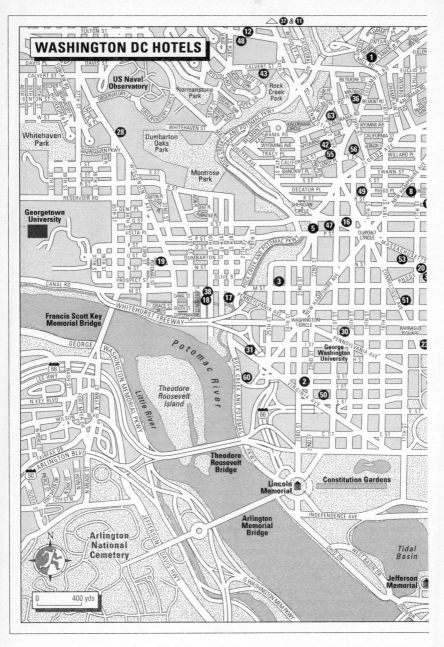

WASHINGTON DC HOTELS

ACCOMMODATION

1 Adams Inn
2 Allen Lee Hotel
3 ANA Hotel
4 Bellevue
5 Brickskeller Inn
6 Capital Hilton
7 Capitol Hill Suites
8 Carlyle Suites
9 Channel Inn Hotel
10 Comfort Inn Downtown
11 Connecticut Avenue Days Inn
12 Connecticut-Woodley Guest House
13 Days Inn Downtown
14 Doubletree Hotel Park Terrace
15 Embassy Inn
16 Embassy Row Hotel
17 Four Seasons Hotel
18 Georgetown Dutch Inn
19 Georgetown Inn
20 Governor's House
21 Grand Hyatt
22 Harrington Hotel
23 Hay-Adams Hotel
24 Henley Park Hotel
25 Holiday Inn Capitol
26 Holiday Inn Central
27 Holiday Inn Franklin Square
28 Holiday Inn Georgetown
29 Holiday Inn on the Hill
30 Hotel Lombardy
31 Howard Johnson Premier Hotel

32 Hyatt Regency Washington on Capitol Hill
33 India House Too
34 Jefferson Hotel
35 JW Marriott
36 Kalorama Guest House at Kalorama Park
37 Kalorama Guest House at Woodley Park
38 Latham Hotel
39 Loews L'Enfant Plaza
40 Marriott at Metro Center
41 Morrison-Clark Inn
42 Normandy Inn
43 Omni Shoreham
44 Phoenix Park
45 Quality Hotel Downtown
46 Ramada Plaza
47 Ritz Carlton
48 Sheraton Washington
49 Simpkins' B&B
50 State Plaza
51 Stouffer Renaissance Mayflower
52 Swiss Inn
53 Tabard Inn
54 The Carlton
55 Washington Courtyard by Marriott
56 Washington Hilton and Towers
57 Washington Hotel
58 Washington International AYH Hostel
59 Washington Vista
60 Watergate Hotel
61 Willard Inter-Continental
62 Windsor Inn
63 Windsor Park Hotel

Accommodation

part of the National Place development and overlooking Freedom Plaza (ask for an avenue-facing room). Weekend rates include breakfast. ⑥.

Washington Hotel, 515 15th St NW ☎638-5900 or 1-800/424-9540, fax 638-4275. Metro Center Metro. Historic hotel next to the *Willard* with a popular rooftop bar and heavily Edwardian rooms; some look across to the White House. It rarely needs to offer discount rates, but off-season weekends can see price reductions. ⑤–⑥.

Willard Inter-Continental, 1401 Pennsylvania Ave NW ☎628-9100 or 1-800/327-0200, fax 637-7307. Metro Center Metro. Few hotels have the style of the *Willard* – in business on and off since the 1850s (see p.176). It's a Beaux-Arts beauty with acres of marble, mosaics and glass, slick service, finely furnished rooms and top-drawer clientele. ⑧.

Foggy Bottom

Nearest Metro to the accommodation listed in Foggy Bottom is Foggy Bottom-GWU.

Allen Lee Hotel, 2224 F St NW ☎331-1224 or 1-800/462-0186. Misleadingly attractive exterior hides musty rooms, with clunky air-conditioning –check a couple before checking in. It's seen much better days, but is in a handy location and is certainly cheap for DC. ②.

ANA Hotel, 2401 M St NW ☎429-2400 or 1-800/262-4683, fax 457-5050. High-class Japanese-owned hotel with extremely comfortable rooms, pool, excellent health club and internal courtyard. It's north of Washington Circle, midway between Foggy Bottom and Georgetown. ⑦.

Hotel Lombardy, 2019 Pennsylvania Ave NW ☎828-2600 or 1-800/424-5486, fax 872-0503. Redbrick townhouse hotel in favoured Pennsylvania Avenue location (it's just as close to Farragut West Metro). Most of the spacious rooms have kitchenettes; the café has open-air seats. ④.

Howard Johnson Premier Hotel, 2601 Virginia Ave NW ☎965-2700 or 1-800/446-4656, fax 965-2700. Decent high-rise rooms, pool and free indoor parking. Earned its reputation as the place from where Nixon's "Plumbers" supervised the Watergate burglary (see p.167). Good weekend discounts. ③–④.

State Plaza, 2117 E St NW ☎861-8200 or 1-800/424-2859, fax 659-8601. Spacious suites with fully equipped kitchens and dining area, plus a rooftop sundeck, health club and good café. Great weekend rates, and there's often room when other places are full. ④–⑤.

Watergate Hotel, 2650 Virginia Ave NW ☎965-2300 or 1-800/424-2736, fax 337-7915. Sniffy hotel with comfortable rooms and suites (some with kitchen and balcony with river views) in the now notorious complex near the Kennedy Center; it's a bit of a hike from good bars and restaurants, though there is a small pool, and shops and services in the complex. ⑦–⑧.

Old Downtown

Comfort Inn Downtown, 500 H St NW ☎289-5959 or 1-800/234-6423, fax 682-9152. Gallery Place-Chinatown Metro. Reasonable rates for this location, with Chinatown on the doorstep; a café serves buffet breakfast (not included in price). Good weekend discounts ④.

Airport-Hotel Connections

The *Washington Flyer Express* bus operates **courtesy shuttle services** from the terminal at 1517 K St NW to the following hotels: *Grand Hyatt* (Old Downtown), *Harrington* (Old Downtown), *Omni Shoreham* (Woodley Park), *Sheraton Washington* (Woodley Park), *Stouffer Renaissance Mayflower* (New Downtown) and *Washington Hilton* (Adams-Morgan/Dupont Circle), as well as the *JW Marriott* and *Washington Renaissance*. There's also a direct service from these hotels back to the airports: see p.38 for more details.

Grand Hyatt, 1000 H St NW ☎ 582-1234 or 1-800/233-1234, fax 637-4797. Metro Center Metro. Nearly 900 rooms, but its location opposite the Convention Center keeps it busy. Rooms are fine but not as flash as the 12-storey atrium, lagoon, waterfalls and glass elevators. ⑥.

Harrington Hotel, 1100 E St NW ☎ 628-8140 or 1-800/424-8532, fax 347-3924. Metro Center Metro. Large, simple, welcoming, family-owned hotel, off Pennsylvania Ave. Adequate rooms (singles to quads) and many foreign guests; cheap parking, too. Book ahead. ③.

Henley Park Hotel, 926 Massachusetts Ave NW ☎ 638-5200 or 1-800/222-8474, fax 638-6740. Mount Vernon Square-UDC or Metro Center Metro. Former apartment building north of the Convention Center turned into a cozy English country-house-style hotel. It's rather at odds with the borderline neighbourhood; take your after-dinner stroll somewhere else. ⑤–⑥.

Marriott at Metro Center, 775 12th St NW ☎ 737-2200 or 1-800/228-9290, fax 347-0860. Metro Center Metro. Revamped downtown hotel with popular bar and grill and sizeable rooms. Weekends can be a real bargain, often including free breakfast and parking. ⑤.

Washington International AYH Hostel, 1009 11th St NW ☎ 737-2333, fax 737-1508. Metro Center Metro. Large (250 beds), clean and very central, just three blocks north of the Metro. Single-sex dorms ($18), some family rooms, kitchen, lounge, laundry, luggage storage, enthusiastic staff and organized activities. Non-members pay $3 more per night (and may be refused in busy spring and summer months). Open 24hr but take care at night around here. Book well in advance, especially in summer; 6-night maximum stay. ①.

New Downtown

Capital Hilton, 1001 16th St NW ☎ 393-1000 or 1-800/445-8667, fax 639-5742. Farragut North, Farragut West or McPherson Square Metro. Art Deco trappings, great location (3 blocks from the White House), buzzing lobby-bar and spacious rooms. Facilities include health club and a good sports bar-restaurant. Weekend rates are among the lowest for quality downtown rooms. ⑥–⑦.

Days Inn Downtown, 1201 K St NW ☎ 842-1020 or 1-800/562-3350, fax 289-0336. Metro Center Metro. Handy sightseeing launchpad near Franklin Square, with small rooftop pool. Some rooms have kitchenettes; all have coffee-makers. ③–④.

Doubletree Hotel Park Terrace, 1515 Rhode Island Ave NW ☎ 232-7000 or 1-800/222-TREE, fax 332-7152. Dupont Circle or Farragut North Metro. European elegance, with comfortable rooms, marble bathrooms, outdoor terrace for summer dining, plus the *Doubletree* trademark – cookies on check-in and free coffee-making facilities. You're near Dupont Circle nightlife, and can start the day with a good-value buffet breakfast. Pick of the bunch in this neighbourhood. ④.

Governor's House, 1615 Rhode Island Ave NW ☎ 296-2100 or 1-800/821-4367, fax 331-0227. Dupont Circle or Farragut North Metro. Decent-sized rooms, some with sofa beds and kitchenettes. There's a pool, too, and use of the nearby YMCA fitness centre. ④.

Holiday Inn Central, 1501 Rhode Island Ave NW ☎ 483-2000 or 1-800/248-0016, fax 797-1078. Dupont Circle or Farragut North Metro. One of downtown's better bargains, with pleasant, modern rooms, rooftop pool, bar, and breakfast included. It's a block up from Scott Circle. ③–④.

Holiday Inn Franklin Square, 1155 14th St NW ☎ 737-1200 or 1-800/465-4329, fax 783-5733. McPherson Square Metro. Actually at Thomas Circle, a couple of blocks north of Franklin Square, but a handy enough location, standard *Holiday Inn* rooms and weekend and off-season discounts. Rooftop pool too. ④–⑤.

Jefferson Hotel, 1200 16th St NW ☎ 347-2200 or 1-800/368-5966, fax 785-1505. Farragut North Metro. Patrician landmark on 16th Street, a favourite with

Accommodation

Price categories:
① *Under $50*
② *$50–70*
③ *$70–100*
④ *$100–140*
⑤ *$140–200*
⑥ *$200–250*
⑦ *$250–300*
⑧ *Over $300*

Accommodation

Nearest Metro for all the places listed in Dupont Circle is Dupont Circle.

politicians since the 1920s. Antique-strewn interior, personal service and all mod-cons in the superb rooms. Weekend rates can fall to under $200 a night. ⑦.

Morrison-Clark Inn, 1015 L St NW ☎898-1200 or 1-800/332-7898, fax 371-0377. Mount Vernon Square-UDC or Metro Center Metro. Twee antique-and-lace accommodation in converted Victorian townhouses. Fifty-odd rooms in overblown styles, balconies overlooking a courtyard, a comfortable lounge and continental breakfast included. Weekend rates, when available, come down to the $100 mark. ⑤.

Quality Hotel Downtown, 1315 16th St NW ☎232-8000 or 1-800/368-5689, fax 667-9827. Dupont Circle or Farragut North Metro. Spacious rooms, many with sofabed and kitchenette, plus pub, café and restaurant and free entry to local health club. Call for weekend rates. ④.

Ramada Plaza, 10 Thomas Circle NW ☎842-1300 or 1-800/272-6232, fax 371-9602. McPherson Square Metro. Convenient location (3 blocks from the Metro), outdoor pool and deck in summer and great views across the Circle from the large rooms. Tourists mingle with convention and business guests in the lobby bar. Good weekend discounts. ④–⑤.

Stouffer Renaissance Mayflower, 1127 Connecticut Ave NW ☎347-3000 or 1-800/468-3571, fax 466-9082. Farragut North Metro. Restoration has left the *Mayflower* (see p.205) better than ever, with the Promenade – a vast, imperially decorated hall – one of DC's great public spaces. Rooms, facilities and service are all top-notch, the bars, café and restaurant much in demand by power-diners. ⑧.

Swiss Inn, 1204 Massachusetts Ave NW ☎371-1816 or 1-800/955-7947. Metro Center Metro. Friendly, guest house with just seven rooms (some with kitchenettes) – book well in advance. Prices don't get much better downtown, and in winter you may score a small discount. ③.

Washington Vista, 1400 M St NW ☎429-1700 or 1-800/847-8232, fax

728-0530. McPherson Square Metro. Contemporary comfort by the *Hilton* group near Thomas Circle. Unexpectedly low prices may be an attempt to shake off the shame of having Mayor Marion Barry arrested here in a drugs sting. Weekend rates include breakfast and parking. ⑥.

Dupont Circle

Brickskeller Inn, 1523 22nd St NW ☎293-1885, fax 293-0996. Simple rooms, most with sinks and a couple with bath, above a late-opening bar (see p.287) near Dupont Circle. The top floor has a view of Rock Creek Park. Good weekly rates. ②.

Carlyle Suites, 1731 New Hampshire Ave NW ☎234-3200 or 1-800/964-5377, fax 387-0085. Comfortable self-catering suites in surprisingly tranquil street near Dupont Circle, with modern furnishings behind the Art Deco exterior. Café, parking, laundry, and weekend discounts. ④–⑤.

Embassy Inn, 1627 16th St NW ☎234-7800 or 1-800/423-9111, fax 234-3309. Welcoming inn, popular with Europeans, on a residential street in northern Dupont Circle, well placed for bars and restaurants. Attractive, good-value rooms, free continental breakfast, coffee and papers available all day, plus an early evening sherry to speed you on your way. ③.

Embassy Row Hotel, 2015 Massachusetts Ave NW ☎265-1600 or 1-800/424-2400, fax 328-7526. Less social cachet – and cheaper – than the nearby *Ritz Carlton* in this top-drawer neighbourhood. Rooftop pool. ⑤.

Ritz Carlton, 2100 Massachusetts Ave NW ☎293-2100 or 1-800/241-3333, fax 466-9867. Embassy Row highlight, once owned by Al Gore's family, and still catering for clubby politicos, media types and business people. Anglo-French country-house chic, with impeccable facilities and service; the *Jockey Club* restaurant has more power in its dining than General Electric. ⑦.

Simpkins' B&B, 1601 19th St NW ☎387-1328. Charming Victorian townhouse with shared or private a/c rooms. Great location, good mix of guests and unbeatable rates (though prices double if you can't produce a passport, US or foreign). Breakfast available. Call well in advance. ①–②.

Tabard Inn, 1739 N St NW ☎785-1277, fax 785-6173. Three converted Victorian townhouses with forty individually decorated, antique-stocked rooms (some with shared bath), two blocks from Dupont Circle. Laidback staff, comfortable if ageing lounges, courtyard and good restaurant. Rates include breakfast. ④–⑤.

Windsor Inn, 1842 16th St NW ☎667-0300 or 1-800/423-9111, fax 667-4503. Under the same welcoming management as the *Embassy Inn*, the *Windsor* is a few blocks further north, its rooms (in twin brick 1920s houses) a shade larger; the spacious suites are a real steal. Ground-floor rooms look onto a terrace; free continental breakfast, coffee and sherry served in the attractive lobby. ③–④.

Adams-Morgan/Kalorama

Adams Inn, 1744 Lanier Place NW ☎745-3600 or 1-800/578-6807, fax 332-5867. Woodley Park-Zoo Metro. Clean, simple B&B rooms, with and without bath, in three adjoining Victorian town houses on a quiet residential street (just north of Calvert St). No TVs, but free breakfast, coffee all day, garden patio and laundry facilities. ②–③.

Kalorama Guest House at Kalorama Park, 1854 Mintwood Place NW ☎667-6369, fax 319-1262. Woodley Park-Zoo Metro. Well-placed Victorian guest house, near Adams-Morgan's restaurants. Spacious rooms (31; 12 en suite) in four spotless houses, filled with period *objets*, plants and handsome furniture (no TV). Free breakfast, papers, coffee and evening sherry, plus washing machine. Booking essential. Also see "Woodley Park". ②–③.

Normandy Inn, 2118 Wyoming Ave NW ☎483-1350 or 1-800/424-3729, fax 387-8241. Woodley Park-Zoo Metro. Quiet hotel in flash neighbourhood, with understated, comfortable rooms (each

with fridge and coffee-maker). Continental breakfast is $5, taken in the garden in summer. Coffee and cookies are served daily and there's a weekly wine and cheese reception. ④.

Washington Courtyard by Marriott, 1900 Connecticut Ave NW ☎332-9300 or 1-800/321-3211, fax 328-7039. Dupont Circle Metro. Dwarfed by the *Hilton* over the road but much nicer rooms in a much nicer building. The top floor has splendid views. Outdoor pool and very keen prices for this area (even better at the weekend). ④–⑤.

Washington Hilton and Towers, 1919 Connecticut Ave NW ☎483-3000 or 1-800/445-8667, fax 265-8221. Dupont Circle Metro. Massive 60s convention hotel midway between Dupont Circle (downhill) and Adams-Morgan (uphill). Most of the anonymous, well-equipped rooms have good views. Facilities include pool, health club, tennis courts and bike rental. ⑦–⑧.

Windsor Park Hotel, 2116 Kalorama Rd NW ☎483-7700 or 1-800/247-3064, fax 332-4547. Pleasant little rooms in a quiet neighbourhood, just off Connecticut Avenue. Continental breakfast included. ③.

Woodley Park and Upper Northwest

Connecticut Avenue Days Inn, 4400 Connecticut Ave NW ☎244-5600 or 1-800/952-3060, fax 244-6794. Van Ness-UDC Metro. A couple of stops beyond the zoo, in a residential-university neighbourhood, with reasonable, if smallish, rooms plus all mod-cons. Call ahead for weekend and special saver rates. ③–④.

Connecticut-Woodley Guest House, 2647 Woodley Rd NW ☎667-0218. Woodley Park-Zoo Metro. Pleasant small guest house opposite the *Sheraton Washington* and near the zoo; rooms (15; some ensuite) are showing their age, but prices are good and there's free parking. Book in advance. ②–③.

India House Too, 300 Carroll St NW ☎291-1195. Takoma Metro. New hostel

Accommodation

Price categories:
① Under $50
② $50–70
③ $70–100
④ $100–140
⑤ $140–200
⑥ $200–250
⑦ $250–300
⑧ Over $300

The Metro stations noted for Adams-Morgan/ Kalorama are the nearest, but that doesn't mean they're particularly close; with luggage and at night, you'll want to take a cab.

Accommodation

in a converted Victorian hotel in a decent neighbourhood. At $12 a night for a dorm bed ($30 private room), it's the cheapest option in DC; 24-hr check-in, kitchen, BBQ (in the lovely garden), laundry and TV room. No curfew. You need passport or student ID. ①.

Kalorama Guest House at Woodley Park, 2700 Cathedral Ave NW ☎328-0860, fax 319-1262. Woodley Park-Zoo Metro. More friendly Victorian charm from the *Kalorama* people, here much nearer the Metro in Woodley Park. Two houses (19 rooms, 12 ensuite), and the same good service and facilities – comfortable brass beds, free continental breakfast, aperitifs, papers and coffee. Book well in advance. ②–③.

Omni Shoreham, 2500 Calvert St NW ☎234-0700 or 1-800/843-6664, fax 332-1384. Woodley Park-Zoo Metro. Plush, grand, Washington institution bursting with history (see p.224). Tasteful, comfortable rooms, recently renovated, many overlooking Rock Creek Park; outdoor pool and tennis courts; the foliage-filled *Garden Court* for drinks; and bargain weekend rates when available. ⑤.

Sheraton Washington, 2660 Woodley Rd NW ☎328-2000 or 1-800/325-3535, fax 387-5436. Woodley Park-Zoo Metro. Second of Woodley Park's historic, celeb-filled hotel-palaces (see p.223), the largest hotel in DC, with two pools, restaurants, and health club and bristling with attentive staff. Very good weekend and off-season discounts make this more affordable than you might think, though convention business keeps rooms full most of the year. ⑥–⑦.

Nearest Metro for Georgetown is Foggy Bottom-GWU; or take bus #30, 32, 34, 35, 36 from Pennsylvania to Wisconsin Ave.

Georgetown

Four Seasons Hotel, 2800 Pennsylvania Ave NW ☎342-0444 or 1-800/332-3442, fax 944-2076. DC's most expensive and luxurious hotel – a sympathetic redbrick at the eastern end of Georgetown – is also its most sought after. Stars, royalty and business high-rollers hanker after the lavish rooms and suites with views of Rock Creek Park or

Student Accommodation

Georgetown University (☎202/687-4560), George Washington University (☎202/994-6688), Catholic University (☎202/319-5277) and American University (☎202/885-2669) all offer a variety of dorms, doubles and apartments at budget rates in summer (June–Aug). Arrangements must be made well in advance; you may find there's a minimum stay (as much as 30 days) since the service is really only for interns or students in summer educational programmes.

the C&O Canal. Service is superb, the *Seasons* restaurant impeccable; there's a pool, fitness centre and *Garden Terrace* bar-lounge. ⑧.

Georgetown Dutch Inn, 1075 Thomas Jefferson St NW ☎337-0900 or 1-800/388-2410, fax 333-6526. All-suite hotel nicely located off M Street, near the canal towpath. Some units are two-level and sleep up to six; all have small kitchens. Free continental breakfast. ⑤.

Georgetown Inn, 1310 Wisconsin Ave NW ☎333-8900 or 1-800/424-2979, fax 333-8308. Stylish, hi-tech redbrick hotel in the heart of Georgetown with a mixed clientele. Rooms are very cheerful and you can hang out in the swish *Millennium* bar. Some weekend rates. ⑤–⑥.

Holiday Inn Georgetown, 2101 Wisconsin Ave NW ☎338-4600, fax 333-6113. The only relative cheapie in Georgetown is just that bit too far up Wisconsin (though the Wisconsin Ave buses get you down to M St pretty quickly). Newish rooms, parking, outdoor pool, fitness room and good discount rates. ④.

Latham Hotel, 3000 M St NW ☎726-5000 or 1-800/368-5922, fax 342-1800. Well-sited hotel insulated from the Georgetown noise, with a pool. Some rooms have canal and river views; there are also split-level carriage suites (in the next category up). ⑤.

Chapter 13

Cafés and Restaurants

The nation's capital has a suitably broad range of places to eat – budget diners to expense-account restaurants, serving African to Vietnamese cuisine – but it can often prove exasperating to try and find exactly the kind of food you want, when you want it. Certain neighbourhoods tend to attract similar kinds of restaurants: homey *trattorias* in businesslike New Downtown are as scarce as staid power-dining spots in Adams-Morgan. For visitors, the most annoying discovery is that the areas in which they spend much of their time – the Mall, around the White House and Federal Triangle – have a positive dearth of good-value cafés and restaurants.

Happily, the Metro system and the sheer number of taxis means that nowhere is really off-limits when it comes to choosing a restaurant. While you can eat well in central neighbourhoods, there's not much in the way of atmosphere – especially at the weekend – even in **Chinatown**, the only central ethnic enclave with its own swatch of restaurants. Only in the outer neighbourhoods can you saunter up and down, checking out the options. There's lots of opportunity to sit outside too, when the weather's clement: patios, sidewalk tables, and opening front windows are all de rigueur in DC.

Georgetown has the most varied selection of places – rowdy saloons, diners, ethnic restaurants of all shades and some rather more sniffy establishments – most of them in the few blocks either side of the M Street/Wisconsin Avenue intersection. **Dupont Circle** (chiefly P St and Connecticut Ave) is generally more upmarket, or at least more refined in its tastes: designer Italian restaurants and espresso bars are typical. The most down-to-earth spot is **Adams-Morgan**, a multi-cultural neighbourhood that throws up the city's best bargains – though prices are moving up slowly, 18th Street at Columbia Road is lined with scores of choices, all still pretty good value.

As for **culinary trends**, naturally Washington keeps up with the times. There's a lot of money about and, consequently, much support for pricey New American and new-wave Italian restaurants. Good southern and southwestern American food isn't hard to find, while Georgetown, in particular, has a rash of renowned New-York-style saloon-restaurants serving everything from oysters to strip steaks. European restaurants tend to be pricey, but there are some good bistros (Georgetown again), while *tapas* is creeping into restaurants and onto menus of many places that aren't strictly Spanish. On the whole, the Chinese restaurants in Chinatown don't hold a candle to their counterparts in similar cities – you'll do better eating Thai or Vietnamese (the best of which are across the river, in Arlington's "Little Saigon"). The city's other major treat is the comparatively large number of Ethiopian restaurants (especially in Adams-Morgan); while fans will also be able to track down places serving food

**Cafés and
Restaurants**

All telephone numbers in this chapter are area code ☎202, unless otherwise stated.

from countries as diverse as Argentina, Burma, Greece and El Salvador.

The **listings** in this chapter are split into two sections: diners, delis, cafés and coffee shops, for keeping you fuelled from breakfast through lunch; and restaurants (starts on p.273). The sections are arranged **geographically**, and correspond largely with the city chapters in the *Guide*; for **listings by cuisine**, turn to the box on p.274.

Diners, delis, cafés and coffee shops

It can be surprisingly difficult downtown to find a place to sit and grab a cup of decent coffee or a sandwich. Ubiquitous drinks and pretzel stands aside, the Mall, in particular, is almost utterly devoid of choice except for the occasional, over-subscribed museum café. The lists below pick out the best of the diners, delis, cafés and coffee shops, concentrating mainly on those where you can get more than just a drink. Most will be good for breakfast, snacks, sandwiches, light lunches and, occasionally, full meals.

City-wide

Burrito Brothers: Well-stuffed tacos and burritos to eat in or go, located at strategic hole-in-the-wall venues. *Hours vary; usually open from 11am; Georgetown branch open until midnight and beyond.*

Chesapeake Bagel Bakery: Early-opening cafés serving a dozen kinds of bagel, breads, sandwiches, and pastries. *Hours vary; usually Mon–Fri 6.30am–5pm; later and weekend opening at some locations.*

Starbuck's Coffee: Cheerful Seattle-based coffee-shop chain with good drinks and cookies, and useful locations. *Hours vary; usually daily 6.30am–6pm; later/weekend opening at some locations.*

Food Courts

There are food courts in the following central locations:

Dupont Down Under, *Dupont Circle*; p.208.

Georgetown Park Food Court, *Georgetown*; p.273.

Old Post Office Pavilion, *Old Downtown*; p.271.

Shops at National Place & Press, *Old Downtown*; p.271.

Union Station Food Court, *Union Station and Capitol Hill*; p.271.

Vie de France Café: Low-priced downtown cafés featuring fresh-baked croissants (plain and stuffed), coffee and cookies. *Hours vary; usually Mon–Fri 8am–6pm.*

Wall Street Deli: New York-style delis serving the downtown office crowd. *Hours vary; usually Mon–Fri 7am–5pm.*

Union Station and Capitol Hill

Bread and Chocolate, 666 Pennsylvania Ave SE ☎547-2875. Popular bakery-cum-coffee house with street-view seating, and tip-top sandwiches. *Eastern Market Metro. Mon–Sat 7am–7.30pm, Sun 8am–6.30pm.*

Center Café, Union Station, 50 Massachusetts Ave NE ☎682-0143. Handsome split-level café-restaurant in the main hall. Also breakfast (8–11am) or coffee – served in large French-style cups – and cake. *Union Station Metro. Mon–Thurs & Sun 8am–10.30pm, Fri & Sat 8am–midnight.*

Ice in Paradise, 615 Pennsylvania Ave SE ☎547-1554. Small Middle Eastern place whose vegetarian food and filling combo platters pull in a mixed crowd. *Eastern Market Metro. Mon–Sat 9am–7pm.*

Le Bon Café, 210 2nd St SE ☎547-7200. Close to the Library of Congress and good for a wholesome lunch of soup, salad or sandwich. *Capitol South*

Metro. Mon–Fri 8am–7pm, Sat & Sun
8am–4pm.

Misha's Deli, 210 7th St SE ☎ 547-5858.
Stuffed cabbage rolls, chicken noodle
soup, blinis and the like, opposite
Eastern Market. Sit inside amid OTT
Russian decor, or on the terrace. *Eastern
Market Metro. Mon–Sat 8am–6.30pm,
Sun 9am–5pm.*

Roasters on the Hill, 666 Pennsylvania
Ave SE ☎ 543-8355. Coffee in a million
guises, near Eastern Market. *Eastern
Market Metro. Mon–Fri 7am–6pm, Sat &
Sun 8am–6pm.*

Union Station Food Court, Union Station,
50 Massachusetts Ave NE. Massive food
court in the renovated bowels of the
station. *Union Station Metro. Mon–Sat
10am–9pm, Sun noon–6pm.*

Yamato, 201 Massachusetts Ave NE
☎ 546-3424. Informal Japanese take-out
sushi and soup; there are a few tables,
too. *Union Station Metro. Mon–Sat
9am–6pm.*

Old Downtown

Café Espresso, *Willard Inter-Continental*,
1401 Pennsylvania Ave NW ☎ 628-9100.
Relaxed Art Nouveau café – come for
coffee, breakfast, lunch or afternoon tea.
*Metro Center Metro. Mon–Fri
6.30am–11pm, Sat 7am–11pm, Sun
7am–10.30pm.*

Ebbitt Express, 675 15th St NW ☎ 347-
8881. Carry-out adjunct to the infinitely
pricier *Old Ebbitt Grill* (see p.276).
Superior salads, sandwiches and snacks
to go. *Metro Center Metro. Mon–Thurs
7.30am–8pm, Fri 7.30am–6pm.*

Harry's, 436 11th St NW ☎ 424-0053. In
the *Harrington Hotel*. Down-to-earth
meals (meatloaf, spaghetti and meat-
balls); the adjacent self-service
Harrington Café (Mon–Fri 7am–2.30pm &
5–9pm) is even cheaper. *Metro Center
Metro. Mon–Thurs & Sun 8am–2am, Fri
& Sat 8am–3am.*

Old Post Office Pavilion, 1100
Pennsylvania Ave NW ☎ 289-4224. Food
court, heaving at lunchtime with office

workers. Twenty-odd outlets, spanning
the spectrum from burgers to
Vietnamese. *Metro Center Metro.
Mon–Sat 10am–9pm, Sun noon–8pm.*

Patent Pending, National Museum of
American Art/National Portrait Gallery, 8th
and G St NW ☎ 357-2700. Just off the
central courtyard in the Patent Building,
with good pastries, sandwiches and hot
food. Some outdoor seating. *Gallery Place-
Chinatown Metro. Daily 10am–3.30pm.*

Reeve's Restaurant and Bakery, 1306 G
St NW ☎ 628-6350. Classic diner, in business since 1886, with an all-you-can-eat
breakfast and fruit bar, crisp-coated
chicken at lunchtime, and famous pies.
Metro Center Metro. Mon–Sat 7am–6pm.

Shops at National Place & Press, 1331
Pennsylvania Ave NW ☎ 783-9090.
Breakfast in the food court before hitting
the White House, or come for pre-theatre
dining. *Metro Center Metro. Mon–Sat
8am–7pm, Thurs until 8pm, Sun
noon–5pm.*

Foggy Bottom

Art Gallery Bar & Grille, 1712 I St NW
☎ 298-6658. Play the Wurlitzer jukebox
and soak up the Art Deco interior as you
tuck into salads, sandwiches, omelettes,
pizza and grills – or sit on the outdoor
patio. *Farragut West Metro. Mon–Fri
7am–10pm.*

Café des Artists, 500 17th St NW
☎ 638-1590. The Corcoran Gallery café
serves coffee, lunches and tea. Book for
the $17 gospel brunch (Sun 11am–2pm).
*Farragut West or Faragut North Metro.
Daily except Tues 11am–4.30pm, Thurs
11am–8.30pm.*

Capitol Grounds, 2100 Pennsylvania Ave
NW ☎ 293-2057. Breakfasts, gourmet
sandwiches, salads and good coffee;
handy GWU location and seats inside
and out. *Foggy Bottom-GWU Metro.
Mon–Fri 7am–6pm, Sat 8.30am–4pm,
Sun 9am–3pm.*

Eye Street Café, 1915 I St NW ☎ 457-
0773. Cosy Mediterranean café-restaurant, serving wood-fired pizzas, pitas,
pastas, salads and grills at reasonable

Cafés and
Restaurants

Cafés and Restaurants

Use Dupont Circle Metro for any of the places we've listed in Dupont Circle.

prices. *Farragut West or Foggy Bottom-GWU Metro. Mon–Thurs 11.30am–3pm & 5.30–9pm, Fri until 10pm.*

World Gourmet, 1917 F St NW ☎371-9048. Large gourmet sandwiches served to an office crowd; grab a hazelnut coffee and sit outside. *Farragut West Metro. Mon–Fri 8am–6.30pm.*

New Downtown

Barista Brava, 1425 New York Ave NW ☎628-2710. New-wave coffee bar with good Italian sandwiches and *cannoli*, and a few seats outside. *Metro Center Metro. Mon–Fri 6.30am–6pm.*

Café Promenade, *Stouffer Renaissance Mayflower*, 1127 Connecticut Ave NW ☎347-3000. A serenading harpist and Mediterranean menu set the tone in this elegant hotel coffee shop-restaurant. *Farragut North Metro. Mon–Sat 6.30am–11pm, Sun 6.30am–2.30pm.*

Cup'a Cup'a, 1911 K St NW ☎466-2872. Upmarket coffee shop on busy K Street with covered outdoor seating; you'll be lucky to find space at lunchtime. *Farragut North Metro. Mon–Fri 7am–6pm, Sat 9am–2pm.*

Sholl's Colonial Cafeteria, 1990 K St NW ☎296-3065. A DC institution, this remarkably cheap self-service café dishes out home-cooked food, cakes and pies – join the lines (enter through the Esplanade Mall), file past the "Patriotism and religion makes this a fine place to work" notice, find a seat and dig in. *Farragut West Metro. Mon–Sat 7am–10.30am, 11am–2.30pm & 4–8pm, Sun 8.30am–6pm.*

Whatsa Bagel, 1216 18th St NW ☎293-8990, also 2000 K St NW. Bagels with *anything* – cream-cheese to Mexican pizza-style – and good coffee. Especially popular on Sun. *Farragut North or Dupont Circle Metro. Mon–Thurs 7am–7pm, Fri 7am–6.30pm, Sat 7.30am–3pm, Sun 8am–3pm.*

Dupont Circle

Afterwords Café, 1517 Connecticut Ave NW ☎387-1462. In the back of

Kramerbooks, serving breakfast, great cappuccino and full meals – salad, pasta and Asian-influenced food, with plenty of vegetarian choices. Live blues and jazz Wed–Sat. *Mon–Thurs & Sun 7.30am–1am, Fri & Sat 24hr.*

Café Luna, 1633 P St ☎387-4005. Italian coffee, breakfast, weekend brunches and substantial meals at other times in a pleasing little spot with sunny sidewalk tables. *Mon–Thurs 8am–11pm, Fri 8am–1am, Sat 10am–1am, Sun 10am–11pm.*

Jolt 'n' Bolt, 1918 18th St NW ☎232-0077. Laidback townhouse tea- and coffee-house with side-alley patio, popular with a local gay crowd. *Mon–Thurs 7am–10.30pm, Fri 7am–midnight, Sat 8am–midnight.*

Luna Grill and Diner, 1301 Connecticut Ave NW ☎835-2280. "Not your usual diner" by virtue of its bright decor, planetary murals and mosaics, and wholesome blue-plate specials, vegetarian dishes, and organic coffees and teas. Outdoor patio, too. *Mon–Fri 11am–10pm, Sat & Sun 10.30am–11pm.*

The Pop Stop, 1513 17th St ☎328-0880. Funky, gay-friendly, late-opening coffee and tea place with (fairly dreadful) modern art on the walls and a patio. Coffee comes in half-pints; good cakes and music too. *Mon–Thurs & Sun 8am–2am, Fri & Sat 8am–3.30am.*

SoHo Tea & Coffee, 2150 P St NW ☎463-7646. Trendy, all-night hangout for the (gay and straight) P Street clubbers, who refuel on coffee, cakes and sandwiches all night long while checking each other out. *Mon–Wed & Sun 6am–4am, Thurs–Sat 24hr.*

Adams-Morgan

Bardia's, 2412 18th St NW ☎234-0420. Small New Orleans café-restaurant with trad jazz washing through the bright interior. All-day breakfasts and omelettes, overstuffed sandwiches, gumbos and Cajun pasta. *Woodley Park-Zoo Metro. Mon–Thurs & Sun 10am–10pm, Fri & Sat 10am–11pm.*

Woodley Park

Woodley Café, 2619 Connecticut Ave NW ☎ 332-5773. Roomy neighbourhood café-bar attracting a laidback crowd for breakfast, late-night snacks and beer, and the popular Sunday brunch. *Woodley Park-Zoo Metro. Daily 9am–1am.*

Georgetown

Booeymonger, 3265 Prospect St NW ☎ 333-4180. Crowded deli-coffee shop at the corner with Potomac St, popular with students. *Daily 8am–midnight.*

Caffe Northwest 3251 Prospect St ☎ 342-9002. Espresso-bar and bakery with sheltered terrace, bagels and good coffees. *Mon–Thurs 7am–midnight, Fri 7am–1am, Sat 8am–1am, Sun 8am–midnight.*

Dean & Deluca, 3276 M St NW ☎ 342-2500. Superior self-service conservatory-style café (and attached deli-market) in one of M Street's most handsome red-brick buildings. Croissants and cappuccino, designer salads, pasta and sandwiches. *Mon–Thurs & Sun 9am–8pm, Fri & Sat 9am–10pm.*

Georgetown Park Food Court, Level One, 3222 M St NW ☎ 298-5577. Cuisines of the world in air-conditioned Victorian splendour. *Mon–Sat 10am–9pm, Sun noon–6pm.*

Patisserie Café Didier, 3206 Grace St NW ☎ 342-9083. Outrageously good (pricey) French cakes and pastries, speciality teas and coffees, thick hot chocolate and changing daily lunches. *Tues–Sat 8am–6pm, Sun 8am–5pm.*

Restaurants

You can, of course, eat lunch or dinner at many of the diners, cafés and coffee shops listed earlier; the establishments reviewed below are special enough to make a night of it. It's always worth a phone call to check on current opening hours; if it's essential to **reserve a table**, the review makes it clear. You'll need to plan ahead to eat at the most renowned restaurants.

We've given each restaurant a **price category** (see box above), which reflects the cost of a three-course meal per person, *excluding drinks, tax and service.* These are only a guideline: most people will be hard pushed to get through three courses in many restaurants and often you'll be able to eat for less than we suggest; on the other hand, don't forget you have to add the price of **drinks** to your bill and (in most places) at least 15 percent **service**. To keep the price of meals at a minimum, look for **set lunches** (from as little as $5) and **early-bird dinners** (usually served before 7pm) – these are not just a feature of budget restaurants, and many fancier establishments are maintaining sensible pricing policies in the face of a volatile restaurant market.

Union Station and Capitol Hill

America, Union Station, 50 Massachusetts Ave NE ☎ 682-9555. Bustling restaurant-bar with a huge menu culled from all corners of the US. Double-decker restaurant inside, concourse or gallery seating outside. *Union Station Metro. Daily 11am–11pm. Moderate.*

The Monocle, 107 D St NE ☎ 546-4488. Elegant saloon-bar-restaurant with a Congress clientele tucking into crab cakes, steaks and the like in between votes. *Union Station Metro. Mon–Fri 11.30am–midnight, Sat 6–11pm. Expensive.*

Cafés and Restaurants

For Georgetown, take buses #30, 32, 34, 35 or 36 from Pennsylvania Ave NW, or Foggy Bottom-GWU Metro and walk (20 min).

Cafés and
Restaurants

Cuisines

Our restaurant reviews are grouped by neighbourhood. To track down a particular
cuisine or restaurant, consult the lists below.

African
Bukom Café p.280

American
Acme p.277
America p.273
Ben's Chili Bowl p.280
Café BaBaBlu p.281
Capitol City Brewing Company p.276
Clyde's p.281
Dixie Grill p.276
Florida Avenue Grill p.280
Fran O'Brien's p.278
Gerard's Place p.278
Hard Times Café p.283
Houston's p.282
J Paul's p.282
The Monocle p.273
Morton's of Chicago p.282
Mr Henry's p.275
New Heights p.281
Old Ebbitt Grill p.276
Old Glory p.282
Peyote Café p.281
Red Hot & Blue p.278 and p.283
Red Sage p.276
Rio Grande Café p.283
Roxanne's p.281
Sign of the Whale p.278
Stoney's p.278
Two Quail p.275

Malaysian/Indonesian
Café Asia p.278
Sarinah Satay House p.282
Straits of Malaya p.279

Brazilian
Coco Loco p.277
The Grill From Ipanema p.280

Burmese
Burma p.277

Caribbean
Hibiscus Café p.282
The Islander p.280

Chinese
City Lights of China p.279
Golden Palace p.277
Go-Lo's p.277
Hunan Chinatown p.277
Tony Cheng's Mongolian Restaurant
p.277

Ethiopian
Fasika's p.280
Meskerem p.280
Red Sea p.281
Zed's p.282

French
Au Pied de Cochon p.281
Bistro Français p.281
La Fourchette p.280
Le Lion d'Or p.278

Greek
Taverna The Greek Islands p.275
Zorba's Café p.280

Indian
The Bombay Club p.278
Madurai p.282

International
Cities p.280
Dante's p.280
Tom Tom p.281

Italian
Ecco Café p.283
Galileo p.278
Notte Luna p.282
Paolo's p.279
Pizzeria Paradiso p.279
Il Radicchio p.279, p.282 & p.283

Mexican/South American
Casa Juanita's p.276
Coco Loco p.277
Lauriol Plaza p.279
Mixtec p.280
Las Pampas p.282

Cuisines (cont')

Middle Eastern
Bacchus p.278
Skewers p.279

Seafood
Fish Market p.283
Gangplank; p.276
Georgetown Seafood Grill p.281
Hogate's p.276
Phillips p.276
Rick's Bar & Grill; p.276
Seaport Inn p.283

Spanish
Jaleo p.276

Thai
Bua p.279
Haad Thai p.276
Star of Siam p.278 & p.281
Thai Roma p.275

Vegetarian
Food For Thought p.279
Madurais p.282

Vietnamese
Little Viet Garden p.283
Miss Saigon p.280
Queen Bee p.283
Saigon Gourmet p.281
Saigonnais p.281
Saigon Inn p.282

Mr Henry's, 601 Pennsylvania Ave SE ☎546-8412. Saloon-bar-restaurant, with outside patio, charcoal grill and loyal gay crowd. Even the most expensive choices – the steak and shrimp plates – don't exceed $10; burgers are half-price on Mon, and jazz trios play weekly. *Eastern Market Metro. Mon–Thurs & Sun 11am–12.30am, Fri & Sat 11am–2am. Inexpensive.*

Taverna The Greek Islands, 307 Pennsylvania Ave SE ☎547-8360. Unsophisticated, rustic Greek joint. Order something from the grill (all meat) and you won't need appetizers. Pricier fish specialities and wine by the carafe (if

you ask). *Capitol South Metro. Mon–Sat 11am–midnight, Sun 5–11pm. Moderate.*

Thai Roma, 313 Pennsylvania Ave SE ☎544-2338. Thai sauces over Italian pasta are not always as successful as you'd hope, but there's a full Thai menu too, and drinks in the adjacent Conrad Pub. *Capitol South Metro. Mon–Fri noon–10.30pm, Sat & Sun 5–11pm. Moderate.*

Two Quail, 320 Massachusetts Ave NE ☎543-8030. Romantic little townhouse bistro serving changing menus of modern American food. Set lunches are good value; call to reserve. *Union Station Metro. Mon–Fri 11.30am–2.30pm &*

Budget:
Under $10
Inexpensive:
$10–15
Moderate:
$15–25
Expensive:
$25–40
Very
Expensive:
Over $40
See p.273 for
more details.

Monument, Museum and Gallery Cafés and Restaurants

Most of Washington's major sightseeing attractions have associated cafés and fast-food restaurants and often they're the only local option for lunch, especially on and around the Mall. Those listed below are particularly good; follow the page numbers for more details.

Corcoran Gallery of Art (*Café des Artists*); p.271.
Library of Congress Cafeteria; p.122.
National Gallery of Art; p.91.
National Museum of American Art/National Portrait Gallery (*Patent Pending*); p.271.

National Museum of American History; p.97.
National Museum of Women in the Arts; p.199.
Supreme Court Cafeteria; p.118.
US Capitol; p.114.

Cafés and
Restaurants

Budget:
Under $10
Inexpensive:
$10–15
Moderate:
$15–25
Expensive:
$25–40
Very
Expensive:
Over $40
See p.273 for
more details.

5.30–10pm, Sat & Sun 5.30–10.30pm.
Moderate–Expensive.

Southwest/Waterfront

Gangplank/Rick's Bar & Grill, 600 Water
St SW ☎554-5000. The elegant upstairs
Gangplank has the better water views,
seafood specials and higher prices;
downstairs in *Rick's* (or on the outdoor
patio) there are tasty burgers and grilled
fish. *Waterfront Metro. Gangplank:
Tues–Thurs 11.30am–1.30pm &
5.30–9.30pm, Fri & Sat 11.30am–2.30pm
& 5.30–10.30pm; Rick's: Mon–Thurs
11.30am–midnight, Fri & Sat
11.30am–2am.*

Hogate's, 800 Water St SW ☎484-6300.
Marina restaurant with zealous nautical
interior, a/c bar and patio. There's a
good spiced shrimp lunch buffet ($13) as
well as full seafood menu. *L'Enfant Plaza
Metro. Mon–Thurs 11am–11pm, Fri
11am–midnight, Sat noon–midnight, Sun
10.30am–10pm. Moderate–Expensive.*

Phillips, 900 Water St SW ☎488-8515.
Renowned city seafood restaurant. Eating
à la carte is pretty much as you'd expect
– good but pricey – but there are lunch
(Mon–Sat $15) and dinner ($25) seafood
buffets and Sunday brunch ($23), too.
*L'Enfant Plaza Metro. Daily 11am–11pm.
Moderate–Expensive.*

Old Downtown

Capitol City Brewing Company, 1100
New York Ave NW, enter at 11th & H
☎628-2222. Better known as a brew-
pub (see p.285), the kitchen serves up
admirable burgers, grilled sausages,
pasta, salads and other bar standards.
Book ahead at weekends. *Metro Center
Metro. Mon–Thurs & Sun 11am–11pm,
Fri & Sat 11am–midnight. Inexpensive.*

Casa Juanita's, 908 11th St NW ☎737-
2520. Family-run Salvadorean-Mexican
restaurant with histrionic Latin American
music, excellent-value combo dishes and
bargain house wine. *Metro Center Metro.
Mon–Thurs & Sun 11am–10.30pm, Fri &
Sat 11am–11pm. Inexpensive.*

Dixie Grill, 518 10th St NW ☎628-4800.

Raucous Southern bar-restaurant where
the main emphasis is on downing pitch-
ers of beer. The menu is short but strong
on meaty roadhouse classics, decor is
flags and licence plates. Sat night jazz.
*Metro Center Metro. Mon
11.30am–10.30pm, Tues–Fri
11.30am–1am, Sat noon–1am, Sun
noon–10pm. Inexpensive–Moderate.*

Haad Thai, 1100 New York Ave NW
☎682-1111. Classy Thai restaurant, featuring coconut-milk curries, tasty
steamed fish and shrimp and spicy
soups. *Mount Vernon Square-UDC Metro.
Mon–Fri 11.30am–2.30pm &
5–10.30pm, Sat & Sun noon–10.30pm.
Moderate.*

Jaleo, 480 7th St NW ☎628-7949.
Upscale *tapas* bar-restaurant with dim
lighting and fashionable young things
draped across the tables. Reserve for
lunch or dinner; or call in early for a
glass of good house wine and *tapas*.
*Gallery Place-Chinatown Metro.
Mon–Thurs 11.30am–2.30pm &
5.30–10.30pm, Fri & Sat
11.30am–2.30pm & 5.30–11.30pm, Sun
5.30–10pm. Inexpensive
(tapas)–Expensive (restaurant).*

Old Ebbitt Grill, 675 15th St NW ☎347-
4800. In business in various locations
since 1856, this plush re-creation of a
nineteenth-century tavern is a joy, with
mahogany bar (serving microbrews), gas
chandeliers, leather booths and gilt mirrors. Everything from burgers to oysters,
breakfasts to late dinners.
Professional/politico clientele. *Metro
Center Metro. Mon–Fri 7.30am–midnight,
Sat 8am–midnight, Sun 9.30am–midnight, bar open Mon–Thurs & Sun until
1.30am, Fri & Sat until 2.30am
Moderate–Expensive.*

Red Sage, 605 14th St NW ☎638-4444.
Landmark Southwestern restaurant
(reservations essential), owned by Mark
Miller and dripping with Santa Fe chic,
featuring rotisserie-grilled meats, fish and
vegetarian specials. The funkily decorated *Chili* bar is less exclusive and easier
to score a table; otherwise sink a

Late-Night Eats

At all the places listed below, you'll be able to order a meal after midnight on at least one night of the week (usually Fri & Sat).

Cafés and
Restaurants

schooner of *Red Sage Ale* at the bar. *Metro Center Metro. Mon–Sat 11.30am–2.15pm & 5.30–10.30pm, Sun 5–10pm. Expensive (Chili Bar)–Very Expensive (restaurant)* .

Chinatown

Burma, 740 6th St NW ☎638-1280. Plain 2nd-floor dining room with Burmese art, approachable staff and very filling food. The noodles are great (try the pork in black bean sauce), and the beer is Thai or Chinese. *Mon–Thurs 11am–3pm & 6–9.30pm, Fri & Sat 11am–3pm & 6–10.30pm, Sun 6–9.30pm. Inexpensive.*

Coco Loco, 810 7th St NW ☎289-2626. Large but relaxed in-crowd restaurant, where you can choose from Mexican *tapas* or all-you-can-eat Brazilian grills. The *tapas* ($4–10 a plate) is the way to go, a mile away in quality from most tired Spanish offerings. Live jazz and Brazilian dancing all week. *Mon–Wed 11.30am–2.30pm & 6–10pm, Thurs & Fri until 11pm, Sat 6–11pm, Sun 6–10pm. Moderate–Expensive.*

Golden Palace, 720–724 7th St NW ☎783-1225. Authentic dim sum restaurant, hugely popular with Chinese families on Sun, when you'll have to wait in line. *Mon & Tues 11am–10pm,*

Wed–Sun 11am–11pm. Inexpensive (dim sum)–Moderate (meals).

Go-Lo's, 604 H St NW ☎347-4656. Friendly spot where local office workers are greeted by name: rice/noodle lunch plates are great value, while meals mix Cantonese and Szechuan influences. *Mon–Thurs & Sun 11am–midnight, Fri & Sat 11am–2am.*

Hunan Chinatown, 624 H St NW ☎783-5858. Sleekly furnished, Western-friendly restaurant (you'll have to ask for chopsticks), where spiciness replaces taste on occasion. You probably won't need appetizers, though the won tun in chilli sauce are good. *Mon–Thurs & Sun 11am–11pm, Fri & Sat 11am–midnight. Moderate.*

Tony Cheng's Mongolian Restaurant, 619 H St NW ☎842-8669. Hot-pots (from $5) and all-you-can-eat Mongolian barbecues ($14) – good participatory affairs in one of Chinatown's more enjoyable spots. *Mon–Thurs & Sun 11am–11pm, Fri & Sat 11am–midnight. Inexpensive.*

New Downtown

Acme, 1207 19th St NW ☎833-2263. Funky little joint on three floors, and with summer patio dining. Burgers, chicken, meatloaf and salads at good prices; live blues on Tues, cheap beer and football nights in season, pool table upstairs.

Gallery-Place-Chinatown Metro for all of the places listed in Chinatown.

Cafés and Restaurants

Budget:
Under $10
Inexpensive:
$10–15
Moderate:
$15–25
Expensive:
$25–40
Very
Expensive:
Over $40
See p.273 for
more details.

Dupont Circle Metro. Mon–Thurs & Sun 11.30am–2am, Fri & Sat 11.30am–3am. Inexpensive.

Bacchus, 1827 Jefferson Place NW, between M and N St ☎785-0734. Somewhat pricey but very good Lebanese restaurant, with excellent hummus and tangy kebabs. *Dupont Circle Metro. Mon–Thurs noon–2.30pm & 6–10pm, Fri until 10.30pm, Sat 6–10.30pm. Moderate–Expensive.*

The Bombay Club, 815 Connecticut Ave NW ☎659-3727. Sleek Indian restaurant a block from the White House (and a Clinton family favourite) – Raj-style surroundings, piano accompaniment and dishes a little out of the ordinary. *Farragut North or West Metros. Mon–Sat 11.30am–2.30pm & 6–11pm. Moderate.*

Café Asia, 1134 19th St NW ☎659-2696. Breezy pan-Asian restaurant featuring dishes from satay to sushi – try the coconut and lemon grass soup. *Dupont Circle or Farragut North Metros. Mon–Sat 11.30am–2.30pm & 5–11pm. Inexpensive.*

Fran O'Brien's, *Capital Hilton*, 1001 16th St NW ☎783-2599. Former Redskins player's steak house-saloon in the *Hilton* basement: check out the Hall of Fame, munch on a bountiful steak or chop and watch the game on TV. *McPherson Square Metro. Mon–Fri 11.30am–3pm & 5–10.30pm, Sat & Sun 5–10.30pm. Moderate–Expensive.*

Galileo, 1110 21st St NW ☎293-7191. Superb Northern Italian cuisine from wonderchef Roberto Donna. Risotto makes a regular appearance on the ever-changing menu; service is snappy, and the wine list impressive. Book well in advance. *Foggy Bottom or Farragut West Metros. Mon–Thurs 11.30am–2pm & 5.30–10pm, Fri until 10.30pm, Sat 5.30–10.30pm, Sun 5.30–10.30pm. Very Expensive.*

Gerard's Place, 915 15th St NW ☎737-4445. Accomplished Michelin-starred New American cuisine. The $55 five-course fixed menu is a good choice; add on $30 if you want a different wine with

every course. Booking essential. *McPherson Square Metro. Mon–Thurs 11.30am–2pm & 5.30–10pm, Fri until 10.30pm, Sat 5.30–10.30pm. Very Expensive.*

Le Lion d'Or, 1150 Connecticut Ave NW ☎296-7972. Classic French cooking at extremely high prices, though the set lunch is affordable. Reserve in advance, dress smartly and brush up on your French if you want to get the best out of the menu. *Farragut North Metro. Mon–Sat 6–10pm. Very Expensive.*

Notte Luna, 809 15th St ☎408-9500. Wood-fired pizzas and trendy Italian dishes in neon-lit power-dining spot with summer patio. *McPherson Square Metro. Mon–Thurs 11.30am–10.30pm, Fri 11.30am–midnight, Sat 5.30pm–midnight. Moderate–Expensive.*

Red Hot & Blue, 1120 19th St NW ☎466-6731. Bright Memphis-style BBQ joint sprayed with Elvis posters, serving ribs – wet (with sauce) or dry – or smoked meat with beans, coleslaw and potato salad. *Dupont Circle or Farragut North Metros. Mon–Thurs 11am–1pm, Fri & Sat 11am–midnight, Sun noon–10pm. Inexpensive.*

Sign of the Whale, 1825 M St ☎785-1110. Downtown saloon best-known for its supreme burgers (half-price on Mon), grilled to perfection, though there's also pasta, fish and other entrees, most well under $10. *Farragut North Metro. Daily 11.30am–10.30pm; bar open until 2am (Mon–Thurs & Sun), 3am (Fri & Sat). Inexpensive.*

Star of Siam, 1136 19th St NW ☎785-2838. Thai townhouse restaurant reputed for its excellently spiced curries, soups and noodles. *Dupont Circle or Farragut North Metros. Mon–Sat 11.30am–11pm, Sun 4–10pm. Inexpensive.*

Stoney's, 1307 L St NW ☎347-9163. Down-to-earth saloon and bar, thirty years old and revelling in its big servings – burgers, fries, chilli and country cooking. *McPherson Square Metro. Daily 9am–1am. Budget–Inexpensive.*

Hotel Restaurants

Some of DC's best power-dining restaurants are in its glitzier hotels. The pick of the bunch are listed below: expect first-rate food and service and high ($60–100 a head) prices. Always call ahead for reservations. And see *Accommodation* (Chapter 12) for hotel reviews.

Four Seasons Hotel, *Seasons*, 2800 Pennsylvania Ave NW ☎342-0444. European.

Hay-Adams Hotel, *Lafayette*, 1 Lafayette Square NW ☎638-6600. Contemporary American.

Jefferson Hotel, 1200 16th St NW ☎347-2200. American regional.

Latham Hotel, *Citronelle*, 3000 M St NW ☎625-2150. Contemporary French-American.

Morrison Clark Inn, 1015 L St NW ☎898-1200. New American.

Ritz Carlton, *Jockey Club*, 2100 Massachusetts Ave NW ☎293-2100. French-European.

Willard Inter-Continental, *Willard Room*, 1401 Pennsylvania Ave NW ☎637-7440. Classic American-European.

Cafés and Restaurants

Dupont Circle

Bua, 1635 P St ☎265-0828. Charming Thai restaurant whose upstairs terrace overlooks P Street. Filling lunch specials ($6) and great noodles. *Mon–Thurs 11.30am–2.30pm & 5–10.30pm, Fri until 11pm, Sat noon–4pm & 5–11pm, Sun until 10.30pm. Moderate.*

City Lights of China, 1731 Connecticut Ave NW ☎265-6688. Above-average, well-priced Chinese restaurant, with spicy Szechuan and Hunan specialties, and a strong emphasis on seafood. *Mon–Thurs 11.30am–10.30pm, Fri 11.30am–11pm, Sat noon–11pm, Sun noon–10.30pm. Inexpensive–Moderate.*

Food for Thought, 1738 Connecticut Ave NW ☎797-1095. DC's original arty (mostly) vegetarian café, keeping its mellow clientele happy with live music, salads, sandwiches, rice plates and organic food, all around $6–9, and cheap lunch combos. *Mon–Thurs 11.30am–12.30am, Fri & Sat 11.30am–2am, Sun 4pm–12.30am. Budget–Inexpensive.*

Lauriol Plaza, 1801 18th St NW ☎387-0035. Lines form early in this packed, family-run restaurant for the excellent Mexican, Spanish and Latin American food – the fajitas are stunning. Eat on the terrace in summer. *Mon–Thurs & Sun 11.30am–11pm, Fri & Sat noon–midnight. Moderate.*

Pizzeria Paradiso, 2029 P St NW ☎223-1245. Arguably DC's best pizzeria, with lines forming nightly on the steps outside the nice old townhouse. Thunderingly good food and house wine at $10 a bottle. *Mon–Thurs 11am–11pm, Fri & Sat 11am–midnight, Sun noon–10pm. Inexpensive.*

Il Radicchio, 1509 17th St NW ☎986-2627. Roberto Donna's designer-rustic pizza-and-pasta emporium, tossing out superb wood-fired pizzas (under $10), or all the spaghetti you can eat ($6) dressed with one of twenty sauces (up to $4). No reservations: expect a wait. *Mon–Thurs 11.30am–11pm, Fri & Sat 11.30am–midnight, Sun 5–11pm. Inexpensive–Moderate.*

Skewers, 1633 P St NW ☎387-7400. Attractive Middle-Eastern restaurant (above *Café Luna*), serving grilled spits of meat or seafood with delicate rice. *Mon–Thurs 11.30am–11pm, Fri 11.30am–midnight, Sat 5pm–midnight, Sun 5–11pm. Moderate.*

Straits of Malaya, 1836 18th St NW ☎483-1483. Popular neighbourhood Southeast Asian restaurant, with particularly good Malaysian choices, great noodles and seafood and a rooftop terrace. The attached, candlelit *Larry's Lounge* bar/coffee house serves snacks and

Use Dupont Circle Metro for all of the places listed in Dupont Circle.

Cafés and
Restaurants

*All places
listed in
Adams-Morgan
are within a
few blocks of
the 18th St,
Columbia Rd,
Calvert St
junction; near-
est Metros are
Woodley Park
Zoo or Dupont
Circle.*

appetizers. *Mon–Fri noon–2pm &
5.30–11pm, Sat 5.30–11pm, Sun
5.30–10.30pm. Moderate.*

Zorba's Café, 1612 20th St NW ☎387-
8555. Filling Greek combo platters,
kebabs and sandwiches. It's self-service,
with sidewalk seating in summer.
*Mon–Sat 11am–11.30pm, Sun
noon–10.30pm. Budget.*

Shaw

Ben's Chili Bowl, 1213 U St NW ☎667-
0909. Venerable U Street hangout, serving
renowned chilli dogs, burgers and fries at
booths and counter stools. A scene in *The
Pelican Brief* was shot here, as photos on
the wall attest. *U Street-Cardozo Metro.
Mon–Thurs 6am–2am, Fri & Sat
6am–4am, Sun noon–7pm. Budget.*

Dante's, 1522 14th St NW ☎667-7260.
On the eastern fringes of Dupont Circle
(take care at night), punky, alternative
Dante's attracts a mix from local theatre-
goers to late-night Generation Xers. Food
is ethnic/Mediterranean, with high veggie
count. *Dupont Circle Metro. Mon–Thurs &
Sun 5pm–3am, Fri & Sat 5pm–4am.
Budget–Inexpensive.*

Florida Avenue Grill, 1100 Florida Ave
NW ☎265-1586. Southern-style diner
serving hearty meals for almost half a
century to locals and stray celebs. *U
Street-Cardozo Metro. Tues–Sat
6.30am–9pm. Budget.*

Adams-Morgan

Bukom Café, 2442 18th St NW ☎265-
4600. Stylish place with laidback bar,
serving delicious West African dishes –
like *obe ila*, a soup with okra and
smoked fish, and *nkatikwan*, chicken
with peanuts, for around $10. All washed
down with African beers and African
music (live Wed–Sat). *Tues–Thurs
4pm–midnight, Fri & Sat 4pm–3am, Sun
4pm–2am. Moderate.*

Cities, 2424 18th St NW ☎328-7194.
Trendy restaurant-bar with regularly
switching (cities-of-the-world) decor and
menu. The outdoor terrace overlooks the
Adams-Morgan streetlife parade; dance

upstairs to World music. *Mon–Thurs
5–11pm, Fri & Sat 5–11.30pm; bar open
until 2am, Fri & Sat until 3am. Moderate.*

Fasika's, 2477 18th St NW ☎797-7673.
Most upscale of the local Ethiopian places,
with sidewalk seating, live music three
nights a week and spicy stews around
$10–12. *Daily noon–1am. Moderate.*

La Fourchette, 2429 18th St NW ☎332-
3077. Longstanding, traditionally furnished brasserie with sidewalk patio,
serving French classics at closely packed
tables. The good-value menu *prix fixé*
(11am–6.30pm) offers three courses for
under $13. *Mon–Fri 11.30am–10.30pm,
Sat 4–11pm, Sun 4–10pm. Moderate.*

The Grill from Ipanema, 1858 Columbia
Rd NW ☎986-0757. Just south of
Calvert, and worth visiting for the name
alone; the *feijoada* (Brazilian meat stew)
is great, too – served on Wed and
weekend nights. Try the baked clams to
start and watch your *caipirinha* (rum
cocktail) intake. *Mon–Thurs 5–11pm, Fri
5pm–midnight, Sat noon–midnight, Sun
noon–11pm. Moderate.*

The Islander, 1762 Columbia Rd NW
☎234-4955. Dingy stairs lead up to a
bright no-frills dining room serving good,
filling Caribbean food. *Mon 5–10pm,
Tues–Thurs noon–10pm, Fri & Sat
noon–1pm. Inexpensive.*

Meskerem, 2434 18th St NW ☎462-
4100. The district's favourite Ethiopian
hangout, with funky decor and cheery
staff. Eat with your hands, scooping food
up with the sourdough *injera* bread; the
messob platter gives you a taste of
everything, and there's lots of vegetarian
and seafood, too. *Daily noon–11pm.
Inexpensive–Moderate.*

Miss Saigon, 1847 Columbia Rd NW
☎667-1900. Reliable Vietnamese food
amid oversized palm fronds. Eager staff
prompt you towards house specials – try
the warming winter seafood hotpot.
*Mon–Thurs noon–10.30pm, Fri
noon–11pm, Sat 5–11pm, Sun 5–10pm.
Moderate.*

Mixtec, 1792 Columbia Rd NW ☎332-
1011. Bright, rather clinical surroundings

for great-tasting, low-priced Mexican food – tacos and tortillas, plus spit-roasted chicken, mussels steamed with chillis, and a soothing *menudo*. *Mon–Thurs & Sun 11am–10.30pm, Fri & Sat 11am–1am. Inexpensive.*

Peyote Café, 2319 18th St NW ☎462-8830. Lively basement Southwestern bar and grill. Food is above average: the faji-tas, particularly, are tip-top. *Roxanne's* upstairs (same phone) has a more adventurous, more expensive menu, also Southwestern, and a roof terrace. *Mon–Thurs 5pm–2am, Fri 5pm–3am, Sat noon–3am, Sun noon–2am. Moderate.*

Red Sea, 2463 18th St NW ☎483-5000. Plentiful portions of spicy food (including vegetarian specials) keep diners coming back to the oldest Ethiopian place in the neighbourhood – the *yetsom wat* gives a taste of six veggie dishes. There's a good beer list, too. *Daily noon–midnight. Inexpensive–Moderate.*

Saigonnais, 2307 18th St NW ☎232-5300. Gourmet Vietnamese food in cozy townhouse – splash out on the whole steamed fish. Prices are cheaper at lunch. The owners have opened *Yin Yang Noodles and Grill* just up the street: more informal but equally highly rated. *Daily 11.30am–3pm & 5.30–11pm. Moderate.*

Star of Siam, 2446 18th St NW ☎986-4133. Warehouse-style restaurant with a great roof terrace and spot-on food. *Mon–Thurs 5–11pm, Fri 5pm–midnight, Sat noon–midnight, Sun noon–11pm. Inexpensive–Moderate.*

Tom Tom, 2333 18th St NW ☎588-1300. Big street-facing windows, booths and a buzzy roof terrace draw in a fancy crowd for wood-fired pizza, *tapas*, sal-ads, mix-and-match pastas, and desserts. *Mon–Thurs & Sun 5–11pm, Fri & Sat 5pm–midnight, bar open until 2am. Inexpensive–Moderate.*

Woodley Park

New Heights, 2317 Calvert St NW ☎234-4110. Fashionable, new-wave American restaurant serving an inventive,

seasonal menu which culls its influences from many cuisines. Book ahead in sum-mer to sit outside, especially for Sun brunch. *Mon–Thurs & Sun 5.30–10.30pm, Fri & Sat 5.30–11pm, bar open until 12.30am. Expensive.*

Saigon Gourmet, 2635 Connecticut Ave NW ☎265-1360. Quality Vietnamese restaurant with lots of surprises, not least that the food isn't overspiced for once – try the roasted quail or a traditional soup. *Daily 11.30am–3pm & 5–10.30pm. Inexpensive.*

Georgetown

Au Pied du Cochon, 1335 Wisconsin Ave NW ☎333-5440. Casual 24-hr bistro with conservatory dining. Breakfast (until noon) and early-bird $10 dinners (3–8pm) are great value, or pick from a *carte* of eggs, fish, coq au vin, steaks and the like. *Daily 24hr. Inexpensive–Moderate.*

Bistro Français, 3124–3128 M St NW ☎338-3830. Late-opening bistro with renowned French cooking, from a simple steak-frites, rotisserie chicken or roast pigeon to more complex, traditional dishes. There's a set dinner (under $20), but check the specials board for what the kitchen does best. *Mon–Thurs & Sun 11am–3am, Fri & Sat 11am–4am. Moderate.*

Café BaBaBlu, 3235 M St NW ☎965-5353. Brick walls, cacti, picture windows and, best of all, an upper-storey glassed in *terrazza*. More Mex than Tex with weekend jazz-blues trios. *Mon–Fri 4pm–2am, Sat & Sun 10.30am–3am. Moderate.*

Clyde's, 3236 M St NW ☎333-9180. Classic New York-style saloon-restaurant featuring the obligatory checked table-cloths, Art Deco lampshades and bur-nished wood interior. It's a Georgetown institution, and prices are accordingly high; good Sun brunch. Book ahead. *Mon–Fri 11am–2am, Sat 9am–3am, Sun 9am–2am. Moderate.*

Georgetown Seafood Grill, 3063 M St NW ☎333-7038. Bustling seafood bar-

Cafés and Restaurants

Budget:
Under $10
Inexpensive:
$10–15
Moderate:
$15–25
Expensive:
$25–40
Very
Expensive:
Over $40
See p.273 for more details.

Woodley Park-Zoo Metro for all the places listed in Woodley Park.

Cafés and Restaurants

Budget:
Under $10
Inexpensive:
$10–15
Moderate:
$15–25
Expensive:
$25–40
Very Expensive:
Over $40
See p.273 for more details.

restaurant, with oysters and clams on ice, and adventurous grilled fish. *Mon–Thurs & Sun 11am–3pm & 6–11pm, Fri & Sat 11am–3pm & 6pm–midnight. Expensive.*

Hibiscus Café, 3401 K St NW ☎338-0408. Cool Caribbean restaurant with hard-to-get outdoor seating, and modish food and style. Book in advance. *Tues–Thurs 11am–2.30pm & 6–11pm, Fri & Sat 11am–2.30pm & 6pm–midnight. Moderate.*

Houston's, 1065 Wisconsin Ave NW ☎338-7760. Flame-grilled burgers, barbecued ribs and other all-American standbys at a popular brick and wood saloon (just south of M). Lines form at peak times; no reservations. *Mon–Thurs & Sun 11am–11pm, Fri & Sat 11am–1am. Moderate.*

Il Radicchio, 1211 Wisconsin Ave NW ☎337-2627. The Georgetown branch of Roberto Donna's pizza-and-pasta house is less frenetically trendy than the Dupont Circle original (see p.279), but the studenty clientele laps up the same great wood-fired pizzas and mix-and-match spaghetti-and-sauce combos. *Mon–Thurs 11.30am–11pm, Fri & Sat 11.30am–midnight, Sun 5–11pm. Inexpensive–Moderate.*

J Paul's, 3218 M St NW ☎333-3450. Rivalling *Clyde's* in clientele and style, this just gets the edge by virtue of brewing its own scrumptious *Amber Ale*. Standard grill/barbecue menu, all of it excellent; try the famous crab cakes. *Mon–Thurs 11.30am–1.30am, Fri & Sat 11.30am–2.30am, Sun 10.30am–1.30am. Moderate.*

Las Pampas, 3291 M St NW ☎333-5151. Reputed Argentinian grill-restaurant: *churrasco* (grilled beef), *parrillada* (mixed grill) and rotisserie chicken are the specialities. *Mon–Thurs & Sun 11am–11pm, Fri 11am–1am, Sat noon–1am. Moderate.*

Madurai, 3316 M St NW ☎333-0997. DC's favourite Indian veg restaurant, now part of the equally good – but meat-serving – *Tandoor* (☎333-3376). There's

an all-you-can-eat Sunday buffet. *Daily 11.30am–2.30pm & 5.30–10.30pm. Inexpensive.*

Morton's of Chicago, 3251 Prospect St NW ☎342-6258. The city's top steak house. Pick your cut or go for entrees ($20 and up) from chicken to swordfish. *Mon–Sat 5.30–11pm, Sun 5–10pm. Very Expensive.*

Old Glory, 3139 M St NW ☎337-3406. Rollicking barbecue restaurant with hickory smoke rising in earnest from the kitchen. Accompany the huge portions of ribs and chicken with one of half-a-dozen sauces on every table. Live R&B three nights. *Mon–Thurs & Sun 11.30am–12.30am, Fri & Sat 11.30am–2am. Moderate.*

Paolo's, 1303 Wisconsin Ave NW, at M St ☎333-7353. Designer dining with a few, hotly contested, tables open to the sidewalk. Gourmet pizza – feta cheese, grappa-cured salmon and broccoli – and even better pasta: make room for dessert. *Mon–Thurs 11.30am–2am, Fri & Sat 11.30am–3am, Sun 11am–2am. Moderate.*

Saigon Inn, 2928 M St NW ☎337-5588. The Vietnamese food served in this pastel-coloured restaurant makes a few concessions to Western tastes, but is still eminently enjoyable – the lunch deal (four dishes for $4, Mon–Fri 11am–3pm) is a bargain. *Mon–Sat 11am–11pm, Sun noon–11pm. Inexpensive.*

Sarinah Satay House, 1338 Wisconsin Ave NW ☎337-2955. Indonesian restaurant, hidden from the street – inside, there's a veritable garden and reasonably authentic food including satay, and noodle rice plates that will suit vegetarians. *Tues–Sat noon–3pm & 6–10.30pm, Sun 6–10.30pm. Inexpensive–Moderate.*

Zed's, 3318 M St NW ☎333-4710. The spot for Ethiopian food in Georgetown, and an intimate one at that. The set lunch is a snip at $5; neither does eating from the menu break the bank. *Mon–Thurs & Sun 11am–11pm, Fri & Sat 11am–1am. Inexpensive.*

Arlington, VA

Little Viet Garden, 3012 Wilson Blvd
☎703/522-9686. Mainstay of "Little
Saigon", with cheap, authentic food served
with gusto. Go for the *pho* (noodle soup)
and sit outside in summer. *Clarendon
Metro. Mon–Fri 11am–2.30pm & 5–10pm,
Sat & Sun 11am–10pm. Inexpensive.*

Queen Bee, 3181 Wilson Blvd
☎703/527-3444. Huge lines outside for
some of the best Vietnamese food in
town, with renowned spring rolls, huge
bowls of noodle soup, Saigon pancakes
and grilled shrimp. *Clarendon Metro.
Daily 11.15am–10pm.
Inexpensive–Moderate.*

Il Radicchio, 1801 Clarendon Blvd
☎703/276-2627. The cross-river branch
of Roberto Donna's pizza-and pasta
empire is great value: wood-fired pizzas
and mix-and-match spaghetti-and-sauce
combos. *Courthouse or Rosslyn Metro.
Mon–Sat 11.30am–10pm, Sun 5–10pm.
Inexpensive–Moderate.*

Red Hot and Blue, 1600 Wilson Blvd
☎703/276-7427. Memphis barbecue
joint that spawned a chain, serving the
best ribs in the district. *Court House
Metro. Mon–Thurs 11am–10pm, Fri &
Sat 11am–11pm, Sun noon–10pm.
Inexpensive–Moderate.*

Rio Grande Café, 4301 N Fairfax Dr,
Ballston ☎703/528-3131. Rollicking Tex-
Mex hangout with in-your-face
Southwestern decor and fine, immense,
combo platters. Come on Thurs for the
cabrito (kid goat) special. *Ballston Metro.
Mon–Thurs 11am–10.30pm, Fri
11am–11.30pm, Sat 11.30am–11.30pm,
Sun 11.30am–10.30pm. Moderate.*

Alexandria, VA

Ecco Café, 220 N Lee St ☎703/684-
0321. Gourmet pizza and pasta joint
with a neighbourhood feel, Sun jazz
brunch and good lunch specials.
*Mon–Thurs 11am–11pm, Fri & Sat
11am–midnight, Sun noon–10pm.
Inexpensive–Moderate.*

Fish Market, 105 King St ☎703/836-
5676. Brick-walled restaurant with terrace, serving oysters and chowder at the
bar or fried fish platters, pastas and fish
entrees. Jazz at night. *Daily 11am–midnight; bar until 2am. Moderate.*

Hard Times Café, 1404 King St
☎703/638-5340. Three styles of chilli,
country music and microbrews add up to
one of Alexandria's better American
restaurants. *Mon–Thurs 11am–10pm, Fri
& Sat 11am–11pm, Sun noon–10pm.
Inexpensive.*

Seaport Inn, 6 King St ☎703/549-2341.
Romantic seafood dinners in an historic
eighteenth-century building at the bottom of King Street. Pricey but thoroughly
nice. *Daily noon–11pm.
Moderate–Expensive.*

Cafés and
Restaurants

*For transport
details for
Alexandria,
see p.249–250.*

Chapter 14

Bars and Clubs

Bars and pubs congregate in distinct neighbourhoods, notably Capitol Hill (near Union Station and along Pennsylvania Ave SE), Georgetown (M and Wisconsin), Dupont Circle (along 17th, Connecticut Ave and P), Adams-Morgan (18th and Columbia) and, latterly, around U Street (near the Metro) in Shaw. The few bars downtown tend to cater for an after-work crowd, and are utterly lifeless at the weekend. There's a thriving – if relatively small-scale – **gay scene**, with most of the action in Dupont Circle, especially on P Street (between 21st and 22nd) and 17th Street (between P and R).

Most bars **open** daily from around noon until 2am, often later at the weekends. Virtually all have **happy hours** where beers and rail drinks are two-for-one, or at least heavily discounted; optimum time for this is Monday–Friday 4–7pm. Many bars also offer free snacks to happy-hour drinkers.

DC's **club scene** moves at a frenetic pace, chronicled in several good **listings papers**: *CityPaper*; the *Washington Post*'s "Weekend" section; *University Reporter*; *Scene* and the gay-oriented *Washington Blade* and *Metro Weekly* all carry schedules, reviews and adverts. The places listed here are some of the more durable venues in a city where clubs open and close with alarming regularity; you're sure to find others that are new or some that have changed hands and style. Many places also feature different nights when the music

and clientele may change radically; call to check if you're aiming for somewhere specific.

Plenty of places have low or no **cover charges**. Where you do need to pay to get in, expect to have to stump up between $5 and $15 (highest at weekends). **Opening hours** vary wildly, though most places don't get going until well after 11pm and stay open until at least 3am, with some continuing (especially at weekends) until 5am. If you're going to be out this late, make sure you have a taxi number with you (see p.44); many clubs are in dubious parts of town where walking around in the small hours invites trouble. It's also as well to take **photo-ID**, or your passport, with you. You won't get in many places without one, and you need to be over 21 to drink alcohol in DC.

Capitol Hill

The Dubliner, *Phoenix Park Hotel*, 520 N Capitol St NW ☎737-3773. As far removed from a regular hotel bar as you could get: a good-time, wooden-vaulted Irish pub, with *Guinness* on draught, boisterous conversation and live Irish music. *Union Station Metro. Mon–Thurs 11am–2am, Fri 11am–3am, Sat 7am–3am, Sun 7am–2am.*

Hawk 'n' Dove, 329 Pennsylvania Ave SE ☎543-3300. Famous old pub with battered bar hung with football pennants, bottles and bric-a-brac. The young, loud crowd come (depending on the night) for the cheap beer, half-price food or football on TV. *Capitol South Metro. Mon–Thurs 10am–2am, Fri & Sat 10am–3am, Sun 3pm–2am.*

Irish Times, 14 F St NW ☎ 543-5433. Crowded student pub with a good range of beers, above-average bar food and live singalongafolk five nights a week (not Mon & Tues). Every June there's an overnight read-through of James Joyce's *Ulysses. Union Station Metro. Mon–Thurs & Sun 11am–2am, Fri & Sat 11am–3am.*

Jenkins Hill, 319 Pennsylvania Ave SE ☎ 544-4066. Eating and bar-room drinking on the main floor, live bands and a dancefloor downstairs in *Underground*, and a sports bar (with pool tables) up top. Bargain drinks 2–8pm most days. *Capitol South Metro. Mon–Thurs & Sun 7am–2am, Fri & Sat 2hr; restaurant 11am–1.30am.*

Phase 1, 525 8th St SE ☎ 544-631. Good-natured lesbian bar and club with dancing, DJs, videos and occasional live appearances. *Eastern Market Metro. Mon–Thurs & Sun 8pm–2am, Fri & Sat 8pm–3am.*

Remington's, 639 Pennsylvania Ave SE ☎ 543-3113. Slip on the cowboy boots and hit the C&W disco nights, wildly popular with a mostly gay clientele. Small cover at weekends. *Eastern Market Metro. Mon–Thurs 4pm–2am, Fri 4pm–3am, Sat 2pm–3am, Sun 2pm–2am.*

Tune Inn, 331 Pennsylvania Ave SE ☎ 543-2725. Crusty neighbourhood bar, which – next to the preppie *Hawk 'n' Dove* – seems in the wrong neighbour-

hood. Settle down in a booth, shoot the breeze and feed the jukebox. *Capitol South Metro. Mon–Thurs & Sun 8am–2am, Fri & Sat 8am–3am.*

Navy Yard

The Edge, 56 L St SE ☎ 488-1200. Frenetic gay club with several bars, entertainment and special events. *Mon–Thurs 7pm–2am, Fri & Sat 7pm–4am, Sun 4pm–2am.*

Tracks, 1111 1st St SE ☎ 488-3320. Thoroughly enjoyable 70s-style dance club with a large gay and lesbian presence and thumping good vibes. Sat is the big gay night; others are straight or nearly straight. *Mon 9pm–3.30am, Tues 8pm–2am, Wed 9pm–3am, Thurs 9pm–4am, Fri & Sat 8pm–5am, Sun 4pm–4am.*

Old Downtown

Capitol City Brewing Company, 1100 New York Ave NW, entrance at 11th and H ☎ 628-2222. Copper vats, pipes and gantries adorn this techno-micro brewery, serving a changing menu of home-brewed beers to an excitable crowd. In Sept, the *Mid-Atlantic Beer and Food Festival* kicks off here. *Metro Center Metro. Daily 11am–2am.*

Chamber of Sound, 925 5th St NW ☎ 898-0761. Cool club for reggae, house and hip-hop, with low cover. *Gallery Place-Chinatown Metro. Tues–Sat 10pm–4am.*

Dock Street Brewing Company, Warner Building, 1299 Pennsylvania Ave NW

Navy Yard Metro is the closest to all places listed in Navy Yard, but it's a dodgy neighbourhood; take a cab.

Bars and Clubs

639-0403. Basement brewhouse and restaurant, more upscale – and less fun – than the *Capitol City*. Half-a-dozen (not cheap) beers on tap, brewery tours (Wed 6pm, Sat 3pm), beer classes, and over-priced food. *Metro Center Metro. Daily 11am–1am.*

Fifth Column, 915 F St NW ☎396-3632. DJs pump out techno, house, rap and hip-hop on three floors of a converted downtown bank. Call for a schedule; lines form early and Mon night is popular. *Gallery Place-Chinatown Metro. Mon–Thurs 9pm–2am, Fri & Sat 10pm–3am.*

The Ritz, 919 E St NW ☎638-2582. Five music bars in one club where fashionable power-dressers wallow in everything from pop and reggae to soul and house. Mainly black crowd, who wait patiently in line after midnight. *Gallery Place-Chinatown Metro. Wed 5pm–2am, Fri 5pm–3am, Sat 9pm–4am, Sun 9pm–2am.*

Sky Terrace, *Washington Hotel*, 515 15th St NW ☎638-5900. Superb rooftop views from its ninth-floor bar-terrace. It's usually very busy – go early or late or expect to wait. *Metro Center Metro. Daily 11am–1am.*

Foggy Bottom

The Bottom Line, 1716 I St NW ☎298-8488. Basement tavern with journalist clientele (and sidewalk patio), short on atmosphere but located in an otherwise alcoholic desert. *Daily 11.30am–2am.*

Red Lion, 2040 I St NW ☎785-2766. Laidback student hangout. *Foggy*

Bottom-GWU Metro. Mon–Thurs 11am–2am, Fri & Sat 11am–3am.

New Downtown

Back Alley, 1111 Rear 19th St NW ☎296-7625. Notorious once-a-week haunt of DC's all-in-black alternative crowd. *Farragut North Metro. Sun 8pm–2am.*

Crow Bar, 1006 20th St NW ☎223-2972. Industrial chic backdrop for rock, grunge, disco and reggae (from DJ and jukebox); drink a microbrew and play pool, or hit the upstairs dancefloor with the mixed yuppie/black-clad posers. *Farragut North or West Metro. Mon–Thurs & Sun noon–2am, Fri & Sat 8pm–3am.*

Deja Vu/Lulu's New Orleans Café, 1217 22nd St NW ☎861-5858. Drinks and Cajun food in the café-bar; DJ rock and pop at the good-natured studenty club every night (small cover at the weekend). *Foggy Bottom-GWU Metro. Bar: Mon–Thurs 6pm–1.30am, Fri–Sun 4pm–2.30am; Club: Mon–Thurs & Sun 8pm–2am, Fri & Sat 8pm–3am.*

15 Minutes, 1030 15th St NW ☎408-1855. College-scene 70s–90s' bar-and-dance club with low or no cover depending on whether there's a band on. *McPherson Square or Farragut North Metro. Mon–Thurs 5pm–1am, Fri 5pm–3am, Sat 9pm–3am.*

Hung Jury, 1819 H St NW ☎279-3212. Popular women's bar and disco, tucked away off an alley; cover charge. *Farragut West Metro. Fri & Sat 9pm–3am.*

The Madhatter, 1831 M St NW ☎833-1495. Homely saloon where the after-

---

Restaurant Bars

Some of DC's restaurants have very funky bars in their own right – you'll be welcome for just a drink in any of the following.

Acme; *New Downtown*; p.277.
America; *Capitol Hill*; p.273.
Bukom Café; *Adams-Morgan*; p.280.
Café BaBaBlu; *Georgetown*; p.281.
Cities; *Adams-Morgan*; p.280.

Jaleo; *Old Downtown*; p.276.
Old Ebbitt Grill; *Old Downtown*; p.276.
Peyote Café; *Adams-Morgan*; p.281.
Red Sage; *Old Downtown*; p.276.
Tom Tom; *Adams-Morgan*; p.281.

Saloons

DC has a wealth of traditional saloon-restaurants, bristling with check tablecloths, panelled wood, good-value food and sharpshooting wait-staff. The checklist below picks out those where the bar action is pretty good, too.

Clyde's; *Georgetown*; p.281.
Fran O'Brien's; *New Downtown*; p.278.
Houston's; *Georgetown*; p.282.
J Paul's; *Georgetown*; p.282.
The Monocle; *Capitol Hill*; p.273.

Mr Henry's; *Capitol Hill*; p.275.
Old Glory; *Georgetown*; p.282.
Sign of the Whale; *New Downtown*; p.278.
Stoney's; *New Downtown*; p.278.

Bars and Clubs

office crowd give way to a free-and-easy student set. DJ Tues–Sat from 9pm. *Farragut North or West Metro. Mon–Thurs 1.30pm–1.30am, Fri 11.30am–3am, Sat 11am–3am, Sun 10.30am–1.30am.*

Quigley's, 1825 I St NW ☎331-0150. College/office bar with decent food, specials and a cover (after 9.30pm) when the DJ spins retro and pop/rock. *Farragut West Metro. Mon–Wed noon–midnight, Thurs 11.30am–1.30am, Fri 11.30am–2.30am, Sat 9pm–2.30am.*

Zei, 1415 Zei Alley NW, 14th St between H and I ☎842-2445. New York-style warehouse dance club, with emphasis on disco, house, funk and hip-hop – look the part (chic and rich), don't turn up until after midnight, and expect to wait. *McPherson Square Metro. Wed–Sat 10pm–4am.*

Dupont Circle

Badlands, 1413 22nd St NW ☎296-0505. Popular, likeable gay chart and house disco with the separate *Annex* bar upstairs. *Mon–Thurs & Sun 9pm–2am, Fri & Sat 9pm–3am.*

The Big Hunt, 1345 Connecticut Ave NW ☎785-2333. As well known for its jungle decor – including the tarantula candelabra – as for the beer. Over 25 brews on tap, good jukebox, and groovy crowd. *Mon–Thurs 4pm–2am, Fri 4pm–3am, Sat noon–3am, Sun 5.30pm–2am.*

The Brickskeller, 1523 22nd St NW ☎293-1885. Renowned brick-lined basement saloon serving "the world's largest selection of beer" – over 500 different types, including dozens from US micro-breweries. Knowledgeable bar staff can advise. *Mon–Thurs 11.30am–2.30am, Fri 11.30am–3am, Sat 6pm–3am, Sun 6pm–2am.*

The Childe Harold, 1722 Connecticut Ave NW ☎483-6701. Friendly old red-brick pub with an outdoor patio, which draws in a mixed crew to chew the fat and watch TV sports. *Mon–Thurs 11.30am–2am, Fri & Sat 11.30am–3am, Sun 10.30am–2am.*

The Circle, 1629 Connecticut Ave NW ☎462-5575. Modern gay bar-club-restaurant, where a mixed, upper-income crowd jostle for window stools and space on the summer terrace. *Mon–Thurs & Sun 11am–2am, Fri & Sat 11am–3am.*

The Fireplace, 2161 P St NW ☎293-1293. Gay-oriented bar with pool tables, jukebox and 7-hr Happy Hour. A staging ground for the cruisey P Street scene. *Mon–Thurs & Sun noon–2am, Fri & Sat noon–3am.*

Fox and Hounds, 1537 17th St NW ☎232-6307. Easygoing bar and grill slap-bang in the middle of the 17th Street action – there's a large sidewalk patio and good punky jukebox. *Mon–Thurs 11am–2am, Fri 11am–3am, Sat 10am–3am, Sun 10am–2am.*

Fraternity House, 2122 P St NW ☎223-4917. Pumping gay bar-disco, mostly house. Mad-for-it crowd (small cover). *Mon–Wed 4pm–2am, Thurs 4pm–4am, Fri 4pm–5am, Sat 8pm–5am, Sun 8pm–3am.*

Dupont Circle Metro for all bars listed in Dupont Circle.

Bars and Clubs

All places listed in Adams-Morgan are within a few blocks of the 18th St, Columbia Rd, Calvert St junction; nearest Metros are Woodley Park Zoo or Dupont Circle.

U St-Cardozo Metro for all places listed in Shaw.

JR's, 1519 17th St NW ☎ 328-0090. Handsome gay saloon-bar with preening clientele; very much the place to be seen for cocktails. *Mon–Thurs 2pm–2am, Fri 2pm–3am, Sat noon–3am, Sun noon–2am.*

Mr Eagan's, 1343 Connecticut Ave NW ☎ 861-9609. Curtained booths, old-time locals and a narrow bar overseen by Mr E himself – not very Dupont Circle and enjoyable for precisely that reason. *Mon–Sat 11am–1am, Sun 7pm–2am.*

Mr P's, 2147 P St NW ☎ 293-1064. Longest-serving gay bar in the neighbourhood, which has given it time to acquire a bit of character and attract a mellow, local clientele. *Mon–Thurs 3pm–2am, Fri & Sat 3pm–3am, Sun noon–2am.*

Planet Fred, 1221 Connecticut Ave NW ☎ 466-2336. Sculpted lunarscapes, space-rocket lamps, wacky art, and DJs playing dance, Indie and alternative music on themed nights (Fri & Sat are best); live bands every other Sun. *Mon–Fri noon–2am, Sat & Sun 4pm–2am.*

Shaw

Asylum in Exile, 1210 U St NW ☎ 319-9353. Always worth checking to see what's on at this alternative bar-club: live music, industrial and Goth DJ nights, beer promotions and an outdoor patio. Happy Hour 8–11pm. *Mon–Thurs & Sun 8pm–2am, Fri & Sat 8pm–3am.*

Bent, 1344 U St NW ☎ 296-1557. Predominantly gay and self-consciously surreal bar/club, with live bands most weekends (cover charge) and dancing to disco, funk and electro. *Mon–Thurs 5pm–1.30am, Fri 5pm–2.30am, Sat 6pm–2.30am, Sun 6pm–1.30am.*

Polly's Café, 1342 U St NW ☎ 265-8385. Neat little brick-and-board café-bar with a few outdoor tables, tap beers and bottled microbrews, good food and acoustic folk nights. *Mon–Thurs 5pm–midnight, Fri 5pm–2am, Sat 11am–2am, Sun 11am–midnight.*

Red Room Bar, *Black Cat*, 1831 14th St NW ☎ 667-7960. Independent, no-cover bar attached to the *Black Cat* music club (see p.291), with pool, pinball, draft beers and amiable, punky clientele. *Mon–Thurs & Sun 8pm–2am, Fri & Sat 8pm–3am.*

State of the Union, 1357 U St NW ☎ 588-8810. Long, red, and dimly lit, festooned with hammer-and-sickles and sporting a fearsome vodka list. DJ's music washes gently from funk, Latin and jazz to acid jazz and hip-hop; occasional low cover. *Mon–Fri 5pm–2am, Sat 6pm–3am, Sun 11am–2am.*

Utopia, 1418 U St NW ☎ 483-7669. Arty bar and grill with regular live blues and jazz and a weekend champagne brunch. *Mon–Thurs & Sun 11am–2am, Fri & Sat 11am–3am.*

Adams-Morgan

Café Lautrec, 2431 18th St NW ☎ 265-6436. Inviting bistro-bar – eat out on the patio or cosy up inside in the dark old bar-room for a beer or coffee. There's live jazz most nights after 9pm. *Mon–Thurs & Sun 4pm–2am, Fri & Sat 4pm–3am.*

Chief Ike's Mambo Room, 1725 Columbia Rd NW ☎ 332-2211. Ramshackle mural-clad restaurant-bar with live R&B on Tues (small cover), or a DJ spinning mostly Latin sounds. The *Chaos* bar upstairs features Indie music and a pool table. *Mon–Thurs & Sun 4pm–2am, Fri 4pm–3am, Sat noon–3am.*

Heaven & Hell, 2327 18th St NW ☎ 234-3455. Funky split-level bar-club with grungy *Hell* downstairs and *Heaven* up, featuring techno, dance and live Indie; Happy Hour 6–8.30pm but no real action until after 10.30pm, when the student/Goth crowd takes the floor. Occasional cover. *Mon–Thurs & Sun 6pm–2am, Fri & Sat 6pm–3am.*

Kala Kala, 2439 18th St NW ☎ 232-5433. Basement African bar announced by a large wooden abstract sculpture. Unusual African beers and great live bands and DJs. *Mon–Thurs & Sun 5pm–2am, Fri & Sat 5pm–3am.*

Kilimanjaro, 1724 California St NW
☎328-3838. Cool club-bar-restaurant
playing reggae and world beat to a black
crowd on two floors; DJ Sun–Wed, bands
other days. *Mon–Thurs & Sun 6pm–2am,
Fri & Sat 6pm–4am.*

Millie and Al's, 2440 18th St NW
☎387-8131. Crusty neighbourhood tavern of a type all too rare in Adams-
Morgan – food, beer and shots for local
wastrels. *Mon–Thurs 4pm–2am, Fri & Sat
noon–3am, Sun noon–2am.*

Mr Henry's, 1836 Columbia Rd NW
☎797-8882. Relaxed bar-cum-cabaret
lounge with a full programme of soul
and African gigs. Grab a seat at the bar
or watch and eat from one of the closely
packed tables. *Mon–Thurs & Sun
4pm–2am, Fri & Sat 4pm–3am.*

Toledo Lounge, 2435 18th St NW
☎986-5416. Hip café-bar with attitude,
zany neon wall sculptures, and windows
onto the local streetlife. The patio seats
are like gold-dust in summer. *Mon–Thurs
6pm–2am, Fri 6pm–3am, Sat noon–3am,
Sun noon–2am.*

Woodley/Cleveland Park

Ireland's Four Provinces, 3412
Connecticut Ave NW ☎244-0860.
Friendly bar with rollicking Irish music
five nights a week (cover some nights);
good atmosphere, and outdoor seats.
*Cleveland Park Metro. Mon–Thurs & Sun
4pm–2am, Fri & Sat 4pm–3am.*

Oxford Tavern, 3000 Connecticut Ave
NW ☎232-4225. Timeless suburban
saloon, near the zoo, with free live
bands three or four nights. *Woodley
Park-Zoo Metro. Mon–Thurs & Sun
11am–2am, Fri & Sat 11am–3am.*

Georgetown

Champions, 1206 Wisconsin Ave NW
☎965-4005. Full-on sports bar awash in
memorabilia, with big games on the TV
and high-calorie food to help the beer
down. A mainstream DJ after 11pm.
*Mon–Thurs 5pm–2am, Fri 5pm–3am, Sat
11.30am–3am, Sun 11.30am–2am.*

Garrett's, 3003 M St NW ☎333-1033.
With the usual brick-and-wood interior
so beloved of DC bars, the *Garrett* stands
out by virtue of the damn big rhino head
by the door, and a pumping jukebox
that keeps the student crowd in party
mood. *Mon–Thurs 11.30am–2am, Fri
11.30am–3am, Sat noon–3am, Sun
noon–2am.*

Mr Smith's, 3104 M St NW ☎333-3104.
Welcoming, brick-walled saloon-bar with
cheapish beer, and live bands at the
weekend. *Daily 11am–2am.*

Sequoia, 3000 K St NW ☎944-4200.
Very popular restaurant-bar at the eastern end of Washington Harbour, with
cane chairs on an outdoor terrace overlooking the river; get there early at weekends. *Mon–Thurs & Sun 11.30am–2am,
Fri & Sat 11.30am–3am.*

Third Edition, 1218 Wisconsin Ave NW,
near M St ☎333-3700. Gung-ho college
bar on several floors. It's a cattle-market
at the weekend (when you'll probably
have to wait in line and pay cover after
10pm); arrive early and enjoy the 4–9pm
Happy Hour. *Mon–Thurs 4pm–2am, Fri
4pm–3am, Sat 11.30am–3am, Sun
11.30am–2am.*

The Tombs, 1226 36th St NW, at
Prospect St ☎337-6668. Busy, basement student haunt, adorned with rowing blades – Bill Clinton, it's said, used
to drink here in his student days.
Occasional live bands and club nights
(small cover). *Mon–Thurs & Sun
11.30am–2am, Fri & Sat
11.30am–3am.*

Arlington, VA

Bardo Rodeo, 2000 Wilson Blvd
☎703/527-9399. Boisterous brew-pub
(claiming to be the largest in the US) in
an old car showroom. *Court House
Metro. Mon–Fri 11.30am–2am, Sat
1pm–2am, Sun 5pm–2am.*

Strangeways, 2830 Wilson Blvd
☎703/243-5272. Different beers on tap,
bar games, and live rock and pop Wed
& Thurs. *Clarendon Metro. Daily
6pm–2am.*

Bars and Clubs

*For transport
details for
Georgetown,
see p.232.*

Chapter 15

Live Music

For a run-down of DC's annual festivals, many of which include live music, see Chapter 18.

Washington DC has a pretty good **live music** scene, with bands right across the spectrum performing every night. To find out **what's on**, consult the "Weekend" section in the Friday edition of the *Washington Post*, or the free weekly *CityPaper* (available in cafés, bars and restaurants all over the city); other sources are the free weekly *Scene* entertainment guide, the monthly, glossy *Washingtonian* magazine, and flyers and posters in book stores and cafés.

Concerts by established stars take place in a variety of **major venues**, in and outside the city: **tickets** tend to be pricey ($20–50), and need to be booked in advance, either direct from the venues (there's a list of the main ones below) or from *TicketMaster* (☎432-

Major Venues

For event and ticket details of concerts at the following venues, call the box office numbers, or *TicketMaster* or *Protix*:

In the City

Carter Barron Amphitheater, 16th St and Colorado Ave NW, Rock Creek Park ☎426-6837. 4250-seat outdoor theatre for pop, jazz and R&B on summer weekends.

DAR Constitution Hall, 1776 D St NW ☎432-7328. Indoor 4000-seat auditorium for major pop, jazz and country acts.

Lincoln Theater, 1215 U St NW ☎328-6000. 1200-seat theatre hosting black pop, jazz, soul and gospel.

Lisner Auditorium, George Washington University, 730 21st St NW ☎994-6800. 1500-seat auditorium on the GWU campus for rock, pop and Indie acts.

RFK Stadium, 2400 E Capitol St SE ☎546-2222. 55,000-seater stadium pulling in the mega-stars.

Warner Theater, 1299 Pennsylvania Ave NW ☎628-1818. Jazz, Latin, Broadway and Vegas stars.

Outside the City

Merriweather Post Pavilion, off Rte 29, Columbia, MD ☎301/982-1800. Pavilion and open-air seating, presenting mid-league and major pop, jazz, country and MOR acts; spring and summer only.

Nissan Pavilion at Stone Ridge, Bristow VA ☎703/549-7625 or 1-800/455-8999. The area's newest outdoor summer stadium (25,000-seater) for rock and country gigs.

USAir Arena, 1 Harry S Truman Drive, Landover MD ☎301/350-3400; exits 15A or 17A off the Beltway. 20,000-seater stadium for pop, rock and country stars.

Wolf Trap Farm Park, Filene Center and The Barns, 1624 Trap Rd, Vienna VA ☎703/255-1900. Jazz, country, folk, zydeco and pop. See p.297 for details.

7328 or 1-800/551-7328) or *Protix*
(☎703/218-6500 or 1-800/955-5566),
who will add on a service charge. Keep
an eye out, too, for concerts at the
Kennedy Center (see p.294), while the
various museums of the **Smithsonian
Institution** (☎357-2700) put on jazz
and folk events throughout the year,
often free and sometimes open-air.

For smaller **gigs** – rock and folk, jazz
to African – check the music-club schedules, where ticket prices run from $5 to
20; the bigger the act, the more advis-
able it is to book ahead. Several of the
places listed below are also bars or
dance clubs, and are reviewed separately in the previous chapter; we've also
listed restaurants where you can catch
live bands. Take **ID** with you wherever
you go: in many clubs you have to be
21 to get in, and in those where the age
limit is 18, under-21s still won't be able
to drink alcohol.

Rock, pop, punk, R&B and reggae

Asylum in Exile, 1210 U St NW ☎319-
9353; U St-Cardozo Metro. U Street
grunge and alternative club with live local
and national bands several times a week.

The Bayou, 3135 K St NW ☎333-2897.
Georgetown's leading headbanger hangout, right on the riverfront, under the
Whitehurst Freeway. Split-level, exposed
brick bar; local and national rock acts.

The Black Cat, 1831 14th St NW ☎667-
7960; U St-Cardozo Metro. Likeable spot
owned by Dante Ferrando (of *Dante's*;
see p.280), DC's premier punk proprietor.
Showcase for new bands and veteran
alternative acts, with a good mix of
music.

Capitol Ballroom, 1015 Half St SE
☎554-1500; Navy Yard Metro. Cutting-
edge Indie and techno bands, and
special club nights, attract a very young,
hip crowd to this large barebones ware-
house-club.

15 Minutes, 1030 15th St NW ☎408-
1855; McPherson Square or Farragut
North Metro. Eclectic music policy sees

very different bands playing at least
three times a week; DJs on other nights,
and one-off open-mike nights. Closed
Sun.

Kilimanjaro, 1724 California St NW
☎328-3838. Live Afro-Caribbean bands
(Thurs–Sat; $5–10 cover) in Adams-
Morgan hotspot.

Madam's Organ, 2003 18th St NW
☎667-5370. Unsophisticated Adams-
Morgan hang-out featuring live, raw R&B
and blues, and funk on Sat nights; usually no cover.

New Vegas Lounge, 1415 P St NW
☎483-3971; Dupont Circle Metro.
Raunch-ridden Chicago R&B Tues–Sat.
Weekends are best for a night out (when
cover runs up to $10); good jam ses-
sions Tues–Thurs.

9:30 Club, 815 V St NW ☎393-0930; U
St-Cardozo Metro. Longest-running DC
venue (in new Shaw premises) for Indie
rock and pop, local, national and foreign.
Separate downstairs bar, too. Book in
advance (through *Protix*) for well-known
names.

Jazz and blues

Blues Alley, 1073 Rear Wisconsin Ave
NW ☎337-4141. Small, celebrated
Georgetown jazz bar, in business for
over thirty years, attracting top names.
Shows usually at 8pm and 10pm, plus
midnight some weekends; cover can run
to $40. Book in advance.

City Blues Café, 2651 Connecticut Ave
NW ☎232-2300; Woodley Park-Zoo
Metro. Live jazz or blues almost every
night in a mural-decorated townhouse.
Get there early for the best seats; there's
a minimum charge of $7 and the food is
overpriced.

Fort Dupont Summer Theater,
Minnesota Ave SE ☎426-7723. Free Fri
and Sat night outdoor jazz June–Aug
under the aegis of the National Park
Service, featuring top national and international acts; arrive early.

The Nest, *Willard Inter-Continental*, 1401
Pennsylvania Ave NW ☎637-7319;

Live Music

*For classical
music con-
certs, see the
next chapter.*

Live Music

Metro Center Metro. Renowned hotel jazz bar attracting quality names, though $10–20 cover and two-drink minimum makes it a pricey night out.

One Step Down, 2517 Pennsylvania Ave NW ☎331-8863; Foggy Bottom-GWU Metro. Intimate neighbourhood jazz bar, with live acts most nights and a fine jazz jukebox.

The Saloun, 3239 M St NW ☎965-4900. Cozy Georgetown bar with nightly jazz trios or bands, and 75 bottled beers. Free Mon and before 8pm, otherwise $2–3 cover.

State of the Union, 1357 U St NW ☎588-8810; U St-Cardozo Metro. Funky bar (see p.288) with progressive and acid jazz bands, and jazz poetry, two or three nights a week.

Takoma Station Tavern, 6914 4th St NW ☎829-1999; Takoma Metro. Laidback club with jazz Mon-Sat, featuring mostly local acts; reggae on Sun, decent food, and no cover.

Acoustic, Irish and folk

There are regular acoustic and folk sessions in the following bars, pubs and restaurants.

The Dubliner; *Capitol Hill;* see p.284.
Food for Thought; *Dupont Circle;* see p.279.
Ireland's Four Provinces; *Cleveland Park;* see p.289.
Irish Times; *Capitol Hill;* see p.285.
Polly's Café; *Shaw;* see p.288.

Alexandria

Birchmere, 3901 Mount Vernon Ave ☎703/549-5919. Longstanding country, blues and folk club with an A-list of current and retro acoustic performers; nightly gigs.

Fleetwood's, 44 Canal Center Plaza ☎703/548-6425. Mick Fleetwood (Mac)'s blues, jazz and R&B joint, attracting high-profile names; often no cover.

Live Music in Restaurants

The following restaurants all feature regular live bands, from jazz to R&B; there's usually no charge over the price of the meal. See the individual reviews for details of the places themselves.

Acme; *New Downtown*; Blues; see p.277.
Afterwords Café; *Dupont Circle*. Jazz/Blues; see p.272.
Bukom Café; *Adams-Morgan*; African; see p.280.
Café des Artists at the Corcoran; *Foggy Bottom*; Gospel; see p.271.
Café Lautrec; *Adams-Morgan*; Jazz; see p.288.
Chief Ike's Mambo Room; *Adams-Morgan*; R&B/Latin; see p.288.
Coco Loco; *Old Downtown*; Jazz/Brazilian; see p.277.
Dixie Grill; *Old Downtown*; R&B/Jazz; see p.276.

Fasika's; *Adams-Morgan*; African; see p.280.
Jenkins Hill; *Capitol Hill*; Rock/R&B; see p.285.
Lulu's New Orleans Café; *New Downtown*; Jazz; see p.286.
Mr Henry's; *Capitol Hill*; Jazz; see p.275.
Mr Smith's; *Georgetown*; R&B; see p.289.
Old Glory; *Georgetown*; R&B; see p.282.
Utopia; *Shaw*; Jazz/Blues/Brazilian; see p.288.

Chapter 16

The Arts and Entertainment

Washington may come a cultural second-best to New York, and a fairly distant one at that, but there's still plenty of choice if you want to take in a play or comedy show, see a movie or attend a concert or recital. The prime mover in cultural and artistic matters is the **John F Kennedy Center for the Performing Arts** – hereafter known as the Kennedy Center – encompassing Concert Hall, Opera House, three theatres and the American Film Institute. It's home to the National Symphony Orchestra and stages seasonal productions by the city's top opera and ballet companies, and also has a full programme of visiting national and international artists, companies and ensembles. The other main promoter is the **Washington Performing Arts Society** (WPAS), which sponsors music, ballet and dance productions across the city.

The city also boasts a whole host of **smaller theatres and venues** dedicated to contemporary, experimental, ethnic or left-field productions, where ticket prices (and availability) tend to be more realistic. There's also plenty that you can **see for free**: the **Smithsonian Institution**, in particular, has a year-round programme of events and concerts, while the Library of Congress' **American Folklife Center** hosts monthly dance and music performances (May–Oct) in front of the library's Jefferson Building.

To find out **what's on**, consult the Friday edition of the *Washington Post* or the free weekly *CityPaper*. Other free guides and magazines (see Chapters 14 and 15) also offer rundowns of events, and the Washington DC CVA (see p.17) publishes a quarterly *Calendar of Events*.

Tickets

Obviously, ticket prices vary considerably according to the event or production. You can expect to shell out a lot for the high-profile events at the Kennedy Center, National Theater, Arena Stage and the like, and in the case of major opera and ballet productions tickets at any price will be hard to come by unless you book well in advance. But many places, the Kennedy Center included, offer half- or cut-price tickets on the day if there's space. In all instances it's worth a call to the box office: students (with ID), senior citizens, military personnel and people with disabilities qualify for discounts in most theatres and concert halls.

You can also buy many tickets over the phone from various **ticket agencies**, which on the whole sell advance-reserved, full-price tickets (plus surcharge) – usually no changes or refunds available.

Cinema

The **movie houses** listed below should cover every eventuality; the *Cineplex Odeons* are the main commercial screens, though the Union Station movie

Many of Washington's annual festivals (see Chapter 18) incorporate arts and music events.

All telephone numbers in this chapter are area code ☎202, unless otherwise stated.

The Arts and
Entertainment

Washington's annual Filmfest DC (April), premiers national and international movies in theatres across the city.

house often proves to be the handiest for visitors. Admission runs $5–7, with many matinees coming in a couple of dollars cheaper – cheapest of all are the bargain daily rates at the *Odeon Foundry*. Check listings in *CityPaper* or the *Washington Post*, which also detail the free films on show in some of the city's **museums and galleries**. With kids in tow, don't forget the IMAX screen at the National Air and Space Museum (see p.74).

AMC Union Station 9, 50 Massachusetts Ave NE ☎703/998-4262; Union Station Metro. Mainstream nine-screen complex inside Union Station.

American Film Institute, Kennedy Center, 2700 F St NW ☎785-4600; Foggy Bottom-GWU Metro. America's national film theatre, showing two to four movies a day in rep: classic, contemporary, national and foreign, often with associated lectures and seminars.

Bethesda Theater Café, 7719 Wisconsin Ave NW ☎301/656-3337; Bethesda Metro. Great retro cinema in suburban Maryland serving food and drink at tables while the movie is screened; minimum age 21.

Borders Books & Music, 1801 K St NW ☎466-4999; Farragut North Metro. Independent/avant-garde films and speakers, last Thurs of every month.

Cineplex Odeon: mainstream movie screens, among others at Dupont Circle (1350 19th St NW, ☎703/714-9037); Georgetown Foundry (M St at Thomas Jefferson St NW ☎703/714-9062); West End (23rd and L St NW ☎703/714-9035); and Uptown (3426 Connecticut Ave NW ☎703/714-9041) – this last an Art Deco classic with massive screen and balcony.

The Key, 1222 Wisconsin Ave NW, Georgetown ☎333-5100. Art-house and foreign movies alongside domestic independent output.

Mary Pickford Theater, Madison Building, Library of Congress, 1st St and Independence Ave SE ☎707-5677. Free classic and foreign historic movies from the library's archives.

Classical music

The Kennedy Center's Concert Hall is the most prestigious in town for classical music; it's also the home of the **National**

Symphony Orchestra (NSO), tickets to whose concerts run from $25 to 50 (though the orchestra also performs free outside the US Capitol on the West Terrace on Memorial Day, 4 July and Labor Day). There are regular concerts at all the places listed below; check newspaper listings for events in museums (particularly the National Gallery of Art and the Corcoran Gallery of Art), historic houses (like Dumbarton House), churches (including the National Cathedral) and embassies. For details of the **Smithsonian Institution** concerts, call ☎357-2700.

Coolidge Auditorium, Madison Building, Library of Congress, 1st St and Independence Ave SE ☎707-5502; Capitol South Metro. Chamber music concerts.

DAR Constitution Hall, 1776 D St NW ☎432-7328; Farragut West Metro. Large (4250-seat) auditorium for major concerts and recitals.

Folger Shakespeare Library, 201 E Capitol St SE ☎544-7077; Capitol South

Metro. Medieval and Renaissance music from the *Folger Consort* ensemble. Oct–May season.

John Phillips Sousa Band Hall, Marine Barracks, 8th and I St SE ☎433-4011; Navy Yard Metro. Free fall and winter chamber recitals by the marine band ensemble, and other occasional concerts.

Kennedy Center, 2700 F St NW, at Virginia and New Hampshire Ave ☎467-4600; Foggy Bottom-GWU Metro. The National Symphony Orchestra performs in the 2800-seat *Concert Hall* (Sept–June); cheaper chamber recitals in the *Terrace Theater*.

Lisner Auditorium, *George Washington University*, 730 21st St NW ☎994-6800; Foggy Bottom-GWU Metro. Regular classical and choral concerts, occasionally free.

National Academy of Sciences, 2101 Constitution Ave NW ☎334-2436; Foggy Bottom-GWU Metro. Pleasing 700-seat auditorium with free chamber recitals by various groups, including the Marine Chamber Orchestra.

The Arts and
Entertainment

Open-Air Concerts

Summer is a good time to catch a free open-air concert in Washington, though certain locations see some activity all year round: look for events at the following places and see DC's festival calendar (p.305) for more.

C&O Canal, Georgetown (p.233). Varied Sun afternoon summer concerts, between 30th and Thomas Jefferson St.

Freedom Plaza, Pennsylvania Ave NW (p.176). Year-round venue for folk events and music festivals.

National Zoological Park, Connecticut Ave NW (p.224). "Sunset serenades" in July, a variety of musical performances.

Neptune Plaza, Jefferson Building, Library of Congress, 1st and Independence Ave SE (p.122). Monthly folk singing and dancing May–Oct.

Netherlands Carillon, Marine Corps (Iwo Jima) War Memorial, Arlington, VA (p.246). Carillon concerts every Sat and national holiday April–Aug.

Sylvan Theater, Washington Monument Grounds, the Mall. Army, Air Force, Navy and Marine Corps bands perform four nights a week June–Aug (including annual *1812 Overture* performance in Aug). Other musical events throughout the year, too.

US Capitol. Armed forces' bands four nights a week (June–Aug) on the East Terrace; NSO on the West Terrace on Memorial Day, 4 July and Labor Day.

US Navy Memorial, 701 Pennsylvania Ave NW (p.174). Spring and summer concert series featuring Navy, Marine Corps, Coastguard and high-school bands. Regular performances June–Aug Tues 8pm.

The Arts and Entertainment

The Phillips Collection, 1600 21st St NW ☎387-2151; Dupont Circle Metro. Classical music concerts in the museum's Music Room (Sun 5pm, Sept–May); free with museum admission (see p.210).

Society of the Cincinnati at Anderson House, 2118 Massachusetts Ave NW ☎785-2040; Dupont Circle Metro. Free chamber recitals once or twice a week in fine mansion surroundings (see p.209).

Comedy and cabaret

Several central and suburban clubs offer the usual mix of big-name **stand-up comedy** acts, improv, local/regional circuit appearances and open-mike nights. As well as the clubs and lounges listed below, there are stand-up nights at spots as diverse as the *Bayou* (see *Live Music*), the *Arena Stage* and the *Kennedy Center*; local listings papers have details. Keep an eye out, too, for comedy troupes which appear in **cabaret** or improv shows at various venues around town. *Capitol Steps* is the best known (and most permanent), but there are also regular shows by ensemble groups like *Dropping the Cow*, *ComedySportz* and *Gross National Product*. Comedy clubs can be expensive, since there's often a drinks-and-food minimum charge on top of the **ticket** price: to see *Capitol Steps* or a big weekend show can cost as much as $40, though tickets for basic stand-up and improv nights are more like $10–15. **Book in advance** at all clubs.

Capitol Steps, *Chelsea's*, 1055 Thomas Jefferson St NW ☎298-8222. Well-established political satire by a group of Capitol Hill staffers. Popular but expensive (see above) perfomances at this Georgetown club (Fri & Sat) and occasionally at other venues.

Comedy Café, 1520 K St NW ☎638-5653; Farragut North Metro. DC's main comedy showcase mixing big names with local and regional acts and open-mike nights; affordable performances, usually Wed–Sat.

The Improv, 1140 Connecticut Ave NW ☎296-7008; Farragut North Metro. Main rival to the *Comedy Café*, with a similar programme plus extended runs.

The Little Café, 2039 Wilson Blvd, Arlington, VA ☎703/522-6622; Court House Metro. Regular Sat night shows with resident improvization team. Tickets under $10.

Marquee Lounge, *Omni Shoreham*, 2500 Calvert St NW ☎745-1023; Woodley Park-Zoo Metro. Celebrity-studded hotel (see p.224) whose exclusive cabaret lounge hosts long-running political satire and musical-comedy improv teams.

Dance, ballet and opera

Opera and **ballet** performances are fairly limited in DC, though what there is – provided principally by *Washington Ballet* and *Washington Opera* – is of the highest quality. There's more scope to see modern and **contemporary dance**, either at the Kennedy Center, the other main theatres or at a specialist venue like *The Dance Place*.

The Dance Place, 3225 8th St NE ☎269-1600; Brookland-CUA Metro. Contemporary and modern dance productions, mainstream and experimental. Hosts *Dance Africa* festival every June.

Summer Opera Theater Company, Hartke Theater, Catholic University, Michigan Ave and 4th St NE ☎526-1669; Brookland-CUA Metro. Independent company staging two operas each summer, usually July and Aug.

Washington Ballet ☎362-3606 or 467-4600. Classical and contemporary ballet performed in rep by the city's major ballet company at the Kennedy Center. Every Dec *The Nutcracker* is performed at the *Warner Theater*. Tickets $30–45.

Washington Opera ☎416-7800 or 1-800/876-7372. Tickets for one of the country's finest resident opera companies (artistic director: Placido Domingo) sell out well in advance, though you may get standing-room at the box office.

Longest-running show in town is Shear Madness *at the* Theater Lab *in the Kennedy Center, a comedy-crime caper with audience participation; call the Kennedy Center for ticket details.*

Wolf Trap Farm Park

Wolf Trap Farm Park (1551 Trap Rd, Vienna VA), about forty minutes from downtown DC, is the country's first national park for the performing arts. Set in 130 acres, the **Filene Center** (☎703/255-1860) stages jazz, pop, and country concerts from June to September with indoor and outdoor seating for seven thousand people; there's also opera, ballet and dance. A **Theatre-in-the-Woods** (☎703/255-1827) puts on free performing arts for children during July and August, while the rest of the year the action switches to the indoor **Barns at Wolf Trap**

(☎703/938-2404), a 350-seat concert hall hosting jazz, blues, folk, world music and zydeco.

The park is outside the Beltway, between Rte 7 and Rte 267 (Dulles Toll Road). For directions on how to get there by public transportation, call ☎703/255-1860 – there's a Metro-shuttle bus service for most performances. Call the **box office** numbers for details about the programme and tickets, which you can buy over the phone. There are concessions stands and a restaurant, but it's nicer to bring a **picnic** in summer – you can eat on the grass. **Parking** is free.

The Arts and Entertainment

Nov–March season; performances in the *Opera House* and the other Kennedy Center theatres.

Theatre and the performing arts

Most **Broadway productions** either preview or tour in Washington; the city also has an enclave of **alternative venues** in the Shaw (14th St NW) district, where relatively low ticket prices reward the adventurous. Come, or at least leave, by taxi, since the area isn't the most salubrious in town.

Arena Stage, 6th St and Maine Ave SW ☎488-3300; Waterfront Metro. The most respected theatrical institution in the city, with three stages (*Arena Stage, Kreeger Theater* and *Old Vat Room*) showing contemporary plays and performance pieces, classics, musicals, comedies and experimental works.

Discovery Theater, Arts and Industries Building, 900 Jefferson Drive SW ☎357-1500; Smithsonian Metro. Year-round, day-time children's theatre, musicals and puppet shows at budget prices.

DC Arts Center, 2438 18th St NW ☎462-7833; Woodley Park-Zoo Metro. Performance art, drama, poetry, dance and a whole range of multi-cultural activities in northern Adams-Morgan; low prices.

Folger Shakespeare Library, 201 E Capitol St SE ☎544-7077; Capitol South Metro. Full programme at the Elizabethan library-theatre (Sept–June), not solely Shakespeare.

Ford's Theater, 511 10th St NW ☎347-4833; Metro Center Metro. Site of Lincoln's assassination (see p.195), this restored nineteenth-century theatre shows mainstream musicals and dramas.

Gala Hispanic Theater, 1625 Park Rd NW ☎234-7174. Specializes in works by Spanish/Latin American playwrights, performed in Spanish or English, as well as performance art and poetry.

Kennedy Center, 2700 F St NW, at Virginia and New Hampshire Ave ☎467-4600; Foggy Bottom-GWU Metro. Site of the *Eisenhower* (drama and Broadway productions), the *Terrace* (experimental/contemporary works) and the *Theater Lab* (almost permanently home to the long-running *Shear Madness*, a comedy-whodunnit). The *Opera House* also puts on musicals.

Lincoln Theater, 1215 U St NW ☎328-6000; U St-Cardozo Metro. Renovated movie/vaudeville house hosting touring stage shows, concerts and dance.

National Theater, 1321 Pennsylvania Ave NW ☎628-6161; Metro Center

Note the Kennedy Center Annual Open House (early Sept) – free concerts, drama and film for all-comers.

The Arts and
Entertainment

Metro. One of the country's oldest
theatres, on this site (if not this building)
since 1835. Premieres, pre- and post-
Broadway productions and musicals.

Shakespeare Theater, *The Lansburgh*,
450 7th St NW ☎ 393-2700; Archives-
Navy Memorial Metro. Four (often star-
studded) plays a year by Shakespeare
and his contemporaries. Each June the
company puts on free, outdoor
Shakespeare at the Carter Barron
Amphitheater in Rock Creek Park (see
p.195).

Source Theater, 1835 14th St NW
☎ 462-1073; U St-Cardozo Metro. New
and contemporary works and classic re-
interpretations. Promotes the Washington
Theater Festival, a showcase for new
works, every summer.

Studio Theater, 1333 P St NW ☎ 332-
3300; Dupont Circle Metro. Independent
theater with two stages presenting classic and contemporary drama and comedy.

Warner Theater, 1299 Pennsylvania Ave
NW ☎ 628-1818; Metro Center Metro.
Erstwhile movie palace now staging
post-Broadway productions and big concerts.

Washington Stage Guild, Carroll Hall,
924 G St NW ☎ 529-2084; Metro Center
Metro. Classics and contemporary productions.

Woolly Mammoth Theater, 1401 Church
St NW ☎ 393-3939; Dupont Circle Metro.
Budget-ticket productions of contemporary, experimental and plain off-the-wall
plays.

Visual arts

Quite apart from the public art galleries
and museums, DC has a massive range
of **commerical art galleries** which often
host changing exhibitions (usually free)
of paintings, prints, sculpture, photography, applied art and folk art. The galleries listed below are some of the more
reliable; call for details of current shows
or check *CityPaper* or the *Washington
Post's* "Weekend" section. There's also a

monthly guide available in bookstores
with comprehensive listings of DC's art
galleries called, appropriately enough,
Galleries. The venues themselves are
grouped in several distinct city areas:
downtown, those along **7th Street NW**
specialize in the works of contemporary
DC-area artists, though the major concentration of galleries is in **Dupont Circle**
where over thirty congregate in a
defined Gallery District (mainly **R Street**
between 21st and 22nd). Most are
closed on Monday and many on
Tuesday.

Downtown

Arts Club of Washington, 2017 I St NW
☎ 331-7282. Changing exhibits from
local artists.

George Washington University:
Colonnade Gallery, Marvin Center, 800
21st St NW ☎ 994-8401; and *Dimock
Gallery*, Lower Lisner Auditorium, 730
21st St NW ☎ 994-1525. Regular changing shows by local, national and international artists.

Mahler Gallery, 406 7th St NW ☎ 393-
5180. Contemporary sculpture and painting, and DC-area artists in mixed-media
shows.

Washington Project for the Arts, 400
7th St NW ☎ 347-4813. Regular contemporary art shows by DC-area
artists, encompassing photography,
painting and sculpture; the entrance is
on D St.

Zenith Gallery, 413 7th St NW ☎ 783-
2963. Mainly works by city-based artists.

Dupont Circle

Affrica, 2010 R St NW ☎ 745-7272.
African masks, figurines, ceramics, textiles
and jewellery.

Fondo del Sol Visual Arts Center, 2112 R
St NW ☎ 483-2777. Pre-Columbian and
other art of the Americas, plus lectures,
poetry and performance art; also sponsors
a summer outdoor Caribbean festival.

Kathleen Ewing Gallery, 1609
Connecticut Ave NW ☎ 328-0955.

Nineteenth- and twentieth-century photography.

Marsha Mateyka Gallery, 2012 R St NW ☎328-0088. Contemporary painting and sculpture.

Tartt Gallery, 2017 Q St NW ☎332-5652. Nineteenth- and twentieth-century photography, plus American folk art.

Venable Neslage Galleries, 1803 Connecticut Ave NW ☎462-1800. One of the longest-established galleries, showing contemporary impressionist and realist works, and modern sculpture.

Washington Center for Photography, 1731 21st St NW ☎234-5517. Changing and challenging photographic exhibitions in a non-profit organization.

Washington Printmakers' Gallery, 2106 R St NW ☎332-7757. Original prints by contemporary artists.

Georgetown

Alif Gallery, 1204 31st St NW ☎337-9670. Arab and Middle Eastern art (as well as concerts, lectures and events).

Guarisco Gallery, 2828 Pennsylvania Ave NW ☎333-8533. Nineteenth- and twentieth-century European and American painting.

Spectrum Gallery, 1132 29th St NW ☎333-0954. Local artists' co-op with regular exhibitions.

The Arts and Entertainment

Chapter 17

Shopping

No one comes to DC to shop, but the city's arty neighbourhood stores, fine range of **book stores** and incomparable museum and **gallery shops** – not to mention the profusion of White House, Capitol, Supreme Court and FBI mugs, key-rings, baseball hats, posters and buttons – means no one needs go home empty-handed.

Nicest areas for **browsing** are Dupont Circle and Georgetown, where art and craft shops co-exist with specialist book and music stores, and student-oriented clothes-and-accessories hangouts; Adams-Morgan has more ethnic soul, and some good shops to match.

The shopping heart has been ripped out of downtown, however, as all the major **department stores**, with the honourable exception of *Hecht's*, have given up the ghost. For day-to-day items you're best off at one of the **mega-malls** on the outskirts of the city.

Stores are usually open Monday–Saturday 10am–7pm; some have extended Thursday night hours. In Georgetown, Adams-Morgan and Dupont Circle many stores open on Sunday, too (usually noon–5pm).

Arts, crafts and antiques

The only indigenous local craft is politics, but specialist stores in DC let you take home a piece of the Southwest or American Victoriana if you so wish. Richest pickings are in arty Dupont

For Alexandria shopping, call in first to the Ramsay House Visitor Center (p.250), which has reams of shopping guides, flyers and information.

Circle, Georgetown, which also has a run of high-ticket antique shops, and Old Town Alexandria, positively dripping with antique/bric-a-brac places aimed at the weekend visitor market. For works of art, visit the galleries of Dupont Circle and those downtown in 7th Street – see p.298.

African Eye, 2134 Wisconsin Ave NW, Georgetown ☎625-2552. African-American clothing, crafts, jewellery and textiles.

American Hand, 2906 M St NW, Georgetown ☎965-3273. Decorative hand-crafted ceramics from American artists.

Appalachian Spring, 1415 Wisconsin Ave NW, Georgetown ☎337-5780; Union Station, 50 Massachusetts Ave NE ☎682-0505. Hand-made ceramics, jewellery, rugs, glassware, kitchenware, quilts and toys.

Artland, 1526 Wisconsin Ave NW, Georgetown ☎333-2481; 739 15th St NW, Old Downtown ☎393-1316. Abstract and traditional African sculpture and art – carvings, wall hangings and furniture.

Beadazzled, 1522 Connecticut Ave NW, Dupont Circle ☎265-2323. Antique and new beads from all over the world, plus ethnic jewellery, folk art and related books.

Indian Craft Shop, Department of the Interior, 1849 C St NW, Foggy Bottom ☎208-4056; *Georgetown Park*, 3222 M St NW ☎342-3918. Quality Native

American arts and crafts – Navajo rugs, Hopi jewellery and assorted ceramics: the first shop is inside the Department, see p.163.

Moon, Blossoms and Snow, 225 Pennsylvania Ave SE, Capitol Hill ☎543-8181. Handmade clothes and contemporary American ceramics, toys, and crafts by over 200 regional artists.

The Old Print Gallery, 1220 31st NW, Georgetown ☎965-1818. Old maps, charts and prints, plus political cartoons, DC scenes and American landscapes.

Santa Fe Style, 1413 Wisconsin Ave NW, Georgetown ☎333-3747. Southwestern chic – decorative arts, household items, ceramics, fabrics, furniture and jewellery.

Washington Antiques Center, 209 Madison St, Old Town Alexandria, VA ☎703/739-2484. Best Old Town antiques spot, with over forty permanent dealers.

Bookstores

Washington's bookstores are one of its high points: you'll find a place to suit whether you want discounted new novels or political science books, flagship superstores with coffee bars or cosy local secondhand shops.

General

Barnes & Noble, 3040 M St NW, Georgetown ☎965-9980. Quality chain bookstore on three floors – heavy discounts, one of the best crime/mystery sections in the city, and *Starbuck's* coffee.

Borders Books & Music, 1801 K St NW, New Downtown ☎466-4999. Huge bookstore with good selection of magazines, newspapers and discount books, full CD and tape selection, readings, gigs, events and an espresso bar.

Chapters, 1512 K St NW, New Downtown ☎347-5495. Notable downtown bookstore with a quality range and full supporting cast of readings and events.

Crown Books, 11 Dupont Circle ☎319-1374; 3131 M St NW, Georgetown ☎333-4493; 1275 K St NW, Old

Downtown ☎289-7170; 1133 19th St NW, New Downtown ☎659-4172; 1710 G St NW, Foggy Bottom ☎789-2277; and others. Local chain with substantial discounts on new books. The Dupont Circle branch is the largest.

Kramerbooks, 1517 Connecticut Ave NW, Dupont Circle ☎387-1462. City institution with a good general selection, a great café-restaurant and long opening hours (round-the-clock at the weekend); see p.272.

Olsson's Books and Records, 1239 Wisconsin Ave NW, Georgetown ☎338-9544; 1307 19th St NW, Dupont Circle ☎785-1133; 1200 F St NW, Old Downtown ☎347-3686; 418 7th St NW, Old Downtown ☎638-7610. Massive range in one of the city's nicest places to browse; regular book signings, plus tapes and CDs.

Used books

Atticus Books, 1508 U St NW, Shaw ☎667-8148. Good used-book store (with records and CDs), a couple of blocks from U St-Cardozo Metro.

Bryn Mawr Lantern Bookshop, 3160 O St NW, Georgetown ☎333-3222. Great general selection of secondhand books, though only open four or five hours a day.

Fuller and Saunders, 1531 33rd St NW, Georgetown ☎337-3235. Strong on the Civil War and local history.

Idle Time Books, 2410 18th St NW, Adams-Morgan ☎232-4774. Large, late-opening used-book store with lots of bargains.

Kulturas Books & Records, 1741 Connecticut Ave NW, Dupont Circle ☎462-2541. Not so much a secondhand bookstore as a yard sale: books, records and arty bits-and-bobs.

Logic and Literature, 1223 31st St NW, Georgetown ☎625-1668. Used-book store with a bent towards the classics, philosophy, science and history.

Second Story Books, 2000 P St NW, Dupont Circle ☎659-8884. Large range

Shopping

*The annual Washington **Antiquarian International Book Fair** is usually held in Sept; check with the CVA for location.*

Shopping

Food and Drink

The city isn't exactly known for the quality of its delis, though a few places stand out. Good **coffee**, at least, isn't hard to find – any of the specialist coffee shops listed in Chapter 13 can sell you the beans. Old-style markets are thin on the ground: **Eastern Market** is your best bet (p.127), while the Waterfront **Fish Wharf** (p.136) has a great selection of Chesapeake Bay seafood; there are Saturday **farmer's markets** in Adams-Morgan (p.221), Alexandria (p.252) and at Arlington Court House. Best general deli is the splendid **Dean & DeLuca** (p.273) in Georgetown. Southwest fanciers should call at the **Red Sage** (p.276) restaurant's associated shop.

of used books and records; a useful spot to find out what's on in the city.

Specialist

Bridge Street Books, 2814 Pennsylvania Ave NW, Georgetown ☎965-5200. Politics, literature, history, philosophy and film.

Lambda Rising, 1426 21st St NW, Dupont Circle ☎462-6969. Gay and lesbian bookstore with a wide choice.

Lammas, 1426 21st St NW, Dupont Circle ☎775-8218. Feminist and lesbian bookstore.

The Map Store, 1636 I St NW, New Downtown ☎628-2608. Maps, atlases and travel guides.

Mystery Books, 1715 Connecticut Ave NW, Dupont Circle ☎483-1600. The city's specialist in detective, spy and crime fiction.

Sidney Kramer Books, 1825 I St NW, New Downtown ☎293-2685. The place for books on politics, economics, business studies, defence matters, foreign affairs and other governmental concerns.

US Government Bookstore, 710 North Capitol St NW, Old Downtown ☎512-0132; 1510 H St NW, New Downtown ☎653-5075. All the official facts and figures you ever wanted from the government's own bookstores; Mon–Fri only.

Vertigo Books, 1337 Connecticut Ave NW, Dupont Circle ☎429-9272. Washington, American and world politics, black and social studies and modern literature. Regular signings and readings.

Yawa, 2206 18th St NW, Adams-Morgan ☎483-6805. African and African-American books, magazines, crafts and cards.

Yes Bookstore, 1035 31st St NW, Georgetown ☎338-7874. Extensive New Age book and music store – eastern religions and personal development to acupuncture and mythology.

Department stores

Flagship department stores – *Neiman Marcus, Nordstrom, Saks Fifth Avenue, Lord & Taylor, Bloomingdale's* and *Macy's* – are all firmly ensconced in the out-of-town malls (see below); the two listed below are the only major downtown survivors.

Filene's Basement, 1133 Connecticut Ave NW, New Downtown ☎872-8430. Famed Boston-based bargain department store with good deals on men's and women's clothing, shoes and accessories.

Hecht's, 1201 G St NW, Old Downtown ☎628-6661; and suburban locations. Classic downtown department store with a full range of clothing and home furnishings. The store is a century old, though this stylish building was put up in 1985.

Miscellaneous

Another Universe, 3060 M St, Georgetown ☎333-8651. Sci-fi specialist for games, comics, cards, toys and posters.

Malls

Although **malls** are flourishing in revitalized downtown areas, they tend to be showy, tourist-oriented collections of gift shops, novelty stores and food courts. Head for the 'burbs for the best malls (and, incidentally, slightly lower local sales taxes); there's direct Metro access to those at Friendship Heights and Pentagon City. Opening hours are usually Monday–Saturday 10am–8pm, Sunday noon–6pm.

Shopping

Downtown
Old Post Office Pavilion, 1100 Pennsylvania Ave NW ☎289-4224.

The Shops at National Place, 1331 Pennsylvania Ave NW ☎783-9090.

Union Station Mall, 50 Massachusetts Ave NE ☎371-9441.

Georgetown
Georgetown Park, 3222 M St NW ☎298-5577.

Out of Town
Chevy Chase Pavilion, 5345 Wisconsin Ave NW ☎686-5335; Friendship Heights Metro.

Fashion Centre at Pentagon City, 1100 S Hayes St, Arlington VA ☎703/415-2400, Pentagon City Metro.

Mazza Gallerie, 5300 Wisconsin Ave NW ☎686-9515; Friendship Heights Metro.

Potomac Mills Outlet Mall, 2700 Potomac Mills Circle, Prince William, VA ☎1-800/VA-MILLS; Sat shuttle from Metro Center, Rosslyn and Pentagon City Metros.

Tysons Galleria, 2001 International Drive, McLean, VA ☎703/827-7700; Capital Beltway exit 11B.

Backstage Inc, 2101 P St NW, Dupont Circle ☎775-1488. Amazingly well-stocked theatrical outfitters.

Capital Coin and Stamp Company, 1701 L St NW, New Downtown ☎296-0440. Not only stamps and coins, but also campaign buttons, stickers and memorabilia.

Commander Salamander, 1420 Wisconsin Ave NW, Georgetown ☎337-2265. Funky T-shirts, sneakers, sportswear, bags, party gear and gimcrack jewellery – open late.

FAO Schwarz, *Georgetown Park*, 3222 M St NW, Georgetown ☎342-2285. Major toy store with massive stock, modern and traditional, dolls to video games.

Movie Madness, 1222 Wisconsin Ave NW, Georgetown ☎337-7064. Small store with thousands of movie posters, old and new.

Political Americana, Union Station, 50 Massachusetts Ave NE ☎547-1685; 685 15th St NW, Old Downtown ☎547-1871. Everything from historic and topical buttons

and bumper stickers to gifts, books and videos on every side of the political divide.

Travel Center, 1108 K St NW, Old Downtown ☎783-4943. Youth-hostel associated one-stop travel shop selling tickets, passes, guides, maps and equipment; IYHF members get a discount off travel accessories.

Museum and gallery stores

Virtually all DC's museums – in particular the Smithsonians – have well-stocked shops. The list below picks out the best; follow the page references for transport and museum details. Note that every other major attraction – US Capitol to Pentagon – has its own store, too, selling enough name-emblazoned souvenirs for even the junkiest of collectors.

Arthur M Sackler Gallery, 1050 Independence Ave SW. Jewellery, prints, waistcoats, fabrics, Asian art, ceramics, rugs, beads and calligraphy. See p.65.

Shopping

Check out the used records, tapes and CDs in Atticus Books, Kulturas Books & Records and Second Story Books. Borders Books & Music and Olsson's Books and Records sell new stuff. See "Bookstores" p.301 for addresses.

B'nai B'rith Klutznick National Jewish Museum, 1640 Rhode Island Ave NW. Jewellery, goblets, ceramics, T-shirts, festival arts and crafts, linen and embroidered goods – all with Jewish motifs. See p.206.

Bureau of Engraving and Printing, 14th and C St SW. Just the place for that Presidential engraving, prints of Washington DC, copies of famous texts, and even bags of shredded cash. See p.135

National Air and Space Museum, Independence Ave and 7th SW. Fantastic array of air- and space-related goodies, books to ray-guns. See p.74.

National Gallery of Art, Constitution Ave, between 3rd and 7th St NW. DC's best art shop – thousands of books, prints, slides, posters and postcards. See p.78.

National Museum of African Art, 950 Independence Ave SW. Splendid displays of African arts and crafts, including great fabrics and jewellery.

National Museum of American History, 14th St and Constitution Ave NW. The Smithsonian's biggest store is great for souvenirs. Everything about America – music, books, T-shirts, kitchenware, ceramics, posters, toys, crafts, jewellery and repro items from the museum. See p.97.

Textile Museum, 2320 S St NW. Unique T-shirts, ethnic fabrics, textile books, silks, cushion covers, ties, kimonos and jewellery. See p.214.

Music stores

Flying Saucer Discs, 2318 18th St NW, Adams-Morgan ☎ 265-DISC. Basement store with good range of used pop, rock, rap, jazz, world and classical CDs.

HMV, 1229 Wisconsin Ave NW, Georgetown ☎ 333-9292. Two floors of music with plenty of range. Open daily until 11pm (midnight at weekends).

Kemp Mill Music, 1254 Wisconsin Ave NW, Georgetown ☎ 333-1392; 1518 Connecticut Ave NW, Dupont Circle ☎ 332-8247; 2459 18th St NW, Adams-Morgan ☎ 387-1011; 1900 L St NW, New Downtown ☎ 223-5310. Local chain for mainstream and chart releases, often with good discount offers.

Smash, 3279 M St NW, Georgetown ☎ 337-6274. Punk, hardcore, new wave and Indie music, T-shirts, boots and clothes.

Tower Records, 2000 Pennsylvania Ave NW, Foggy Bottom ☎ 331-2400. Biggest music store in town, with in-store appearances. Daily until midnight.

Chapter 18

DC's Festival Calendar

The best of DC's major **festivals, parades and annual events** are picked out below, month by month, though for a comprehensive list contact the *Washington DC Convention and Visitors Association*. Note that many festivals vary their dates from year to year while birthday celebrations for famous people generally take place on the nearest weekend; call the numbers given, check with one of the organizations listed below and watch the local press for exact dates.

Annual music festivals are detailed in chapters 15 (*Live Music*) and 16 (*The Arts and Entertainment*); while **open days** at museums, galleries and attractions are covered where appropriate in the text. For a list of **national public holidays**, see *Basics*, p.22.

January

Dr Martin Luther King Jr's Birthday (Fri before the Mon national holiday): wreath-laying at the Lincoln Memorial, reading of the "I have a dream" speech, concerts and speeches. ☎619-7222.

Information Lines

National Park Service ☎ 619-7222
Post-Haste ☎ 334-9000
Smithsonian ☎ 357-2700
Washington DC CVA ☎ 789-7000
Washington DC Events Office
☎ 619-7222
For more details see p.40.

Robert E Lee's Birthday (19th): celebrations, music and food at Arlington House in Arlington Cemetery (p.245); special events in Old Town Alexandria, VA (p.251). ☎703/557-0613.

February

Chinese New Year (date varies): dragon-dancers, parades and fireworks on H St NW in Chinatown. ☎724-4093.

African-American History Month (all month): special events, exhibits and cultural programmes. Information from the Smithsonian, National Park Service or Martin Luther King Memorial Library (p.195).

Abraham Lincoln's Birthday (12th): wreath-laying and reading of the Gettysburg Address (p.60) at the Lincoln Memorial. ☎619-7222.

Frederick Douglass' Birthday (14th): wreath-laying and other events at Cedar Hill, Anacostia (see p.139). ☎619-7222.

George Washington's Birthday Parade (22nd): spectacular parade and events in Old Town Alexandria, VA. ☎703/838-4200. Also, events, concerts and wreath-laying at Mount Vernon (p.225).

March

St Patrick's Day (17th): big parades down Constitution Ave NW, as well as celebrations in Old Town Alexandria and at Arlington House, Arlington Cemetery, VA. ☎637-2474 for grandstand seats on Constitution Ave. Also an Irish festival of arts, music and dance – ☎347-1450.

All telephone area codes in this chapter are ☎202 unless otherwise stated.

DC's Festival
Calendar

US Botanic Gardens Spring Flower Show: runs through April. ☎225-7099.

Smithsonian Kite Festival (end of the month): kite-flying competitions for all at the Washington Monument. ☎357-3030.

April

National Cherry Blossom Festival (early April): the famous trees around the Tidal Basin (see p.64) bloom in late March/early April; celebrated by a massive parade down Constitution Ave NW, crowning of the festival queen, free concerts, lantern-lighting, dances and races. Parade ticket information ☎728-1137; other events ☎646-0366.

Blessing of the Fleet (mid-month): nautical celebrations and services at US Navy Memorial (p.174). ☎737-2300. Associated events at Southwest Waterfront marina (p.136).

Easter Sunrise Service (Easter Sun): sunrise memorial service at Arlington National Cemetery. ☎475-0856.

White House Easter Egg Roll (Easter Mon): entertainment and egg-rolling (eggs provided) on the White House South Lawn. Special garden tours on one weekend after Easter. Call well in advance. ☎456-2200.

Thomas Jefferson's Birthday (13th): wreath-laying and military drills at the Jefferson Memorial. ☎619-7222.

Duke Ellington's Birthday (20th): music and events at Freedom Plaza, Pennsylvania Ave NW. ☎331-9404.

Smithsonian Craft Show (late April): craft exhibitions in the National Building Museum (p.184).

Marvin Gaye/Save the Children Day (end of the month): downtown street festival sponsored by the African-American Music Foundation. ☎678-0503.

May

Flower Mart (1st weekend): flowers, booths, children's entertainment and displays at Washington National Cathedral. ☎537-6200.

Asian-Pacific American Heritage Festival (first weekend): cultural displays, food stalls and activities in Freedom Plaza, Pennsylvania Ave NW. ☎659-2311 or 703/354-5036.

Malcom X Day (mid-month): commemorative concerts, films and speeches in Anacostia Park. ☎724-4093.

Bob Marley Commemorative Day Festival (mid-month): reggae concerts and events at Freedom Plaza, Pennsylvania Ave NW. ☎724-9060.

Worldfest (date varies): two-day, outdoor array of ethnic music, food and events on Pennsylvania Ave between 9th and 14th streets. ☎724-5430.

Memorial Day (last Mon): wreath-layings, services and speeches at Arlington Cemetery ☎475-0856; Vietnam Veterans Memorial ☎619-7222, and US Navy Memorial ☎737-2300. The NSO performs on the Capitol's West Lawn (on the Sun) and there's a jazz festival in Old Town Alexandria ☎838-4200.

June

Phillipine Independence Day Parade (3rd): Pennsylvania Ave parade and a fair on Freedom Plaza. ☎724-4093.

Dance Africa (mid-month): festival of African dance, open-air market and concerts at Dance Place, 3225 8th St NE ☎269-1600.

Marvin Gaye Jr Appreciation Day (mid-month): street events and music on Pennsylvania Ave between 13th and 14th streets. ☎724-4093.

Festival of American Folklife (end of June and first two weekends in July). One of the country's biggest festivals: American music, crafts, food, and folk heritage events on the Mall (between 7th and 14th). ☎357-2700.

July

National Independence Day Celebration (4th): reading of the Declaration of Independence at National Archives (p.179), parade along Constitution Ave NW, free concerts at the Sylvan Theater near the Washington Monument, NSO performance on west steps of US Capitol, finishing with superb firework display – get there as early as possible for all events. ☎619-7222.

Mary McLeod Bethune Celebration (date varies): wreath-laying, gospel choir and speakers at Bethune statue, Lincoln Park (p.126). ☎619-7222.

Caribbean Summer in the Park (mid-month): outdoor music, food and dancing, at RFK Stadium. ☎249-1028.

Hispanic-Latino Festival (end of the month): Constitution Ave parade; food, crafts, music, dance and theatre in Adams-Morgan and Mount Pleasant. ☎835-1555 or 454-2464.

August

Arlington County Fair (mid-month): fair with rides, crafts, entertainment, food stalls and concerts at Thomas Jefferson Center, 3501 2nd St, Arlington, VA ☎703/358-6400.

Georgia Avenue Day (end of the month): parade along Georgia Ave (at Eastern Ave NW), plus carnival rides, music, food and stalls. ☎723-5166.

September

Labor Day Weekend Concert (Sun before the holiday): NSO plays on west lawn of the US Capitol to mark the end of the summer season. ☎619-7222.

Adams-Morgan Day (first Sun after Labor Day): one of the best of the neighbourhood festivals, with live music, crafts and cuisine along 18th St NW – always packed and great fun. ☎332-3292.

Constitution Day Commemoration (17th): Constitution displayed at the National Archives (p.179) to celebrate the anniversary of its signing; naturalization ceremonies, parade and concerts. ☎501-5215.

National Frisbee Festival (date varies): frisbee-related activities on the Mall, near the Air and Space Museum. ☎301/645-5043.

African Cultural Festival (date varies): ethnic music, dance, cuisine, arts and crafts at Freedom Plaza. ☎667-5775.

Black Family Reunion (date varies): weekend festival on the Mall celebrating the African-American family. ☎628-0015.

German-American Day (end of the month): Teutonic food and entertainment in Freedom Plaza. ☎554-2664.

October

Taste of DC (date varies): restaurant festival mixing tastings with arts and crafts, children's shows, and entertainment on Pennsylvania Ave NW ☎724-4093.

Columbus Day Ceremonies (2nd Mon): wreath-laying, speeches and music at the Columbus Memorial in front of Union Station. ☎301/434-2332.

White House Fall Garden Tours (mid-month): garden tours and military band concerts. Call well in advance. ☎456-2200.

Halloween (31st): unoffical block parties, costumed goings-on and fright-nights in Georgetown, Dupont Circle and other middle-class neighbourhoods.

November

Annual Seafaring Celebration (date varies): the Navy Museum (p.137) hosts a family event with maritime activities, food, arts and children's performances. ☎433-4882.

Veteran's Day Ceremonies (11th): solemn services and wreath-laying at 11am at Arlington Cemetery (p.241), Vietnam Veterans Memorial (p.61), and US Navy Memorial (p.174).

December

Christmas Tree Lightings (beginning of the month): separate ceremonies for the lighting of the Capitol (west side) and National (Ellipse) Xmas trees – the latter lit by the President. The entire month on the Ellipse sees nativity scenes, choral groups, and other seasonal displays. ☎619-7222.

Washington National Cathedral Christmas Services (all month): carols, pageants, choral performances and bell-ringing. ☎537-6200.

White House Candlelight Tours (usually 26th–28th): extremely popular evening White House tours. Call well in advance. ☎456-2200 or 619-7222.

DC's Festival Calendar

Chapter 19

City Directory

All telephone numbers are area code ☎202 unless otherwise stated.

AIRLINES *Air Canada* ☎1-800/776-3000; *Air France* ☎1-800/321-4538; *Alitalia* ☎331-1841; *America West* ☎1-800/235-9292; *American Airlines* ☎1-800/433-7300; *British Airways* ☎1-800/247-9297; *Continental Airlines* ☎1-800/525-0280; *Delta* ☎1-800/221-1212; *Finnair* ☎1-800/950-5000; *Icelandair* ☎1-800/223-5500; *Japan Airlines* ☎1-800/525-3663; *KLM* ☎1-800/284-6210; *Korean Air* ☎1-800/438-5000; *Lufthansa* ☎1-800/645-3880; *Northwest* ☎1-800/225-2525; *SAS* ☎1-800/221-2350; *Swissair* ☎1-800/221-4750; *TWA* ☎1-800/221-2000 or 737-7400; *USAir* ☎1-800/428-4322; *United Airlines* ☎1-800/241-6522 or 703/742-4600; *Valujet* ☎1-800/825-8538; *Virgin Atlantic* ☎1-800/862-8621.

BUS DEPARTURES Call *Greyhound* (☎1-800/231-2222) or *Peter Pan Trailways* (☎371-2111 or 1-800/343-9999); departures to Baltimore, Philadelphia, New York, Boston and beyond are from the terminal at 1005 1st St NE.

CITY TAXES DC sales tax is 6 percent; restaurant tax 10 percent; hotel tax 13 percent plus $1.50 occupancy charge.

DOCTORS AND DENTISTS Lists of doctors can be found in the Yellow Pages under "Clinics" or "Physicians and Surgeons". Most large hotels either have a doctor on call or will direct you to a private surgery. For a doctor referral service call ☎362-8677, or contact your embassy (see below). The basic consultation fee is $50–100, payable in advance. Contact the *DC Dental Society* ☎547-7613 (Mon–Fri 8am–4pm) for dentist referral.

EMBASSIES AND CONSULATES
Australia, 1601 Massachusetts Ave NW, 20036 ☎797-3000
Canada, 501 Pennsylvania Ave NW, 20001 ☎682-1740
Ireland, 2234 Massachusetts Ave NW, 20008 ☎462-3939
Netherlands, 4200 Linnean Ave NW, 20008 ☎244-5300
New Zealand, 37 Observatory Circle NW, 20008 ☎328-4800
United Kingdom, 3100 Massachusetts Ave NW, 20008 ☎462-1340

GAY AND LESBIAN CONTACTS Gay and Lesbian Hotline ☎833-3234, a counselling and referral service; Gay Info and Assistance ☎363-3881; Gay Community Yellow Pages ☎1-800/849-0406. Also visit *Lambda Rising*, 1426 21st St NW, Dupont Circle ☎462-6969, a gay/lesbian bookstore which acts as a clearing-house for information and events. See p.285 for bar and club details.

HOSPITAL *George Washington University Medical Center*, 901 23rd St NW ☎994-4782 has a 24-hr medical advice line.

City Directory

LIBRARIES The general public can use the Library of Congress (see p.121 for details), while the main city library is the Martin Luther King Memorial Library, 901 G St NW (see p.195).

NEWSPAPERS AND MAGAZINES The relatively liberal *Washington Post* is DC's main and most respected daily newspaper, challenged in news coverage (though not style or balance) only by the conservative, Moonie-published *Washington Times*. Free weeklies include the investigative *CityPaper* – best in the city for news and listings – and the gay *Washington Blade* and *Metro Weekly*; glossy monthlies include the *Washingtonian* and *Where Washington*; while there's a host of other local/neighbourhood papers and magazines, all available in bars, restaurants, shops and hotels.

PHARMACIES *CVS* has forty different locations throughout DC, with convenient downtown and Georgetown sites and 24-hr stores at 14th St NW and Thomas Circle ☎628-0720, and 7 Dupont Circle ☎785-1466. Foreign visitors should bear in mind that many pills available over the counter at home need a prescription in the US – most codeine-based painkillers, for example – and that local brand names can be confusing; ask if you're unsure.

POLICE In an emergency call ☎911. For non-emergency help, information and location of local stations call ☎727-1010. The Metro Transit Police are on ☎962-2121.

RADIO STATIONS Local AM stations include: WMAL (630) for news, sports and talk; WJFK (1300) for jazz; WOL (1450) for soul and talk; WTOP (1500) for news; WPGC (1580) for hip-hop. Local FM stations include: WAMU (88.5) for news, talk and music; WDCU (90.1) for jazz and talk; WHFS (99.1) for rock; WARX (106.9) for golden oldies; WRQX (107.3) for 70s–90s pop and rock.

SPORTS Washington Redskins play at the RFK Stadium, 2400 E Capitol St SE ☎546-2222, but you'll never get a ticket unless you're prepared to pay ridiculous prices to scalpers, agents and newspaper advertisers (pre-season games are easier). Closest decent baseball team is the Baltimore Orioles, Oriole Park at Camden Yards, 333 Camden St, Baltimore, MD ☎410/685-9800 – *Maryland Rail Commuter Service (MARC;* ☎1-800/325-7245) trains from Union Station run right there. A surprising success has been the new soccer team, DC United, which plays Major League games at RFK Stadium ☎478-6600. The basketball team, Washington Bullets, play at the USAir Arena, 1 Harry S Truman Drive, Landover MD ☎301/622-3865.

TRAIN DEPARTURES Amtrak ☎1-800/872-7245 or 484-7540 – buy tickets either at Union Station, the *Amtrak Travel Center,* 1721 K St NW, or New Carrollton (MD) or Alexandria (VA) stations. *Maryland Rail Commuter Service (MARC;* ☎1-800/325-7245) connects DC to Baltimore – tickets from Union Station.

TRAVELERS AID SOCIETY Useful help, emergency and information desks run by a voluntary, non-profit agency. Main office is 1015 12th St NW (☎546-3120; Mon–Fri 9am–5pm); other offices at Union Station (☎546-3120; Mon–Sat 9.30am–5.30pm, Sun 12.30–5.30pm); National Airport (☎703/419-3972; Mon–Fri 9am–9pm, Sat & Sun 9am–6pm); Dulles Airport (☎703/661-8636; Mon–Fri 10am–9pm, Sat & Sun 10am–6pm).

TV STATIONS Channel 4 (WRC/NBC); Channel 5 (WTTG/Fox); Channel 7 (WJLA/ABC); Channel 9 (WUSA/CBS); Channel 26 (WETA/PBS).

Part 4

Contexts

A History of Washington DC

In the two centuries since Washington DC was founded – purpose-built as the nation's capital – it's been at the heart of American government, a showcase city embodying the ideals and aspirations of the United States of America. However, it's also a city where people live and work, a fact that's easy to forget among the mighty monuments and memorials. The history below provides a brief exposition of the main themes in the city's development; for more detail on specific matters – from biographies of famous people to histories of buildings – follow the pointers at the end of each section.

Early settlers

The first white settlers to clap eyes on the Potomac River region – site of modern DC – were the pioneers under Captain John Smith of the Virginia Company in 1608. Sponsored by the English King James I, they had established the first successful English colony in America the previous year at Jamestown on the coast, to the south, and lost little time exploring their surroundings. Despite early setbacks and conflict with the local native population, the colonists flourished on the back of a thriving tobacco trade: Virginia, and then Maryland (created as a haven for Catholics in 1632), expanded as English, Irish and Scottish settlers poured into the region, displacing the indigenous population and introducing slaves from Africa to work the plantations. Not least of these pioneers was one Captain John

Washington, George's great-grandfather, who in 1656 arrived from Essex in England, and immediately set about establishing a plantation on the river. The Potomac remained an important commercial thoroughfare and vibrant new towns sprang up alongside it: notably Alexandria in Virginia (1749) and Georgetown in Maryland (1751).

Establishment of the capital

In 1775, in the context of increasing hostilities with the British, the colonies – now calling themselves states – drafted the Declaration of Independence. Following the ensuing American War of Independence (1775–83), during which Virginia's George Washington served as commander-in-chief of the Continental Army, came proposals for the establishment of a permanent capital city. There was no obvious site: the exigencies of war and conflicting political interests in the new republic meant that early meetings of Congress had gathered in several different cities. The Constitutional Convention of 1787, which devised a permanent system of government for the nation, was held in Philadelphia, while George Washington was elected as first President of the United States in New York City in 1789. Extended political wrangling between the mercantile North and agrarian South, who both wanted the capital, came to an end when a southern site on the Potomac was chosen (near George Washington's beloved estate at Mount Vernon), with land to be donated by Virginia and

Maryland. Washington hired surveyors Andrew Ellicot and the African-American Benjamin Banneker to conduct the preliminary survey.

Building the city

In 1791, French engineer Pierre Charles L'Enfant began work on a grand plan for the new city, and though he was fired the following year, his blueprint was largely followed by his successors. The first stone of the Executive Mansion (later known as the White House) was laid in 1792, construction of the US Capitol followed in 1793, and in 1800 Congress and second president John Adams moved from Philadelphia to the nascent city. The following year, Thomas Jefferson became the first president to be inaugurated in Washington DC. The population of 3500 was then little more than that of a village, based largely around Capitol Hill and the Executive Mansion, overseen by a mayor and council. Its numbers were boosted by over three thousand slaves who laboured on the new buildings, wharves and streets and lived in the swamp-ridden reaches near the river. Progress was interrupted by the War of 1812 with England; in 1814, English occupying forces burned the White House, Capitol and other public buildings to the ground. President Madison was forced to relocate to a private house, known as the Octagon, while Congress met in a hastily assembled Brick Capitol until the US Capitol was fully restored in 1819.

Mid-nineteenth-century malaise

Between the War of 1812 and the Civil War, the new capital struggled to make its mark. The Mall – L'Enfant's showpiece thoroughfare – remained a muddy swamp, and construction was slow and piecemeal. Foreign ambassadors collected hardship pay while stationed in this marshy outpost, and criticism was heaped upon the place, not least by visitors like Charles Dickens (in the 1840s) and Anthony Trollope (1860s). Despite its detractors, however, the city was slowly beginning to look the part. Pennsylvania Avenue was spruced up (and the Treasury Building added in 1836), and work started on the Washington Monument in 1848. British gentleman scientist and philanthropist James Smithson made a huge bequest in 1829, which led to the foundation of the Smithsonian Institution; its first home, the Smithsonian Institution Building (or the "Castle") on the Mall, was completed in 1855.

Though the population increased slowly, throughout the first half of the century it never grew above 60,000. The balance of the steadily increasing black population shifted, however, as the number of runaway slaves and free blacks (migrants from Southern plantations) increased dramatically. Separate black schools and churches were established as debate intensified between abolitionists and pro-slavery adherents – the so-called Snow Riots (1835) saw intimidation and destruction by white mobs intent on maintaining slavery in the capital.

The Civil War

Following the Confederate attack on Fort Sumter, which finally propelled the country into war, Abraham Lincoln's call to defend the Union in 1861 brought thousands of volunteer soldiers to Washington, virtually doubling the city's population. Others left to join the Confederate cause; not least Robert E Lee, who abandoned his home at Arlington and his Union Army post to take command of the Virginian military. Washington DC became the epicentre of the Union effort and the North's main supply depot, surrounded by defensive forts, its public buildings turned over to massive makeshift hospitals. Lincoln determined to continue construction in the capital (symbolically, the Capitol dome was added in 1863), despite fear of imminent attack by Southern forces – the city was never overrun, though several of the bloodiest and most decisive battles (including Bull Run, Antietam and

Gettysburg) were fought within ninety miles. As Lincoln's war aims became more focused, the Civil War became a war about slavery. The system was outlawed in DC in 1862 and Lincoln signed the Emancipation Act in 1863, freeing all slaves in the rebel states; thus defeated by the North's superior strength and economic muscle, and legally stripped of the right to operate a system crucial to their economic survival, the Confederate South was effectively vanquished. The war ended in April 1865 with Lee's surrender to General Ulysses S Grant. Five days later, President Lincoln was assassinated in the capital while attending a play at Ford's Theater.

Reconstruction and expansion

The period after the Civil War was an era of tremendous growth in DC as ex-slaves from the South and returned soldiers settled in the city – within thirty years, the population stood at 300,000, and distinct neighbourhoods were emerging. Black residents now comprised 40 percent of the population and enjoyed unprecedented rights and privileges in the aftermath of emancipation. Suffrage was extended to all adult men for local DC elections (1866); black public schools became established and the all-black Howard University was founded (1867); segregation was prohibited; and ex-slave, orator and abolitionist Frederick Douglass was appointed marshal (and, later, recorder of deeds) of DC. In 1867, when Congress granted the District of Columbia territorial status, for the first time the city embarked on a coherent public works programme under Alexander "Boss" Shepherd – a short-lived exercise in local democracy that ended in 1874, when control of the debt-ridden city passed back to Congress. Washington's cultural profile, however, went from strength to strength, boosted after the 1876 Philadelphia Centennial Exhibition when the Smithsonian

Institution built America's first National Museum (now the Arts and Industries Building) on the Mall to provide a permanent home for the exhibition's artefacts. The Renwick and Corcoran galleries – two of the earliest public art galleries in the country – both opened during this period. The Washington Monument, first of the city's grand presidential memorials, was finally completed in 1884, as DC began to reshape itself as a national showpiece. As its stock rose, place-seekers and lobbyists (a term first coined during Grant's presidency) flooded into the city, seeking attachment to the administration of the day; in 1881, just four months after his inauguration, President James Garfield became the second President to be assassinated in Washington, shot by a man denied a civil service post.

The turn of the century

By the turn of the century, Washington had established itself as a thriving, modern capital city with civic and federal buildings to match: in a flurry of construction, Patent Office, Post Office, Pension Building and fine new premises for the Library of Congress (1897) were erected, while Theodore Roosevelt carried out the first full-scale expansion and renovation of the White House (1901). Meanwhile, LeDroit Park, Adams-Morgan and Woodley Park became fashionable suburbs; Georgetown was formally merged with DC, and the Smithsonian branched out again with the establishment of the National Zoo. In 1901, a committee under Senator James McMillan proposed the development and extension of the city's park system, and later the National Commission of Fine Arts was established to coordinate public improvements and new building design: the country's largest train station, Union Station, was completed in the prevailing Beaux Arts style in 1908 and, in 1910, height restrictions were imposed on downtown buildings to pre-serve the cityscape. However, after the high hopes of the Reconstruction years, the city's black population suffered from increasing segre-gation and loss of civil rights. Housing in black neighbourhoods like Foggy Bottom and Georgetown was in poor shape, federal jobs became harder to come by, and the black popu-lation actually decreased.

World War I and the Depression

The US entered World War I in 1917, despite President Woodrow Wilson's avowed efforts to remain neutral; after the war, Washington's population increased again as soldiers returned home. The post-war years in DC were as troubled as for the rest of the US. Under Wilson (the only president to remain in the city after his term of office), Prohibition was imposed in an attempt to improve the morality of the nation, and a num-ber of strikes were violently broken. Racial ten-sion increased in this uneasy climate, which saw segregation entrenched, the Ku Klux Klan parad-ing at the Washington Monument, and race riots, fanned by demobbed white soldiers, breaking out in the city in 1919. Ironically, segregation also worked to boost the fortunes of DC's black neigh-bourhoods: prevented from socializing else-where, blacks made Shaw's U Street famous as the "Black Broadway", nurturing stars such as Duke Ellington. Downtown, the Phillips Collection opened in 1921 as America's first modern art museum, while the building of the Lincoln Memorial (1922) and Freer Gallery (1923) repre-sented the last cultural gasps of the McMillan Commission. The capital, with its government agencies and large federal payroll, was not as hard hit as rural or industrial areas by the Great Depression; unemployed marchers from the rest of the country descended upon the Capitol to register their distress in 1931 and 1932 (the lat-ter march dispersed by the army). Franklin D Roosevelt's New Deal, and, specifically, the Works Progress Administration (WPA), put thousands of jobless men to work – in DC, among other pro-

jects, building Federal Triangle and the Supreme Court (1935). If proof were needed that racial prejudice was still institutionalized in America's capital it came in 1939 with the banning by the Daughters of the American Revolution (DAR) of black contralto Marian Anderson from singing in their building – she subsequently appeared in front of a huge desegregated crowd at the Lincoln Memorial.

World War II to 1968

1941 saw the entry of the US into World War II. The third great wartime influx boosted the popu-lation again; guards were posted at the White House and Capitol, air defences installed in case of Japanese attack, and the Pentagon built in 1943 to accommodate the expanding War Department. The war years also saw the opening of the National Gallery of Art (1941), the nation's finest art gallery, and the completion of the Jefferson Memorial (1943). Following the war, under presidents Truman and Eisenhower, Washington grew as the federal government expanded and by 1960 the population touched 800,000: the White House was completely over-hauled, neighbouring Foggy Bottom – once a poor, black neighbourhood – became the seat of various departments and organizations, and new housing proliferated in suburban Maryland and Virginia.

The war had gone some way to changing racial perceptions in America, as black soldiers had again enlisted in their droves to fight for free-dom, and in the post-war years the Civil Rights movement began to gain strength. Segregation of public facilities was finally declared illegal by the Supreme Court ruling on *Brown vs. Topeka Board of Education* and schools in DC were desegregated in 1954. In the trenchant southern states, however, the ruling was obeyed only in name, leading to an increasingly politicized, nationwide stream of demonstrations, boycotts, sit-ins and marches in the 1950s and early

1960s. A nascent feeling of widespread hope culminated in John F Kennedy's close election victory in 1961 – the youngest president ever to take office, and the first Catholic – and was epitomized by Rev Dr Martin Luther King Jr's famous "I have a dream" speech during the March on Washington for Jobs and Freedom at the Lincoln Memorial in August 1963. Just three months later, however, JFK was assassinated in Dallas, and buried in Arlington Cemetery. In 1964 DC citizens voted in a presidential election for the first time, following the 23rd Amendment of 1961, which gave them new electoral rights. The contest was won with a huge majority by Lyndon Johnson, who as vice-president had been governing the country since Kennedy's death.

By the late 1960s protest had broadened beyond the realm of Civil Rights, and demonstrations in Washington were called against poverty (notably the Poor People's March, in 1968) and the war in Vietnam. Discrimination against blacks forced itself explosively back on to the agenda with the assassination of Dr Martin Luther King, in Memphis in 1968. His death sparked off nationwide riots, including the worst in DC's history; Shaw and the old downtown neighbourhoods were devastated. The white flight to the suburbs began in earnest and DC became predominantly black.

The 1970s

The 1970s put politics centre stage in DC. In 1970, DC got its first non-voting delegate to the House of Representatives; three years later, the Home Rule Act paved the way for the city's first elected mayor – Walter Washington – for more than a century; and the Watergate scandal of 1974 led to the resignation of a president. Meanwhile, divisions within the city became increasingly stark. Downtown areas continued to reshape themselves – the Kennedy Center opened in 1971, the Hirshorn Museum (1974) and East Wing of the National Gallery of Art

(1979) were added to the Mall, the K Street business district in New Downtown thrived, the new Southwest Waterfront acquired character, and arty Dupont Circle became one of the city's trendiest neighbourhoods – while Shaw and areas of southeast and northeast Washington slipped further into degradation, with a drug-and-crime problem that earned DC the enduring tag as "Murder Capital" of America. Such contradictions were largely ignored, however, and in 1976, Bicentennial year, the city celebrated by opening its Metrorail system and the National Air and Space Museum – still the top museum attraction in Washington.

The 1980s

Under Ronald Reagan, the nation's economy boomed and bust as taxes (and welfare and aid programmes) were cut, and the federal budget deficit soared. In DC, the souped-up economy paved the way for drastic downtown renovation projects: the building of the Convention Center (1980) signalled the revitalization of Old Downtown; Pennsylvania Avenue and its buildings – an eyesore for three decades – were restored; and the yuppies moved into Adams-Morgan. Reagan survived an assassination attempt in DC in 1985, but his reputation (and that of his successor, George Bush) were put through the mill by the various Iran-Contra proceedings, whose revelations (in an echo of Watergate) were carried live on TV from hearings in the city. As American military spending increased dramatically, major new patriotic memorials were built to the Vietnam Veterans (1982) and US Navy (1987). Culturally, the city went from strength to strength. The Smithsonian expanded its collections on the Mall with the addition of the Sackler Gallery and African Art Museum in 1987; the National Postal Museum opened (1986) and Union Station was restored (1988). City politics took a colourful turn with the successive administrations of Mayor Marion Barry (first elected in 1978), whose initial success in attracting investment soon gave way to conflict with Congress that was to become the hallmark of the following decade. The city began its slide into insolvency just as Bill Clinton was elected on promises to turn the economy around and restructure welfare.

Modern times: into the 1990s

On the surface, it was business as usual in tourist DC – now one of the most visited cities in America – as new attractions continued to open, notably the National Law Enforcement Officers Memorial in 1991, Holocaust Memorial Museum in 1993 and the Korean War Veterans Memorial and White House Visitor Center in 1995. Behind the scenes, though, Washington lurched into crisis in the first half of the 1990s, as the federal budget deficit spiralled. Amazingly, Marion Barry returned from a drug-related prison sentence to be re-elected as mayor in 1994 – only for Congress to revoke Washington's home rule charter a year later. A Congressionally appointed control board now has responsibility for the city's affairs, which look as bleak as they have ever done. Underfunding, unemployment and service

cuts have left the poorer parts of a city now 75 percent black in dire straits, while the showpiece downtown areas remain targeted at tourists and big business. Arguments over the budget between the Republican-dominated Congress and President Clinton briefly closed DC's museums and federal offices in 1995; following the 1996 general election, which merely entrenched each side in their positions, such conflicts are likely to occur again. Meanwhile, security scares at the White House in 1995 restricted access to Pennsylvania Avenue, leading many to question the traditional open-house policy at federal institutions in DC – there are now heightened security measures in place at most major government buildings. Businesses still find downtown DC an attractive investment, as the massive new building around Chinatown attests, but on a local level the city is in a parlous state. The total population is at its lowest since the 1930s – down to around 600,000 – as the mostly white well-to-do continue to leave in their droves. Away from the Mall, the museums, galleries and memorials, parts of the city look more like the Third World than capital of the First.

The American System of Government

In a self-governing republic – good government in some places, dubious in others – three thousand miles wide, eighteen hundred miles long, with fifty separate states which in many important matters have almost absolute powers – with two hundred million people [sic] drawn from scores of nations, what is remarkable is not the conflict between them but the truce.

Alistair Cooke, *Letter from America*, 1969

The American system of government derives squarely from the articles of the **Constitution of the United States**, thrashed out by the original thirteen states at the Constitutional Convention in Philadelphia and signed on September 17, 1787. Deriving its authority from the essential force of popular sovereignty – "We the People" – this gave a federal administration certain designated powers so that it could both resist attack from abroad and prevent the fragmentation of the nascent nation. Two centuries and 27 amendments later, the Constitution's provision of "checks and balances" on the exercise of power still provides the basis for the fundamental democratic stability of a country which, often and awfully, has looked less than united at times.

The idea was simple enough. The earlier **Articles of Confederation** (adopted during the Revolution) had joined a loose grouping of independent states together in Congress under a weak central legislature, but by the late 1780s it was clear that the system lacked internal logic – with no separation of executive powers, Congress had to request permission from the states every step of the way; each state retained the right to refuse consent (whether for money, permission for new laws or soldiers) and exercised the power in its own interest. What was needed, according to Federalists like Alexander Hamilton and James Madison, was a strong central government buttressed by a supreme Constitution; the Antifederalists who opposed them, fearing encroachment upon the sovereignty of the individual states, were appeased by the promise of the ratification of various amend-ments (adopted in 1791 in the ten-point Bill of Rights) which would encompass many of their demands. What was produced at the Constitutional Convention was nothing less than a triumph: eighty percent of the original text of the Constitution remains unchanged today; only seventeen more amendments have been added in the two centuries following the Bill of Rights; and the United States remains, on paper at least, one of the world's most enduring democracies.

As a **federal republic**, the country splits its powers between the government and the fifty individual states, basically protecting the states from unnecessary intrusions from an overbearing central government while allowing federal decisions to be made to benefit (or protect) the whole country: thus the states can police themselves, make local laws and raise taxes, but they can't issue currency, conclude foreign treaties, or maintain armed forces; on the other hand, the Constitution pledges that the federal government shall protect each of the states against invasion or "domestic violence". Moreover, those who framed the Constitution took great pains to emphasize that individual states should retain all powers not specifically removed or curtailed by the Constitution; reinforced by the 10th Amendment, this notion remains a fundamental tenet of American democracy, in which local and national powers are stringently defined within the framework of a federal, and not centralized, republic. Thus each state has a significant amount of autonomy, while their political structures duplicate the federal system, with their own legislative chambers, state courts and constitutions.

The Constitution and the Bill of Rights are on display in the National Archives; see p.179.

The **federal government** itself is comprised of three distinct **arms**: the legislative, executive and judiciary. Each operates as a check and balance on the other, and each directly affects individual liberties and not just those of the states.

Article 1 of the Constitution vests all **legislative** powers in a bi-cameral **Congress** made up of a House of Representatives and a Senate, which both meet in the US Capitol. When established in the eighteenth century, the House of Representatives was conceived as the body whose directly elected members would represent the people; the addition of a Senate, or upper house, would not only be a check on the House's power, but also a way of balancing the interests of the smaller states against the larger, since each state in the Senate has an equal vote. Moreover, the separation of powers between House and Senate was institutionalized from the start – Representatives and Senators are elected at different times, from differently sized constituencies for different lengths of office.

See p.109, p.144 and p.113 for histories of the US Capitol, the White House and Senate.

The **House of Representatives** (or simply House) has 435 members (the size fixed in 1929), with states allocated a number of representatives based on their population (which is reassessed, or "reapportioned", every ten years; each state is entitled to at least one representative). Members are elected from defined congressional districts (each containing around 500,000 people), serve for two years and receive around $125,000 per annum (plus the support of up to thirty staff members). The House is the more representative of the two chambers in more ways than just name: more frequent elections mean a sharper convergence with the general public's mood, while the House always has a significantly higher percentage of women and ethnic members than the Senate (though neither barely reflects the demographic make-up of modern America). Apart from the fifty states thus represented, there are also non-voting delegates in the House, representing the territories of Samoa, Guam and the Virgin Islands, and since 1973, Washington DC itself (see p.182 for more on Washington's peculiar status within the Union). The chief officer of the House is the **Speaker** (chosen from the ranks of the majority party); both parties also elect a leader in the House, known accordingly as the House Majority or House Minority leader, and a whip (to ensure the party members vote).

The **Senate** comprises two Senators from each state. At first, in rather aristocratic fashion, senators were chosen by the individual state legislatures, but in 1913, the 17th Amendment allowed for the direct election of Senators by state voters. Senators are elected for six years, with one third being elected every two years; they get paid less than representatives, earning a shade over $100,000 a year. Presiding officer in the Senate is the Vice-President (though on a day-to-day basis the Senate Majority Leader takes the chair); the V-P doesn't have a vote unless it's to break a tie.

In Congress, the House and the Senate share certain **responsibilities**, like assessing and collecting taxes, borrowing money, overseeing commerce, minting currency, maintaining the armed forces, declaring war and, crucially, making "all Laws which shall be necessary and proper for carrying into Execution" these matters. But each separate chamber also has its own responsibilities: all revenue-raising (ie tax) bills originate in the House of Representatives, though the Senate can propose changes to such bills; only the Senate offers advice to the President on foreign treaties or on nominations to Presidential appointments; and while the House has the sole power of impeachment of the President or other federal officer, the Senate is the body which decides whether to remove the person from office or not.

The House and Senate have separate chambers in the US Capitol, in which their debates take place. In practice, however, the **bills** that Congress debates as a prelude to making laws are generally put together and taken apart ("marked up", in the jargon) in over 250 smaller **standing committees** and **subcommittees** (not to mention *ad hoc* committees and joint committees), which meet in rooms in the Capitol building or in the various relevant House or Senate Office Buildings; the committees are made up of members from both parties, in rough accordance with their overall strength, and are usually chaired by senior members of the controlling party.

If a bill survives this process (and many don't), it is "reported" to the full House for consideration, where **amendments** may be added before the particular bill is voted upon. It can be defeated at this stage, and if it passes it's sent to the Senate, which can also make amendments before returning it to the House. Any differences are resolved by wrangles in a joint House-Senate **conference committee** to produce a final bill, acceptable to a majority in Congress. In addition to the standing committees of Congress, on occasion **select committees** are established to deliberate on special Congressional investigations or matters of national importance – most famously, perhaps, the unravellings of the Watergate affair.

Voting in Congress doesn't always divide upon party lines as it usually does in parliamentary democracies. Although the Speaker and the Rules Committee (which arranges the work of the House) can ensure that the majority party influences the make-up of various committees, the order of debates and nature of proposed amendments, strict party discipline is becoming less important. In the House, members often vote along state lines on particular issues, while specific matters increasingly are agreed and voted upon by members grouped into caucuses (or interest groups) which can cut across party loyalties.

Once a bill passes Congress it goes to the **executive** branch of government for approval, whose head is the **President**, or Chief Executive (on a current salary of $200,000; the V-P gets $160,000) – presidential powers are defined in Article 2 of the Constitution. The President can either sign the bill, when it becomes law, or veto it, in which case the bill goes back to the chamber where it originated; a two-thirds majority in that house, followed by the same in the other, and Congress can override the President to make the bill law. As well as being Chief Executive, the President is also **Commander-in-Chief** of the armed forces; he can make treaties with foreign powers (provided two-thirds of the Senate agrees) and, also under the Senate's advisement, can appoint ambassadors, Supreme Court judges and other federal officers. Lest the Chief Executive get too bold, though, the Constitution provides **parameters** for his power: under the terms of the 22nd Amendment, ratified in 1951, the President (and the Vice-President) is elected to office for four years and may only serve two terms. The amendment was a direct result of the presidency of Franklin Delano Roosevelt, who determined to preserve his New Deal programme and wary of impending war, served an unheard-of four consecutive terms. Moreover, the President is not above the law and can be removed from office by Congress "on impeachment for, and convic-

tion of, treason, bribery, or other high crimes and misdemeanors". If the President is removed from office, or he dies or resigns, the Vice-President gets the job until the next election; the Speaker of the House is third in line in the order of succession, followed by the Senate Majority Leader and then the Secretaries of the various executive departments in order of precedence. For more on the role of the presidency, see the feature on p.148–149.

This entire system is underpinned by the third arm of government, the **judiciary**, whose highest form is manifested in the **Supreme Court**, established by Article 3 of the Constitution. Right from the outset, the Court was designed as the final protector of the Constitution, its task to uphold its articles and the laws made under it – in effect, to maintain what the Constitution calls "the supreme law of the land". Consequently, every Congress member, and all executive and federal officers, are bound by oath to support and uphold the Constitution since they derive their powers from it. Ultimately, this notion of judicial supremacy boils down to the Constitution being what the Supreme Court says it is: the country has an "inferior" federal court system, in which legal decisions are made, and states are empowered to pass their own laws, but the appointed justices of the Supreme Court have the absolute right to throw out any legislation or legal argument which, in their opinion alone, violates the Constitution. Naturally, for this reason, the executive branch in the shape of each president is keen to appoint sympathetic justices to the Supreme Court bench. This, fortunately, for the system, is not as easy or as predictable as it might appear. For more on the make-up of the Supreme Court itself, see the feature on p.118–119.

Over the years, constitutional developments have also taken place outside the Constitution – that is, **informal changes** have been introduced to the system of government through custom or historical event. The Constitution makes no mention of political parties, primary elections or the Congressional committee system for example, though each is now firmly entrenched in the system.

That's the theory of American government. In practice, depending on whom you listen to, the entire structure – carefully crafted over two hundred years ago – is in a state somewhere between bare working order and terminal decline. Political historian David McKay puts his finger on the nub when he says that the "federal system, with its myriad governments and what amounts to fifty-one distinct constitutional structures, is the very essence of fragmentation". The most obvious drawback of the system of "checks and balances" is that it can work both for and against political progress. The Constitution forces the President to work with Congress on policy, and some of the wilder presidential excesses are certainly curtailed by Congressional deliberations. But in an entrenched **two-party system** such as exists today, much depends on the prevailing political climate in either House or Senate: stalemate (like that which engineered the federal shutdowns of 1996) or ineffective compromise tend to be the natural outcome of the checks and balances system.

Real-world Congressional politics, as opposed to the theoretical marvel of American democracy, can be an unedifying spectacle, involving the often squalid trading of political favours, known as "logrolling". Moreover, the people are increasingly isolated from their elected representatives by the simple fact that candidates now need to be very rich to stand in the first place. Partly in response to the Watergate revelations, the 1974 Federal Election Campaign Act limited party and corporate contributions to a candidate's campaign, though failed to place a limit on the candidate's own contributions – a **campaign** for a prospective House seat can now cost $250,000, and up to ten times that for a Senate seat. Hardly surprisingly, becoming a member of Congress is now seen as a career move: having invested the time and money, incumbent members are less likely to stand down whatever their personal or political failings and, statistically, more likely to be re-elected than a challenger (who doesn't have the same access to the media and to the reflected political glories of Congress colleagues).

As both Democrats and Republicans scramble to occupy the increasingly crowded middle ground, the **electorate** it seems is becoming more sophisticated in its intentions. A reasonably high (though ultimately futile) protest vote went to third-party candidate Ross Perot in 1992 and again in 1996. Moreover, the voters are both becoming less willing to give a president's party control of both houses of Congress at the same time (viz, the 1996 general election) and to give a president an overwhelming popular mandate. Since Richard Nixon's landslide in 1972, the Presidential victor's share of the popular vote has bobbed under and around fifty percent – the only one to buck the trend was Ronald Reagan in 1984 (who gained almost 59% of the vote). In the end, though, the general disdain felt for what goes on on Capitol Hill is perhaps best indicated by the fact that the **turnout** for Presidential and House elections only ranges from 30 to 50 percent – one of the lowest in any democracy in the world.

Presidents of the USA

In our brief national history we have shot four of our presidents, worried five of them to death, impeached one and hounded another out of office. And when all else fails, we hold an election and assassinate their characters.

P | O'Rourke, *Parliament of Whores*, 1991

Name	Party	Date	State of birth
George Washington	–	1789–97	Virginia
John Adams	Federalist	1797–1801	Massachusetts
Thomas Jefferson	Democratic-Republican	1801–09	Virginia
James Madison	Democratic-Republican	1809–17	Virginia
James Monroe	Democratic-Republican	1817–25	Virginia
John Quincy Adams	Democratic-Republican	1825–29	Massachusetts
Andrew Jackson	Democrat	1829–37	South Carolina
Martin Van Buren	Democrat	1837–41	New York
William H Harrison	Whig	1841 [died in office]	Virginia
John Tyler	Whig	1841–45	Virginia
James Polk	Democrat	1845–49	North Carolina
Zachary Taylor	Whig	1849–50 [died in office]	Virginia
Millard Fillmore	Whig	1850–53	New York
Franklin Pierce	Democrat	1853–57	New Hampshire
James Buchanan	Democrat	1857–61	Pennsylvania
Abraham Lincoln	Republican	1861–65 [assassinated]	Kentucky
Andrew Johnson	Union	1865–69	North Carolina
Ulysses S Grant	Republican	1869–77	Ohio
Rutherford B Hayes	Republican	1877–81	Ohio
James A Garfield	Republican	1881 [assassinated]	Ohio
Chester A Arthur	Republican	1881–85	Vermont
Grover Cleveland	Democrat	1885–89	New Jersey
Benjamin Harrison	Republican	1889–93	Ohio
Grover Cleveland	Democrat	1893–97	New Jersey
William McKinley	Republican	1897–1901	Ohio
Theodore Roosevelt	Republican	1901–09	New York
William H Taft	Republican	1909–13	Ohio
Woodrow Wilson	Democrat	1913–21	Virginia
Warren G Harding	Republican	1921–23 [died in office]	Ohio
Calvin Coolidge	Republican	1923–29	Vermont
Herbert Hoover	Republican	1929–33	Iowa
Franklin D Roosevelt	Democrat	1933–45 [died in office]	New York
Harry S Truman	Democrat	1945–53	Missouri
Dwight D Eisenhower	Republican	1953–61	Texas
John F Kennedy	Democrat	1961–63 [assassinated]	Massachusetts
Lyndon B Johnson	Democrat	1963–69	Texas
Richard M Nixon	Republican	1969–74 [resigned]	California
Gerald Ford	Republican	1974–77	Nebraska
James (Jimmy) Carter	Democrat	1977–81	Georgia
Ronald Reagan	Republican	1981–89	Illinois
George Bush	Republican	1989–93	Massachusetts
William (Bill) Clinton	Democrat	1993–	Arkansas

Books

There are plenty of books which touch upon the history, politics and personalities of Washington DC; the problem is in getting an overall picture of the city. There's no one single straightforward and up-to-date history of DC, while visitors through the ages have tended only to include their observations of the capital as part of wider works about America. However, every book on American history contains at least a few pages about the founding of the capital city; Civil War treatises highlight DC as Lincoln's headquarters (and place of assassination), while Presidential autobiographies and biographies, from those of George Washington onwards, necessarily recount the daily experience of political and social life in the capital.

In this chapter we've picked out some of the better, and more widely available, books about Washington DC, including novels set in the city. Many are available in good bookshops everywhere, and most in good **bookstores** in DC itself (see p.301 for a list) – where you'll also find local guides to ethnic restaurants, political trivia, cycling in the city, what to do with kids, and the like. Every major museum, gallery and attraction in DC sells related books, too, and these are a good first stop if you're looking for something arcane or specific – say a *History of Cats in the White House* or *101 Things to do with a Beltway Journalist*. The selection in the National Museum of American History (p.96) is perhaps the finest, while the Smithsonian Institution itself produces a wide range of titles on a variety of city-related topics. Finally, the White House Historical Association (740 Jackson Place, DC 20560,

☎ 202/737-8292) publishes a series of informative accounts of the White House, its contents and historical occupants.

In the list below, the US publisher is listed first, followed by the UK publisher. Where the book is published by the same company in both countries, the name of the company appears just once, and where books are published in only one of these countries, UK or US follows the publisher's name.

History

David Brinkley *Washington Goes to War* (Ballantine/Deutsch). Acclaimed account of the capital during World War II under FDR, charting its emergence onto the international stage.

Alistair Cooke. Over sixty years as a correspondent has left Cooke with a wealth of American stories, personal histories and snapshots of cities, times and crises that adorn everything he writes and broadcasts. The capital appears as a bit player in much of his work, though its presidents, politicians and people provide substance.

Francine Curro Cary *Urban Odyssey: A Multicultural History of Washington DC* (Smithsonian Institution Press). A readable historical account of settlement (and racial discrimination) in the city.

David Lewis *District of Columbia: A History* (Norton, US). Useful standard history of the District, although written as it was in 1976, it stops well short of contemporary times.

Lloyd Lewis *The Assassination of Lincoln: History and Myth* (University of Nebraska Press). Lyrical, minute-by-minute account of the city's most notorious assassination and its aftermath, first written in 1929 (as *Myths After Lincoln*) and still entertaining.

Politics and politicians

Anonymous *Primary Colors* (Warner/Random House). Highly readable, barely disguised account of a presidential primary campaign by young, charismatic, calculating, philandering, Southern governor Jack Stanton. Published amid

Presidential Biographies

Any good bookshop can provide a massive range of presidential biographies and memoirs. It's a growth industry – more books were written about Bill Clinton during his first term than about all the other presidents put together – which means it's difficult to pick the wheat from the chaff, but recent, well-received biographies have included David Herbert Donald's *Lincoln* (Simon & Schuster/Pimlico), Roy Jenkins' *Truman* (Harper Collins/Pan McMillan), Jonathan Aitken's *Nixon: A Life* (Regnery/Wiedenfeld & Nicholson) and Martin Walker's *Clinton: the President We [They] Deserve* (Crown/Fourth Estate).

great controversy in 1996, the book threw into the public domain the more reprehensible antics of press and politicians – its author was eventually unmasked as journalist and Washington insider Joe Klein.

Carl Bernstein and Bob Woodward *All the President's Men* (Simon & Schuster, US), *The Final Days* (Touchstone, US). America's most famous journalistic sleuths tell the gripping story of the unravelling of the Nixon presidency. *All the President's Men* is a great book, later made into a great film; *The Final Days* saw the duo wrapping up the loose ends. Although both have written investigative books since, none has matched these early classics.

Paul F Boller *Presidential Anecdotes, Presidential Campaigns, Congressional Anecdotes* (all OUP). Amusing, inconsequential political factoids – who did what, where and when, and with whom.

Nigel Cawthorne *Sex Lives of the US Presidents* (Prion). Cawthorne turns his scurrilous eye to the horizontal pleasures of the world's most powerful men. Entertaining ephemera.

Frederick Douglass *The Life and Times of Frederick Douglass* (Carol/ Wordsworth). The third volume (1881) of statesman, orator and ex-slave Frederick Douglass' autobiography sees him finally living in DC as US marshal and recorder of deeds. However, the early first volume (*Narrative of the Life of Frederick Douglass: An American Slave*, 1845, Penguin) is actually more gripping.

David McKay *Politics and Power in the USA* (Penguin). Most up-to-date (written in 1991) and best general introduction to who does what, why and when in the United States government.

P J O'Rourke *Parliament of Whores* (Random House/Picador). All O'Rourke's demented political insights and raving rightwing prejudices brought together in a scabrous critique of the American political system as practised in Washington DC. It's also very, very funny.

Hunter S Thompson. Gonzo's at his best taking sideswipes at corrupt politicians full of cant, and any of his books or collected essays feature a Washington villain or twenty – shot down in flames by a man for whom politics isn't the only drug.

Architecture

Christopher Weeks *AIA Guide to the Architecture of Washington DC* (John Hopkins University Press). Authoritative illustrated guide to the architecture of the city, covering buildings from every period since its founding.

Visitors to DC

David Cutler *Literary Washington* (Madison, US). The words and wisdom of celebrated writers, past and present, who have visited, worked and lived in DC.

Charles Dickens *American Notes* (Penguin). One of the most quoted of all visitors, Dickens came in the early 1840s, when it was still, famously, a "City of Magnificent Intentions". Highly enjoyable satirical banter from a British writer at ease with America.

Jan Morris *Destinations* (OUP). Typically dry observations of Washington high and low life, one of a series of pieces (about international cities) first written in the early 1980s for *Rolling Stone* magazine.

Anthony Trollope *North America* (Da Capo/Alan Sutton). Two-volume account of Trollope's visit to the US in the early 1860s. Picking up where his pioneering mother, Fanny, had left off in her contentious *Domestic Manners of the Americans* (1832), Trollope lays about him with ire and verve – in Volume II, Capitol building, White House, DC's streets and hotels, Washington Monument and the Smithsonian all come in for undiluted carping and moaning. Great stuff.

Watergate

If Washington has one domestic scandal it can call its own it's **Watergate** (see p.166), whose various aspects have been exhaustively covered since Bernstein and Woodward first set the ball rolling with *All the President's Men*. For the full story you could consult Fred Emery's *Watergate: The Corruption and Fall of Richard Nixon* (Simon & Schuster/Pimlico) or a host of other witnesses, not least Nixon's own *Memoirs* (Simon & Schuster, US), the *Haldeman Diaries: Inside the Nixon White House* (Berkley/Putnam), John Dean's *Blind Ambition* (Simon & Schuster, US) and *Lost Honor* (Stratford Press, US) and John Erlichman's *Witness to Power* (Simon & Schuster, US) – first-hand (if not completely reliable) testimony from those who were there at the time. Virtually everyone else involved has written about the affair at some time or other, too, from Watergate burglar James McCord to judge John Sirica, while *Nixon: An Oliver Stone Film* (Hyperion/Bloomsbury) presents the original screenplay of said movie alongside transcripts of taped Watergate conversations, previously classified memos and essays by key protagonists.

DC in fiction

Henry Adams *Democracy* (NAL-Dutton/Meridian). A story of electioneering and intrigue set in 1870s DC, written (anonymously) by the historian grandson of John Quincy Adams.

Jeffrey Archer *Shall We Tell the President?* (Pocket Books/Harper Collins). The "master storyteller" serves up the usual offering – risible characterization, feeble plot development and leaden prose wrapped around a DC-set tale of an assassination plot against "President Edward Kennedy".

William Peter Blatty *The Exorcist* (Harper Collins/Corgi). Blatty's seminal horror story about the possession of a teenage girl, written in 1971, was set around Georgetown University and made into the scariest film ever produced.

Tom Clancy. One of the best of the blockbuster thriller writers, Clancy weaves DC scenes (or at least the White House, Capitol building, FBI and CIA HQ at Langley in Virginia) into nearly every tale of spook and terrorist intrigue – most explosively in *Debt of Honor* (Berkley/Harper Collins) in which the President, Cabinet and most of Congress perish in an attack on the US Capitol.

Richard Timothy Conroy *The India Exhibition, Mr Smithson's Bones, Old Ways in the New World* (St Martin's Press, US). Murder, mystery and labyrinthine goings-on in a series of engaging thrillers set in the Smithsonian Institution.

Allen Drury *Advise and Consent* (Avon, US). Blackmail and slippery politics in Washington's upper echelons in the late 1950s; the novel was turned into a fine film by Otto Preminger starring Henry Fonda.

John Grisham *The Pelican Brief* (Dell/Arrow). Renowned legal whodunnit (capably filmed) starting with the assassination of two Supreme Court judges and delving into dodgy politics and murky land deals.

Elliott Roosevelt *Murder in the . . .* (St Martin's Press & Avon/Severn House). White House murder tales (with the dark deed committed in the Blue Room, West Wing, etc) by FDR's son, with the highly improbable First Lady-turned-sleuth Eleanor riding to the rescue every time.

Margaret Truman *Murder . . .* (Fawcett/Severn House). Harry's daughter churns out wooden murder-mystery stories set in various neighbourhoods and buildings of DC, from Georgetown to the National Cathedral.

Gore Vidal *Burr, Lincoln, 1876, Empire, Washington DC* (all Ballantine/Abacus). DC's – and America's – most potent, cynical chronicler sustains a terrific burst of form in five hugely enjoyable novels that trace the history of the US from the Revolution to modern times and rely heavily on Washington set-piece scenes. The moving epic *Lincoln* is the real tour-de-force.

Poetry

Walt Whitman *Leaves of Grass* (OUP/Everyman). The first edition of *Leaves of Grass* appeared in 1855, and Whitman added sections to it for the rest of his life. His war poems, *Drum-Taps* (1865), were directly influenced by his work in DC's Civil War hospitals; later, *Memories of President Lincoln* were added after the assassination – including the famous and affecting *O Captain! My Captain!*.

Index

direct orders from

		£	US$	CAN$
Amsterdam	1-85828-086-9	£7.99	US$13.95	CAN$16.99
Andalucia	1-85828-094-X	8.99	14.95	18.99
Australia	1-85828-141-5	12.99	19.95	25.99
Bali	1-85828-134-2	8.99	14.95	19.99
Barcelona	1-85828-221-7	8.99	14.95	19.99
Berlin	1-85828-129-6	8.99	14.95	19.99
Brazil	1-85828-102-4	9.99	15.95	19.99
Britain	1-85828-208-X	12.99	19.95	25.99
Brittany & Normandy	1-85828-224-1	9.99	16.95	22.99
Bulgaria	1-85828-183-0	9.99	16.95	22.99
California	1-85828-181-4	10.99	16.95	22.99
Canada	1-85828-130-X	10.99	14.95	19.99
China	1-85828-225-X	15.99	24.95	32.95
Corsica	1-85828-089-3	8.99	14.95	18.99
Costa Rica	1-85828-136-9	9.99	15.95	21.99
Crete	1-85828-132-6	8.99	14.95	18.99
Cyprus	1-85828-182-2	9.99	16.95	22.99
Czech & Slovak Republics	1-85828-121-0	9.99	16.95	22.99
Egypt	1-85828-188-1	10.99	17.95	23.99
Europe	1-85828-159-8	14.99	19.95	25.99
England	1-85828-160-1	10.99	17.95	23.99
First Time Europe	1-85828-270-5	7.99	9.95	12.99
Florida	1-85828-184-4	10.99	16.95	22.99
France	1-85828-124-5	10.99	16.95	21.99
Germany	1-85828-128-8	11.99	17.95	23.99
Goa	1-85828-156-3	8.99	14.95	19.99
Greece	1-85828-131-8	9.99	16.95	20.99
Greek Islands	1-85828-163-6	8.99	14.95	19.99
Guatemala	1-85828-189-X	10.99	16.95	22.99
Hawaii: Big Island	1-85828-158-X	8.99	12.95	16.99
Hawaii	1-85828-206-3	10.99	16.95	22.99
Holland, Belgium & Luxembourg	1-85828-087-7	9.99	15.95	20.99
Hong Kong	1-85828-187-3	8.99	14.95	19.99
Hungary	1-85828-123-7	8.99	14.95	19.99
India	1-85828-200-4	14.99	23.95	31.99
Ireland	1-85828-179-2	10.99	17.95	23.99
Italy	1-85828-167-9	12.99	19.95	25.99
Kenya	1-85828-192-X	11.99	18.95	24.99
London	1-85828-231-4	9.99	15.95	21.99
Mallorca & Menorca	1-85828-165-2	8.99	14.95	19.99
Malaysia, Singapore & Brunei	1-85828-103-2	9.99	16.95	20.99
Mexico	1-85828-044-3	10.99	16.95	22.99
Morocco	1-85828-040-0	9.99	16.95	21.99
Moscow	1-85828-118-0	8.99	14.95	19.99
Nepal	1-85828-190-3	10.99	17.95	23.99
New York	1-85828-171-7	9.99	15.95	21.99
Pacific Northwest	1-85828-092-3	9.99	14.95	19.99

In the UK, Rough Guides are available from all good bookstores, but can be obtained from Penguin by contacting: Penguin Direct, Penguin Books Ltd, Bath Road, Harmondsworth, West Drayton, Middlesex UB7 0DA; or telephone the credit line on 0181-899 4036 (9am–5pm) and ask for Penguin Direct. Visa, Access and Amex accepted. Delivery will normally be within 14 working days. Penguin Direct ordering facilities are only available in the UK and the USA. The availability and published prices quoted are correct at the time of going to press but are subject to alteration without prior notice.

Paris	1-85828-235-7	8.99	14.95	19.99
Poland	1-85828-168-7	10.99	17.95	23.99
Portugal	1-85828-180-6	9.99	16.95	22.99
Prague	1-85828-122-9	8.99	14.95	19.99
Provence	1-85828-127-X	9.99	16.95	22.99
Pyrenees	1-85828-093-1	8.99	15.95	19.99
Rhodes & the Dodecanese	1-85828-120-2	8.99	14.95	19.99
Romania	1-85828-097-4	9.99	15.95	21.99
San Francisco	1-85828-185-7	8.99	14.95	19.99
Scandinavia	1-85828-039-7	10.99	16.99	21.99
Scotland	1-85828-166-0	9.99	16.95	22.99
Sicily	1-85828-178-4	9.99	16.95	22.99
Singapore	1-85828-135-0	8.99	14.95	19.99
Spain	1-85828-240-3	11.99	18.95	24.99
St Petersburg	1-85828-133-4	8.99	14.95	19.99
Thailand	1-85828-140-7	10.99	17.95	24.99
Tunisia	1-85828-139-3	10.99	17.95	24.99
Turkey	1-85828-242-X	12.99	19.95	25.99
Tuscany & Umbria	1-85828-243-8	10.99	17.95	23.99
USA	1-85828-161-X	14.99	19.95	25.99
Venice	1-85828-170-9	8.99	14.95	19.99
Vietnam	1-85828-191-1	9.99	15.95	21.99
Wales	1-85828-245-4	10.99	17.95	23.99
Washington DC	1-85828-246-2	8.99	14.95	19.99
West Africa	1-85828-101-6	15.99	24.95	34.99
More Women Travel	1-85828-098-2	9.99	14.95	19.99
Zimbabwe & Botswana	1-85828-186-5	11.99	18.95	24.99

Phrasebooks

Czech	1-85828-148-2	3.50	5.00	7.00
French	1-85828-144-X	3.50	5.00	7.00
German	1-85828-146-6	3.50	5.00	7.00
Greek	1-85828-145-8	3.50	5.00	7.00
Italian	1-85828-143-1	3.50	5.00	7.00
Mexican	1-85828-176-8	3.50	5.00	7.00
Portuguese	1-85828-175-X	3.50	5.00	7.00
Polish	1-85828-174-1	3.50	5.00	7.00
Spanish	1-85828-147-4	3.50	5.00	7.00
Thai	1-85828-177-6	3.50	5.00	7.00
Turkish	1-85828-173-3	3.50	5.00	7.00
Vietnamese	1-85828-172-5	3.50	5.00	7.00

Reference

Classical Music	1-85828-113-X	12.99	19.95	25.99
Internet	1-85828-198-9	5.00	8.00	10.00
Jazz	1-85828-137-7	16.99	24.95	34.99
Opera	1-85828-138-5	£16.99	24.95	34.99
Rock	1-85828-201-2	17.99	26.95	35.00
World Music	1-85828-017-6	16.99	22.95	29.99

IF KNOWLEDGE IS POWER, THIS ROUGH GUIDE IS A POCKET-SIZED BATTERING RAM.

Written in plain English, with no hint of jargon, it will make you an Internet guru in the shortest possible time . . .
Internet 2.0 cuts through the hype and makes all others look like nerdy text books.

ROUGH GUIDES ON THE WEB

Visit our websites www.roughguides.com and www.hotwired.com/rough for news about the latest books, online travel guides and updates, and the full text of our Rough Guide to Rock – all 1058 entries!

AT GOOD BOOKSHOPS · DISTRIBUTED BY PENGUIN

Stay in touch with us!

ROUGH*NEWS* is Rough Guides' free newsletter. In three issues a year we give you news, travel issues, music reviews, readers' letters and the latest dispatches from authors on the road.

NOTES

NOTES

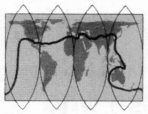